CHINA AS A POLAR GREAT POWER

China has emerged as a member of the elite club of nations that are powerful at both global poles. Polar states are global giants, strong in military, scientific, and economic terms. The concept of a polar great power is relatively unknown in international relations studies; yet China, a rising power globally, is now widely using this term to categorize its aspirations and emphasize the significance of the polar regions to its national interests. China's focus on becoming a polar great power represents a fundamental reorientation. It is a completely new way of imagining the world. China's push into these regions encompasses maritime and nuclear security, the frontlines of climate change research, and the possibility of a resources bonanza. As shown in this book, China's growing strength at the poles will be a game-changer for a number of strategic vulnerabilities that could shift the global balance of power in significant and unexpected ways.

Anne-Marie Brady is a professor of politics and international relations at the University of Canterbury, New Zealand, and a global fellow at the Woodrow Wilson Center in Washington. In 2014 she was appointed to a two-year term on the World Economic Forum's Global Action Council on the Arctic. She is editor-in-chief of *The Polar Journal*, and has published ten books and more than forty scholarly papers on a range of issues, including China's modernized propaganda system, China's activities in the South Pacific, and competing foreign policy interests in Antarctica.

China as a Polar Great Power

ANNE-MARIE BRADY

Woodrow Wilson Center Press
Washington, D.C.
and
 CAMBRIDGE
UNIVERSITY PRESS

CAMBRIDGE
UNIVERSITY PRESS

University Printing House, Cambridge CB2 8BS, United Kingdom

One Liberty Plaza, 20th Floor, New York, NY 10006, USA

477 Williamstown Road, Port Melbourne, VIC 3207, Australia

314-321, 3rd Floor, Plot 3, Splendor Forum, Jasola District Centre, New Delhi - 110025, India

79 Anson Road, #06-04/06, Singapore 079906

Cambridge University Press is part of the University of Cambridge.

It furthers the University's mission by disseminating knowledge in the pursuit of education, learning and research at the highest international levels of excellence.

www.cambridge.org
Information on this title: www.cambridge.org/9781316631256
DOI: 10.1017/9781316832004

Woodrow Wilson Center Press
Woodrow Wilson International Center for Scholars, One Woodrow Wilson Plaza,
1300 Pennsylvania Avenue nw, Washington, DC 20004–3027 www.wilsoncenter.org

First published 2017

A catalogue record for this publication is available from the British Library

ISBN 978-1-107-17927-1 Hardback
ISBN 978-1-316-63125-6 Paperback

Wilson Center

The Wilson Center, chartered by Congress as the official memorial to President Woodrow Wilson, is the nation's key nonpartisan policy forum for tackling global issues through independent research and open dialogue to inform actionable ideas for Congress, the Administration, and the broader policy community.

Conclusions or opinions expressed in Center publications and programs are those of the authors and speakers and do not necessarily reflect the views of the Center staff, fellows, trustees, advisory groups, or any individuals or organizations that provide financial support to the Center.

Please visit us online at www.wilsoncenter.org.

Jane Harman, Director, President, and CEO

Contents

Figures

Acronyms and Abbreviations

AFoPS	Asian Forum for Polar Science
ASEAN	Association of Southeast Asian Nations
ATCM	Antarctic Treaty Consultative Meeting
ATCPs	Antarctic Treaty Consultative Parties
ATS	Antarctic Treaty System
CAA	China Arctic and Antarctic Administration
CCAMLR	Commission for the Conservation of Antarctic Marine Living Resources
CCP	Chinese Communist Party
CNNC	China National Nuclear Corporation
CNOOC	China National Offshore Oil Company
CNPC	China National Petroleum Company
COLTO	Coalition of Legal Toothfish Operators
COMNAP	Council of Managers of National Antarctic Programs
COSCO	China Ocean Shipping (Group) Company
EU	European Union
GBI	Ground-Based Interceptor
GPS	Global Positioning System
IASC	International Arctic Science Committee
ICBM	intercontinental ballistic missile
IGY	International Geophysical Year
IMO	International Maritime Organization
IPY	International Polar Year
ISA	International Seabed Authority
NASA	National Aeronautics and Space Administration (United States)
NySMAC	Ny-Ålesund Science Managers Committee
PBSC	Politburo Standing Committee
PLA	People's Liberation Army
PLAN	People's Liberation Army-Navy

PRC	People's Republic of China
PRIC	Polar Research Institute of China
ROC	Republic of China
SCAR	Scientific Committee on Antarctic Research
SIPRI	Stockholm International Peace Research Institute
SLOC	sea lane of communication
SOA	State Oceanic Administration (China)
SSBN	Nuclear powered ballistic missile submarine
UN	United Nations
UNCLOS	United Nations Convention on the Law of the Sea
UNEP	United Nations Environment Programme
USPACOM	US Pacific Command
VTS	Vehicle Traffic Service

Acknowledgments

China as a Polar Great Power is an in-depth study of the place that the polar regions plays in China's emerging global strategy. My research on China's polar interests has demonstrated to me that the polar regions offer front-row seats to observe the changing global order, and early on it was clear that the perspectives and interests of both established and emerging polar players were neither well understood nor transparent. A further understanding of my early research was that China, like all other major powers, is not interested solely in either the Arctic or the Antarctic. This realization led me on a massive learning journey to not only discover the range of interests—many of them hidden from public view—that China has at the poles, but also to be able to interpret China's polar interests within the context of the interests of other major polar players. I also had to learn the complex governance structures of the Arctic and Antarctic, which both enhance and constrain the interests of those few states such as China that have the economic ability and political will to access the poles.

As I worked on this project, some of my early findings were published in *Asian Survey, China Brief, World Politics Review*, two policy papers for the Wilson Center, and two chapters in edited books, and were rehearsed and refined in papers given at many international conferences and public talks. I am indebted to the editors of those journals and books for permission to republish those findings in this book and for the valuable feedback I received from scholarly audiences as I developed my research project. Every effort has been made to contact copyright holders for their permission to reprint material in this book. The publishers would be grateful to hear from any copyright holders that are not acknowledged here, and will undertake to rectify any errors or omissions in future editions of this book.

China's polar policies are an undeclared foreign policy; hence, this has been an extremely difficult topic to research. Gathering data on China's polar interests has taken assiduousness, patience, persistence, and sometimes a very thick skin. I am very grateful to Richard McGregor, Andy Nathan, Ari Overmars, Karen Scott, Michael Yahuda, and Oran Young, who read early book drafts and gave crucial support that has enabled the book to come to fruition. I am extremely grateful to the staff of the library at the University of Canterbury and the library of the Wilson Center for help in gathering many of the scholarly resources used in this project.

I began writing this book in Washington, from a spacious office in the Ronald Reagan Building overlooking the Woodrow Wilson Plaza, while on a ten-month residential fellowship at the Woodrow Wilson International Center for Scholars. In 2015, I was awarded an eight-month Gerda Henkel Stiftung Fellowship, which facilitated the final completion of this book project. I finished up the book while based in my sixth-floor eyrie overlooking the Southern Alps at the University of Canterbury in Christchurch, New Zealand. I have thus been privileged to observe how China's growing polar interests look from the angle of both an ailing polar superpower and a polar small state. I benefited enormously from the intellectual leadership and camaraderie of the Wilson Center and its extraordinary collection of resident experts and visiting fellows, as well as from the intensely political atmosphere of Washington, D.C. I would like to express my thanks to a number of people who helped and encouraged this project in D.C. and Christchurch. First, special thanks to my Wilson Center writing partner, Maria Cristina Garcia, and to my writing group members, Amal Fadlalla, Hope M. Harrison, and Donny Meertens. You helped make the Wilson Center feel like home, and it has been extremely exciting and inspiring to watch your own projects emerge. Rob Litwak, vice president for scholars and director of international security studies, was an inspiration, and I felt very lucky to have him as a next-door neighbor at the Wilson Center. Robert Daly was always encouraging and supportive and helped make me feel part of the team at the Wilson Center's Kissinger Institute on China and the United States. I am also very grateful to Arlyn Charles, Lindsay Collins, Kim Conner, Kent Hughes, and Janet Spikes for making my stay at the Center so pleasant and productive; to my intern Scott Wingo for his work in compiling the charts in the book; for the steady support and good humor of Woodrow Wilson Center Press director Joe Brinley; and for the thoroughness and fine attention to detail of Woodrow Wilson Center Press editor Shannon Granville, who helped make the book ready for publication in partnership with Cambridge University Press. I have benefited greatly from local research funds and technical support at the University of Canterbury that has facilitated the continuance of this research, and I have been able to draw on the vast pool of polar knowledge at the university over the years. Special thanks to Neil Gilbert, Alan D. Hemmings, Daniela Liggett, Michelle Rogan-Finnemore, and Karen Scott in this regard.

I would like to especially thank my husband, Z. J., who has been a patient and loyal support person throughout this book project. I dedicate this book with love to our children, Francesca, Silas, and Matteo. I have greatly enjoyed sharing the many eureka moments on this project with you all, and have valued your support and encouragement throughout the long journey of completing the book.

Glossary

Beiji (北极): literally, "the Northern Extreme"; the North Pole, and more broadly also used to described the Arctic as a whole

Beiji diqu (北极地区): the Arctic region

Beiji Huanghe zhan (北极黄河站): Arctic Yellow River Station (China)

Beiji shiwu xietiao xiaozu (北极事物协调小组): Arctic Affairs Coordination Group (China)

bingjie (冰结): frozen

bingzhan (冰站): Arctic iceberg stations

bu zhan er qu ren zhi bing, shanzhi shan zhe ye (不战而屈人之兵, 善之善者也): "the ultimate technique is to get the enemy to submit without actually going to war"

Caizhengbu (财政部): Ministry of Finance (China)

Changcheng zhan (长城站): Great Wall Station, Antarctica (China)

changxiang zhuxuanlü (唱响主旋律): "sing with one voice"

Daguo jueqi (大国崛起): *The Rise of Great Powers* (documentary)

dang de houshe (党的喉舌): "[the Chinese media as] the tongue and throat of the Chinese Communist Party"

dang de jilü (党的纪律): CCP instructions or disciplinary measures for party members

disanji (第三极): "the third pole"; the Tibetan Plateau

Donghua dajie (中华大街): "China Boulevard"; the dedicated Antarctic traverse route from Zhongshan Station to Dome A via Taishan Station

Dong Nanji da duanmian yanjiu zhanlüe gouxiang (东南极大断面研究战略构想): East Antarctic Sector Strategic Research Vision

duinei xuanchuan (对内宣传): information or activities aimed at Chinese citizens

duiwai xuanchuan (对外宣传): information or activities aimed at foreigners

erdeng gongmin (二等公民): second-class citizen

fen fa youwei (奋发有为): "proactive"

fu guo qiang bing (富國強兵): "rich country with a strong army"

furen julebu (富人俱乐部): rich man's club

fu zeren de daguo (负责任的大国): "responsible great power"

fu zeren de liyi xiangguan zhe (负责任的利益相关者): "responsible stakeholder"

gonghai (公海): high seas

Gongye he xinxihuabu (工业和信息化部): Ministry of Industry and Information Technology (China)

guoji gonggong haiyu (国际公共海域): international waters

guoji xingxiang (国际形象): international image

Guojia anquan weiyuanhui (国家安全委员会): National Security Council (China)

guojia anquan xitong (国家安全系统): China's national security *xitong*

Guojia cehui dili xinxi ju (国家测绘地理信息局): National Administration of Surveying, Mapping and Geoinformation (China)

Guojia haiyangju (国家海洋局): State Oceanic Administration (China)

Guojia haiyangju weiyuanhui (国家海洋局委员会): National Antarctic Expedition Committee (China)

Guojia haiyangju jidi kaocha bangongshi (国家海洋局极地考察办公室): China Arctic and Antarctic Administration (CAA)

Guojia Nanji kaocha weiyuanhui bangongshi (国家南极考察委员会办公室): Office of the National Antarctic Expedition Committee (China)

Guojia weisheng yu jihua shengyu weiyuanhui (国家卫生和计划生育委员会): National Health and Family Planning Commission (China)

Guojia ziran kexue jijin weiyuanhui (国家自然科学基金委员会): Natural Science Foundation of China

Guotu ziyuanbu (国土资源部): Ministry of Land and Natural Resources (China)

Guowai jidi kaocha xinxi huibian (国外极地考察信息汇编): *Foreign Polar Expedition News Report*

haiyang qiangguo (海洋强国): maritime great power

haiyang quanli (海洋权利): sea power

haiyang xitong (海洋系统): maritime *xitong*

haiyang zhengce (海洋政策): maritime strategy

huayu quan (话语权): "right to speak"

huoban (伙伴): partnership

Jiaotongbu (交通部): Ministry of Transport (China)

Jiaoyubu (教育部): Ministry of Education (China)

jidi (极地): polar

Jidi ban (极地办): CAA (abbreviation of the China Arctic and Antarctic Administration)

jidi fazhan zhanlüe (极地发展战略): polar strategy

jidi guihua (极地规划): polar plan

Jidi guojia zhengce yanjiu baogao (极地国家政策研究报告): *Polar National Policy Research Report*

jidi kaocha (极地考察): polar expeditions

Jidi keji dongtai (极地科技动态): *Polar Scientific Trends*

jidi qiangguo (极地强国): polar great power

jidi sheshi (极地设施): polar facilities

Jidi xinxi (极地信息): *Polar Information*

jidi yanjiu (极地研究): polar research

Jidi yanjiu jianbao (极地研究简报): *Polar Bulletin*

jidi zhanlüe (极地战略): polar strategy

Jidi zhanlüe yanjiuzu (极地战略研究组): Polar Strategic Research Group

Jidizhanlüe yanjiu tongxun (极地战略研究通讯): *Polar Strategy Research Bulletin*

jidi zhengce (极地政策): polar policies

jin'an (近岸): coastal waters

jin'an fangyu (近岸防御): coastal defense

jin hai (近海): near seas

jinhai fangyu (近海防御): offshore defense

jiti baquan (集体霸权): collective hegemony

Kexueyuan jidi kexue weiyuanhui (科学院极地科学委员会): Polar Science Committee

Kexue jishubu (科学技术部): Ministry of Science and Technology (China)

kongcheng ji (空城计): empty fort

kou (口): CCP policy suprabureaucracies that link policy areas; usually, but not always, on smaller policy areas than the *xitong*

Kunlun zhan (昆仑站): Kunlun Station, Antarctica (China)

laoshi zuoren, zhashi zuoshi; bu shi zhangyang, zhi qiu shiji; wu wang renmin, gan zuo fengxian; jugong jincui, fenfa you wei (老实做人, 扎实做事; 不事张扬, 只求实绩; 勿忘人民, 甘作奉献; 鞠躬尽瘁, 奋发有为):"be honest, do solid work; be unassuming, get on with things; do not forget the people, be willing to make sacrifices; spare no effort; and be proactive" (Xi Jinping's motto)

lengjing guancha, wenzhu zhenjiao chenzhuo yingfu, taoguang yanghui, shanyu shouzhuo, jue bu dangtou, you suo zuowei (冷静观察; 稳住阵脚; 沉着应付; 韬光养晦; 善于守拙; 决不当头, 有所作为): "be calm and observe the situation; hold our ground; hide our strengths and bide our time; be good at keeping a low profile; don't take the lead, do what you can" (Deng Xiaoping foreign policy strategy)

liangge zhan yige chuan (两个站，一个船): "two stations, one boat"

liyong (利用): to exploit, to utilize, to use

minjian waijiao (民间外交): people-to-people diplomacy

Nanji (南极): literally, "Southern Extreme"; the South Pole, also used to describe the Antarctic as a whole

Nanji 2049 (南极2049): *Antarctica 2049* (movie title)

Nanji, women lai le! (南极，我们来了!): *Antarctica: We're Here!* (1985 documentary)

neiwai you bie (内外有别): insiders and outsiders are different

Nongyebu (农业部): Ministry of Agriculture

qiu tong cunyi (求同存异): look for points in common, put aside differences

quanmian waijiao (全面外交): total diplomacy

quanyi (权益): rights and interests

quan renlei de Beiji (全人类的北极): the North Pole belongs to all humanity

quan shijie de gonggong lingtu (全世界的公共领土): global commons

Renmin ribao (人民日报): *People's Daily* (CCP official newspaper)

ruan cunzai (软存在): soft presence

Sanshiliu ji (三十六計): *Thirty-Six Stratagems*

sha ji jing hou (杀鸡儆猴): "kill the chicken to scare the monkeys"

Shekeyuan (社科院): Chinese Academy of Social Sciences

shengmingxian (生命线): "lifeblood [of the CCP]"; the CCP's perspective on the role of propaganda

Shijie Nanji kuanwu ziyuan guanli tiaoyue (世界南极矿物资源管理条约): the (nonexistent) World Treaty on Managing Antarctic Minerals

suzao guoji yulun (塑造国际舆论): mold global public opinion

Taishan zhan (泰山站): Taishan Station

tici (题词): political slogan

tifa (提法): politically correct language

tongzhan (统战): United Front

tuanjie da duoshu, daji yi xiaocuo (团结大多数，打击一小撮): "uniting with the majority, while attacking a minority"

Waijiaobu (外交部): Ministry of Foreign Affairs

waishi xitong (外事系统): foreign affairs *xitong*

waixuan (外宣): foreign propaganda; information targeted at foreign audiences

Weiduoliyadi changnian zhan (维多利亚地常年站): Victoria Land Permanent Base

wei renlei heping liyong Nanji zuochu gongxian (为人类和平利用南极做出贡献): peacefully exploit Antarctica on behalf of the whole of humanity

weixie lun (威胁论): the "[China] threat" narrative

wenhua jianshe (文化建设): cultural construction

xiao kang shehui (小康社会): a comfortable standard of living as a basic minimum

xitong (系统): CCP suprabureaucracies that group policy areas

xuanchuan (宣传): propaganda, communications, information management

xuanchuan yu sixiang gongzuo (宣传与思想工作): "propaganda and thought work"; persuasion and censorship

xuanjiao xitong (宣教系统): the CCP propaganda *xitong*

yao mianzi (要面子): face-seeking

yaomohua (妖魔化): "demonization [of China]"

yidai yilu (一带一路): "One Belt, One Road"; the New Silk Road

yongyu (用语): politically correct language

yuan yang zuozhan (远洋作战): offshore battle readiness

zhanlüe xin jiangyu (战略新疆域): new strategic frontiers

zhanju (占据): occupied or held

zhengming (正名): the Confucian concept of the rectification of names

zhidao sixiang (指导思想): guiding strategy

zhidao yulun (指导舆论): "guide public opinion"

Zhongguo (中国): China, "the Middle Kingdom"

Zhongguo dizhenju (中国地震局): China Earthquake Administration

Zhongguo duiwai xuanchuan bangongshi (中共对外宣传办公室): the CCP Office for Foreign Propaganda

Zhongguo gongchengyuan (中国工程院): Chinese Academy of Engineering

Zhongguo guanli qu (中国管理区): China's Management District

Zhongguo jidi yanjiusuo (中国极地研究所): Polar Research Institute of China (PRIC)

Zhongguo jidi yanjiu zhongxin (中国极地研究中心): Polar Research Institute of China

Zhongguo jidi kaocha zixun weiyuanhui (中国极地考察咨询委员会): Chinese Advisory Committee for Polar Research

Zhongguo kexueyuan (中国科学院): Chinese Academy of Science

Zhongguo qiang (中国墙): China's Great Wall (in Antarctica)

Zhongshan zhan (中山站): Zhongshan Station

Zhongyang caijing lingdao xiaozu (中央财经领导小组): CCP Finance and Economics Leading Group

Zhongyang haiyang gongzuo lingdao xiaozu (中央海洋工作领导小组): CCP Maritime Affairs Leading Group

Zhongyang haiyang quanyi lingdao xiaozu bangongshi (中央海洋权益领导小组办公室): CCP Maritime Rights Office

Zhongguo qixiangju (中国气象局): Chinese Meteorological Administration

Zhongyang quanmian shenhua gaige lingdao xiaozu (中央全面深化改革领导小组): Party Leading Group for Comprehensively Deepening Reform

Zhongyang waishi lingdao xiaozu (中央外事领导小组): CCP Foreign Affairs Leading Group

zhuquan meiyou guishu de dalü (主权没有归属的大陆): a continent with no attribution of sovereignty

zhuquan quanli (主权权利): sovereign rights

zhuazhu Nanji (抓住南极): "seize" Antarctica

Zongcan zuozhanbu haijun ju (总参作战部海军局): PLAN General Staff Operations Department

Zouxiang haiyang (走向海洋): *To the Oceans* (2011 PLAN-funded CCTV documentary)

zou xiang haiyang, jinglüe haiyang (走向海洋, 经略海洋): "going out on the oceans" policy

zuo er bu shuo (做而不说): "do, but don't say"

zuzhi yu lingdao (组织与领导): organize and lead

Introduction

The Rise of a New Polar Power

On September 2, 2015, the Pentagon reported the visit of five People's Liberation Army-Navy (PLAN) vessels to US territorial waters off the coast of Alaska.[1] It was the first ever incursion by Chinese navy boats into the Arctic region. Occurring only the day before China's biggest-ever military parade, and just as US president Barack Obama was making his own first visit to Alaska to announce his new Arctic policies, PLAN's brief voyage showcased China's growing naval reach and desire to expand operations into Arctic waters. The five boats, consisting of three surface warships, an amphibious vessel, and a supply ship, had been participating in a military exercise with Russian forces near Vladivostok. They then voyaged thousands of kilometers north to the Bering Sea, where they transited the US Aleutian Islands, before heading home to Chinese waters.

The official US response was muted: China was simply playing the same game that the US Navy has played for years in the South China Sea and Taiwan Strait, exercising the right of innocent passage to show off its sea power. Behind the scenes, however, the message was clear – China was announcing that it had military interests in the Arctic and intended to expand its operations there. One month later, in late September and early October 2015, PLAN drove this point home, giving a further demonstration of emerging Arctic sea power by sending a destroyer, a frigate, and a supply ship on goodwill visits to Denmark, Finland, and Sweden.

The incursion into US territorial waters was much more than a stunning example of China's growing maritime capacities and its ability to reach the polar regions. The frenzied international media attention over the boldness of

---

[1] Andrea Chen, "Chinese Navy Sends Washington a Message by Patrolling Near Largest US State Alaska," *South China Morning Post*, September 4, 2015, http://www.scmp.com/news/china/diplo macy-defence/article/1855448/chinese-navy-sends-america-message-patrolling-near.

China's display, which drowned out Obama's visit to the Arctic, underscored the broader import of China's actions. The controversy associated with China's expansion into the polar regions reflects its potential to upend the global order, just as it has done in multiple sectors of the global economy, in its nearby oceans through projection of its naval power, and even in outer space. In the past ten years, as part of its overall expanding global foreign policy, China has become a leading polar player with wide-ranging and complex interests in both the Arctic and Antarctic. China is now emerging as a member of the unique club of nations that are powerful at both poles. Polar states are global giants, strong in military, scientific, and economic terms. China's leaders view their country's expanding polar presence as a way to demonstrate China's growing global power, and to achieve international recognition for this new status.[2]

To anyone who was watching closely, China's polar push has been advancing on numerous fronts, both public and private. In 2014, the Chinese polar icebreaker *Xue Long* helped in the dramatic rescue of the trapped Russian research vessel *Akademik Shokalskiy* in Antarctic waters. In 2012, Chinese entrepreneur Huang Nubo tried and failed to purchase a section of remote Iceland farmland to build a luxury hotel and eco-resort;[3] in 2014, he tried to purchase land in Svalbard, and finally succeeded in purchasing a massive tract of land in Tromsø, Norway.[4] In 2014, the China National Space Administration constructed a ground receiving station for the civil-military BeiDou-2 satellite navigation system in Antarctica, which will extend coverage to a global scale.[5] And in November 2015, China's polar science program announced that it had attained "fully self-sufficient land, sea, and air capabilities at the poles."[6]

[2] "Chen Lianzeng fu juzhang chuxi Zhongguo jidi kaocha gongzuo zixun weiyuanhui di 13 ci huiyi" [Vice Director Chen Lianzeng attends 13th meeting of the China Polar Expedition Work Group], State Oceanic Administration, May 20, 2011, http://www.mlr.gov.cn/xwdt/hyxw/201105/t20110520_868036.htm.

[3] Alëx Elliott, "Chinese Investor Still Hot on Iceland Despite Politicians," *Iceland Review*, April 25, 2014, http://icelandreview.com/news/2014/04/25/chinese-investor-still-hot-iceland-despite-politicians.

[4] Knut-Eirik Lindblad, "Norwegian Landowner Sells Huge Amount of Land to Chinese Billionaire Huang Nubo," *Nordlys*, May 16, 2014, http://www.nordlys.no/nyheter/article7362483.ece.

[5] Andrew Darby, "China's Antarctica Satellite Base Plans Spark Concerns," *Sydney Morning Herald*, November 12, 2014, http://www.smh.com.au/world/chinas-antarctica-satellite-base-plans-spark-concerns-20141112-11l3wx.html.

[6] Luo Sha, "Wo guo jidi kaocha jiang xin gou feiji xinjian pobingchuan" [China's polar expedition will purchase new airplane and icebreaker], Xinhua, February 3, 2014, http://tech.sina.com.cn/d/2014-02-03/11279140668.shtml.

China's rise as a polar power has been dramatic and rapid. When, in 2004, Chinese polar officials voiced the desire for China to overtake the level of research and involvement of developed countries active in Antarctica,[7] it seemed a far-off goal. In 2005, China's leading polar scientist first mentioned in public the aspiration for China to become a "polar great power" (*jidi qiangguo*).[8] In 2013, a senior Chinese polar official stated that China was beginning the transition to achieving this status.[9] In 2013, senior Chinese polar officials publicly stated for the first time that China's goal of becoming a polar great power was a key component of Beijing's maritime strategy.[10]

Then, in a speech given in Hobart, Australia, in November 2014, Chinese Communist Party (CCP) general secretary Xi Jinping used the term "polar great power" for the first time. Xi stated that due to "profound changes in the international system" and China's unprecedented level of economic development over the past twenty years, China soon would be "joining the ranks of the polar great powers." Xi told his audience, "Polar affairs have a unique role in our marine development strategy, and the process of becoming a polar power is an important component of China's process to become maritime great power."[11] Having China's top leader refer to his country as a future polar great power was a signal to the entire Chinese political system that polar affairs had moved up the policy agenda. Following this speech, the polar regions were officially included in Xi's bold new foreign policy direction, China's "New Silk Road" (*yidai yilu*). In China's bureaucratic system, the polar regions are categorized within maritime affairs. The goal of becoming a polar great power is now a key component of Beijing's emerging maritime strategy.[12] China's emerging status as a polar power is directly linked to its

---

7 Wang Qian, "Twenty Years of Antarctic Research," *China Daily*, November 3, 2004, accessed October 18, 2009, http://china.org.cn/English/2004/Nov/111106.htm (link discontinued). Links, with access dates, are given here and in subsequent notes for sources that are no longer available online.

8 "Ben bao jizhe zhuanfang Zhongguo jidi yanjiu zhongxin fuzhuren Yang Huigen boshi wo guo yunliang quanqiu kaocha" [A discussion with PRIC deputy director Yang Huigen about China's polar expeditions], *Dalian wanbao*, December 5, 2005, http://news.sina.com.cn/s/2005-12-05/00437617786s.shtml.

9 "Chen Lianzeng fu juzhang chuxi Zhongguo jidi kaocha gongzuo zixun weiyuanhui di 13 ci huiyi."

10 "2013 Zhongguo jidi kexue xueshuhui zhaokai" [2013 polar conference at the Chinese Academy of Science begins], Polar Research Institute of China (PRIC), September 26–29, 2013, accessed November 19, 2013, http://www.pric.gov.cn/detail/News.aspx?id=1440d741-0486-4ab1-a 6db-60e717df893c (link discontinued).

11 "Er lun shenru xuexi guanche Xi Jinping zhuxi zhongyao jianghua jingshen" [Study and implement the important speech of Chairman Xi Jinping], *Zhongguo haiyang ribao*, November 20, 2014, http://www.oceanol.com/redian/shiping/2014-11-25/38013.html.

12 "2013 Zhongguo jidi kexue xueshu nianhui zhaokai."

desire to seek a greater global role.[13] China's thinking on the polar regions and global oceans demonstrates a level of ambition and forward planning that few, if any, modern industrial states can achieve. If China succeeds in its goals in the polar regions, the high seas, outer space, and cyberspace, then its quest for international status and power will be assured.

It has been difficult for China and international relations experts to grapple with China's polar policies because the field is divided into different silos of specialists who do not have the requisite skill sets to connect the proverbial dots. Paradoxically, China's dramatic polar rise has therefore flown under the radar – until this book. Political and strategic research on the polar regions has tended to be the preserve of a select number of Arctic-focused, and a very small group of Antarctic-focused, social scientists. Although scientists frequently integrate their research on both poles, very few social scientists talk about "polar studies" or discuss the two poles as a region. Meanwhile, the world's most powerful polar powers, the United States and Russia, rarely use the term "polar great power" to describe their status and interests in the polar regions. Yet China is now widely using this term to sum up its aspirations and symbolize the significance of the polar regions to China's national interests.

China's focus on becoming a polar great power represents a fundamental reorientation – a completely new way of looking at the world. Nothing symbolizes this shift more than China's vertical world map, the cover image for this book. This map, devised by Hao Xiaoguang, a brilliant geophysicist from Wuhan, has been used since 2004 by China's State Oceanic Administration to chart voyages to the Arctic and Antarctic and, since 2006, by the People's Liberation Army (PLA) as an official military map. The map was finally released to the public in 2014.[14] Hao also designed China's new vertical national boundaries map, which for the first time included China's controversial nine-dash-line claims in the South China Sea as part of Chinese territory, provoking a media storm of commentary.[15] Yet the international media missed the more far-reaching significance of China's vertical world map, which was released at exactly the same time. Unlike the traditional world map, which has the Arctic and Antarctic at the edges of the world, China's new

---

[13] Guo Peiqing, *Beiji hangdao de guoji wenti yanjiu* [Research on the matter of the internatio-nalizing of the Arctic sea route] (Beijing: Haiyang chubanshe, 2009), 320.

[14] "Jiemi shu ban ditu: Mibu jiefangjun dui Mei junshi buju zhiming shiwu" [Unmasking of secret vertical map: The PLA offsets the fatal mistake of the United States' military layout], *Qianzhan*, October 21, 2014, http://xw.qianzhan.com/military/detail/275/141021-3937a19b .html.

[15] "China's New Weapon in the South China Sea Is… a Vertical Map," China Real Time Report, *Wall Street Journal*, June 25, 2014, http://blogs.wsj.com/chinarealtime/2014/06/25/chi na-new-weapon-in-the-battle-for-the-south-china-sea-is-a-vertical-map/.

vertical world map is dominated by a peacock-shaped Antarctic Continent and depicts the Arctic as a central ocean ringed by North America and Europe. The PLA has been using this vertical world map to help determine the location of satellites and satellite receiving stations for BeiDou-2, China's strategic weapons navigating system,[16] in order to chart China's new direction in the most literal sense. The map is the visual representation of China's new global *Realpolitik*: pragmatic, assertive of China's national interests, cooperative where it is possible to be cooperative, and yet ready to face up to conflict.

As the founder of modern geopolitics, H. J. Mackinder, pointed out early in the twentieth century, each era has its own geographical perspective.[17] China's vertical map completely resets the world map to highlight the significance of the world oceans and the polar regions, creating a new geographical perspective more in keeping with modern realities. It exposes what Mackinder called the "World-Island" – the joint continent of Europe, Asia, and Africa.[18] Thus, China's new global vision confronts the observer with how the various land masses, big continents and smaller islands, connect in one interlinked, inseparable world ringed by vast oceans. The vertical map places the rooster-shaped Chinese territory at the center of the new world order: visually dominating the Asia-Pacific, sidelining the United States, and dwarfing Europe. For centuries, geopolitical contention has centered on Europe and focused on land-based territories. And since the breakup of the Soviet Union in 1991, the United States has been the unchallenged global hegemon. But a new geopolitics is taking shape that reflects the unprecedented level of global interconnectedness of trade, communication, and people movement; the pressing concerns of the future, including food supplies and energy security; the consequences of climate change on geopolitics; and, ultimately, the rise of a new global power. China aims to be at the heart of this new order.

China's declaration that it is poised to enter the ranks of the "polar great powers" reveals both a deep need for status change in the international system and an awareness of a gap in global geopolitics that China alone has the unique ability to fill. In setting its sights on the polar regions now, China is looking to the mid- to long term and planning for its future economic, political, and strategic needs.[19] The Chinese government's stated core

---

[16]   Wang Pu, "Shu qilai de ditu, gaibianle ni de 'shijieguan' ma?" [Put up a map and change your "world view"?], *Zhidao ribao*, July 13, 2014, http://zhidao.baidu.com/daily/view?id=522.

[17]   H. J. Mackinder, *Democratic Ideals and Reality: A Study in the Politics of Reconstruction* (London: Constable and Company, 1919), 39.

[18]   Ibid., 81.

[19]   Guojia haiyangju haiyang fazhan zhanlue yanjiusuo ketizu, ed., *Zhongguo haiyang fazhan baogao* [Report on China's maritime development] (Beijing: Haiyang chubanshe, 2012), 367.

national interests in the current era – to maintain China's social system and state security, to preserve state sovereignty and territorial integrity, and to ensure the continued stable development of the economy and society[20] – all require access and engagement in the polar regions.[21] China has global interests and is well on the way to becoming a global great power. To succeed in this evolution, it must be dominant in the polar regions.

China, like other rising powers before it, seeks to improve its national security, and in doing so it inevitably will challenge the existing order. The polar regions are key sites for these new geopolitics. As Xi Jinping pointed out in his Hobart speech, the Arctic and Antarctic are ripe with economic, political, and military-strategic potential.[22] A new "Great Game" is well underway at both the Arctic and Antarctic, as various states compete for access and opportunities there.

Great powers are states that exhibit "global structural power," or the ability to shape governance frameworks in the economic, military, and political-diplomatic sectors.[23] So how should we define *polar* great powers? In the polar regions, the measures – and means – of power are somewhat different. Along with more traditional forms of power and influence, in the Arctic and Antarctic a state's investment in polar-related science is a fundamental indicator of power and intentions. Thus, to be considered a polar great power, a state must have high levels of polar scientific capacity and scientific research funding; a significant level of presence in the polar regions; and significant economic, military, political, and diplomatic capacity there; as well as a high level of international engagement in polar governance. This last factor is particularly important because, in the polar regions of the world – more perhaps than anywhere else – "structural power" comes from cooperation and participation in existing governance structures.

Going it alone in the polar regions is a strategy that only a regional hegemon, such as Russia in the Arctic, might consider taking. States that are able to dominate militarily at the two poles are truly powerful, controlling key choke points into strategic regions. Currently, only the United States, with its strong military presence in both the Arctic and the Antarctic, has this capability. Yet massive pressures on the US federal budget since the 2008 global financial

[20] "Shoulun Zhong Mei jingji duihua" [First round of US-China relations], Chinanews.com, July 29, 2009, http://www.chinanews.com/gn/news/2009/07–29/1794984.shtml.
[21] *Zhongguo haiyang fazhan baogao*, 362 and 374.
[22] "Er lun shenru xuexi guanche Xi Jinping zhuxi zhongyao jianghua jingshen."
[23] Liselotte Odgaard, *China and Coexistence: Beijing's National Security Strategy for the Twenty-First Century* (Washington, DC: Woodrow Wilson Center Press; Baltimore: Johns Hopkins University Press, 2012), 45.

crisis, which has capped spending on polar-related infrastructure and science, means that US polar capacity is steadily slipping backwards.

China's modern strategic thought has long been greatly influenced by the ideas of late-nineteenth-century US naval strategist Alfred T. Mahan,[24] who advocated that rising powers should expand their navy, aim for global markets, and either establish colonies or else garner privileged access to resources.[25] China is following this advice to the letter. By China's definition, the polar regions, the deep seabed, and outer space are all *res nullius* (literally, "no one's property"), and hence are ripe for "colonization." In 2015, the Chinese government announced that the polar regions, the deep seabed, and outer space are China's "new strategic frontiers" (*zhanlüe xin jiangyu*),[26] strategically important areas from which China will draw the resources needed to become a global power.[27] Although this vision has only recently been made public by China's senior leader Xi Jinping, the thinking behind it has been developing for many years.

China does not yet have a formal document outlining the government's strategy for the polar regions, let alone formal individual strategies for the Arctic and Antarctic, but it does have a clear agenda and set of priorities and can be expected to make a formal public statement on some – but not all – aspects of its Arctic strategy during the 13th Five-Year Plan (2016–2020). China's polar policymakers are coy on the topic of China's polar strategy, and in news stories aimed at foreign audiences they have publicly denied that China has one.[28] Yet in meetings for polar officials reported in specialist websites, and in classified materials, the topic of China's current polar strategy (*jidi zhanlüe / jidi guihua*) and policies (*jidi zhengce*) are freely discussed, as are plans to formulate a more long-term, overarching, and possibly public strategy. China's polar strategic priorities are focused on security (traditional and nontraditional), resources, and strategic science. Without a formal polar

---

24 Liu Huaqing, *Liu Huaqing huiyilu* [The memoirs of Liu Huaqing] (Beijing: Jiefang jun chubanshe, 2005), 432.

25 Alfred T. Mahan, *The Influence of Sea Power upon History, 1660–1783* (Boston: Little, Brown and Co, 1890).

26 "Guojia anquan fa cao'an ni zengjia taikong deng xinxing lingyu de anquan weihu renwu" [The draft national security law will increase security in space and other new areas], Xinhua, June 24, 2015, http://www.chinanews.com/gn/2015/06-24/7363693.shtml.

27 "Fangwen Zhongguo Nanji kaocha shouxi kexuejia: wei shenme qu Nanji" [Interview with China's chief polar scientist: Why go to Antarctica], Sina.com, December 5, 2005, http://tech.sina.com.cn/d/2005-12-05/1202782841.shtml.

28 "Jidi baozang zhi zheng: Duoshao shiyou jutou zai 'zhan dipan' guafen beiji" [Polar treasure dispute: How many oil giants will carve up the Arctic basin], Xinhua, February 21, 2012, http://news.xinhuanet.com/finance/2012-02/21/c_122731902_5.htm.

security strategy document in place, whether public or classified, China is currently acting out an undeclared foreign policy in the polar regions, and its actions provide a useful indicator of the Chinese attitude toward global governance issues more widely. In contrast to China's opacity on its polar interests, both Russia and the United States have made formal public statements on their Arctic and Antarctic priorities and agenda in recent years, as has Norway, the only state with territorial claims at both poles, and prominent Antarctic states such as Australia, the United Kingdom, and New Zealand.

China has a long-term agenda in the polar regions. Many of the opportunities in the Arctic and Antarctic that attract Chinese interest will not be available for several decades, and they will take considerable planning, coordination, and international diplomacy to maximize. The Chinese government is thus employing strategic ambiguity to defend its interests to the wider world. Hence, as two of China's leading polar scholars point out, China works hard to "create an international image of China as a peaceful and cooperative state" in order to further China's goals in the polar regions.[29] If international public opinion were to turn against China's plans in the polar regions, it would harm the government's abilities to achieve these goals. Thus, persuasion, framing, information management, and strategic communication play an extremely important role in China's current polar strategy, and they are used to shape both domestic and global perceptions of China's polar agenda.

GREAT POWER POLITICS AT THE POLES

In the Cold War era, the United States and the Soviet Union dominated both the Arctic and the Antarctic. For most of the post–Cold War era, the United States has been the dominant power on the Antarctic ice, while it has treated the Arctic as somewhat of a geostrategic backwater. However, as US global power has declined, especially since 2008, a host of emergent states are beginning to take advantage of the power vacuum, and China is at the head of the pack. The Obama administration tried to rebalance to the Asia-Pacific, but became preoccupied in the Middle East and Europe. Now the Trump administration is alienating allies, accentuating perceptions of the decline of US power. The Arctic is important to the United States, as an Arctic littoral state, and yet it pays little attention to its own northern regions.[30] Relative to other foreign policy commitments, Antarctic

---

[29] Guo Peiqing and Li Zhenfu, *Beiji hangdao de guoji wenti yanjiu* [Research on the international issues regarding the Arctic shipping routes] (Beijing: Haiyang chubanshe, 2009), 317.
[30] Jim Paulin, "A Conflict between Alaska and Feds over Arctic Policy?" *Alaska Dispatch News*, September 8, 2013, http://www.alaskadispatch.com/article/20130908/conflict-between-alaska-and-feds-over-arctic-policy.

affairs are even less of a priority for Washington. US capacities there are in a slow decline, as symbolized by the US administration's inability to finance new icebreakers to service its bases in Antarctica and protect its interests in the Arctic.[31]

Russia has more at stake in the Arctic than most countries do. It controls one-quarter of the Arctic coastline and 40 percent of the land area, and it is home to three-quarters of the Arctic's population. Russia has been active in the Arctic region since the 1600s and receives 20 percent of its gross domestic product from Arctic economic activities such as natural resource extraction. Yet Moscow too has neglected its Arctic interests for many years. It is only now reasserting itself militarily in the region and looking for partners to open up its Arctic regions for development.[32] In the Antarctic, since the fall of the Soviet Union, Russia has become a weak but sometimes belligerent player, beset by aging infrastructure and limited budgets.

The Arctic is a vast sea surrounded by continents, while Antarctica is a continent surrounded by sea. Although the two poles have some physical and climactic similarities, from the point of view of governance they are vastly different. Arctic governance is in somewhat of a state of flux, whereas Antarctic governance mechanisms are considerably more settled and ordered. However, tensions are rising in both regions, and China's emergence as a significant polar player is a contributing factor to these tensions. China's economic power and increasing interest in garnering global influence is perceived by the more established Arctic and Antarctic states as a potential threat. Yet some also recognize China's polar interests as an opportunity: as a chance to adjust existing balances of power, as a new source of polar scientific funding and capacity, as a source of new consumer markets, and as a deep-pocketed investor.

The Arctic has global significance as a region for a number of factors. In 2009, the US Geological Survey's Circum-Arctic Resource Appraisal study found that 22 percent of the total undiscovered oil and natural gas left on the planet is located above the Arctic Circle.[33] The Arctic region is also rich in uranium, rare earth metals, gold, diamonds, zinc, nickel, coal, graphite, palladium, and iron ore. All of these mineral resources are located on the

---

[31] Rather than expanding, from 2012 the US Coast Guard – which provides the US polar icebreakers – has had its funds cut significantly.

[32] Marlene Laruelle, "Resources, State Reassertion and International Recognition: Locating the Drivers of Russia's Arctic Policy," *The Polar Journal* 4, no. 2 (2014): 253–70.

[33] USGS Energy Resources Program, "Regional Studies – Circum-Arctic Resource Appraisal," US Geological Survey, November 12, 2005, http://energy.usgs.gov/RegionalStudies/Arctic .aspx.

territory of the Arctic states. The Arctic has rich fisheries and forestry, and is an important site for scientific research of global significance. Major climate change was first observed in the Arctic; the impact of climate change is much stronger there than in other parts of the world, and it has a global impact. The Arctic region is also an important site for strategic space-related research in such areas as the earth's magnetic field and auroras.

The Arctic has also attracted intense international interest as a new shipping route. With the rapid onset of melting Arctic ice during the Northern Hemisphere summer months, many ocean-going nations are now exploring the possibility of the North and Northwest passages through Arctic seas as an alternative route between the Asia-Pacific and into northern Europe and the Americas. Though the Arctic route is hazardous and only seasonal, shipping companies are attracted to it because it can shave off a third of the time it takes to get between markets in Asia and Europe and the Americas, and it avoids chokepoints such as the Malacca Strait and conflict zones such as the Somali coast. The Arctic sea route will also be useful for the shipping of raw materials from the Arctic to industrial sectors in China, South Korea, and Japan.

The Arctic was a key site for US-Soviet military confrontation in the Cold War era, with both sides hosting significant military bases and strategic missile launch sites in the Arctic region. Virtually all of these sites were closed down or downsized in the 1990s. However, as the Arctic ice melts and tensions grow over access to Arctic resources and sea routes, many of the Arctic littoral states have been boosting their Arctic military presence. In 2013, the US government announced a 50 percent increase in the number of missiles stationed at its ground-based interceptor missile defense base in Fort Greely, Alaska. The missiles at Fort Greely are targeted at "rogue states" and the "theatre-missile threat";[34] in other words, at North Korea, Russia, and China. In 2014, Russia announced that it planned to "militarize the Arctic," that it was reopening a Cold War–era Arctic military base, and that its navy had begun patrolling the Northern Sea Route along Russia's Arctic coast from the Kara Sea to the Pacific Ocean.[35] As a consequence of all these developments, Arctic geopolitics are experiencing a sea change. There is an increasingly complex Arctic security environment, while Arctic states are divided on a number of issues.

---

[34] Mark Thompson, "Possible North Korean Threat Triggers Beefed Up Missile Shield," *Time*, March 15, 2013, http://ti.me/ZbUoBO.

[35] "Russia to Form Arctic Military Command by 2017," *Moscow Times*, October 1, 2014, http://www.themoscowtimes.com/business/article/russia-to-form-arctic-military-command-by-2017/508199.html.

Antarctica was the site for imperialist expansion, exploration, and exploitation by leading states and their agents from the 1800s through the mid-twentieth century. Russia, the United States, Great Britain, Norway, France, Germany, and Japan were early key actors in the region, reflecting their respective power – or aspiration to power – in the global system at the time. States geographically close to Antarctica, such as Chile, Argentina, Australia, and New Zealand, took a propriety interest in the territory, though they frequently lacked the capabilities of major powers to back up these interests. Then, as now, Antarctica has always been a mirror for the changing global balance of power and geopolitical rivalry. It is significant that Germany and Japan, the losers of the two major conflicts of the twentieth century, were both forced to renounce any rights to territorial claims in Antarctica as part of the terms of peace: Germany in the 1919 Treaty of Versailles, and Japan in the 1951 Treaty of San Francisco.

Antarctica is widely believed to be rich in mineral resources; however, the scientific evidence of this so far is scant. Until recently, only relatively preliminary research had been done to ascertain the extent of the continent's mineral, oil, and natural gas resources.[36] After the oil crisis of the 1970s, a number of countries engaged in exploratory mineral research in Antarctica. In a series of reports and maps published in the 1980s, a team of international researchers working with the US Geological Survey divided the Antarctic continent into three major geologic zones: the Andean metallogenic province, which is believed to contain mainly copper, platinum, gold, silver, chromium, nickel, diamonds, and other minerals; the Trans-Antarctic metallogenic province, which is speculated to be the world's largest deposit of coal, along with copper, lead, zinc, gold, silver, tin, and other minerals; and the East Antarctic iron metallogenic province, which contains significant amounts of iron ore, as well as gold, silver, copper, uranium, and molybdenum. The reports identify the key locations likely to have oil and natural gas deposits as the Ross Sea, Weddell Sea, Amundsen Sea, and the Bellingshausen Sea, with the Ross and Weddell seas likely to have commercially significant supplies.[37]

---

[36] D. I. M. MacDonald et al., "A Preliminary Assessment of the Hydrocarbon Potential of the Larsen Basin, Antarctica," *Marine and Petroleum Geology* 5 (1988): 34–53; and David I. M. MacDonald, "Coal, Oil and Gas," in *Encyclopedia of the Antarctic*, ed. Beau Riffenburgh (Abingdon, UK: Routledge: 2006), 1 and 268–69.

[37] "Regional Studies – Circum-Arctic Resource Appraisal"; and N. A. Wright and P. L. Williams, eds., *Mineral Resources of Antarctica*, Geological Survey Circular 705 (Reston, VA: US Geological Survey, 1974).

CHINA AS A POLAR GREAT POWER

China's emergence as a polar great power marks an important shift in its global presence and influence. Unlike the more established players in the polar regions, China has an increasing polar budget and program and plans for political, economic, scientific, and military expansion into the polar regions. China's expanding polar program demonstrates the resources that Beijing now has at hand to project power globally. Current analysis of China's growing power is essentially concerned with the question: As China becomes more powerful, will it attempt to change the existing global order? Power depends on the ability to influence others and achieve one's own goals. This book analyzes China's polar strategy, currently in the stage of doctrine formation and implementation, as a framework for understanding China's global ambitions, its ability to achieve them, and its attitude toward existing norms and governance structures. It also examines the extent to which existing polar regimes will be able to cope with the changing balance of power and other new pressures.

Many observers speculate that China's increased Arctic and Antarctic activities may challenge the interests of other states active in the Arctic and Antarctica. In recent years, there has been a flurry of policy papers and academic papers in English published on China and the Arctic.[38]

---

[38] Olga Alexeeva and Frédéric Lassare, "The Snow Dragon: China's Strategies in the Arctic," *Chinese Perspectives*, no. 3 (2012): 61–68; Caitlin Campbell, *China and the Arctic: Objectives and Obstacles*, US-China Economic and Security Review Commission Staff Report (Washington, DC: US-China Economic and Security Review Commission, 2012); Chen Gang, "China's Emerging Arctic Strategy," *The Polar Journal* 2, no. 2 (2012): 358–71; Aldo Chircop, "The Emergence of China as a Polar-Capable State," *Canadian Naval Review* 7, no. 1 (2011): 9–14; Kyle D. Christensen, "China in the Arctic: Potential Developments Impacting China's Activities in an Ice-Free Arctic," *On Track* 15, no. 4 (2010–11): 19–22; Malte Humpert and Andreas Raspotnik, "China in the 'Great White North,'" *European Geostrategy*, August 17, 2012; Linda Jakobson, *China Prepares for an Ice-Free Arctic*, SIPRI Insights on Peace and Security, 2010/2 (Stockholm, SIPRI, 2010); Linda Jakobson and Peng Jingchao, *China's Arctic Aspirations*, SIPRI Policy Paper No. 34 (Stockholm, SIPRI, 2012); Linda Jakobson, "China Wants to Be Heard on Arctic Issues," *Global Asia* 8, no. 4 (2013): 98–101; Linda Jakobson, "China's Security and the Arctic," in *Routledge Handbook of Chinese Security*, ed. Lowell Dittmer and Yu Maochun (Abingdon, UK: Routledge, 2015), 155–66; Mark Lanteigne, *China's Emerging Arctic Strategies: Economics and Institutions*, Institute of International Affairs, Centre for Arctic Policy Studies (Reykjavik: University of Iceland, 2014); Frédéric Lassare, *China and the Arctic: Threat or Cooperation Potential for Canada*, China Papers No. 11 (Toronto: Canadian International Council, June 2010); Paul McLeary, "The Arctic: China Opens Up a New Strategic Front," *World Politics Review*, May 19, 2010; Vijay Sakhuja, *China: Breaking into the Arctic Ice* (New Delhi: Indian Council of World Affairs, 2012); K. Joseph Spears, "China and the Arctic: The Awakening Snow Dragon," *China Brief* 9, no. 6 (2009): 10–13; K. Joseph Spears, "The Snow Dragon Moves in the Arctic Ocean Basin," *China Brief* 11, no. 2

In contrast, much less scholarly writing in English has been done on China and the Antarctic.[39] Yet China, like all the leading states in the global system, does not focus on one of the polar regions to the exclusion of the other. There is, as yet, no scholarly study in Chinese, English, or other languages of the range of China's polar interests and current government policy, their possible effects on other polar players, and their potential position in China's growing global role. Thus, *China as a Polar Great Power* breaks new ground to provide a detailed, in-depth study of China's long-standing polar interests and their implications for global governance. It is also the first study to examine China's overall polar activities and policies and locate them where they properly belong, within China's evolving maritime strategy (*haiyang zhengce*). It will discuss the part that China's polar initiatives play in other key concerns of the Chinese government, such as planning for China's long-term energy needs, maintaining its economic development, developing a strategic space program, and boosting the Chinese government's national and international prestige.

China as a Polar Great Power aims to help fill a gap in our understanding of China and its international relations and the challenges faced by current polar regimes. It explores a series of questions, including the following: What are China's strategic interests in the polar regions? Will China's rise in Antarctica impinge on the interests of other Antarctic Treaty nations, or of those that have not yet joined the treaty but have expressed an interest in the affairs of the Antarctic continent? Will China demand an upheaval of the Arctic Council to allow itself more of a voice in Arctic governance? Will China demand the establishment of a new Arctic body? Does China support the continuance of

(2010); Shiloh Rainwater, "Race to the North: China's Arctic Strategy and Its Implications," *Naval War College Review* 66, no. 2 (2013): 62–82; Roger W. Robinson Jr., "China's Long-Term Arctic Strategy," *Inside Policy*, October 12, 2013; Aki Tonami, "The Arctic Policy of China and Japan: Multi-layered Economic and Strategic Motivations," *The Polar Journal* 4, no. 1 (2014): 105–26; David Curtis Wright, *The Panda Bear Readies to Meet the Polar Bear: China Debates and Formulates Foreign Policy Towards Arctic Affairs and Canada's Arctic Sovereignty* (Calgary: Canadian Defence and Foreign Affairs Institute, 2010); David Curtis Wright, *The Dragon Eyes the Top of the World: Arctic Policy Debates and Discussion in China*, China Maritime Studies Institute No. 8 (Newport, RI: US Naval War College, 2011); and David Curtis Wright, "China's Growing Interest in the Arctic," *Journal of Military and Strategic Studies* 15, no. 2 (2013): 50–70.

39 Phillipe Forêt, "Mapping 'Ancient' Chinese Antarctica," *Bulletin of the Museum of Far Eastern Antiquities*, no. 73 (2001): 192–213; Wei-chin Lee, "China and Antarctica: So Far and Yet So Near," *Asian Survey* 30, no. 6 (1990): 576–86; Zuoyue Wang, "China Goes to the Poles: Science, Nationalism, and Internationalism in Chinese Polar Exploration," in *Extremes: Oceanography's Adventures at the Poles*, ed. Keith R. Benson and Helen M. Rozwadoski (Sagamore Beach, MA: Science History Publication, 2007), 269–302; and Zou Keyuan, "China's Antarctic Policy and the Antarctic Treaty System," *Ocean Development and International Law* 24, no. 3 (1993): 237–55.

the Antarctic Treaty and its 1991 Protocol on Environmental Protection? What are China's views on polar governance more broadly? Who are the actors in China's polar decision-making? What are China's polar strengths and weaknesses? What position does China take on key policy issues in the polar regions such as sovereignty and the exploitation of resources? Will China's growing interest in the Arctic impinge on the interests of the Arctic littoral states? And will China's perspective on polar issues appeal more widely to other states, helping to shape new global norms?

This book places China's polar involvement within the context of its evolving domestic and foreign policy, over eight chapters of analysis and discussion. Chapter 1 outlines the governance systems that manage the Arctic and Antarctic, and the range of rights that China and other states can access in these regions. Chapter 2 shows how China uses different framing techniques (including coded language and audience-specific messaging) to influence foreign and domestic public opinion on the polar regions, and examines the place of the polar regions in China's national narrative. Chapter 3 discusses the three strategic drivers of China's activities in the polar region – security, resources, and science – and chapter 4 discusses the CCP-state-military-market nexus in China's polar policymaking. Chapter 5 evaluates China's polar power from the point of view of polar presence, logistics capacity, budgets, scientific achievements, and polar leadership. Chapter 6 discusses China's position on contentious issues in polar governance such as Arctic and Antarctic sovereignty, access to resources, and environmental protection. Chapter 7 analyzes what China's polar engagement tells us about Beijing's attitude toward global governance, and the extent to which China can now be considered a global great power. Finally, chapter 8 concludes and summarizes the findings.

China as a Polar Great Power draws on a combination of Chinese-language primary source materials, classified policy papers, discussion documents, and interviews. In addition, careful use has been made of open-source writing by Chinese scholars and policymakers on polar affairs, supported by interviews, primary documents, and secondary source materials in English and other languages. In many polar states, nongovernmental organizations, business interests, and public intellectuals play a major role in polar politics and policymaking. Currently, in China their influence is much more curtailed, but as this book will show, these external actors are already helping to shape some aspects of polar policymaking in China and may become more prominent in further aspects as time goes by. Every effort has been made to accurately reflect internal Chinese policy discussion on polar issues in this book. Because of the political sensitivity of this research, all Chinese interview sources have been protected with anonymity. Throughout the book, the realist (in international relations theory terms) perspectives of the Chinese-language sources are presented as an accurate reflection of official opinion on the polar regions. The level of forward planning within the Chinese bureaucratic system is a symptom of this realist theoretical mindset, which has an underlying assumption of states as the most important actors in the global system, competition for resources as a key driver of global politics, and the international order as a hierarchy of states.

My research into China's polar interests was inspired by senior colleagues at the research center Gateway Antarctica in the University of Canterbury, who in 2006 asked me to investigate the topic of China and Antarctica because, as they told me, "China is spending a lot of money there, and we don't know why." The answer to that question has taken me in directions neither they nor I ever could have predicted. Researching this book has been like putting together a giant jigsaw puzzle, requiring a massive amount of academic detective work. In the following pages, I lay out the various pieces of this puzzle – China's polar interests, its polar capacity, and its polar policymaking process – and show how the pieces fit in to China's current global economic, political, and military expansion.

China's push into the polar regions encompasses maritime and nuclear security, the frontlines of climate change research, and the possibility of a resources bonanza. China's growing strength at the poles will be a game changer for a number of strategic vulnerabilities that could shift the global balance of power. The Chinese navy is not far off from developing a credible sea-based deterrent, and access to the polar regions is crucial to this endeavo – as is China's strategic space science which will enhance the PLA's C⁴ISR (command, control, communications, computers, intelligence, surveillance, and reconnaissance) and cyberwarfare capacities. In the past ten years, China has spent a lot of money at the poles – investing more in capacity than any other nation – because access to all the opportunities available in the Arctic and Antarctic are essential for China to achieve its goal of restoring its international status and becoming "a rich country with a strong army" (*fu guo qiang bing*). Both the Arctic and Antarctic have unresolved sovereignty issues, so China has acted like any great power would, dramatically extending its presence there and responding to any initiatives to restrict access to the poles with great resistance. A new international order is emerging, and the polar regions offer front row seats to observe this changing geopolitics.

1

Polar Governance

From the Chinese government's perspective, the polar regions belong to the common heritage of humankind which means that all states should have the right to participate in, and help shape, their future global governance. The unique features of Arctic and Antarctic governance offer extensive rights for influence and access to nonlittoral states such as China. China is assiduously researching every angle on these polar rights and is trying to access every aspect of them.

ARCTIC GOVERNANCE AND POLITICS

Most people can pinpoint the Arctic by the North Pole, but few know or understand its boundaries. There are several different definitions of what comprises the Arctic zone: (1) the area within 66°32′ N, known as the Arctic Circle; (2) the area north of the Arctic tree line, where only lichen and shrubs grow; and (3) any locations at a high latitude where average daily summer temperatures do not rise above 10 degrees Celsius.[1] Broadly speaking, the Arctic region encompasses the Arctic Ocean and the surrounding land territories, including all of Greenland and the Svalbard archipelago, plus the northern parts of the US state of Alaska, Canada, Norway, and Russia. (See figure 1.1 for a Chinese map of the Arctic region, and figure 1.2 for a China National Petroleum Corporation map of Arctic mineral resources.) Thus, the Arctic is a mixture of sovereign territories, internal waters, and high seas. As a consequence, the governance of the Arctic region is a complex combination of national law, established international instruments, and evolving regional management.

---

[1]   "What Is the Arctic?" National Snow and Ice Data Center, 2016, https://nsidc.org/cryosphere/arctic-meteorology/arctic.html.

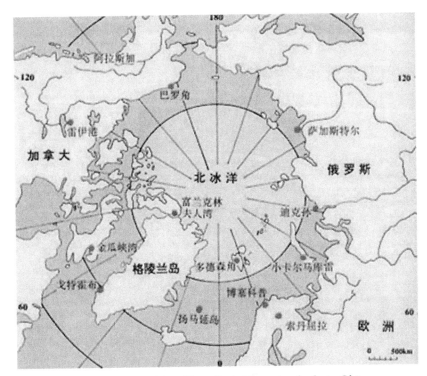

FIGURE 1.1 Chinese Arctic Map: How the Arctic region looks in Chinese maps – a vast expanse of ice-free international waters.

Source: "Beiji diqu" [The Arctic region], Xinhua, July 13, 2006, http://news .xinhuanet.com/ziliao/2006-07/13/content_4826007.htm.

Rather than one single regime or treaty system, Arctic governance involves a number of issue-specific arrangements.[2] The most prominent instrument of Arctic governance is the Arctic Council, established in 1996 as a forum for cooperation on a broad range of Arctic-related matters. In 2013, the Arctic Council's permanent secretariat was opened in Tromsø, Norway.

There are eight permanent members of the Arctic Council: Canada, Denmark, Finland, Iceland, Norway, Russia, Sweden, and the United States. Six Arctic indigenous communities have permanent participant status in the council. In addition, eleven non-Arctic states – China, France, Germany, Italy, Japan, the Netherlands, Poland, Singapore, South Korea, Spain, and the United Kingdom – have been granted observer status. This status is reviewed every four

[2] O. R. Young, "Governing the Arctic: From Cold War Theater to Mosaic of Cooperation," *Global Governance* 11, no. 1 (2005): 9–15.

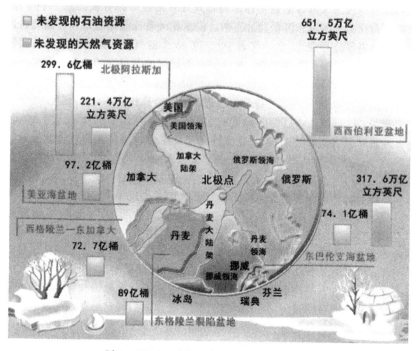

FIGURE 1.2 China National Petroleum Corporation Map of Arctic Mineral Resources

Source: Ding Huang, ed., *Jidi guojia zhengce yanjiu baogao 2012–2013* [Annual report on national polar policy research 2012–13] (Beijing: Kexue chubanshe, 2013), 22.

years. Observer states are expected to contribute to Arctic Council working groups, but they may make only written statements at Arctic Council meetings and must propose any new projects through an Arctic state or participant. In 2008, five Arctic Council states (Canada, Denmark, Norway, Russia, and United States), announced the Ilulissat Declaration which aimed to block any new international regime being imposed on the Arctic region. In 2009, the council established guidelines for the development of oil and natural gas in the Arctic region; in 2011, it adopted a binding agreement on search-and-rescue cooperation. Yet many of the challenges facing the Arctic, such as rapid climate change and toxic damage, originate outside the region, and the solutions for these problems also must come from outside the region.[3] International pressure

---

[3]   See Olav Schram Stokke, "Can Asian Involvement Strengthen Arctic Governance?," in *Asian Countries and the Arctic Future*, eds. Leiv Lunde, Yang Jian, and Iselin Stensdahl (Singapore: World Scientific Publishing, 2016), 51–60.

is growing to devise an integrated management regime for Arctic seaways and for agreements on military activities, environmental protection, airspace rights, and marine safety.

The Arctic Council is an important actor in Arctic governance, but its significance should not be overinflated. It has very limited resources and powers, and will only deal with issues on which all participants can agree. Other organizations have a greater say in Arctic governance matters, such as the International Tribunal for the Law of the Sea, the United Nations (UN) Commission on the Limits of the Continental Shelf, the International Maritime Organization (IMO), the Secretariat of the UN Framework Convention on Climate Change, and the United Nations Environment Programme (UNEP). The 1982 United Nations Convention on the Law of the Sea (UNCLOS) is one of the most significant international agreements pertinent to the Arctic Ocean. All of the Arctic Council members are coastal states, and with the exception of the United States, all have signed and ratified UNCLOS.

One of the potentially most contentious aspects of UNCLOS, in terms of the Arctic, is the right for coastal states to delineate the outer limits of their continental shelf. Under UNCLOS, a coastal state exercises *sovereign rights* – but not *sovereignty* – over its continental shelf "for the purpose of exploring it and exploiting its natural resources."[4] Since 2001, four of the eight Arctic Council members (Canada, Denmark, Norway, and Russia) have been preparing their submissions to the UN Commission on the Limits of the Continental Shelf, the international body involved in evaluating these limits and making recommendations regarding coastal status. All four submitting states have claims in the Arctic Ocean, and it could take at least twenty years to resolve them. Where claims overlap, the commission does not have decision-making powers to resolve the dispute; instead, this process must be managed by negotiation and diplomacy between the affected states.[5] The commission itself is mostly made up of scientists from developing, non-Arctic states. China has a Chinese scientist working on the commission, but of the claimant Arctic states, only Canada and Russia have scientists on the commission.[6]

---

4   See UNCLOS, December 10, 1982, Article 77, 54, http://www.un.org/depts/los/convention_agree ments/texts/unclos/unclos_e.pdf.
5   Peter J. Cook and Chris M. Carleton, eds., *Continental Shelf Limits: The Scientific and Legal Interface* (Oxford: Oxford University Press, 2000), 312–13.
6   "Members of the Commission on the Limits of the Continental Shelf, 2012–2017," UNCLOS, August 8, 2014, http://www.un.org/depts/los/clcs_new/commission_members.htm.

In the 2008 Ilulissat Declaration, the Arctic littoral states asserted that they would resolve any disputes among themselves, but this may not be easy to achieve. Russia's intervention in Crimea in 2014 is a portent of the risks involved in future negotiations on Arctic sovereignty. Since 2007, Russia has been increasingly nationalistic regarding its Arctic rights. When these Arctic Ocean boundaries are resolved – and some of them are likely to be contentious – the rights to mine the resources in the area beyond national jurisdiction will be managed by the International Seabed Authority (ISA), the international body established by UNCLOS to regulate mineral-related activities in the international seabed. China's scientist at the UN Commission on the Limits of the Continental Shelf is on this body as well. China currently has three deep seabed mining contracts with ISA.

The Law of the Sea Convention is a globally applicable governance model for managing most, though not all, aspects of Arctic Ocean governance. However, UNCLOS cannot resolve the issue of shared fish stocks, some of which are in international waters. The UN's Food and Agriculture Organization has a role here; it has a sustainable fishing ecosystem management program, as well as the UN Fish Stocks Agreement (in force since 2001) that puts the sustainable fishing principles established in UNCLOS into action.[7] The UN Convention on the Prevention of Marine Pollution by Dumping of Wastes and Other Matter 1972, also known as the London Convention, applies to the Arctic Ocean as well.[8] Furthermore, UNEP supports governance in the Arctic, and the Arctic and the Antarctic are included in UNEP's regional seas program which helps neighboring states develop cooperative measures to manage environmental risks in shared waters as "independent regions."[9] The International Convention for the Regulation of Whaling governs whaling in the Arctic (and Antarctic); currently, both Iceland and Norway harvest whales in Arctic seas.

[7] "Overview – Convention and Related Agreements," Division for Ocean Affairs and the Law of the Sea, United Nations, July 31, 2013, http://www.un.org/depts/los/convention_agreements/convention_overview_fish_stocks.htm; and United Nations, Agreement for the Implementation of the Provisions of the United Nations Convention on the Law of the Sea of 10 December 1982 Relating to the Conservation and Management of Straddling Fish Stocks and Highly Migratory Fish Stocks, A/CONF.164/37, September 8, 1995, http://www.un.org/depts/los/convention_agreements/texts/fish_stocks_agreement/CONF164_37.htm.
[8] "Convention on the Prevention of Marine Pollution by Dumping of Wastes and Other Matter," IMO, 2016, http://www.imo.org/en/OurWork/Environment/LCLP/Pages/default.aspx.
[9] "Regional Seas Programs," UNEP, 2016, http://www.unep.org/regionalseas/programmes/independent/default.asp.

The IMO is a UN agency that regulates international shipping focusing on safety and antipollution measures.[10] In 2015, it announced a new polar code, a binding international framework aimed at governing shipping standards for the polar seas and protecting them from environmental risks.[11] In 2012, the IMO's Marine Safety Committee adopted a mandatory ship reporting system for certain categories of ships passing through the Barents Sea region. As a result, all ships with a gross tonnage of over 5000 tons, all tankers, all ships carrying hazardous cargoes, all vessels towing another when the length of the tow exceeds 200 meters, and any ship with defective navigational aids must report to either Norway's Vardø Vehicle Traffic Service (VTS) or Russia's Murmansk VTS when they enter the Barents Sea area.[12] A further global governance body, the International Hydrographic Organization, is managing a project to map Arctic waters; however, only Arctic littoral states can join this activity.[13] Finally, the Convention on the Conservation and Management of Pollock Resources in the Central Bering Sea manages fishing in this zone; China is a signatory to this convention, as are South Korea and Japan.

Polar law specialist Christopher C. Joyner argued in 2009 that the existing body of international law relevant to the Arctic region was a "patchwork," and that some aspects were difficult to implement. He said that rapid changes in the Arctic environment necessitated a new "comprehensive legal regime for protecting, conserving, and managing the Arctic Ocean."[14] However, the Ilulissat Declaration drew a line in the sand about the possibility of an Arctic Treaty being formed. Without the consent of the five Arctic littoral states, no new international legal instrument can be created for the region.

There is one Arctic region-specific treaty of global interest: the 1920 Spitsbergen Treaty.[15] This treaty granted sovereignty over the Spitsbergen archipelago (now called Svalbard) to Norway, while permitting all

10   IMO website, 2016, http://www.imo.org/en/Pages/Default.aspx.
11   "Ships Operating in Polar Regions," IMO, 2016, http://www.imo.org/en/OurWork/Safety/Saf etyTopics/Pages/PolarShippingSafety.aspx.
12   "Shipping in Polar Waters," IMO, 2016, http://www.imo.org/en/MediaCentre/HotTopics/po lar/Pages/default.aspx.
13   "Fourth Arctic Regional Hydrographic Commission Meeting, January 29–30, 2014," International Hydrographic Organization, July 21, 2014, http://www.iho.int/mtg_docs/rhc/Ar HC/ArHC4/ArHC4Docs.htm.
14   Christopher C. Joyner, "The Legal Regime for the Arctic Ocean," *International Journal of Transnational Law and Policy* 18, no. 2 (2009), 244.
15   "Treaty Concerning the Archipelago of Spitsbergen, and Protocol (Paris, February 9, 1920)," Australian Treaty Series 1925 No. 10, Department of Foreign Affairs and Trade, Canberra, 1999, http://www.austlii.edu.au/au/other/dfat/treaties/1925/10.html.

signatories to the treaty equal rights to resource exploitation and trade.[16] Since the 1980s, Norway has defined scientific research as a key economic activity in the Svalbard archipelago, thereby permitting many non-Arctic states to have a foothold in the Arctic through their involvement in scientific activity.[17] Currently, there are more than forty signatories to this treaty. China, as the Republic of China, signed the Spitsbergen Treaty in 1925. In recent years, many non-Arctic states that wish to have a role in setting future norms in Arctic governance have set up research stations at Ny-Ålesund, a research town on Spitsbergen Island. This was advantageous to them when, in 2013, the Arctic Council decided which new states could become permanent observers at its meetings. Having a significant Arctic science program was one of the criteria for observer status. The Ny-Ålesund Science Managers Committee (NySMAC) was established in 1994 to enhance cooperation and coordination among research activities at the Ny-Ålesund International Arctic Research and Monitoring Facility.[18] Each country with a research station at Ny-Ålesund is entitled to have a representative on the committee.

A number of other regional bodies are engaged in Arctic-related political, economic, and scientific cooperation. The most recently formed is Arctic Circle, a nongovernmental organization sponsored by the government of Iceland. It was launched in 2013 by President Ólafur Ragnar Grímsson of Iceland at a high-profile ceremony in Washington, D.C. Arctic Circle aims to be a forum for debate among Arctic nations, non-Arctic states, and other actors such as commercial interests that wish to be active in the Arctic region. The formation of this new group is an implicit criticism of the Ilulissat Five which wanted to place limits on non-Arctic states' involvement in the region. In time, Arctic Circle may be able to take on the same relationship to the Arctic Council that the ASEAN Regional Forum has to the Association of Southeast Asian Nations (ASEAN). The ASEAN Regional Forum has seventeen members and meets regularly with ASEAN to discuss regional concerns. International relations scholar Jon M. Van Dyke has suggested that a similar organization of non-Arctic states with an interest in the region could participate in decision-making on Arctic issues with global relevance, as well as help

---

[16] "The Svalbard Treaty (Paris, February 9, 1920)," University of Oslo Faculty of Law, accessed April 27, 2016, http://www.jus.uio.no/english/services/library/treaties/01/1-11/svalbard-treaty.xml.

[17] Adam Grydehøj, Anne Grydehøj, and Maria Ackrén Ilisimatusarfik, "The Globalization of the Arctic: Negotiating Sovereignty and Building Communities in Svalbard, Norway," *Island Studies Journal* 7, no. 1 (2012), 112.

[18] See the NySMAC website, http://nysmac.npolar.no/.

fund programs and working groups.[19] So far, the Arctic littoral states, of which Iceland is not a member, have not budged on their resistance to any further internationalization of Arctic governance.

The Northern Forum, established in 1993, is a further Arctic political association of note. It groups twenty-four subnational and regional units of government, and focuses on economic concerns and the issue of sustainable development in Arctic and near-Arctic areas that tend to be heavily dependent on resource extraction. The forum has observer status in the Arctic Council.[20] Other Arctic cooperation groupings include the Conference of Parliamentarians of the Arctic regions; the World Winter Cities Association for Mayors; the International Arctic Science Committee; the International Arctic Social Sciences Association; and regional groupings such as the Nordic Council, the Barents Euro-Arctic Council, and the Pacific Northwest Economic Region's Arctic Caucus.

ANTARCTIC GOVERNANCE AND POLITICS

Defining Antarctic territory is much simpler than defining the Arctic. The Antarctic continent is surrounded by the Southern Ocean and takes up most of the area south of the Antarctic Circle (latitude 66° 33′ 45.9″). Antarctica is remote from human settlement and did not undergo significant human exploration until the end of the 1800s. Unlike the Arctic, there is no international instrument that recognizes special rights in Antarctica by virtue of proximity. But, inevitably, the eight countries closest to the Antarctic continent (Argentina, Australia, Brazil, Chile, France through its French Southern and Antarctic Lands in the Indian Ocean, New Zealand, South Africa, and the United Kingdom through its Falkland Islands territory), and the seven countries that have territorial claims there (Argentina, Australia, Chile, France, New Zealand, Norway and the United Kingdom), all have vested interests in Antarctica and the Southern Ocean that set them somewhat apart from the other states active there. Yet under the current Antarctic governance model, which puts aside the issue of sovereignty drawing attention

---

[19] Jon M. Van Dyke, "Regional Cooperation in the South China Sea and the Arctic Ocean," in *Maritime Security Issues in the South China Sea and the Arctic: Sharpened Competition or Collaboration?*, ed. Gordon Houlden and Hong Nong (Beijing: China Democracy and Legal System Publishing House, 2012), 233.

[20] See the Northern Forum's Mission and Structure page at the Northern Forum website, http://www.northernforum.org/en/the-northern-forum/about-the-northern-forum/mission-and-structure.

to those interests in the same way that Arctic littoral states do, is sure to provoke ire from other interested parties.

Since 1961, Antarctica has been managed under the Antarctic Treaty System (ATS), a series of international agreements that began with the Antarctic Treaty. The Antarctic Treaty was initiated by the United States and its allies, in the words of US secretary of state John Foster Dulles in 1956, so as "to keep Antarctica in friendly hands."[21] This point was made even more explicit when the US negotiator of the Antarctic Treaty, Paul Daniels, argued the case for setting up an international regime in Antarctica in 1958, stating it might be easier to control the Russians if they were in a regime than if they were out of one.[22] The Antarctic Treaty was signed in 1959 and entered into force in 1961. The treaty was a product of the Cold War and the rivalry between the United States and the Soviet Union, as well as of escalating tensions over the overlapping territorial claims of the seven Antarctic claimant nations (see figure 1.3). It aimed to balance all these interests as well as those of other interested states. The Antarctic Treaty privileges science as the core legitimate activity on the continent and the primary resource to be extracted from the continent. Antarctic scientific activities are the sole justification for states to be allowed to participate in Antarctic governance.

In spite of its international scope, the Antarctic Treaty did not resolve the issue of sovereignty for the original seven claimants; for the United States and Russia, which have maintained a basis of claim on the continent, or for other countries that have also signed the treaty and regard Antarctica as an international space, *res nullius*, or else as part of the common heritage of humankind. Article IV (1) of the Antarctic Treaty deals with the issue of Antarctic sovereignty claims by putting them on hold. Article IV (2) further states that no new activity in Antarctica will be allowed to "constitute a basis for asserting, supporting, or denying a claim to territorial sovereignty in Antarctica or create

---

[21] Agenda Paper, Commonwealth Prime Ministers Conference, 1956, A1838/1495/3/2/1 Part 2, National Archives of Australia, as cited in David Day, *Antarctica: A Biography* (Oxford: Oxford University Press, 2013), 479. For an in-depth discussion of US polar policy and strategy in the Cold War era, see Department of State Policy Statement, "Polar Regions," July 1, 1951, *Foreign Relations of the United States, 1951, National Security Affairs; Foreign Economic Policy*, Vol. 1 (Washington, DC: US Government Printing Office, 1979), doc. 765, https://history.state.gov/historicaldocuments/frus1951v01/d765.

[22] Memorandum of Conversation, January 30, 1958, Department of State, Bureau of Inter-American Affairs, Office of the Deputy Assistant Secretary, Office files, 1956–1959, box 25, Antarctica file, US National Archives and Records Administration, as noted in Day, *Antarctica*, 483.

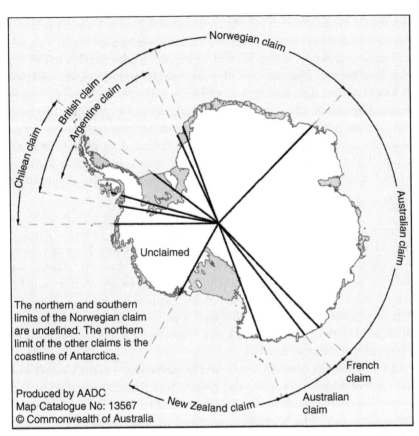

The northern and southern
limits of the Norwegian claim
are undefined. The northern
limit of the other claims is the
coastline of Antarctica.

Produced by AADC
Map Catalogue No: 13567
© Commonwealth of Australia

FIGURE 1.3 Antarctica: Territorial Claims: Antarctic map showing territorial
claims and base locations.

Source: Commonwealth of Australia, 2016, https://data.aad.gov.au/aadc/mapcat/
display_map.cfm?map_id=13567.

any rights of sovereignty in Antarctica."[23] The treaty permits the orderly
exploitation of certain Antarctic resources: free access to the continent for
scientific research, free access to the continent for individual exploration and
adventure, managed fishing, and unlimited tourism and bioprospecting.
However, since the 1991 Protocol on Environmental Protection (also known
as the Madrid Protocol or the Antarctic Environmental Protocol) entered into
force in 1998, mineral exploitation and exploration have been banned,

23 "The Antarctic Treaty," Secretariat of the Antarctic Treaty, December 1, 1959, http://www.ats
    .aq/documents/ats/treaty_original.pdf.

although scientific research into Antarctic minerals has not (as per Article 7 of the abovementioned protocol). However, the definition of which mineral-seeking activities are "scientific" and which are "exploration" is left to the individual nations. Each nation with a research station in Antarctica acts as if its bases are sovereign territory and applies its national laws there, including the right to exclude others. As this has been the norm for more than fifty years and no state, whether claimant or nonclaimant, has ever objected to it, this situation amounts to local customary law, independent of the Antarctic Treaty.[24] This means that the more scientific bases and work sites a nation has in Antarctica, the more *de facto* control their government has over territory there.

The Antarctic Treaty and all its instruments highlight the "freedom of scientific investigation" as a key activity on the continent. From the point of view of polar scientists Antarctica is a perfect laboratory for many areas of scientific research, and the privileged research budgets granted for Antarctic projects by many governments is an added incentive. But from the perspective of many national governments, establishing national Antarctic science programs is the means to establish political influence in Antarctic affairs, while setting up Antarctic scientific bases enables effective control over key swathes of Antarctic territory.

In addition to the Antarctic Treaty and its various instruments, a number of other international agreements also govern Antarctic affairs, including the International Convention for the Regulation of Whaling, UNCLOS, and the IMO's polar code. The Scientific Committee on Antarctic Research (SCAR) also plays an important role in Antarctic governance by initiating, coordinating, and developing international Antarctic scientific research, while also providing advice to the ATS on scientific matters. The Council of Managers of National Antarctic Programs (COMNAP) coordinates Antarctic logistics links and other forms of cooperation between Antarctic states and offers policy advice to the Antarctic Treaty members on issues such as environmental management.[25]

Fifty-three states have signed the Antarctic Treaty, though only the twenty-eight Antarctic Treaty Consultative Parties (ATCPs), have a say in how the continent is governed. The ATCPs are an exclusive group of states with the resources and scientific infrastructure needed to conduct Antarctic science.

[24] Anne-Marie Brady, "Democratising Antarctic Governance," *The Polar Journal* 2, no. 2 (2012): 451–61.
[25] Council of Managers of National Antarctic Programs (COMNAP), accessed April 27, 2016, https://www.comnap.aq/SitePages/Home.aspx.

In the decade following the signing of the Antarctic Environmental Protocol in 1991, the number of signatories to the treaty had been fairly static. But since 2011, reflecting the changes in the international system, five new states (Iceland, Kazakhstan, Malaysia, Mongolia, and Pakistan) have signed the treaty. Both Turkey and Iran have announced plans to set up Antarctic bases: Turkey joined the Antarctic Treaty in 1995, but Iran has not yet said whether it will sign the treaty. Meanwhile, global environmental groups are lobbying governments and attempting to sway public opinion to preserve and extend environmental management in Antarctica. Their concern is not unwarranted. In the past five years, Bulgaria, Belarus, China, India, Iran, South Korea, Turkey, and Russia have all publicly expressed an interest in assessing Antarctic mineral resources. Regulated and unregulated fishing in the Antarctic Ocean is on the increase. Meanwhile, Japan continues its whaling program in the Southern Ocean, despite strenuous international censure. Ever-growing global energy needs and heightened food security concerns are reawakening international interest in the resources of the Antarctic continent and its oceans. With their unwieldy, nonenforceable structures, the treaty and its associated instruments appear inadequate to deal with these many new challenges.

In addition to its potential abundance of minerals, Antarctica is rich in many other resources, all of which are available to states that are able to exploit them. Up to 72 percent of the world's freshwater is locked up in Antarctic ice, and there is no restriction within the Antarctic Treaty to harvest it other than the Environmental Protocol. Antarctica is also filled with unique biological organisms that may have commercial potential. The ATCPs have resisted suggestions that the practice be regulated, or the idea that any income resulting from bioprospecting belongs to all of humanity under the principle of the common heritage of humankind. Antarctic waters are rich in krill and other fishing resources which are managed by the Commission for the Conservation of Antarctic Marine Living Resources (CCAMLR), a treaty agency. Antarctic tourism is a lucrative industry, cornered by a few boutique agencies. Tourists now vastly outnumber scientists. In the 2015–16 season, 38,478 tourists visited Antarctica, while the number of Antarctic scientists visiting that year was less than 4000. According to information released in May 2016, the International Association of Antarctica Tour Operators expects that the numbers of tourists in Antarctica will surge to 43,000 in 2016–17.[26] Many observers believe that this

---

[26] "Antarctic Tourism Figures Released as IAATO's 25th Anniversary Meeting Begins," International Association of Antarctica Tour Operators, May 3, 2016, http://iaato.org/docu ments/10157/1278700/News+Release+IAATO+2016+opens++Final.pdf/.

growing tourism industry is unsatisfactorily regulated, yet ATCPs have resisted calls for it to be better managed through a new treaty mechanism. Instead, the International Association of Antarctic Tour Operators has set a voluntary code of practice which has repeatedly proven ineffective at properly managing the environmental risks associated with taking large numbers of people and boats into the fragile Antarctic environment.

Antarctica is a valuable research site for militarily significant strategic research on space and climate. Moreover, engagement in Antarctic affairs is a high-prestige activity that many nations – big and small – use to demonstrate that they want to be global players with global foreign policies. Article I (2) of the Antarctic Treaty restricts military activities in Antarctica and the surrounding seas to "peaceful purposes" only, a rather wide definition that is open to interpretation. Article I (1) says that states may not engage in any measure of a military nature, such as establishing military bases and fortifications, carrying out military maneuvers, or testing any type of weapon. Argentina, Australia, Brazil, Chile, New Zealand, and the United States all currently use their militaries in Antarctica for logistics. For Antarctic claimant states, the use of militaries in logistics is a subtle, politically acceptable means of signifying occupation. For global powers such as the United States, utilizing military forces in logistics enables them to maintain familiarity with polar conditions which would be useful in the event of a global military crisis that affected strategic air and sea chokepoints such as the Panama and Suez canals and the North Pacific. In addition, whether or not states use their militaries for Antarctic logistics, the satellite receiving stations and telescopes housed at the Antarctic bases of rising and leading global powers such as China, India, France, Norway, Russia, and the United States have strategic dual civil-military capabilities that provide an additional motivation for maintaining a physical presence there. The Antarctic Treaty and subsequent agreements are silent on the issue of how to deal with the military, nonpeaceful aspects of this technology.

Antarctic Treaty Consultative Meetings are usually pro forma affairs attended by government officials who have only limited power for setting new agendas or responding to governance challenges. The meetings have consistently failed to address potentially high-conflict issues such as the claimant states' Antarctic continental shelf applications to the UN Commission on the Limits of the Continental Shelf. From the perspective of some non-claimant states – of which China has been the most vocal – the claimant states' submission of information to the commission amounted to an attempt to expand their territorial claims on the continent. However, even though the commission accepted submissions from claimant states, decisions about the status of these claims were set aside in keeping with the provisions of the Antarctic Treaty.[27]

The Antarctic Treaty requires full consensus for all decision-making. This structure enables the established Antarctic players to maintain the status quo but does not allow them to address new challenges; in fact, it appears to be getting more cumbersome as the years progress. In many ways, the term "Antarctic governance" is a misnomer. There is very little oversight of the various countries active there, and almost no enforcement through ATS instruments when nations break the governance rules. The treaty permits and encourages base inspections, but such inspections are not in-depth and inspectors do not ask hard questions about the extent to which science is the main activity or whether the bases follow environmental management and reporting guidelines.

The Antarctic Treaty was designed to keep conflict out of the Antarctic region and maintain the interests of the existing players. Under those terms it was a success, but more than two decades after the end of the Cold War, the Antarctic Treaty now has the air of an antiquated gentleman's club that is out of touch with present-day geopolitics. Poorer countries are effectively excluded from Antarctic governance because only those nations with recognized Antarctic scientific interests, whether as original claimant states or through established Antarctic scientific research programs, may become ATCPs. The restrictions on which states can have a say on Antarctic affairs undermines the treaty's political legitimacy. As with any international instrument, the treaty's efficacy will be measured by the number of states that sign up to it, as well as the extent to which signatories respect its principles.

The 1991 Protocol on Environmental Protection can be modified or amended at any time, but unanimous agreement by all consultative parties is required to change its provisions. However, from 2048, the protocol will have been in force for fifty years. At that time, according to Article 25 of the protocol, any of the ATCPs can request that a conference be held to review its terms, and a simple three-quarters majority of the ATCPs, which must include all those who signed the original protocol, could alter those terms. This review is not automatic, but judging from the recent statements of many Antarctic states, it should not be difficult to find a government willing to put forward the motion. Many oil-poor states, especially those that lack guaranteed access to oil and natural gas through their allies, regard Antarctica's potential mineral

---

27 Tina Schoolmeester and Elaine Baker, eds., *Continental Shelf: The Last Maritime Zone* (Arendal, Norway: UNEP/GRID-Arendal, 2009), http://www.unep.org/dewa/Portals/67/pdf/Continental_Shelf.pdf.

resources as part of the solution to their medium-term energy needs. However, before the ban on mineral resource activity can be lifted, a comprehensive minerals treaty would have to be in place. This is why countries such as China, that are interested in the potential of Antarctic minerals, are now engaging in the strategic planning and research that will help construct a new instrument of global governance to protect their interests. If the amendment to the minerals ban does not enter into force within three years of it having been proposed, then any party may withdraw from the protocol.

Much groundbreaking science has come out of Antarctica, such as the identification of the ozone hole, the reconstruction of the past million years of global climate history from ice cores, the establishment of a sustainable management system for Southern Ocean fisheries, the mapping of Antarctica's subglacial lakes, and the continuation of innovative research into the origin of the southern continents. However, for all of the governments engaged in these scientific activities, the main goal is meeting their strategic needs, both political and economic. Science is the currency of Antarctic politics; high-level science garners high-level influence, and having at least a basic scientific program in Antarctica is the fig leaf for maintaining a base there. Though many scientists work cooperatively on international projects, scientific bases in Antarctica are run by national programs and act as effective diplomatic posts. National Antarctic bases are a way to signal presence and establish effective control over strategic regions. This approach generates a significantly larger environmental footprint in Antarctica than if scientific activities and environmental protection, as opposed to simply maintaining a physical presence there, were truly the focus of Antarctic Treaty partners. Many of the ATCPs lack sufficient resources to engage in meaningful Antarctic science and fill their bases with support personnel. Many Antarctic stations, in contravention of the treaty, are essentially military camps. Currently, at least three ATCPs openly rent out beds on their bases to visiting tourists. This practice is not technically illegal under the treaty, but it contravenes the norms of behavior among signatory states.

Some critics of the Antarctic Treaty say that Antarctica should be run by the UN. Throughout the 1980s and 1990s, Malaysia, supported by many other developing countries, unsuccessfully raised this point at UN meetings. The proposal failed to gain traction due to the stonewalling of Antarctic Treaty stakeholders. Other critics argue that a whole new set of international laws applying to all nations, not just Antarctic Treaty members, should govern the continent. In the post–Cold War, post-unipolar global order, the clash of values and interests of emerging players such as China, against those of established Antarctic players, is putting the treaty and its instruments under increasing pressure.

CHINA'S RIGHTS AND INTERESTS IN THE POLAR REGIONS

The Arctic and Antarctic are both intrinsically important to China as the location of significant natural resources, scientific research sites, and key waterways. They are also understood as sites where rising powers can expand, test, and protect their increasing international interests and prestige. In 2011, Chen Lianzeng, the deputy director of China's State Oceanic Administration, stated that the overall goal of China's current five-year polar plan was to increase China's "status and influence" in polar affairs to better protect its "polar rights."[28] So just what are China's polar rights?

In the Arctic, along with all non-Arctic states, China has the following rights:

- To engage in scientific and economic activities in the Svalbard islands;
- To apply for observer status at the Arctic Council;
- To access Arctic seas for scientific research, transportation, tourism, and fishing;
- To utilize cross-Arctic air routes;
- To participate in international decision-making on Arctic matters under international governance;
- To bid for mineral rights and other economic opportunities with Arctic states; and
- To bid for deep-sea mineral exploration licenses in Arctic international waters.

In Antarctica, along with other states in the world, China has the following rights:

- To engage in Antarctic science;
- To set up scientific bases in Antarctica;
- To inspect the Antarctic bases of other nations;
- To access the science data of other Antarctic states;
- To participate in Antarctic governance under existing norms and agreements;
- To participate in Antarctic Treaty committees and working groups;

[28] "Wo guo xinjin jidi kexue kaocha pobingchuan lizheng 2013 nian touru shiyong" [Our new polar expedition icebreaker should be ready by 2013], Xinhua, June 22, 2011, http://news .xinhuanet.com/tech/2011-06/22/c_121566754.htm.

- To participate in setting any new norms in Antarctic governance;
- To fish in Antarctic waters;
- To access Antarctic freshwater;
- To engage in bioprospecting in Antarctica;
- To send tourists to Antarctica;
- To exercise jurisdiction over its own citizens in Antarctica;
- To use Antarctic seas and airspace for peaceful activities;
- To utilize its military for peaceful purposes in Antarctica;
- To set up polar-orbiting satellites, to locate polar satellite receiving stations and strategic airfields in Antarctica; and
- To bid for deep-sea mineral exploration in the Southern Ocean through the ISA (after sovereignty rights there are decided).

China is currently utilizing almost all of its Arctic and Antarctic rights, or has plans to take action on them and develop them further in the future.

2

The Polar Regions in China's National Narrative

In February 2015, China's official news service, Xinhua, published an article promoting a new film by one of the most remarkable players in China's growing polar industry, entrepreneur-cum-filmmaker Fang Li. The film's title alone underscored the fusion between China's commercial ambitions in the Antarctic and their ties with the ruling Chinese Communist Party. Fang told journalists that the title, *Antarctica 2049* (*Nanji 2049*), refers to the date when "humanity will open up a new area of mineral resource exploitation" in Antarctica – as well as being the 100-year anniversary of the founding of the People's Republic of China, when the Chinese nation "will have completed its modernization process." Fang said that he is targeting his film at Chinese youth audiences.[1]

Antarctica 2049 is a collaboration between China's national polar entity, the Polar Research Institute of China (PRIC), and Fang's company, Beijing Laurel Films. The film was made under the supervision of some of China's leading polar scientists and policymakers, including PRIC deputy head Qin Weijia and glaciologists Sun Bo and Liu Xiaohan.[2] Fang Li is well connected in polar affairs in China. As well as being a film producer of some notoriety, he is chief executive officer of Laurel Industrial, one of the world's largest marine geophysical survey instruments and systems integration firms. Laurel Industrial supplies the technology used in China's deep sea mining, seabed bathymetrics, and polar marine exploration.

[1] "Zhongguoren jinru Nanji 30 duo nian" [Thirty years of Chinese people in the Antarctic], Xinhua, February 18, 2015, http://news.xinhuanet.com/tech/2015–02/18/c_1114404858.htm.
[2] "Zhipianren Fang Li tou xin pian jihua mingnian pai Nanji kehuan pian" [Producer Fang Li plans to shoot Antarctic science fiction movie next year], *Sina yule*, April 18, 2013, http://ent .sina.com.cn/m/c/2013–04-18/14543903215.shtml; and "Kexuejia de guangyingjie" [Scientist's glamorous world], *Huanqiu qiyejia*, August 2013, http://www.gemag.com.cn/15/33019_1.html.

Fang Li's new film demonstrates how the importance of polar resources have penetrated the national narrative on multiple levels. China's polar frames – the official positions on the polar regions and China's role within them – are very carefully managed. Fang's new movie received explicit approval from China's state censorship body, unlike the official censorship and restrictions placed on several of his earlier films that were more critical of Chinese society.[3] As China strengthens its polar capacities, the Chinese government is now incorporating the polar regions into its metanarrative on national identity, national interests, and China's global rise as an economic and political power.

In Chinese sources, China's expanded polar presence and expanded scientific program are explained to the Chinese public as being part of China's efforts to secure a share of polar resources in the future, which will help underwrite China's continued economic growth, as well as an indicator of China's improved comprehensive national strength. Yet in information aimed at foreign audiences, a very different line is promoted. Negative public opinion can have a severe impact on Chinese interests. For example, Chinese businessman Huang Nubo's effort in 2012 to purchase land in Iceland for an eco-resort was thwarted by hostile media attention and popular objections, as was his bid in 2014 to purchase land in Norway's Svalbard islands. According to two of China's leading polar policymakers, since at least 1989, when the Convention on Regulating Antarctic Mineral Resource Activities failed to be ratified and then was replaced by the 1991 Protocol on Environmental Protection to the Antarctic Treaty, China's emerging polar foreign policy has been to "understand the status quo, be proactive, hide our strengths, and bide our time."[4] Now that China's polar capacities have grown exponentially, China is even more cautious about revealing its full intentions in the polar regions to global public opinion. The head of the China Arctic and Antarctic Administration (CAA), Qu Tanzhou, says that the international community needs time to "make a psychological adjustment" to accept China's new strength in polar affairs.[5] In the meantime, careful information management is an essential component in achieving this "adjustment" in

---

[3] "Lost in Beijing Awaits Final Decision from Censors," *Screen Daily*, February 7, 2007, http://www.screendaily.com/lost-in-beijing-producer-awaits-final-decision-from-censors/40306 51.article.

[4] Yan Qide and Zhu Jiangang, *Nanjizhou lingtu zhuquan yu ziyuan quanshu wenti yanjiu* [Research on the issue of Antarctic sovereignty and resources] (Shanghai kexue jishu chubanshe, 2009), 35. Yan and Zhu work for the PRIC. The PRIC's duties and authority are explained in greater detail in chapter 4.

[5] "Zhengzhan Nanji, Zhongguo zai hangdong" [China is on the move in Antarctica], *Science in China Daily*, January 14, 2014, http://blog.sciencenet.cn/blog-1208826–759893.html.

global public opinion. This strategy even has an impact on what Chinese polar scientists are allowed to research. China's polar leaders are well aware that other polar states are closely watching what Chinese scientists choose to research for clues to the Chinese government's polar agenda and intentions. Hence, as stated in China's 2014 annual polar report, the government has made a point of selecting for funding polar scientific projects with "low political sensitivity" – research on climate change is given as one example of this – in order to "ease the suspicion and resistance of the major powers against China and make them more supportive and cooperative towards China's polar activities."[6]

China's polar strategy is an undeclared foreign policy, and hence is extremely politically sensitive, so even within the Chinese-language public sphere varying levels of censorship are applied to polar policy discussions. Knowledge of the Chinese government's information management systems (*xuanchuan*, *waixuan*) and the ability to read Chinese sources is therefore essential for unearthing the details of China's polar interests, understanding the policy guiding them, and discovering the bureaucratic actors and corporate interests helping to shape the national narrative on the polar regions.

HOW CHINA FRAMES THE POLES

National narratives have an important role in state-building and creating national identities. They also have a flow-on effect in foreign policy. Framing theory can help decode the process involved when political actors attempt to shape a national narrative on a given topic and help identify the meaning behind these frames.[7] States utilize official frames when there is a perceived legitimacy deficit that must be addressed, as part of an ongoing process of legitimation of their interests. Frames provide "psychological weight" to contentious issues in the public and private domain;[8] weight that has a discernable effect on public opinion. China has a credibility gap when it comes to being involved in Arctic affairs, so it needs to try to shape the international narrative on the Arctic Ocean and Arctic region as a global concern. China is also a relative latecomer to Antarctic affairs, and has some perspectives on Antarctic affairs that are not yet mainstream; much as in the

---

6 Ding Huang, ed., *Jidi guojia zhengce yanjiu baogao 2013–2014* [Annual report on national polar policy research 2013–2014] (Beijing: Kexue chubanshe, 2014), 138.

7 David A. Snow and Robert D. Benford, "Master Frames and Cycles of Protest," in *Frontiers in Social Movement Theory*, ed. Aldon D. Morris and Carol McClurg Mueller (New Haven, CT: Yale University Press, 1992), 137.

8 Ibid.

Arctic, it needs to work to protect its present and future interests by building a positive global public opinion about Chinese activities there.

One of the main means by which the Chinese Communist Party government sets "frames" in the Chinese and global public sphere is through guiding what can and cannot be said in public (in other words, exercising censorship) and through setting the correct political terminology to refer to contentious matters (the Chinese terms for such language are *tifa*, *yongyu*, and *tici*).[9] The Chinese media is heavily involved in this endeavor. The media is tasked by the CCP with "guiding public opinion" (*zhidao yulun*) and has traditionally been described as the "tongue and throat of the CCP" (*dang de houshe*).[10] Propaganda and "thought work" (*xuanchuan yu sixiang gongzuo*) – or "strategic communication and agenda-setting," to put it in terms more familiar to Western readers – are regarded by the CCP as core tasks of government. The CCP divides strategic communication and agenda-setting activities into those that are targeted at foreign audiences (*duiwai*) and those that are targeted at domestic audiences (*duinei*). "Propaganda" (*xuanchuan*) is not a negative term in CCP usage; rather, it is believed to be the "lifeblood" (*shengmingxian*) of the party and, along with censorship, it is a core means of maintaining political power in China.

Although scientists have freedom of speech in polar scientific matters, when it comes to polar governance, Chinese scientists and policymakers are working from a well-defined "script" of what can and cannot be said publicly on polar affairs. Social science debates in China, especially on such a sensitive matter as an undeclared foreign policy, are also highly managed. Social science is part of the CCP propaganda system and must conform to the limits of political censorship in China.[11] The boundaries are much wider than many might think, but certain topics are definitely off-limits. There are internal and external, Chinese-language and foreign-language "playbooks" of polar affairs, depending on the audience. As a state where the media, culture, education, and historiography are under the strict control of the ruling political party, this process is readily apparent in China, compared with societies with a more open political environment.

9   For more on China's modernized censorship and information management, see Anne-Marie Brady, *Marketing Dictatorship: Propaganda and Thought Work in Contemporary China* (Lanham, MD: Rowman and Littlefield, 2008), and Anne-Marie Brady, ed., *China's Thought Management* (Abingdon, UK: Routledge, 2012).

10 Brady, *Marketing Dictatorship*, 79–80.

11 Xuexi chubanshe, ed., *Quan guo xuanchuan sixiang gongzuo huiyi wenjian huibian* [Collected articles from the National Conference on Propaganda and Thought Work] (Beijing: Xuexi chubanshe, 1994), 143.

China seeks to enhance perceptions of its status in polar affairs because it will help the government obtain the support it needs from other like-minded states, and it will ensure that global public opinion is not aligned against China's polar interests. An important influence on the frames for China's polar policies is China's research funding priorities, which reflect national interests. Chinese polar scientists and social scientists locate the bulk of their research funding within national research funds that focus on China's economic development and work to find ways for China to acquire privileged access to resources. This skews their work, setting the trajectory for enquiry within those frames of scientific analysis as well as public debate.

China's External Message on Polar Affairs

The Chinese government spares no effort to hide its designs on Antarctic mineral resources from possible foreign criticism, to the extent of even deliberately mistranslating a speech of its supreme leader. One of the tasks of China's media sector targeted at foreign audiences – which includes the broadsheet newspaper *China Daily*, the tabloid newspaper *Global Times*, China Radio International, china.com, and CCTV International – is to manage and respond (usually indirectly) to international controversy about China. In November 2014, when CCP general secretary Xi Jinping visited Australia, the Australian media was full of speculation about concerns on the implications of China's expansion of its BeiDou satellite navigation system to Antarctica. *China Daily* avoided commenting on the controversy explicitly, but instead translated a quote from Xi's speech given while visiting China's icebreaker *Xue Long* in port in Hobart, Australia. Xi was quoted as saying that "scientific research in Antarctica is important work that will benefit humankind, and China has contributed to peaceful use of the continent."[12] The Chinese Ministry of Foreign Affairs website had a more complete version of the speech in English that might have aroused greater misgivings if any of the journalists following the story had looked at it. According to the ministry's official English-language account, Xi Jinping was reported as having said, "The Chinese side stands ready to continuously work with Australia and the international community to better understand, protect and *exploit* the

---

[12] Wu Jiao and Wang Qian, "Nations Join Hands for Antarctic Study," *China Daily*, November 19, 2014, http://usa.chinadaily.com.cn/epaper/2014–11/19/content_18942303.htm. Xinhua has an identical version of the news report in Chinese (dated November 18, 2014), which enables the reader to compare the differences between *China Daily*'s and the Ministry of Foreign Affairs' translation: http://news.xinhuanet.com/world/2014–11/18/c_1113301920.htm.

Antarctic" (emphasis added).[13] This was a factually accurate translation of Xi's actual words. The *China Daily* article, however, changed the last part of Xi's remarks, stating that he had expressed China's continued interest in cooperating with Australia and other nations to "know, protect and *explore* Antarctica" (emphasis added).[14]

To alter the words of China's senior leader is an extremely serious matter. However as *China Daily* editors would know, in materials aimed at foreign audiences China's polar officials scrupulously avoid mentioning China's strong interest in exploiting polar resources, whereas in Chinese-language materials it is continually highlighted as the main reason for China's investment in polar activities. The assumption is that foreigners will not be able to read Chinese, and so they will not know what Chinese officials and commentators are saying in Chinese about the polar regions – and mostly, they are right.

The full version of Xi's speech is available only in Chinese. In the speech, Xi referred explicitly to China's strong strategic interests at the poles and described China as a "polar great power" for the first time in public.[15] Although Xi was giving the speech in a foreign country, his target audience was in China and aimed at those working within polar affairs, so the full speech was not made available in English and it did not appear in the mainstream Chinese-language media. Since few foreign journalists have the Chinese-language skills to read the full speech, the polar knowledge to recognize the speech's significance, or the time to pursue the story, it was surprisingly easy for China to promote two separate versions of Xi's visit to Hobart to foreign and Chinese publics.

To influence governance in the polar regions, China needs its interests in the polar regions to be accepted by other actors as legitimate. China needs allies that accept Beijing's perspective on polar matters and are willing to cooperate with it. China is extremely sensitive about foreign analysis of its Arctic or Antarctic activities. Even the more obscure coverage will usually receive a rebuttal in the Chinese media – and even when the facts of the foreign reporting are actually true. In 2012, China scholars Linda Jakobson and

---

[13]   "Xi Jinping Visits Chinese and Australian Antarctic Scientific Researchers and Inspects Chinese Research Vessel 'Snow Dragon,'" Ministry of Foreign Affairs of the People's Republic of China, November 18, 2014, http://www.fmprc.gov.cn/mfa_eng/topics_665678/xj pzxcxesgjtldrdjcfhdadlyxxlfjjxgsfwbttpyjjdgldrhw/t1212943.shtml.

[14]   "Nations Join Hands for Antarctic Study."

[15]   "Er lun shenru xuexi guanche Xi Jinping zhuxi zhongyao jianghua jingshen" [Study and implement the important speech of Chairman Xi Jinping], *Zhongguo haiyang ribao*, November 20, 2014, http://www.oceanol.com/redian/shiping/2014-11-25/38013.html.

Peng Jingchao published a report on China in the Arctic for the Stockholm International Peace Research Institute (SIPRI) titled *China's Arctic Aspirations*.[16] The *Global Times*, which is part of the CCP's *People's Daily* newspaper group, published a lengthy riposte to the report titled "China's 'Arctic' Dream Misread as the Chinese Dragon's Arctic Ambitions." In the Chinese-language edition, PRIC director Yang Huigen was quoted responding to the Jakobson and Peng article as follows:

> PRIC Director Yang Huigen told the *Global Times* that China indeed puts great value on polar expeditions and research, but Arctic resources are not the main focus of research for expeditions there. This kind of assumption is just based on media speculation. Yang Huigen said that China is more ambitious in its Antarctic expeditions, because Antarctica is a region without sovereignty. As everyone knows, the Arctic region belongs to various sovereign states and China is very clear that it must not enter those countries' territorial waters and exclusive economic zones to do research. Strictly speaking the international waters of the Arctic are a very small area, and much of it is covered by thick ice where China's icebreaker *Xue Long* cannot reach.[17]

Yang's comments that Arctic resources are "not the main focus" of China's Arctic science expeditions was certainly factual; but they were disingenuous, or at least the reporting on them was. China's Arctic science is not primarily focused on Arctic mineral resources; however, as the Chinese-language press and Chinese scholarly sources frequently emphasize, Arctic mineral resources – as Jakobson and Peng rightly pointed out – are one of the main reasons why China is interested in the Arctic region.

International media coverage of China's Arctic and Antarctic initiatives is often negative and questioning of China's motives. The positive reports on China's involvement in the rescue of the Russian research ship *Akademik Shokalskiy*, in Antarctic waters in 2014, were a rare exception and consequently received high-profile attention in the Chinese media. As in other aspects of Chinese foreign policy, China tends to attract negative international commentary on polar affairs, and many of its potential partners do not completely trust its intentions. A 2011 survey of public opinion in Arctic states, for instance, found that China was the least attractive partner to all Arctic Council

[16] Linda Jakobson and Peng Jingchao, *China's Arctic Aspirations*, SIPRI Policy Paper No. 34 (Stockholm, SIPRI, 2012).

[17] "Zhongguo 'Beiji' mengxiang bei wudu wei julong dui Beiji de yexin" [China's "Arctic" dream misread as the Chinese dragon's Arctic ambitions], *Huanqiu shibao*, December 12, 2012, http://mil.huanqiu.com/paper/2012–12/3372436.html.

countries, with the sole exception of Russia.[18] Chinese analysis of foreign scholarly and media commentary on China's Arctic and Antarctic activities dismisses such negative coverage as simply "[China] threat" (*weixie lun*) rhetoric and accuses it of "demonizing China" (*yaomohua*).[19] Chinese polar scholars Guo Peiqing and Li Zhenfu say that "China threat rhetoric" is preventing China's active participation in polar international regimes, and that it is being used to prevent China's rise.[20] To further China's goals in the polar regions, they advise that the Chinese government focus on "creating an international image of China as a peaceful and cooperative state."[21] Improving China's international image (*guoji xinxiang*) is a key project of China's emerging foreign policy strategy. Chinese polar officials say that China will need to strengthen both its "hard" (polar capacity) and "soft" (persuasion) power in the polar regions in order to achieve its national goals there.[22]

Rather than recognizing that foreign reporting and analysis on China's polar interests reflects individual views and analysis, Chinese analysis erroneously assumes foreign scholars and journalists who write on China's polar activities write for their governments or publish within frames set by their governments in much the same way Chinese scholars and journalists do. China's 2013–14 *Annual Report on Polar Research* lists a number of foreign scholars who have written on China's polar interests – including myself – and says that if their "China threat" coverage is not dealt with "appropriately," then it will not only affect China's polar interests but also negatively affect the nation's global strategy.[23]

As China has expanded its polar program, Chinese polar officials have dealt with critical coverage of China's polar activities by making use of long-standing CCP techniques to win friends and neutralize enemies. The CCP has an extensive tradition of building positive relationships with influential foreign

18 FKOS Research Associates, *Rethinking the Top of the World: Arctic Security Public Opinion Survey* (Toronto: Walter and Duncan Gordon Foundation and the Canada Centre for Global Security Studies at the Munk School of Global Affairs, January 2011), ix.

19 "Zhongguo 'Beiji' zhi meng bei wudu wei julong dui Beiji de yexin"; and "Zhuanjia: 'Zhongguo zai Beiji gao junshi kuozhang' guandian duo ren ermu" [Expert opinion that "China to engage in military expansion in the Arctic" draws attention], *Nanfang Daily*, August 5, 2013, accessed March 5, 2014, http://news.takungpao.com/military/world/2013–08/1807183.html (link discontinued).

20 Guo Peiqing and Li Zhenfu, *Beiji hangdao de guoji wenti yanjiu* [Research on the international issues regarding the Arctic shipping routes] (Beijing: Haiyang chubanshe, 2009), 315.

21 Ibid., 317.

22 "Zhongguo Nanji kaocha 25 zhounian: Heping liyong Nanji yong buguo shi" [Twenty-fifth anniversary of Chinese Antarctic expeditions: peaceful exploitation will never go out of date], Xinhua, October 14, 2009, http://news.xinhuanet.com/tech/2009–10/14/content_12232453.htm.

23 Ding, *Jidi guojia zhengce yanjiu baogao 2013–2014*, 41 and 47–48.

elites who will speak up for China's interests. These individuals are officially described as "friends of China."[24] Foreign non–Chinese-speaking polar social scientists, scientists, politicians, and business interests friendly to China's agenda are the usual targets to be designated "friends of China," and polar affairs are no different. In the past five to ten years, China has only had to dangle the carrot of lucrative polar research funding partnerships and investment projects – or threaten to withdraw cooperation – to silence many potential critics and buy powerful friends among Arctic and Antarctic states.

It certainly is the case that China's official perspective on polar affairs is sometimes misinterpreted by the foreign media. Setting aside potential political biases that may be affecting reporting, the Chinese communist government's traditional secrecy and lack of transparency of its intentions is one factor in this, as is the terminology used in Chinese to discuss polar issues. "Polar" is translated in Chinese as the compound word *jidi*: the two characters in the word are *ji* ("extreme") and *di* ("earth"), or in other words, "the extremes of the earth." Thus, in Chinese, the Arctic is the "Northern Extreme" (*Beiji*); the Antarctic is the "Southern Extreme" (*Nanji*); while the Tibetan Plateau, which contains the world's highest mountains, is the "Third Extreme" (*disanji*) or Third Pole. According to Chinese international law specialist Zou Keyuan, China and Antarctica's close links were forged millions of years ago as part of the history of the ancient supercontinent of Gondwana.[25] These claims are not made lightly; the implication is that although the two continents are now far apart, China has as much right to make a claim on the territory as other nations that currently are physically much closer. From a Chinese government perspective, the geographical connection between China and "the poles" gives added cogency and legitimacy to its claim for rights and interests in the polar regions and China's "right to speak" on polar affairs.

In Chinese, *Beiji* can refer to both the North Pole and the Arctic region as a whole, while *Nanji* means both the South Pole and the continent of Antarctica. This subtle difference in terminology between Chinese and English is the source of statements made by many Chinese commentators that have been translated as "the Arctic belongs to the whole of humanity." Such phrases understandably cause alarm in Arctic littoral states. Chinese public discourse also talks of the Arctic as a region (*Beiji diqu*). Yet the eight Arctic states are collectively still some way off from thinking of themselves in

[24] See Zhao Pitao, *Waishi gaishuo* [Foreign affairs summary] (Shanghai, Shanghai shehui kexue chubanshe, 1989), 166–67.

[25] As cited in Zou Keyuan, "China's Interests in and Policy toward Antarctica," in *Asia in Antarctica*, ed. Bruce Davis and Richard Herr (Canberra: Australian National University Centre for Resource and Environmental Studies, 1994), 94.

terms of a region. Each Arctic state has its own "High North," Arctic interests, and national identity. Geography, economics, politics, and recent history have given them few reasons to be unified or aligned.

Bread and Circuses, or the Role of China's Polar Activities in the Chinese Media

Beijing needs the support of its own people for its polar investments. Perceived success in polar affairs adds to the CCP government's legitimacy to rule, as well as greater buy-in and participation in the national vision for China's role as a polar state. The stress on China's Arctic and Antarctic triumphs contributes to the CCP's narrative of patriotism and ethnic pride. If China succeeds in its economic and security goals in the polar regions, then it will be a game changer in terms of China's international standing. Thus, the CCP regime's survival is greatly enhanced by access to, and success in, achieving its goals in the polar regions. China's polar program is heavily promoted to Chinese-language audiences as part of ongoing political education efforts. In addition to their scientific duties, leading Chinese polar scientists are given the task of promoting their research in thousands of talks to Chinese youth. The stated aim of these talks is to teach Chinese youth to "love science" and "love their country."[26] Chinese youth are now the primary target of the CCP's ongoing activities to build legitimacy and public support.[27]

China's polar agencies put considerable effort into public education on polar affairs through introducing polar information into the curriculum, giving scientific talks to the public, developing museum exhibits, and building close links with the Chinese media. Chinese high school geography tests require students to identify the key natural resources in the polar regions and ask, for example, "Which mineral does the Antarctic have in greatest quantities: a. coal, b. natural gas, c. oil, d. gold?"[28] Many other governments also engage in polar public education, but the focus on mineral resources and exploitation that the Chinese authorities promotes to young audiences would be anathema to most polar states.

---

[26] State Bureau of Survey and Mapping, "Zhongguo Nanji cehui kexue kaocha 22 nian chengjiu yu gongxian" [22 years of achievements of China's Antarctic mapping], 2007, accessed April 29, 2015, http://www.sbsm.gov.cn/article/ztzl/jdch/jdch/200711/20071100027867.shtml (link discontinued).

[27] See Xuanchuan wenhua zhengce fagui bianweihui, ed., *Xuanchuan wenhua zhengce fagui* [Policies and regulations on propaganda and culture] (Kunming: Yunnan renmin chubanshe, 1999), 10.

[28] See a sample test at "Jidi diqu" [Polar regions], accessed November 7, 2014, http://www.doc88.com/p-854247175909.html.

Xue Long, China's polar icebreaker, has both a scientific and a propaganda function. Each polar expedition departure is the occasion for a public event hosted not just at *Xue Long*'s home port of Shanghai but alternating with China's other major ports. This is done to popularize China's polar activities to a wide audience. Similar events are hosted when *Xue Long* docks at foreign ports where China wishes to strengthen its polar collaborations. China's polar expeditions have always been incorporated into the government's ongoing propaganda and thought work activities. In 1985, China's first Antarctic expedition was commemorated with a full-length television documentary titled *Antarctica: We're Here!* (*Nanji women lai le!*), which described the journey to build Great Wall Station, China's first Antarctic research station, from beginning to end. Every Chinese Arctic or Antarctic expedition always contains a substantial media presence. Since 2005, there has been an even bigger push to promote China's polar activities to the Chinese public, as well as awareness of the political issues surrounding the polar regions and the government's strategy for dealing with them. A CCTV camera crew was part of China's seventeen-member team to conquer Dome Argus (also known as Dome A), the highest ice dome in Antarctica, in January 2005, recording the team's exploits and their triumph for Chinese audiences via live satellite link. The Chinese media tends to talk up China's polar activities and achievements in Chinese-language materials, whereas it downplays the same activities and achievements in materials aimed at foreigners. The challenge for the interested observer is to sift the facts out of the political messaging.

THE OFFICIAL (AND UNOFFICIAL) HISTORY OF CHINA'S POLAR ENGAGEMENT

During Xi Jinping's November 2014 visit to Hobart, he was photographed viewing an exhibition outlining the history of China's polar science. According to the version of events portrayed in that exhibition, China's interest in Antarctica dates only from 1980.[29] In an analysis aimed at Chinese officials, Chinese polar specialists narrate a chronology of China's Antarctic activities in four stages: (1) 1980 to 1984: deliberations and preparations; (2) 1984 to 1990: setting up bases and sending expeditions; (3) 1991 to 2004: a focus on basic science; (4) and 2005 to the present, which they describe as "great leap" – style development.[30]

---

[29] As viewed by the author on the *Xue Long*, February 2015.

[30] Ling Xiaoliang et al., "Guowai Nanji kaocha guanli jigou yu kaocha guanli moshi de duibi fenxi" [Research on foreign Antarctic organization administration], *Haiyang kaifang yu guanli*, no. 3 (2008): 49.

Meanwhile, foreign analysis usually dates China's Arctic geopolitical interests from 2007, when Russian scientists planted a titanium flag on the Arctic seabed, provoking a strong reaction in China as well as among other nations.[31] Because of political and military sensitivities, Chinese reports also commonly use that event as a starting point for discussing China's interest in Arctic affairs.[32] Foreign accounts also highlight the origin of China's interest in Antarctic affairs to debates on Antarctic minerals in the late 1970s, which culminated in the Convention on the Regulation of Antarctic Mineral Resource Activities. However, China's interest in the polar regions began well before the dates offered by official Chinese and foreign media accounts. The backstory to China's official history helps to flesh out a deeper understanding of why the polar regions are so important to China. China's steadily expanding presence and engagement in the polar regions over the decades reflects the progress of modern China's economic and political development and the nation's ever-increasing engagement in global economic and political affairs.

The Early Years through to the International Geophysical Year

Chinese scientists were involved in both the first and second International Polar Years (IPY) held from 1882 to 1883 and from 1932 to 1933.[33] China's Beiyang government, the nominal government of the Republic of China (ROC) from 1911 to 1928, signed the Spitsbergen Treaty in 1925, guaranteeing China a share of economic rights in the Svalbard archipelago. Chinese official accounts highlight the Beiyang government's signing of the Spitsbergen Treaty as a noteworthy justification for China's contemporary participation in Arctic affairs and indicative of China's long-standing interests in the Arctic region.[34] Certainly, the excitement about polar exploration that was a feature of international public discourse from the early 1900s and up until World War II filtered into China also. In the 1920s and 1930s, popular books on Arctic and Antarctic discoveries were translated into Chinese, which brought the

[31] Jakobson and Peng, *China's Arctic Aspirations*, 1.
[32] See the 2011 People's Liberation Army-Navy–funded CCTV documentary *Zouxiang haiyang* [To the oceans], at CCTV.com, December 21, 2011, http://tv.cntv.cn/video/C33446/479129c42bf6440bb04430c978f622bc.
[33] Zuoyue Wang and Jiuchen Zhang, "China and the International Geophysical Year," *Globalizing Polar Science: Reconsidering the International Polar and Geophysical Years*, ed. Roger D. Launius, James Rodger Fleming, and David H. DeVorkin (New York: Palgrave Macmillan, 2010), 143.
[34] Qu Tanzhou et al., *Beiji wenti yanjiu* [Research on Arctic issues] (Beijing: Ocean Press, 2011), 327n7.

international competition to be the first explorer to conquer the poles to a wide Chinese readership.[35] In the same period, Chinese scientists studying in the United States and other nations that took part in polar exploration and science, brought awareness of the significance of the polar regions back to China when they came home to teach at Chinese universities.

The ROC was overthrown in a two-year civil war against the CCP from 1947 to 1949, leading to the establishment of the People's Republic of China (PRC) and a new government led by Mao Zedong. After the PRC took the North Korean side in the Korean War in 1950, the United States vetoed the recognition of the new Chinese state and forced its allies to comply. This veto meant that for much of the Cold War, the ROC, despite controlling only the island of Taiwan and a few tiny islands off the coast of mainland China, was able to retain all of China's seats on international organizations such as the United Nations until the early 1970s. This made it almost impossible for Chinese scientists to continue their international research linkages with Western counterparts. In 1951, a Chinese scientist joined in Soviet projects in geomagnetic research at the North Magnetic Pole, becoming the first Chinese citizen to go to the Arctic. In 1958, two Xinhua journalists toured Soviet Arctic research stations, and one published a book of his experiences.[36] From 1958 to 1959, Chinese glaciologist Xie Zichu went on fieldwork to the Arctic as part of his studies in the Soviet Union.[37] These individual efforts notwithstanding, Chinese scientists' ability to conduct international research was greatly reduced in these early years of the PRC.

Chinese scientists were keen to be involved in the International Geophysical Year (IGY) 1957–1958, a global scientific survey that included Antarctic research programs. They hoped to take advantage of the IGY to expand China's scientific capabilities, and some were interested in working in Antarctica. Prominent Chinese geologist and meteorologist Zhu Kezhen argued that China should join in the IGY scientific explorations in Antarctica, stating that it would be the "last repository of oil when all other

---

[35]   "Bingwan A" [Dome A], China Association for Science and Technology, July 14, 2010, http://www.cast.org.cn/n35081/n12101561/12103482_3.html.

[36]   "Wo guo tansuo Beiji licheng" [China's history of Arctic exploration], n.d., accessed February 24, 2014, http://tech.sina.com.cn/focus/beiji_kekao/; and "Zhongguo Beiji kaocha zhi 'di yi'" [China's "first" Arctic expedition], n.d., accessed February 24, 2014, http://baike.baidu.com/view/704599.htm?fromtitle=%E3%80%8A%E5%8C%97%E6%9E%81%E6%8E%A2%E9%99%A9%E3%80%8B&fromid=135863&type=syn#1.

[37]   Baike Baidu, s.v. "Xie Zichu," accessed November 7, 2014, http://baike.baidu.com/view/1563069.htm?tp=0_00.

sources had been exhausted globally."[38] However, the PRC had an extremely limited scientific budget in the 1950s and very few polar specialists. The PRC's final IGY program did not include any Antarctic projects; even the China-based projects were severely curtailed by budgetary problems.[39] But political reasons were also a factor in the PRC not taking up its earlier interest in being involved in the IGY. The PRC sought assurances from the IGY organizing committee that the ROC would not be accepted as a participant. This was not agreed, so the CCP government withdrew its application to participate in the IGY.[40]

The twelve countries that engaged in Antarctic science during the IGY were the same twelve states that would take part in the series of meetings from 1958 to 1959 that led to the Antarctic Treaty. As China had not undertaken any Antarctic science in the IGY, it was automatically excluded from discussions. As noted earlier, the United States had initiated the Antarctic Treaty negotiations in order to keep Antarctica in "friendly hands."[41] The Soviet Union pushed to open the meetings to "all interested states," meaning the PRC and the Eastern bloc countries, but it did not force the issue. Even if it had, the United States and its ten allies in these meetings would not have allowed any "unrecognized Communist regimes" – in other words, the PRC – to participate.[42] Thus, a combination of economics and politics led to China missing out on being an early signatory to the Antarctic Treaty.

The 1960s and 1970s – The Beginnings of Active Polar Engagement

In 1964, China's State Oceanic Administration (*Guojia haiyangju*; SOA) was established with a brief to "engage in polar expeditions in the future."[43] However, within a year and a half of this agency being set up, China was

[38] Liu Xiaohan, "Zhongguo qiangzhan Nanji zui gaodian ling Meiguo shiliao weiji" [China's seizing of the highest point in Antarctica has made the United States anxious], Sohu.com, August 22, 2008, http://news.sohu.com/20090108/n261650601.shtml.

[39] See the list of China's final IGY program in Wang and Zhang, "China and the International Geophysical Year," 149.

[40] Wei-chin Lee, "China and Antarctica: So Far and Yet So Near," *Asian Survey* 30, no. 6 (June 1990), 580; and Wang and Zhang, "China and the International Geophysical Year," 151.

[41] Agenda Paper, Commonwealth Prime Ministers Conference, 1956, A1838/1495/3/2/1 Part 2, National Archives of Australia, as cited in David Day, *Antarctica: A Biography* (Oxford: Oxford University Press, 2013), 479.

[42] Dian Olson Belanger, *Deep Freeze: The United States, the International Geophysical Year, and the Origins of Antarctica's Age of Science* (Boulder: University Press of Colorado, 2006) 38 and 373.

[43] "Bingwan A."

engulfed in the ten-year tragedy of the Cultural Revolution (1966–76). In this period, SOA staff, along with other scientists and government officials in China, were swept up in political struggle for several years, and were sent down to the countryside to "learn from the peasants" until the mid-1970s. China's own domestic turmoil, diplomatic isolation, and dire economic straits of the 1960s were all key factors in Beijing not following up the initial expressions of interest in both Arctic and Antarctic science and governance.

Remarkably, though, in 1966 the Antarctic continent was part of the planned trajectory for Chinese intercontinental ballistic missiles (ICBMs). US nuclear weapons historians John Wilson Lewis and Hua Di have said that if these ICBMs had been successfully deployed, they would have penetrated US defenses at their weakest point.[44] The strategic significance of the Arctic and Antarctic to Chinese security must have been obvious to Chinese military planners at least as early as 1951, when the United States set up the still-extant regional security architecture against the PRC and the Soviet Union. The US-led "hub and spoke" security agreements that link the Arctic to the Antarctic were established to keep the Soviet Union out of the Pacific Ocean and to protect Asia and the Pacific from the further spread of communism.[45] As a consequence of this strategy, the PRC had to endure an extremely damaging US naval blockade that lasted from 1950 until 1953, as well as US spy plane flights, and what the United States refers to as "freedom of navigation" missions in Chinese territorial waters that began in the 1950s and have continued through the present day.

Chinese nuclear security is directly connected to the Arctic. The shortest route for ballistic missiles and bombers to fly between the US mainland and China is over the Arctic. The Soviet Union was China's bulwark against the US nuclear threat until the Sino-Soviet split in 1960, but by 1969 the Soviet Union was threatening to use a nuclear strike against China. The trajectory of Soviet weapons also came via China's High North. So from a military point of view, China's greatest security threats have long come from the Northern Pacific and the Arctic region. During the Cold War era, the United States and

---

44 John Wilson Lewis and Hua Di, "China's Ballistic Missile Programme: Technologies, Strategies, Goals," *International Security* 17, no. 2 (1992), 19.

45 "Background Papers for the Australia–New Zealand–United States (ANZUS) Council Preparations, July 24, 1952," Acheson Memoranda of Conversations Files, 1949–1953, Box 70, July 1952, Dean G. Acheson Papers, Harry S. Truman Library and Museum, Independence, MO, at www.trumanlibrary.org; see also "The 1951 ANZUS Treaty – Volume 21," *Documents on Australian Foreign Policy* (Canberra: Department of Foreign Affairs and Trade, 2001), http://dfat.gov.au/about-us/publications/historical-documents/Pages/volume-21/the-1951-anzus-treaty-volume-21.aspx.

the Soviet Union dominated the Arctic Ocean and Northern Pacific airspace with their planes, submarines, and missiles. China could only keep a watching brief.

In 1971 – after twenty-two years of debate and voting on the issue – the UN General Assembly finally voted in favor of the PRC taking over the China seat at the UN and on the Security Council. Thus began a new era of international diplomacy for Beijing, when the PRC could become more involved in international organizations and participate in global governance, from which it formerly had been excluded. The Chinese media also took note of the 1975 Antarctic Consultative meeting in Oslo – which began a fifteen-year debate on the issue of the commercial exploitation of Antarctic minerals and concluded with the 1991 Madrid Protocol – as well as the discovery of North Sea oil and other Arctic resources.[46] However, Chinese diplomats could not attend the deliberations on Antarctica, as China was not yet a signatory to the Antarctic Treaty. By 1975, the PRC was gradually coming out of international isolation, but it was still held back by the political divides of the latter Mao years.

Mao Zedong died in September 1976, and the major political and economic changes that followed restored China's ability to act on the CCP government's long-standing political, military, and scientific interests in the polar regions. In 1977, the PRC's London embassy asked the British Foreign and Commonwealth Office to provide briefings both before and after the 9th Antarctic Treaty Consultative Meeting, which was to be held in London that year.[47] A few months later, an internal publication of the CCP newspaper, *People's Daily*, released a top-secret report on Antarctic governance and natural resources.[48] In May 1977, the SOA's CCP Committee set three key goals for the future: "explore China's marine territories; go out into the oceans; and land in Antarctica."[49] At the spring 1978 meeting of the Chinese National Science Conference, leading Chinese glaciologist Xie Zichu advocated "seizing Antarctica" (*zhuazhu Nanji*) as China's next big scientific challenge.[50] In August 1978, the SOA issued a report on "Preparations for an Antarctic

---

[46] Renmin Ribao guoji bu ziliao zu, "Shijie 'zuihou de bianjiang'—Nanjizhou de ziyuan zhengduo zhan" [The world's "last frontier"—The fight for control over Antarctic resources], *Neibu ziliao* 158, (1977), 2.

[47] External Intelligence Bureau, "Antarctica: possible PRC interest," March 23, 1979, IR 41/79, Box 186 Miscellaneous Material Bob Thomson, Archives New Zealand, Christchurch.

[48] Renmin Ribao guoji bu ziliao zu, "Shijie 'zuihou de bianjiang'—Nanjizhou de ziyuan zhengduo zhan," 2.

[49] *Baike Baidu*, s.v. "Wu Heng," accessed November 7, 2014, http://www.baike.com/wiki/%E6%AD%A6%E8%A1%A1.

[50] *Baike Baidu*, s.v. "Xie Zichu."

Expedition."[51] The first stage of the preparations for China's first Antarctic expedition was to gather background materials. However, in China at that time, all of the background materials on Antarctica that could be located were a few newspaper articles and a translation of a 1927 book by British polar explorer R. N. Rudmose-Brown (published in Chinese in 1936) on the geography of the polar regions, which a scientist found in a secondhand shop in Beijing. The paucity of available information illustrated how isolated the PRC had become over the years.[52]

On January 2, 1978, Xinhua News Service published an open-source review of Antarctic affairs, focusing on the issue of unresolved sovereignty and the conflict over resources.[53] As with the classified report published in 1977, the Xinhua article was extremely scathing of the United States' and Soviet Union's dominance in Antarctica, and it highlighted the richness of Antarctica's natural resources. Between 1977 and 1983, multiple Chinese media reports adopted an extremely combative tone on Antarctic affairs, criticizing the two major powers for wanting to divvy up Antarctic spoils between themselves. Such views can be regarded as authoritative and representative of government policy at the time. However, after China signed the Antarctic Treaty in 1983, Chinese news coverage began to focus on China's own Antarctic program and adopted a more neutral tone toward Antarctic disputes. It is noticeable that at this early stage of Chinese interest in Antarctic affairs, every Chinese newspaper report emphasized the significance of Antarctic strategic resources and the desirability of exploiting them – much as recent Chinese media coverage has done.[54]

In the 1970s, China's public discussion of Arctic issues focused in particular on Soviet and US military and political interests in the Arctic region, frequently noting the threat that these posed to Chinese interests. Thousands of such open-source articles are available in the Chinese media. In 1979, a *People's Daily* internal publication featured a top-secret report on the Arctic

51 "Zhongguo tingjin Nanji, Nanji tiaoyue fuyi" [China advances in the Antarctic, reviews the Antarctic Treaty], *Ocean World*, accessed April 3, 2014, http://www.ocean360.net/?action-view news-itemid-107-page-2 (link discontinued).

52 R. N. Rudmose Brown, *The Polar Regions: A Physical and Economic Geography of the Arctic and Antarctic* (London: Methuen, 1927).

53 "US, USSR Compete for Antarctic Dominance," OW041041Y Peking NCNA Domestic Service in Chinese, 0754 GMT 2 January 1978, Foreign Broadcast Information Service (FBIS).

54 My comments are based on a database survey of Chinese-language news media sources collected in FBIS from 1974 to 1985.

region and its strategic resources.[55] In the same year, an open-source Xinhua report noted the strategic significance of the Svalbard archipelago, pointing out that the islands lie at the intersection of the US and Soviet missile trajectories against each other – and at China.[56] In the 1980s and 1990s, public reports in the Chinese media on the Arctic emphasized the Arctic's wealth of untapped mineral resources, its rich fishing grounds, the strategic significance of the Arctic Ocean for the militaries of the great powers, and the Arctic as the shortest shipping route between Asia and northern Europe and North America. Interestingly, neither Xinhua nor the *People's Daily* recorded the signing of the historic Arctic Environmental Protection Strategy in 1991 or the founding of the Arctic Council in 1996 – demonstrating that participating in Arctic governance was not yet high on China's political agenda.

In 1978, glaciologist Xie Zichu made use of his scholarly contacts to ask for Australian help to go to Antarctica on fieldwork. As a result of this approach, in the 1979–80 austral summer, two Chinese scientists were sent to participate in Australia's annual Antarctic expedition; the unlucky Xie, however, missed out on being selected.[57] In 1980, the SOA requested places for "between three and five" scientific researchers and one Chinese navigator to be accommodated on Australia's 1981 Antarctic expedition. Australian officials agreed to this additional request for help in the hope that, through this assistance, it could influence China's future policies on Antarctica in Australia's favor.[58] In the same year, China sent two observers to the Scientific Committee on Antarctic Research meeting in Queenstown, New Zealand.[59] The SOA also asked Argentina, Chile, Japan, New Zealand, the United Kingdom, and the United States to host Chinese scientists and other personnel and enable them to develop Antarctic experience. By the time that China joined the Antarctic Treaty in 1983, it had thirty-five scientists working in various international expedition teams on the Antarctic continent. China's first woman scientist in Antarctica arrived that same year, staying three months at New Zealand's Scott Base. Chinese Antarctic scientists were given special travel allowances to recognize the hardship and difficulty of working in Antarctica

---

[55]   Renmin Ribao guojibu, "Beiji diqu de zhuyao nengyuan he kuangchan ziyuan" [The main energy and mineral resources of the Arctic region]; and "Beihai youtian gaikuang" [An overview of North Sea oil fields], *Neibu ziliao* 188 (1979).

[56]   "People's Daily Discusses USSR Designs on Svalbard Islands," January 29, 1979, FBIS-CHI-79–029.

[57]   *Baike Baidu*, s.v. "Xie Zichu."

[58]   Peter Forsythe, "China: Interests in Antarctica," CAYP CH805 2802, Box 1296, Antarctic Division General, Archives New Zealand. I am grateful to David Walton for alerting me to these papers and to Ari Overmars for copying them for me.

[59]   Ibid.

on these early expeditions. Under the terms of their contracts, any Chinese scientist who died while in Antarctica would be given the same status as CCP revolutionary martyrs.[60] These regulations are still in force.

The 1980s and China's Entry into the Antarctic Treaty System

In 1981, China set up the National Antarctic Expedition Committee (*Guojia haiyangju weiyuanhui*) to coordinate Antarctic research nationwide and facilitate cooperation with other countries. The Office of the National Antarctic Expedition Committee (*Guojia Nanji kaocha weiyuanhui bangongshi*) was established in the same year. Reflecting the strong political and strategic focus of China's early Antarctic interests, the committee director and deputy directors of this office were senior CCP officials experienced in propaganda, diplomacy, and the navy, while the ordinary committee members were representatives from the scientific community.[61] However, in interactions with foreign counterparts, the scientific focus of China's Antarctic interests was emphasized, rather than the political component.[62]

China signed the Antarctic Treaty in 1983 and attended its first ATCM in Canberra in that same year. Thanks in no small part to the help of its various international partners, China was able to begin annual expeditions to Antarctica in 1984, and in the same year it set up a base, Great Wall Station (*Changcheng zhan*) on King George Island in the Chilean Antarctic claim. Initially, China had sought advice from New Zealand on setting up an Antarctic base in the Ross Sea area in West Antarctica.[63] The New Zealand government had been very encouraging and actually offered China the choice of seven sites on New Zealand's Antarctic territorial claim, along with maps

---

[60]   "Wo guo bu Nanji kaocha renyuan shenghuo daiyu de zhanxing guiding" [China Antarctic expedition members' supplementary payment regulations], *China Baike*, 1983, accessed November 7, 2014, http://www.chinabaike.com/law/zy/bw/0972/1416611.html.

[61]   See *Baike Baidu*, s.v. "Guojia Nanji kaocha weiyuanhui" [National Antarctic Expedition Committee], April 2, 2013, accessed November 7, 2014, http://www.baike.com/wiki/%E5%9B %BD%E5%AE%B6%E5%8D%97%E6%9E%81%E8%80%83%E5%AF%9F%E5%A7%94%E. 5%91%98%E4%BC%9A.

[62]   Forsythe, "China: Interests in Antarctica," 3.

[63]   "Meeting with Mr. Wu Heng, Chairman of China National Committee for Antarctic Research at the State Science and Technology Commission," April 3, 1984, New Zealand Embassy, Beijing (copy held in the personal collection of Dr Ian J. Shearer). I am grateful to Dr. Hon. I. J. Shearer for discussing New Zealand's policy at the time and sharing his files from the period when he was New Zealand's Minister of the Department of Scientific and Industrial Research (DSIR).

and other advice,[64] but there was a catch: China had to agree to recognize that New Zealand had special rights in the Ross Dependency.[65] This did not suit China's interests at all, so it set up a base on the Chilean territorial claim, on an island near the Antarctic peninsula. Unlike New Zealand, Chile did not attach any conditions to China's base development. Likewise, the Australian government has continually facilitated China's expansion in East Antarctica; it did not demand that China recognize its claim, and so China set up its second, third, and fourth bases on the Australian claim area. It would be another thirty years before China would initiate plans to set up a research station in the strategically important Ross Sea. China is loath to indicate any prior rights to Antarctic claimant states. Rather than give away potential rights and interests, it prefers to wait a while to achieve what it wants.

The arrangements for China's first Antarctic expedition were led and coordinated by People's Liberation Army-Navy Admiral Liu Huaqing, founder of the modern Chinese navy. Liu Huaqing believed that PLAN's participation in the expedition would be useful preparation for the force's expansion to become a blue-water navy – thereby challenging the US island chain strategy.[66] Two PLAN vessels provided transportation and crew for the 1984 expedition and base-building project. Both boats experienced mechanical difficulties during the voyage. The breakdowns were a visible demonstration of how far off China was in achieving its goal of developing a blue-water navy. Of the 531 personnel sent on this first expedition, 308 were from the navy. It was China's largest ever Antarctic expedition, and more than sixty government departments supported the project to set up the base.[67] In 1984, China was having financial difficulties, and the cost of setting up the base was considerable: 20 million renminbi (US$2.4 million).[68] Yet senior leaders Deng Xiaoping, Chen Yun, and Zhao Ziyang personally approved the construction budget and gave messages of support for the initiative. It was understood at the time that the political gains of this investment far outweighed the cost.

---

[64] "Implications of Potential Base Sites in the Ross Sea Region," DSIR, INT 8/1/1, 1984, Archives New Zealand, Christchurch.

[65] "PRC Offered Permanent Antarctic Research Base," Xinhua (English), April 10, 1984, FBIS BK101247.

[66] "1984 nian tianjin Nanji: Liu Huaqing biaotai 'Haijun yi bu rongci'" [1984 advance in Antarctica: Liu Huaqing commits Navy support], Guofangsheng, May 14, 2013, http://www .guofangsheng.com/show.aspx?id=9068&cid=38.

[67] "Zhongguo shouci Nanji kaocha" [China's first Antarctic expedition], Xinhua, November 13, 2013, http://news.xinhuanet.com/tech/2013-11/13/c_125694947.htm.

[68] Wang Qian, "Twenty Years of Antarctic Research," *China Daily*, November 3, 2004, accessed October 18, 2009, http://china.org.cn/English/2004/Nov/111106.htm (link discontinued).

Great Wall Station was formally opened on February 22, 1985. The head of the National Antarctic Expedition Committee made use of Chile's air link to King George Island to join the ceremony. Great Wall Station is only 2.5 kilometers from Chile's Frei Montalva Station. As so many other Antarctic states had done before it, China immediately set up a post office on its new research base, issuing stamps and postmarks indicating that the mail had been sent from China's first piece of Antarctic real estate.

China was made a consultative party to the Antarctic Treaty at the next ATCM in October 1985, and was made a full SCAR member in June 1986. Having the PRC join the Antarctic Treaty was not just advantageous for Beijing; it was also regarded as a coup for the treaty members because it kept China from lending its support to the anti-treaty movement at the UN, which was led by Malaysia.[69] For twenty years, Malaysia had tried unsuccessfully to get the "Question of Antarctica" discussed at the UN, acting on behalf of many developing states that regarded the Antarctic Treaty as a form of neocolonialism.

In 1985, the SOA was granted funding to purchase its own ice-capable vessel from Finland to launch China's annual Antarctic expeditions. The ship, named *Jidi* ("Polar"), ferried supplies for China's Antarctic mission from 1986 to 1994, until it was replaced by *Xue Long*, a converted cargo boat purchased from Ukraine. A further big breakthrough in capacity came in 1988, on China's fifth expedition, when a group of scientists and workers were sent to survey suitable sites in eastern Antarctica for China's second Antarctic base. The Chinese polar scientists who worked with Australian scientists in the early 1980s had identified the Prydz Bay region as a good location for China to establish a base, because it was believed to have resource potential. Once the site was decided on, Zhongshan Station was built in just under a month.

In the 1980s, Antarctic involvement and the international collaborations that stemmed from activities there greatly increased China's international partnerships and global standing. However, 1989 was a turning point in terms of Chinese domestic and foreign policy. After the violent crackdown on the pro-democracy movement in Beijing's Tiananmen Square in June 1989, international public opinion turned against China. From that year, China's Antarctic strategy adjusted to a consolidating phase. Meanwhile, in Shanghai in October 1989, China established the Polar Research Institute of China (*Zhongguo jidi yanjiusuo*; PRIC),[70] a new polar organization that was the first public indication that China had aspirations beyond Antarctica.

---

[69] Lee, "China and Antarctica," 585.
[70] In 2003, PRIC changed its Chinese, but not its English name, to *Zhongguo jidi yanjiu zhongxin*.

Consolidation Phase

From 1989 to 2004, China shifted its priorities in the Antarctic from base construction to building a meaningful polar scientific research program and exploring Antarctic resource potential. As early as 1990, the SOA vessel *Ocean 4* was sent to Antarctic waters to investigate deep seabed mineral resources from Antarctica to the Indian Ocean.[71] Chinese science in Antarctica gradually became more ambitious. In 1996, Chinese scientists began the first of four attempts to reach Dome A, the last unexplored zone of geological significance in Antarctica.[72] In 1998, Chinese scientists launched their first expedition to the previously unexplored Grove Mountains. The Grove Mountain area is rich in meteorites, and as a result of exploration there, China quickly became the country with the third-largest collection of Antarctic meteorites, after the United States and Japan.

In the Arctic, China began exploring the scientific and political links that it would need to help it become a polar player. In 1990, a Chinese scientist visited the North Pole and planted a Chinese flag there.[73] In 1994, the Chinese Advisory Committee for Polar Research (*Zhongguo jidi kaocha zixun weiyuan-hui*) was established. This committee is led by China's SOA, but has cross-agency functions to advise all Chinese government departments with polar interests. Another group of Chinese scientists, with journalists in tow, visited the Arctic in 1995,[74] and in the same year the Chinese Academy of Sciences set up a Polar Science Committee (*Kexueyuan jidi kexue weiyuanhui*). In 1996, the National Antarctic Expedition Committee Office was renamed in both English and Chinese as the China Arctic and Antarctic Administration, or CAA (*Guojia haiyangju jidi kaocha bangongshi*; abbreviated in Chinese as *Jidi ban*). Also in 1996, China joined the International Arctic Science Committee (IASC), one of the key governing bodies of the Arctic. In 1999, the CAA dispatched the *Xue Long* on China's first Arctic scientific voyage, traveling to the Bering and Chukchi seas. A follow-up voyage was sent in 2003; after that date, China began biannual Arctic voyages. Then, in 2004, China set

[71] "Zhongguo di qici Nanji kaocha" [China's seventh Antarctic expedition], Xinhua, November 13, 2013, http://news.xinhuanet.com/tech/2013–11/13/c_125695016.htm.

[72] "The Draft Comprehensive Environmental Evaluation for the Construction and Operation of Chinese Dome A Station in Antarctica," Committee for Environmental Protection (CEP) 6 (a), Antarctic Treaty Consultative Meeting, Kiev, 2008.

[73] "Zhongguo jiaru Beiji lishihui" [China enters the Arctic Council], accessed November 7, 2014, http://wap.tyread.com/goChapterContent.action?bookId=100000214796423&chapterI d=2 (link discontinued).

[74] Ibid.

up a new polar research site, the Arctic Yellow River Station (*Beiji Huanghe zhan*), at Ny-Ålesund, a hub for international Arctic research in Svalbard.[75]

China's "Great Leap" in Polar Affairs

Chinese polar specialists say that from 2005 on, China's polar activities entered a period of "great leap"-style development.[76] This is a politically significant choice of words to use to describe China's polar strategic evolution. China's Great Leap Forward was launched by Mao Zedong in 1958. The method of the Great Leap Forward was to maximize economic production through extremely intensive means; its goal was that China's economy first would overtake that of the Soviet Union, and ultimately those of the developed world. Similarly, as China's polar plan evolved, China first set itself the goal of overtaking developing countries' capabilities,[77] then of overtaking the capabilities of the leading polar developed states. It has now set the ultimate goal of becoming a polar great power between 2015 and 2030.[78]

China's "great leap" into Antarctica began dramatically in January 2005, when Chinese expeditioners entered the ranks of significant Antarctic exploration, discovery, and leadership. The first breakthrough in this new era of China's Antarctic activity was carefully scripted and broadcast live to domestic and international audiences; a feat that previous Antarctic explorers could only have imagined. According to *China Daily*, at precisely 3:16 a.m. (Beijing time) on January 18, 2005, a seventeen-member team finally reached the peak of Dome A and planted an enormous Chinese flag to show that they had conquered the spot for China.[79] Later in the same year, a Chinese expedition team spent 130 days exploring the Grove Mountains, some 400 kilometers from Zhongshan Station. Like other explorers before them, the Chinese expeditioners marked their presence by naming the various points of geological significance they discovered, with names rich in cultural meaning such as Gui Shan (Turtle Mountain), She Shan (Snake Mountain), and Xi Hu (Western Lake).[80] China's Antarctic personnel were following well-

---

75   PRIC, "Zhongguo Beiji zhan Huang He jieshao" [An introduction to China's Arctic Yellow River Station], Shanghai, 2006, accessed November 7, 2014, http://www.pric.gov.cn/newinfo .asp?sortid=4&subid=39&id=465 (link discontinued).

76   Li et al., "Guowai Nanji kaocha guanli jigou yu kaocha guanli moshi de duibi fenxi," 49; and Guojia haiyangju haiyang fazhan zhanlue yanjiusuo ketizu, ed., *Zhongguo haiyang fazhan baogao* [Report on China's maritime development] (Beijing: Haiyang chubanshe, 2012), 374.

77   Wang, "Twenty Years of Antarctic Research."

78   "Er lun shenru xuexi guanche Xi Jinping zhuxi zhongyao jianghua jingshen."

79   Guan Xiaofeng, "Explorers Conquer 'Inaccessible Pole,'" *China Daily*, January 18, 2005.

80   Yu Dawei, "Nanji 'sanji tiao'" [Triple Jump in Antarctica], *Caijing*, no. 16, August 4, 2008.

established symbolic acts that help to build up a case for sovereignty in an unclaimed territory, just as many other generations of Antarctic explorers had done before them.[81]

In 2005, former PRIC director Zhang Zhanhai was elected to a two-year term as vice president of SCAR, an important "eyes and ears" role and a first for China.[82] Also in 2005, two China-based polar scholars, Li Shenggui and Pan Min, urged Chinese social scientists to pay greater attention to researching Antarctic issues. They stated that up until this point, China had focused its attention on the "hard" sciences while neglecting the important role of social scientists in exploring and articulating China's Antarctic agenda. The authors asserted that this "neglect has been restricting China's voice, rights, and interests" in international Antarctic affairs and influencing the country's international status, making it too passive.[83] Following the authors' rallying cry, there was a steady increase in Chinese social science publishing on Antarctica, compared with the output of previous years. This new emphasis was directly encouraged by senior government leaders.[84]

China's "great leap" in Antarctic (and Arctic) affairs since 2005 has been all the more noticeable in terms of capacity-building. China's future economic development is measured in five-year plans, and its polar agenda is no different. In the 11th Five-Year Plan, from 2006 to 2010, China refurbished Zhongshan and Great Wall Stations, set up a new summer-only research base at Dome A, refitted the *Xue Long*, established a dedicated berth for the ship and warehouse space in Shanghai, increased the budget for polar research threefold, and stepped up domestic and international promotion of China's polar program. Chinese leaders also became increasingly outspoken on Arctic issues, and China's polar officials began talking up China's new polar capabilities, stating in 2006 that China's Antarctic capacities would soon be on a par with those of the developed countries active there.[85]

---

[81] On the history of Antarctic exploration, see Day, *Antarctica*.

[82] "Zhang Zhanhai churen Nanji yanjiu kexue weiyuanhui" [Zhang Zhanhai takes up a post at SCAR], *Zhongguo haiyang bao*, no. 1429 (March 20, 2007), http://www.soa.gov.cn/hyjww/jdsy/2007/03/20/1174381011512817.htm (link discontinued).

[83] Li Shenggui and Pan Min, "Zhongguo Nanji ruankexue yanjiu de yiyi, xianzhuang yu zhanwang" [The significance, status quo, and prospect of Antarctic soft science research], *Jidi yanjiu* 17, no. 3 (September 2005): 214–31.

[84] Author's discussions at the PRIC, December 2009. See also Zhang Jiansong, "Zhuanjia chengying zhengzhi Nanji ziyuan fenzheng, qi guo you guafen lingtu yaoqiu" [Experts call for facing up to the struggle over Antarctic resources, seven countries put in a request to carve up the territory], *Liaowang*, June 18, 2007, http://news.sohu.com/20070618/n250625161.shtml.

[85] "Chen Lianzeng: Zengqiang wo guo zai Nanji de shizhi cunzai" [Chen Lianzeng: Strengthen China's physical presence in Antarctica], Xinhua, January 6, 2006, http://news.xinhuanet.com/world/2006-01/02/content_4000473.htm.

In 2007, China was for the first time accepted as an observer at the Arctic Council. France, Germany, the Netherlands, Poland, Spain, and the United Kingdom were already permanent observers to the council, but China was given only temporary status, valid solely for that meeting. China applied for a permanent observer position in 2009 and 2011, but each time was unsuccessful. Chinese polar officials and scholars were extremely resentful of what they regarded as China's exclusion from this important forum for Arctic affairs. China and other applicants were turned down by the Arctic Council owing to concerns about their motivations for being active in the Arctic and fear that increasing the number of Arctic Council participants would water down the rights of the council members. But in 2013, China (along with Japan, India, and South Korea, but not the European Union) was finally accepted as an "observer" at the Arctic Council. Dropping "permanent" from the terminology of the role helped shift the impasse on the matter.

From 2008, the global economic crisis gave further significance to China's polar expansion because other leading polar players had to cut back their Arctic and Antarctic capacity. The United States had 8 percent cuts in polar spending from 2012 on, while other previously strong players in Antarctic affairs such as Australia, New Zealand, Russia, and the United Kingdom had their budgets frozen for the first three years after 2008, with subsequent budget increases barely matching inflation. By contrast, in 2009 China's Ministry of Foreign Affairs set up the Department of Boundary and Ocean Affairs to better coordinate China's participation in global governance of international land and maritime boundaries.[86] Also in 2009, the PRIC started coordinating teams of social scientists to investigate Arctic and Antarctic governance and law, and the polar policies of the various leading players. In that same year, SOA deputy director Chen Lianzeng announced that China's polar strategy aimed to beef up China's soft and hard power, and that China was poised to become a "polar great power."[87]

During the 12th Five-Year Plan from 2011 to 2015, China continued to expand polar capabilities and engagement, notably extending China's polar presence by setting up a fourth Antarctic Base, Taishan. According to a report in the official SOA newspaper, the goal of this expansion was to

> steadily increase China's polar presence so as to increase China's status and influence and conduct research and assessments of polar oil and natural gas,

---

[86] "Bianjie yu haiyang shiwusi" [Department of Boundary and Maritime Affairs], accessed January 6, 2013, http://www.fmprc.gov.cn/mfa_chn/wjb_602314/zzjg_602420/bjhysws_603700/ (link discontinued).

[87] "Zhongguo Nanji kaocha 25 zhounian: heping liyong Nanji yong bu guoshi."

biological, and other resources, in order to explore the possibilities and means for future use.[88]

During the 2011–2015 Five-Year Plan, China was scheduled to build a new icebreaker; invest in a polar plane; set up air fields at Kunlun, Zhongshan, and Taishan bases; expand the PRIC logistics base in Shanghai and develop an international polar campus there; and increase the scientific budget. However, some of these ambitious plans were slowed by the strict fiscal constraints on government spending imposed by the Xi Jinping government after 2012. They will now be completed during the next Five-Year Plan (2016–2020).[89] Yet despite this reduction of pace, by the end of the 12th Five-Year Plan, China had achieved its stated goal of improving its polar soft and hard power through producing high-quality scientific research, had steadily expanded its multi-level presence in the Arctic and Antarctic, and certainly had met its target of equaling the capacity of the leading developed states operating in Antarctica.[90]

So far China's current Five-Year Plan, which will end in 2020, is also going through a few hiccups due to the economic slowdown. During the 2015–16 austral summer, China took delivery of its new polar plane, set up an intercontinental airplane network in Antarctica to transport its Antarctic scientists, significantly increased its polar science budget, and finally began construction on the new polar icebreaker. However, in April 2016, Chinese officials quietly admitted at the ATCM in Chile that China was delaying its previously announced plan to establish a fifth Antarctic research station in the strategically important Ross Sea region.[91] In July 2016, the SOA's *Ocean 6* research vessel set sail on a one-year voyage to engage in comprehensive maritime, geological and geophysical research in and around Antarctica, as well as in the Western Pacific.[92] Also in July 2016, the *Xue Long* set off on its seventh annual Arctic expedition, expanding the route and program covered on previous years. But the construction of China's second Arctic research station, in Iceland, was one year behind schedule – although it was expected to open by 2017.

[88]   "Wenbu tuijin jidi kaocha qiangguo jianshe jingcheng" [Steady progress in the project to become a polar great power], *Zhongguo haiyang bao* (China Institute for Maritime Affairs), July 19, 2011, http://www.cima.gov.cn/_d271688467.htm.
[89]   Chinese polar official, interview with author, October 2014.
[90]   Wang, "Twenty Years of Antarctic Research."
[91]   Eyewitness account from nongovernmental organization attendee at the 2016 ATCM.
[92]   "Wo guo shouci zai Nanji Luosi Hai faxian xin de maodi" [China discovers new anchorage in Antarctica's Ross Sea], Xinhua News Agency, January 9, 2015, http://www.ocofo.com/news/201501/09/list96087.html.

China's polar work plans have had to adjust to the new economic environment, yet the achievements of the past few years cannot be denied. In the next five years, China's polar expedition plan will undergo three major new changes: (1) increasing emphasis on national strategic priorities in polar natural science research, (2) a shift to a more unified polar management structure, and (3) a shift from reliance on foreign-made polar equipment to made-in-China equipment.[93] As Xi Jinping announced at Hobart in November 2014, due to "profound changes in the international situation," China is now "confidant" and "motivated" and willing to step up to a new level of strategy in its polar and maritime policies.[94]

---

[93] "'Shisanwu' jidi jiang tui san ge zhuanbian zengqiang san da nengli" [Polar 13th Five-Year Plan: Pushing for three changes in order to enhance a further three], *Haiyang ribao*, October 30, 2015, http://www.oceanol.com/shouye/jdkc/2015–10-30/52443.html.

[94] "Er lun shenru xuexi guanche Xi Jinping zhuxi zhongyao jianghua jingshen."

3

China's Geostrategic Interests in the Polar Regions

In 2015, the Chinese Communist Party government identified the polar regions, the deep seabed, and outer space as China's new strategic frontiers, noting that they are ripe with opportunities and open to all states with the capacity to exploit them.[1] As China's comprehensive national power grows, the government is taking advantage of every available opportunity in these three zones. China has strong geostrategic, political-military, economic, and scientific interests in the polar regions. China's strategic interests in the polar regions can be divided into three core categories, ranked as follows:

- **Security (traditional and nontraditional):** China has economic, political, military, and strategic interests in the polar regions.
- **Resources:** China wants access to Arctic and Antarctic minerals and hydrocarbons, fishing, tourism, transportation routes, water, and bioprospecting.
- **Science and technology:** Access to the polar regions is essential for the rollout of the BeiDou navigational system, China's space science program, and accurate weather forecasting in China.

These categories have many overlaps. For example, China's energy interests in the polar regions have strategic, economic, political, and scientific components. Using the three categories, the following sections will examine China's core strategic interests in the polar region and discuss how they connect to the Chinese government's broader geopolitical and geoeconomical plans.

---

[1] "Guojia anquan fa cao'an ni zengjia taikong deng xinxing lingyu de anquan weihu renwu" [The draft national security law will increase security in space and other new areas], Xinhua, June 24, 2015, http://www.chinanews.com/gn/2015/06-24/7363693.shtml.

CHINA'S SECURITY AND THE POLAR REGIONS

There are several dimensions to China's security interests in the polar regions, and they reflect the traditional concerns of a rising or a great power. China's core polar traditional security interests interconnect, but they can be divided into three areas: preserving freedom of transportation, particularly sea lanes of communication (SLOCs); projecting global maritime power; and strengthening defense. In terms of nontraditional security, China's economic and strategic science interests in the polar regions also require a stable and peaceful political environment in the Arctic and Antarctic, one where Chinese interests are protected and able to flourish. All these categories are both separate and intertwined and reflect the new geopolitics of the current era, in which maintaining global connectivity and cooperation are as prized as dominating one geographical site would be. China's core interests in the polar regions connect to, and are part of the justification for, the Chinese government's increased investment in military spending in the last twenty years, particularly on naval forces. They reflect Beijing's steady shift to project military power globally, one of the traditional indicators of a great power.

Freedom of Transportation

In the past twenty years, China has become a global economic power dependent on the sea for much of its commerce. China now has the world's third-largest merchant marine, exceeded only by Panama and Liberia, most of whose boats are simply flying flags of convenience.[2] Since 2010, China has been the world's largest shipbuilding nation,[3] and since 2014 it has been the world's largest trader in goods and the largest importer of oil.[4] The majority of China's trade by value and volume travels by sea,[5] and so the security of sea routes has become a key preoccupation of the Chinese government. The main international shipping routes are designed to link Asia, North America, and Western Europe, the world's most significant markets. China's SLOC to Western Europe is via the Suez Canal, and the SLOC to the United States is via the Panama Canal. China's maritime transportation also has to pass through a number of key chokepoints: the Malacca, Lombok, Bali, and Miyako straits;

[2] Howard J. Dooley, "The Great Leap Outward: China's Maritime Renaissance," *Journal of East Asian Affairs* 26, no. 1 (2012), 56.
[3] Ibid., 59–63.
[4] Jamil Anderlini and Lucy Hornby, "China Overtakes US as World's Largest Goods Trader," *Financial Times*, January 10, 2014, http://on.ft.com/1hBumUe.
[5] Wu Shicun and Zou Keyuan, ed., *Maritime security in the South China Sea: Regional Implications and International Cooperation* (Farnham, UK: Ashgate, 2009), 70.

the Somali coast; and the Suez and Panama canals. All of these potential chokepoints are controlled by other states; even in peacetime, they are prone to economic and political difficulties outside China's control. The Chinese leadership is particularly worried about China's overreliance on the Malacca Strait. Eighty-five percent of China's maritime trade passes through this strait, which connects the Indian Ocean and South China Sea. Meanwhile, the Panama Canal is operating at capacity, despite recent expansions. Insurance costs for the Suez Canal are very high, owing to piracy in the region, and it is close to areas of military conflict in the Middle East. A further but less-well-known sea route is strategically important for access to China's near seas: the Miyako Strait. This lies between Japan's Okinawa and Miyako islands, and it is the main passage for the People's Liberation Army-Navy North and East Sea Fleets to access the Pacific Ocean. The strait is controlled by the Japanese Self-Defense Forces, which positioned surface-to-ship missiles there in 2013.[6]

As the world's largest shipping nation with the world's largest economy, China is now acting prudently and looking for ways to reduce its dependence on these maritime chokepoints. Polar transportation routes are among a number of options China is exploring.[7] In a 1999 article that has been extremely influential on Chinese analysis of the importance of the Arctic and Antarctic sea routes, R. Douglas Brubaker and Willy Ostreng wrote, "The relative importance of different avenues of the oceans in the future will depend on techniques, contexts, and needs, which cannot be envisaged now. In a world where military capabilities take years to construct, but where political intentions can change overnight, the prudent course is not to surrender any of these maritime routes if at all avoidable."[8] Following this sound advice, Chinese investment is currently involved in projects to expand the Panama Canal, to develop a new canal through Nicaragua, and to establish cross-continent rail links through Colombia. China is also setting up pipelines that will link it to energy sources in Central Asia and Russia and avoid the need for sea access. For the same reason, it is expanding and improving rail and road links with neighboring states and helping neighbors with sea boundaries such as Burma, Pakistan, and Sri Lanka to develop new ports. China also has expressed an interest in investing in a cross-Thailand canal that would help ease congestion in the

---

6   Sun Xiaobo, "Japan Deploys Missiles on Strategic Strait," *Global Times*, November 7, 2013, http://www.globaltimes.cn/content/823106.shtml.

7   Ding Huang, ed., *Jidi guojia zhengce yanjiu baogao 2012–2013* [Annual report on national polar policy research, 2012–13] (Beijing: Kexue chubanshe, 2013), 64.

8   R. Douglas Brubaker and Willy Ostreng, "The Northern Sea Route Regime: Exquisite Superpower Subterfuge?," *Ocean Development and International Law* 30, no. 4 (1999), 331.

Malacca Strait, and it is exploring the possibility of a high-speed Arctic rail route that would link Asia with North America.[9]

Accessing the polar seas would greatly expand China's range of transportation possibilities. The Southern Ocean offers three potential alternative shipping routes linking China with the Indian and Atlantic Ocean: (1) via South Africa's Cape of Good Hope, (2) via Chile's Cape Horn, and (3) via Australia's Southeast Cape in Tasmania. For centuries before the Panama and Suez canals were constructed or the cross-continental railways of North America built, these first two capes, and to a lesser extent the third, were core ocean highways for merchant shipping, and global and regional navies continue to use them. Thus, as Chinese naval analysts note, in a time of military conflict in the vicinity of China's main SLOCs, these three capes would provide useful alternative routes for Chinese shipping.[10] Although the areas suffer from extreme weather conditions, all three are free of conflict. Chinese analysis comes to the surprising conclusion that from the point of view of security, the transit via Tasmania's Southeast Cape is a "golden route," as it is completely under the control of the Royal Australian Navy.[11]

The Arctic shipping route has also been famously described by Chinese maritime specialists as a "golden route" for maritime transportation.[12] Historically, explorers looked for a shortcut across the Arctic from Europe to Asia, the fabled Northwest Passage. Since 2009, climate change has increasingly opened up the possibility of three Arctic sea routes as alternative oceanic highways during the Northern Hemisphere summer months: (1) the Northeast and Northern sea routes, which follow the Russian coast; (2) the Transpolar Route, which crosses the North Pole; and (3) the Northwest Passage, which passes through the Canadian Arctic Archipelago. Accessing these three routes will increase shipping options for China, as well as for a host of other countries, and open up a previously closed-off zone to development. In the long run, China favors the Northern Sea Route; it crosses directly over

---

9   "Fan ya gaotie xia yue donggong jianshe" [Pan-Asia high-speed rail to start construction next month], *Jinghua shibao*, May 8, 2014, http://epaper.jinghua.cn/html/2014–05/08/con tent_87865.htm.
10 Shen Kong, Sha Weiliang, and Yuan Xiansheng, "Nan Dayang zhanlüe diwei tuxian" [Highlighting the strategic position of the Southern Ocean], *Dangdai haijun*, no. 9, (2007); and Liu Jiangping and Yan Min, "Rijian tuxian de Nan Dayang zhanlue diwei ji quyu haijun qiangguo" [The increasing strategic significance of the Southern Ocean and regional naval power], *Xiandai junshi*, no. 1, (2003). Similar points about the strategic significance of the polar air and sea routes can be seen in Ding, *Jidi guojia zhengce yanjiu baogao 2012–2013*, 64.
11 Liu and Yan, "Rijian tuxian de Nan Dayang zhanlue diwei ji quyu haijun qiangguo," 48.
12 See the first five minutes of Part 1 of *Zou xiang haiyang* [To the oceans] (CCTV, 2011). The film promotes China's polar strategy as an important component of China's maritime strategy.

the Arctic Ocean, thus avoiding coastal state control, and it is shorter.[13] China is keen to be included in setting the norms for international shipping on this route.[14] However, in the current climate conditions, the Northern Sea Route will not be open for more than a few weeks at a time until mid-century.

There has been a lot of hype about China's interest in Arctic shipping, not least from Chinese sources. In 2011, *To the Oceans* (*Zouxiang haiyang*), a twelve-part documentary by Chinese Central Television on China's maritime strategy (jointly funded by the PLAN and the State Oceanic Administration) began with a well-known quote from maritime studies scholar Li Zhenfu: "Whoever controls the Arctic Ocean will control the new corridor for the world economy."[15] Many Chinese polar scholars concur with Li's analysis. As Chinese maritime specialist Shi Chunlin wrote in 2010, "The Arctic sea route is a strategic military route; whoever controls the Arctic will have the upper hand over other opponents."[16] Other Chinese researchers stress the usefulness of the Arctic sea route in enabling China to evade existing chokepoints.[17] However, the opening up of Arctic shipping routes would also create further potential chokepoints for Chinese shipping heading to the far north: (1) in the straits that divide the Japanese archipelago; (2) at the Bering Strait; then in Canada's Queen Elizabeth Islands on the Northwest Passage; and (3) Russia's Severnaya Zemlya and New Siberian islands along the Northern Sea Route.

Accessing Arctic routes will help China to diversify its overdependence on existing SLOCs, using paths that are much less contested and vulnerable to attack than traditional shipping routes. If any of its usual SLOCs are blocked or restricted by military conflict, China will have to take alternative routes for its strategic shipping, even going as far as the Southern Ocean. Regardless of how uneconomic this is or whether the passage was shorter or longer, in the short term it could be expedient for Chinese shipping to take such routes. Under this scenario, routes that go by way of either polar region have to be considered and prepared for. However, in statements aimed at foreign

---

[13]   Zhang Xia of the Polar Research Institute of China, cited in "Xifang guafen Beiji chunudi: Zhongguo charu rang Mei E shiliao bu zhu" [The West divides up Arctic virgin soil: China's engagement worries US and Russia], *Heyang xinwen*, February 22, 2012, http://wap.tiexue.net/touch/thread_5718734_1.html.

[14]   Guo Peiqing and Li Zhenfu, *Beiji hangdao de guoji wenti yanjiu* [Research on the international issues regarding the Arctic shipping routes] (Beijing: Haiyang chubanshe, 2009), 317.

[15]   *Zou xiang haiyang*, Part 1.

[16]   Shi Chunlin, "Bei bingyang hangxian kaitong dui Zhongguo jingji fazhan de zuoyong ji Zhongguo liyong duice [Opening up the Arctic Oceanic route: China's economic interests and policies], *Jingji wenti shensuo*, no. 8 (2010), 50.

[17]   Guo and Li, *Beiji hangdao de guoji wenti yanjiu*, 1.

audiences, China's official news agency Xinhua emphasizes the cost- and time-saving opportunities of Arctic shipping routes.[18]

When the Arctic sea routes open up, China's trade routes could indeed be shortened by about 4000 miles. China also would no longer have to worry about current size restrictions on boats passing through the Panama Canal or high transit fees.[19] In a 2009 report, Zhang Xia, director of polar strategy at the Polar Research Institute of China, estimated that if Arctic shipping is completely opened up, then China could save around US$533 billion to US$1.274 trillion per year.[20] A 2013 study in a Chinese commercial shipping publication calculated that Arctic shipping could reduce China's marine transportation costs by 40 percent. This figure does not include fuel savings, the reduction of ship emissions on the atmosphere, or the wider economic benefits of shortening the operation cycle of the voyage, such as lower wage bills.[21] The Arctic sea route would be most suitable for shipping minerals rather than containers, owing to the short window currently available for shipping goods through the Arctic Ocean. Russian icebreaking fees would have to decrease by 25 percent in order for the Arctic sea route to be competitive with the current costs of utilizing the Suez and Panama canals for container shipping. This could possibly be achieved if greater numbers of shipping were to use the route,[22] but sanctions imposed on Russia since its 2014 intervention in Ukraine have drastically slowed the expansion of the Arctic sea route.[23] Arctic shipping also attracts high insurance costs. Moreover, China would need to prepare for Arctic transits by making adjustments in port facilities to allow them to be capable of handling the size of boats that will service Arctic traffic.[24] Specially designed Arctic cargo boats that are able to

---

[18] "Bigger Chinese Role Sought in the Arctic," Xinhua, February 18, 2014, http://news.xinhuanet .com/english/china/2014-02/18/c_133123759.htm.

[19] Guo and Li, *Beiji hangdao de guoji wenti yanjiu*, 322.

[20] Zhang Xia, "Beiji hangxian de haiyun jingji qianli pinggu ji qi dui wo guo jingji fazhan de zhanlue yiyi" [Evaluation of the economic potential of the Artic shipping route and China's economic development and strategic interests], 2009 *Zhongguo jidi kexue xueshu nianhui lunwen zhaiyaoji* [Abstracts from the 2009 China polar science conference] (Shanghai: PRIC, 2009), 94–95.

[21] "Beiji hangyun de xianzhuang yu mianlin de tiaozhan [The current situation of Arctic shipping and challenges ahead], *Zhongguo yuanyang shangwu*, October, 2013, accessed July 8, 2014, http://www.maritime-china.com/ztjj/hxbj/275612.htm (link discontinued).

[22] Julia Nanay, "Russian Arctic Strategies and Recent Deals" (paper presented at Wilson Center, Washington, D.C., July 12, 2012), http://www.wilsoncenter.org/sites/default/files/NanayArcti c7-12-12.pdf.

[23] Alister Doyle and Alistair Scrutton, "Sanctions Sap Allure of Russia's Arctic Shipping Route," Reuters, January 22, 2015, http://reut.rs/1yMjOb2.

[24] Joseph Spears, "China and the Arctic: The Awakening Snow Dragon," *China Brief* 9, no. 6 (2009), 2.

withstand Arctic conditions will load or offload cross-Arctic shipments at hub ports, which will then distribute the shipments to smaller ports.

Plans are already under way for Shanghai to become the Arctic shipping hub in northeast Asia, linked with Qingdao, Dalian, Hong Kong, and Taiwan's Kaohsiung as the supporting ports.[25] Meanwhile, Iceland, Norway, and Russia are contenders for the future site of the Arctic shipping hub on the European side. The opening of Arctic voyages will support China's coastal economic development strategy in its northeastern rustbelt, providing opportunities for the expansion of polar shipbuilding industries, logistics support, fisheries, mining, and tourism.[26] China is already experienced in managing modern mega-ports and is the world's third-lowest cost container shipper. Chinese shipping companies are experienced in building commercial ports, logistics centers, and transportation systems to support China's trade in locations from the Indian Ocean to the Mediterranean. The northeast Arctic hub would also be a processing center for Arctic resources. Hosting the site for the Asian Arctic hub port will increase the profitability of Arctic shipping for China and reduce costs, and it will help raise China's international profile. A SOA-funded analysis of the Arctic route envisions Shanghai as the new Venice and China being able to create a new Sinocentric maritime order in East Asia.[27] The Arctic sea route and the Southern Ocean are part of China's New Silk Road policies, which link China with its trading partners in a new global order.[28] But these plans rely on a peaceful strategic environment in China's near neighborhood. In particular, China needs to amicably settle territorial disputes in the East China and South China seas and gain acceptance for its preeminence among its neighbors – a goal that has eluded Beijing so far.

With the help of nuclear icebreakers, by 2020 the Arctic Northern sea route could be operational for several months of the year. By 2030, it would be open for three to four months; the Northwest Passage and Transpolar routes would be open for slightly less time, on a similar time frame.[29] The utilization of

---

[25]   Guo and Li, *Beiji hangdao de guoji wenti yanjiu*, 333–43; on the potential role of Kaohsiung, see Ibid., 340.

[26]   "Beiji hangyun de xianzhuang yu mianlin de tiaozhan,"

[27]   Guo and Li, *Beiji hangdao de guoji wenti yanjiu*, 333–43.

[28]   "Liaoning canyu 'yidai yilu' dazao santiao zhi ouzhou jiaotong yunshu tongdao" [Liaoning participates in "New Silk Road" to create three new European transportation routes], *Zhongguo xinwen wang*, January 27, 2015, http://www.chinanews.com/sh/2015/01-27/7009502 .shtml; and "2015 Nian Zhongguo jidi kexue zhanlüe yanjiu jijin shenbao zhinan" [Guide to 2015 Polar Strategic research fund], Chinese Antarctic Center of Surveying and Mapping, June 29, 2015, http://pole.whu.edu.cn/cacsm/gb_news.php?id=128104&modid=02001.

[29]   Navy Task Force Climate Change, "US Navy Arctic Roadmap, 2014–2030," US Department of the Navy, February 2014, http://www.navy.mil/docs/USN_arctic_roadmap.pdf, 11.

Arctic shipping routes will open up a whole new zone of economic development, one that presently is extremely underdeveloped. Greenland, Russia, Canada, Norway, and the US state of Alaska all have untapped mineral and natural gas resources, and the new shipping route could help stimulate the currently stagnant economies of the US Eastern seaboard and Northern Europe. China does not yet have many boats suitable for sailing in the Arctic (though it is starting to build them) and Chinese shipping companies have only minimal experience sailing in Arctic waters. Detailed charts on Arctic sailing routes are in short supply; only Russia has precise route charts. Chinese shipping specialists point out that there are many risks involved in Arctic shipping: some areas of the potential shipping route pass through US military zones; apart from ice conditions, Arctic waters are hazardous due to a high risk of floating logs and uncharted wrecks; while navigation in the high latitudes is difficult due to magnetic variation.[30] Because of these risks and the additional costs associated with Arctic passage, the Arctic sea route is not yet economically viable for Chinese shipping companies, and despite the hype of recent years they are not very interested in it at present.[31] In 2012, the China Ocean Shipping (Group) Company (COSCO), China's largest shipping company, commissioned a navigation study on Arctic sea routes,[32] and it released the study in 2015. However, so far COSCO sent only one vessel via the Arctic route in 2013, and one in 2015, although three were sent in 2016.[33] COSCO said that it was considering opening an Arctic tourism line in 2014, but nothing progressed from this initial expression of interest. Thus, when China signals its interest in the Arctic routes it should be understood as essentially reflecting geopolitical and geostrategic priorities rather than commercial ones.

Arctic shipping routes are recognized as having strategic advantages for China, and the economic, political, and military significance of these advantages will only grow as Arctic development unfolds. For now, as polar politics specialists Guo Peiqing and Sun Kai point out, Beijing's well-known interest in the Arctic sea route is a clever way to position China as having legitimate interests in the Arctic region, so that it can ensure that it has a seat at the table in any future negotiations there.[34] Although China's shipping companies are

[30] "Beiji hangyun de xianzhuang yu mianlin de tiaozhan."

[31] Chinese shipping official, interview with author, November 2014.

[32] "Cosco Seeks to Study Arctic Shipping with Iceland," *Lloyd's List*, September 17, 2012, http://www.lloydslist.com/ll/sector/ship-operations/article407505.ece.

[33] "Zhongguo shangchuan chenggong shouhang Beiji hangdao" [Chinese merchant ship makes first successful Arctic transit], *Renmin ribao*, September 12, 2012, http://news.12371.cn/2013/09/12/ARTI1378938013311706.shtml.

[34] Guo Peiqing and Sun Kai, "Beiji lishihui de 'Nuke biaozhun' he Zhongguo de beiji canyu zhi lu" [The Arctic Council's 'Nuuk standard' and China's path to participation in the Arctic], *Guoji jingji yu zhengzhi*, no. 12 (2013), 136.

required to make a profit, as state-owned enterprises (SOEs) they must also follow national policy and in the case of the Arctic, geostrategic needs will trump commercial interests.[35] Shi Chunlin echoes these points, arguing that unlike the Malacca Strait or the Suez or Panama canals, China should not allow the Arctic sea routes to be dominated by other states, and that subsidies for Chinese shipping on the Arctic sea route will shore up the Chinese government's right to participate in Arctic norm-setting.[36]

Large sections of the three possible Arctic Ocean highways pass through or near Russian territorial waters, so Russia obviously will have the main role in controlling the Arctic sea route. But because new infrastructure will need to be developed along the route, and other littoral states will be involved in the route and most likely will be heavy users, Arctic shipping will need to rely on international cooperation and investment to take off. There is potential for a new model of international relations here, with China taking a prominent role in helping to set up the new order in the Arctic.

China views the Arctic sea routes as international straits, as does the United States; however, neither Russia nor Canada accepts this position. Both Russia and Canada define the sections of the Arctic sea routes that pass by their territories as internal waters. They assert that Article 234 of UNCLOS (which affects human activity in ice-covered waters) applies to these routes, and therefore they impose many restrictions on vessels wishing to transit them. Currently, the Arctic Northern Route sees the most use. Russian authorities require that all boats using the Northern Route be guided by a Russian icebreaker going in convoy, a situation that a senior Chinese strategic analyst described as "extremely irksome." The convoy fees make this route uneconomical compared to the Panama Canal route.[37] If the Chinese navy or coast guard had its own nuclear icebreaker, Chinese Arctic shipments would be more self-sufficient. More international shipping on the Arctic sea routes will strengthen the case for the Northern Sea Route and Northwest Passage being accepted as international straits. From the point of view of China's long-term strategic interests in the Arctic, therefore, the more that the Arctic shipping route opens up, the better. Arctic shipping will not solve all of China's SLOC worries, but it will be a useful alternative to traditional routes during the Northern Hemisphere summer months. It will open up strategically important, resource-rich areas in the circumpolar north to Chinese investment,

---

[35] Guo and Li, *Beiji hangdao de guoji wenti yanjiu*, 325.
[36] Shi Chunlin, "Bei bingyang hangxian kaitong dui Zhongguo jingji fazhan de zuoyong ji Zhongguo liyong duice" [Opening up the Arctic oceanic route: China's economic interests and policies], *Jingji wenti shensuo*, no. 8 (2010), 52 and 51.
[37] "Beiji hangyun de xianzhuang yu mianlin de tiaozhan."

especially mining and fishing interests, and will give new economic opportunities to China's struggling northeast.

Polar shipping is only one aspect of China's focus on polar transportation. The opening up of the Arctic to more transpolar flights is also of great interest, as improved international air links are an important means of further boosting China's economic development. Crossing the North Pole to travel between Asia and North America and Europe significantly cuts travel distances. It also opens up alternative flight routes, which is why Chinese sources refer to polar air routes as "air resources."[38] The flight path from Beijing to New York via the Pacific is 19,000 kilometers; whereas via the Arctic it is only 11,000 kilometers. During the Cold War, polar civilian routes across the Soviet Union were restricted due to political and military sensitivities. Commercial cross-polar routes did not open up until 2000. In 2001, Arctic states adopted the "Guidance for Polar Operations," a joint policy on polar air flights that lists specific requirements for polar flight operations, including cold-weather conditions, special communication capabilities, fuel freeze strategy, and evacuation and recovery plans. China's first cross-Arctic flight was launched in 2001.[39] In 2010, there were 10,025 cross-polar commercial flights, a 10 percent increase over the previous year.[40] By 2016, the numbers of cross-polar flights had nearly doubled, with around fifty flights per day or approximately 18,300 annually.[41] The International Air Transportation Association's Pacific Project is developing polar User Preferred Routes between key Asian cities and European and Northern American cities; this has required careful negotiation among Chinese, Russian, and US interests, as flights cross militarily-significant air defense identification zones in the Arctic and near-Arctic regions. The benefits of improved cross-polar route planning are easily visible: polar air routes cut travel time, save on fuel, and help manage the ever-increasing air traffic demand between Asia and North

---

[38] Guojia haiyangju haiyang fazhan zhanlue yanjiusuo ketizu, ed., *Zhongguo haiyang fazhan baogao* [Report on China's maritime development] (Beijing: Haiyang chubanshe, 2012), 362.

[39] Lu Junyuan, *Beiji diyuan zhengzhi yu Zhongguo yingdui* [Geopolitics in the Arctic and China's response] (Beijing: Shishi chubanshe, 2010), 45.

[40] United Airlines, "Polar Operations, 1996–2010," Briefing to Cross-Polar Working Group, November 2010; and Edgar Vaynshteyn / Global Aviation Consulting LLC, "Transpolar Operations/Diversions Planning and Support" (presentation at International Winter Operations Conference, Montreal, October 5–6, 2011), United Kingdom Flight Safety Committee, October 21, 2011, http://www.ukfsc.co.uk/files/External%20Meetings/Speciali st%20Subject/Intl%20Winter%20Ops%20Conference%20E.%20Vaynshteyn%20Oct%2020 11.pdf.

[41] See the day-to-day routings for cross-polar flights at "Crosspolar Routes," Unified Air Traffic Management System of the Russian Federation, n.d., https://app.matfmc.ru/publique/Cross Polar/flights.aspx.

America.[42] However, China is the main obstacle to further expansion in cross-Arctic flights between Asia, North America, and Europe, as the Chinese government has restricted entry and exit points for polar routes to a mere seven cross-border points. China also charges among the highest fees among partner countries for international flights to cross its airspace. A large percentage of Chinese airspace is dedicated to military use, and the PLA is reluctant to release its access to domestic or foreign commercial interests.[43]

The Antarctic transpolar air route is less commercially significant than the Arctic transpolar route, but Chinese military analysts noted its strategic significance as early as the 1960s.[44] In 1977, a classified Chinese report on Antarctica pointed out that the continent was a strategic air route linking Oceania, South America, and Africa.[45] Any state that dominates the air space of Antarctica – currently, only the United States is in this situation – potentially could control air access to all three regions. In a 2007 report, *People's Daily* highlighted the "military-strategic" significance of Antarctica, noting that the US Coast Guard was stationed there and that the United States has a substantial air force presence in Antarctica, while Chile has armed military bases there.[46] Within the next few years, China is likely to follow nations like Argentina, Brazil, Chile, New Zealand, and the United States in using military personnel for the bulk of its logistics in Antarctica. This will enable the Chinese polar program to greatly expand its operations in Antarctica,[47] and enable the PLA to develop operational capacity in the polar regions. It also will help China achieve its emerging polar military-security and civilian-scientific goals.

China's Rise as a Maritime Power

China's political and geostrategic interests in the polar regions are intertwined with the government's wider foreign and defense policy concerns and global strategy. China's significant global shipping interests are the official

---

[42]   *Report on the 38th Meeting of the Informal Pacific Air Traffic Control Coordinating Group,* Mountain View, CA, April 22–26, 2013.

[43]   International air industries official, interview with author, June 2015.

[44]   John Wilson Lewis and Hua Di, "China's Ballistic Missile Programme: Technologies, Strategies, Goals," *International Security* 17, no. 2 (1992), 19.

[45]   Renmin ribao guojibu ziliaozu, "Shijie 'zuihou de bianjiang': Nanjizhou de ziyuan zhengzhuo zhan" [The world's "final frontier": The struggle for Antarctica's strategic resources], *Neibu ziliao (Renmin ribao)* (May 1977), 1.

[46]   "Ling ren danyou de Nanji 're'"[The worrying "heating up" of Antarctica], *Renmin ribao,* December 4, 2007, http://scitech.people.com.cn/GB/6607386.html.

[47]   Chinese polar official, interview with author, October 2012.

justification for the PLAN's expanded maritime strategy and capabilities.[48] The PLAN is the world's largest navy in terms of personnel and it is second only to the US Navy in fleet tonnage. In military terms, China is steadily moving from being a land-based regional power to becoming a maritime power with a global reach. China wants not only to be able to protect its own sea borders, but also to develop a blue-water navy capable of patrolling the high seas (*gonghai*) to protect China's trading routes, as well as new sites for resource exploitation. In a 2009 internal report on Antarctic resources, PRIC researchers linked China's maritime strategy with Antarctica, saying that "[China] needs to be able to compete with other states on the high seas, this is the only way to obtain the resources there; these will be a key source for our economic growth and development."[49] In 2012, the Central Party School, the CCP's dedicated higher education institute, set up a special research group to analyze China's maritime policies. A report published in CCP policy journal *Theoretical Trends* (*Lilun dongtai*) stated that as part of China's maritime policies, China "will protect its rights on the open seas and pay close attention to the Arctic and Antarctic."[50] The authors of the report noted:

> The existing international maritime norms have been set by the West, and in many ways they are disadvantageous to our maritime strategy. Under the present-day situation, whereby the international legal system is dominated by Western states, China must defend its national interests and be very involved in the process and application of international law in order to strengthen its right to speak on the setting of international maritime law and to protect its national interests.[51]

China has 9.6 million square kilometers of land territory and 18,000 kilometers of coast line; its combined territorial seas, exclusive economic zones, and continental shelf (if accepted by other states) would extend to around 3 million square kilometers. China's double-digit growth since the early 1990s means that, more than ever before, the Chinese government is finally in a position to improve its maritime security and access to maritime rights both within its own region and globally.

---

[48] Liu Yijian, *Zhi haiquan yu haijun zhanlüe* [The command of the sea and the strategic employment of naval forces] (Beijing: Jiefangjun guofang daxue chubanshe, 2004), 233.

[49] Zhu Jiangang, Yan Qide, and Ling Xiaoliang, "Nanji ziyuan ji qi kaifa liyong qianjing fenxi" [An analysis of Antarctic resources, their exploitation, and potential utilization], *Zhongguo ruan kexue*, no. 8 (2005), 18.

[50] "Zhongguo haiyang anquan xianzhuang yu yingdui jucuo" [The state of China's maritime security and coping measures], *Lilun dongtai*, no. 1937 (2012), 15.

[51] Ibid., 24.

China does not have a strong maritime tradition. However, ever since the devastating Opium Wars (1839–42), when Western gunboats defeated China's land-based forces and forced China into a series of unequal treaties, Chinese political elites have understood the need for China to develop a modern navy in order to protect its national interests. US naval strategist Alfred T. Mahan's 1890 publication *The Influence of Sea Power upon History* had a major impact on the thinking of military leaders in the late Qing Dynasty.[52] In 1921, Dr. Sun Yat-sen, first president of the Republic of China, devised a plan for national construction and guidelines for China's national defense that laid out a strategy to enable China to become a maritime power.[53] The ROC built a modest naval and air force to defend Chinese interests; however, when the People's Republic of China was founded in 1949, its military forces, the People's Liberation Army, were solely land-based. The CCP's lack of navy and air force was the main weakness that prevented it from completely routing the ROC government from its final redoubt on Taiwan. From 1950, the ROC's naval defenses were backed up by security guarantees from the United States with which the nascent PLAN and PLA–Air Force could not compete. In the Mao era, Chinese thinking on naval doctrine was also very much shaped by the Soviet Union's naval doctrine, which rejected Mahan as an "apologist of imperial sea power" and advocated a focus on coastal defense.[54]

US naval dominance in the Asia-Pacific was set up in the early stages of the Cold War to defend a series of island chains – "from the Aleutians to Australia and New Zealand" – against the spread of communism.[55] Since the early 1950s, a series of "hub and spokes" security pacts – including the US-

[52]   Pi Mingyong, "Haiquan lun yu Qingmo haijun jianshe lilun" [Sea power theory and modern construction theory in the late Qing dynasty], *Jiandai shi yanjiu*, no. 2 (1996), 37.

[53]   Chang Chi-Yung, ed., *The Complete Works of Dr. Sun Yat-sen* (Taipei: National Defense Institute, 1960), 40–42, 50–63, and 69–74. For more on the history of China's maritime strategy, see Kuo Tsung-chin, "China's Maritime Strategy," in *Report of the Seventh International Conference on the Security of Sea Lines of Communication in the Western Pacific and Indian Oceans* (Warrenton, VA, May 7–10, 1990), 179–92.

[54]   Quotes from Admiral Vladimir Chernavin, the last naval commander of the Soviet Union, cited in Norman Polmar, *The Naval Institute Guide to the Soviet Union* (Annapolis, MD: United States Naval Institute Press, 1991), 25.

[55]   Background Papers for the Australia–New Zealand–United States (ANZUS) Council Preparations, July 24, 1952, Acheson Memoranda of Conversations File, 1949–1953 (July 1952), Dean G. Acheson Papers, Harry S. Truman Library and Museum, available at http://www.trumanlibrary.org; see also the Australian government papers on the 1951 ANZUS Treaty, in *Documents on Australian Foreign Policy*, Vol. 21: *The ANZUS Treaty* (Canberra: Department of Foreign Affairs and Trade, 2001), http://dfat.gov.au/about-us/publications/historical-documents/Pages/volume-21/the-1951-anzus-treaty-volume-21.aspx.

Philippines Mutual Defense Treaty (1951); the ANZUS Treaty between Australia, New Zealand, and the United States (1951); the Mutual Cooperation and Security between the United States and Japan (1952); the United States–Republic of Korea Mutual Defense Treaty (1953); the United States–ROC Mutual Defense Treaty (1955); and the Antarctic Treaty (1959) – has enabled US armed forces in the Asia-Pacific to dominate key chokepoints leading to the Arctic Ocean, the Indian Ocean, and the Southern Ocean.[56]

The island chain concept – which is now more often referenced with regard to China's response, rather than to its US defense strategy origins – links the North Pole to the South Pole, extending US strategic control over the gateways to the seas and skies of the Asia-Pacific region from the entrance to the Arctic at the Bering Sea chokepoint, all the way down to Antarctica and as far as the South Pole where the United States's Scott-Amundsen Base is located. The first island chain begins in Japan, passes through the Liuqiu Islands to Taiwan, and on to the Philippines; it includes the East China and South China Sea. The second island chain begins southwest of Japan and continues through to the Ogasawa-gunto (Bonin) Islands and the Mariana Islands. The third island chain is more geopolitical than geographical, running from the Aleutians in the northernmost Pacific to the southernmost islands of New Zealand and Australia and on down to Antarctica. The vast region of territories within the island chain, consisting of more than 50 percent of the globe, is managed under the control of the US Pacific Command (USPACOM). Formed in 1947, USPACOM is the oldest and largest of the US armed forces' unified combatant commands. USPACOM currently has around 360,000 military personnel under its command in the Asia-Pacific regions.[57] This figure includes 49,347 personnel in Hawaii, 5666 in Guam, and 185 in Antarctica,[58] as well as those stationed outside US territory such as in South Korea and Japan. Put in US military terms, USPACOM is an integral part of the US military's "forward posture" strategy in the interests of "deterrence and

---

56 On the continuing importance of US naval dominance and preeminence in Asia-Pacific waters, see the comments of Admiral Timothy Keating, chief of USPACOM from 2007 to 2009, "Remarks at the IFPA-Fletcher Conference on National Security and Policy," Washington, D.C., September 27, 2007, http://ifpafletcherconference.com/oldtranscripts/2007/Keating.pdf.

57 See the Headquarters US Pacific Command website, http://www.pacom.mil/About-USPACOM/.

58 "Antarctic Treaty Electronic Information Exchange System: United States 2012/2013 Annual Information," Secretariat of the Antarctic Treaty, accessed February 19, 2014, http://eies.ats.aq/Ats.IE/ieGenRpt.aspx?idParty=42&period=2&idYear=2012.

reassurance" and its activities are defensive in nature.[59] China has long perceived it as nothing more than a strategic blockade.[60]

After China entered the Korean War in support of North Korea in October 1950, the United States imposed an extremely damaging sea blockade on China that lasted throughout the 1950s.[61] Even up to the present day, the US Navy periodically conducts military exercises and "freedom of navigation" exercises in the South China Sea, Taiwan Straits, and other strategic seas within or near to Chinese territorial waters as part of the US deterrence strategy. Since 2012, there have been repeated clashes and near-misses between the PLA and US military planes and boats. Breaking the US military's strategic dominance in the Asia-Pacific would greatly enhance China's security and enable it to gain the upper hand in multiple maritime territorial disputes: the status of Taiwan and the Offshore Islands; the Diaoyu/Senkaku Islands territorial dispute with Japan; and territorial disputes with Brunei, Malaysia, the Philippines, and Vietnam in the South China Sea. Another critical issue involves the maritime component of nuclear balance. The United States currently has 1538 nuclear warheads.[62] Experts estimate that China has around 250 warheads.[63] But if Chinese submarines armed with nuclear weapons were able to access the Arctic Ocean without detection, this would alter the nuclear balance between the two states. More than any other new initiative, it also would significantly strengthen China's position in northeast Asia – which would have an impact on territorial disputes – and would bolster China's growing status as a global leader. In this light, China's sea power display in September 2015, when five PLAN vessels entered US territorial waters in the Aleutians, should be seen as a warning shot of the Xi government's ambition to transform the strategic balance in the Asia-Pacific.

In 1986, PLAN commander Admiral Liu Huaqing laid out a blueprint for China to gain control over its maritime boundaries and to defend the key

[59]   Timothy Keating, "PACOM: Moving the Throttle Forward in the Pacific," *Asia-Pacific Defense Forum*, 4th Quarter (2007).

[60]   Liu Zhongmin, *Shijie haiyang zhengzhi yu Zhongguo haiyang fazhan zhanlue* [World maritime politics and China's maritime development strategy] (Beijing: Shishi chubanshe, 2009), 179.

[61]   You Ji, "The Evolution of China's Maritime Combat Doctrines and Models: 1949–2001," Working Paper No. 22, Institute of Defence and Strategic Studies Singapore, 2002, 1. http://www.rsis.edu.sg/publications/WorkingPapers/WP22.pdf.

[62]   "World Nuclear Weapon Stockpile: 2015," Ploughshares Fund (updated March 2, 2016), http://www.ploughshares.org/world-nuclear-stockpile-report; and "New START Treaty Aggregate Numbers of Offensive Weapons," US State Department, October 1, 2015, http://www.state.gov/t/avc/rls/247674.htm.

[63]   Hans M. Kristensen and Robert S. Norris, "Chinese Nuclear Forces, 2013," *Bulletin of the Atomic Scientists* 69, no. 6 (2013), 79.

chokepoints on which its SLOCs depend. The initial goal was to bring China's coastal waters (*jin'an*) under control; then, when Chinese economic and technological capabilities permitted, to take control of China's near seas (*jin hai*).[64] Since 2012, China has built three unsinkable aircraft carriers on reclaimed coral reefs in the contested waters of the South China Sea, and in 2013 it declared an air defense identification zone over the Diaoyu/Senkaku Islands. PLAN ships and submarines regularly venture into the Indian Ocean, and in 2015 PLAN vessels entered Arctic waters twice. China's 2015 White Paper on Defense announced that the PLAN was transitioning from "offshore waters defense" to a combination of "'offshore waters defense' with 'open seas protection.'"[65] China is trying to gain control of the area within the first island chain, is moving to achieve sea denial capabilities in the second island chain, and has plans to go well beyond that zone to the third island chain and into the high seas. Thus, as Arctic shipping, tourism, scientific expeditions, and Arctic oil and mineral exploitation become more significant for China, so too will the PLAN become more active in protecting Chinese interests in the Arctic. The PLAN is integrating the recent political, economic, and strategic developments in the Arctic and Antarctic region into its current global maritime strategy, and it is a key actor in helping to set China's evolving polar strategy and agenda. We can expect to see more forays of PLAN vessels into Arctic waters in the coming years.[66]

Surprisingly, the PLAN's first-ever international expedition was to the other end of the third island chain, Antarctica. In 1984, PLAN sent 308 armed personnel and two ships, *Xiang Yang Hong 10* and *J-121*, to accompany and protect the scientists and technicians on China's first Antarctic expedition.[67] Once China's first Antarctic base was set up, PLAN involvement in logistics was downsized. Nonetheless, PLA scientists and engineers still regularly participate in China's polar projects. The PLA has provided some of the equipment used by China's Antarctic program, and pilots and other technical personnel have had a small role in logistics during many Antarctic seasons.[68]

[64]   Liu Huaqing, *Liu Huaqing huiyilu* [The memoirs of Liu Huaqing] (Beijing: Jiefang jun chubanshe, 2005), 436–37.

[65]   "Full Text: China's Military Strategy," *China Daily*, May 26, 2015, http://www.chinadaily.co m.cn/china/2015-05/26/content_20820628_4.htm.

[66]   "Zhongguo heqianting xunhang chenggong tupo dao lian xia yibu Beibingyang" [Chinese nuclear submarines successfully breakthrough the island chain: the Arctic Ocean is next], *Huanqiu junshi wang*, July 21, 2015, http://www.armystar.com/m/view.php?aid=26980&pageno=4.

[67]   Senior Chinese polar scientist, interview with author, August 2014.

[68]   See, e.g., the list of personnel on the following Chinese Antarctic expeditions: "Zhongguo 29ci Nanji kexue kaocha [China's 29th Antarctic expedition], Gate to the Poles, November 12, 2015, http://www.polar.gov.cn/expeditionDetail/?id=759; "Li Zhongdong," Gate to the Poles, November 12, 2015, http://www.polar.gov.cn/personDetail/?common_id=88164; "Wang

For polar great powers, having their military provide logistics in Antarctica (which is permitted under the rules of the Antarctic Treaty) can be useful in training military personnel to work in an extreme cold environment and conduct military-related scientific experiments.[69] This strategy has multiple advantages, including enabling states to prepare for situations in which conflict might prevent access to traditional transportation routes. The world's current polar great powers, the United States and Russia, have military personnel and equipment that can operate in alternative air and shipping routes through the polar regions in crisis periods. These capabilities also enable their militaries to operate in conflict situations in the polar regions if necessary.

As China's polar interests have grown and as China's maritime strategy has become an increasingly important policy area under the Hu Jintao (2002–12) and the Xi Jinping (2012–) administrations, so too has the level of the PLA's contribution to polar affairs increased. Chinese polar analysts have highlighted the military-strategic importance of the Arctic and Antarctic as sites for key strategic routes, as strategically vital territories with unresolved sovereignty, and as ideal sites for military-related research.[70] PLA analysts frequently publish on polar strategic issues in military open-source journals. PLA personnel took part in the Chinese government's multiagency 2012–16 project to assess polar governance and resources.[71] A search of Chinese-

Zhaojun," Gate to the Poles, November 12, 2015, http://www.polar.gov.cn/personDetail/?common_id=89052; "Zhongguo 30ci Nanji kexue kaocha" [China's 30th Antarctic expedition], Gate to the Poles, November 12, 2015, http://www.polar.gov.cn/expeditionDetail/?id=814; as well as the following media stories on PLA personnel and equipment in Antarctica: "Yang Shenggao zhu meng Nanji, yong xingdong zhanxian junren dandang" [Yang Shenggao's Antarctic dream shows a soldier in action], *Jiefang ribao*, June 27, 2015, http://military.people.com.cn/n/2015/0627/c172467-27216076.html; "Wo zai Nanji shang kong fei hang" [I flew in Antarctica], *Ba-yi fengcai*, July 2007, accessed November 19, 2013, http://www.am765.com/ztl/ztfl/ypzt/pla80/history/200707/t20070725_272470.htm (link discontinued); Zhongguo zai Nanji xiujian gao pin leida chang: Meiguo jinzhang budeliao" [China builds HF radar in Antarctica and makes USA very nervous], *Junshi kongjian*, April 22, 2008, accessed November 19, 2013, http://www.armsky.com/army/JGKYGL/mavin/200804/9411.html (link discontinued); and "Jiefangjun Q ban shuilu liangqi quan dixing che jiang zhengzhan Nanji" [PLA Q-type all terrain amphibious vehicles will go to Antarctica], *Tiexue shequ*, October 12, 2007, http://bbs.tiexue.net/post2_2309351_1.html.

69   Ding, *Jidi guojia zhengce yanjiu baogao 2012–2013*, 64.
70   On Chinese analysis on the military significance of the Antarctic see: no author, "Zhongguo Nanji guojia liyi qianxi" [Analysis of China's Antarctic national interests], *Jidi zhanlue yanjiu dongtai*, no. 1, (2012), 14; on the military significance of the Arctic, see Qu Tanzhou et al., *Beiji wenti yanjiu* [Research on Arctic issues] (Beijing: Haiyang daxue chubanshe, 2011), 291–311.
71   Cheng Baozhi, "'Zhili yu hezuo: 2011 Zhongguo jidi zhanlue yu quanyi yantao hui' huiyi zongshu" ["Governance and Cooperation: 2011 Symposium on China Polar Strategy and Rights" Conference], January 29, 2012, http://www.17net.net/Article/Class7/705/17074026900.html.

language, open-source military-related journals published between 2000 and 2013 identified close to sixty articles discussing various aspects of the Arctic, Antarctic, and polar regions from a military perspective. The articles analyze security-military trends in the Arctic; describe the polar regions as "global commons"; and highlight the future economic, scientific, and military significance of the polar regions to China. One representative 2008 article noted that "the polar regions are extremely important to China's future," as they are the repository of so many undiscovered natural resources.[72] China's 2012–13 annual report on polar policy states that Antarctica is an extremely significant zone from a military-strategic point of view, highlighting the continent's value as an alternative transportation route in times of crisis, as a site for strategic satellite installations, and as a potential site of military conflict if sovereignty rights are not resolved peacefully.[73]

Since 2009, the PLA has engaged in public military diplomacy activities, aimed at strengthening China's soft and hard power.[74] A handful of senior military experts are authorized to speak to the Chinese media on Chinese military matters. In 2010, Yin Zhuo, a retired senior naval officer and member of the Chinese People's Political Consultative Conference, caused an international furor when he was interviewed on the question of China's maritime interests. The conference is a political body without any political powers that gathers various interest groups in China. Yin is an authorized PLA spokesperson, and his reported views are a mainstream position in Chinese policy discussions on the Arctic and are worth citing in full:

> Why are we talking about a maritime strategy? China is trying to get a sense of trends in maritime affairs, such as the Antarctic and the Arctic. The Antarctic and the Arctic are part of the common heritage of mankind. I have said on many occasions: China's population accounts for one-fifth of the world's population, so why shouldn't we get a fifth of the interests in the Antarctic and Arctic? It belongs to the common heritage of mankind, everyone can have a share, and if you do not defend it, do not fight for it, then you have no say. The Antarctic Treaty has a very clear requirement: it is the common heritage of mankind, and those who do not have the ability to build a long-term research station in the Antarctic, have no say in Antarctic governance, they can only attend [meetings], the right to have a say only

---

72 "Beiji junshi zhanlue zhongda" [The Arctic region has major strategic military value], *Bingqi zhishi*, September 15, 2008, 15–18.

73 Ding, *Jidi guojia zhengce yanjiu baogao 2012–2013*, 64.

74 Peng Guangqin, "Junshi waijiao yi cheng Zhongguo ying shili yu ruan shili de jiehe dian" [China's military diplomacy is a combination of hard and soft power], *Tianxia junshi*, July 20, 2009, http://txjs.chinamil.com.cn/zhuanjia/2011–12/23/content_4749989.htm.

comes with the establishment of a station in the Antarctic. So in the 1980s, we built a station in the Antarctic. The Arctic is such a large body of water; Antarctica has a continent, the Arctic does not, but the Arctic deep seas are very rich in various resources; the sea lanes will also be important in the future. We cannot leave it all to others; the Chinese people have rights there.[75]

Most of the other leading official PLA media commentators have also been outspoken on Arctic issues in recent years. Their comments reflect a number of factors, including the PLA's desire to help shape the polar policy process in China, the military-strategic importance of the polar regions to China's security, and the role of the polar regions as a theme in CCP patriotic education. In 2011, PLAN commentator Zhang Zhaozhong said that the struggle for dominance in the Arctic had only just begun;[76] in 2014, he stated that the United States was trying to carve up the Arctic Basin for itself.[77] In 2013, high-profile PLA commentator Du Wenlong highlighted the global importance of the Arctic region as an indicator for the future global balance of power.[78] In the same year, Du added his public support to commercial interests that were bidding to make China's next polar icebreaker nuclear-powered.[79] In 2013, yet another leading PLA public commentator Luo Yuan said that China should copy Russia's behavior when it sought to preempt sovereignty rights disputes by putting a titanium flag on the Arctic seabed, and it should put its own titanium flags on the seabed of the Diaoyu/Senkaku Islands.[80]

The PLAN works in close partnership with the SOA (which is in charge of China's polar program and the Chinese Coast Guard) to coordinate China's

[75]   "Meiguo haishang baquan yinxiang Zhongguo anquan" [US maritime hegemony affects China's security], Chinanet, March 9, 2010, http://news.163.com/10/0309/10/61AVODO T000147GI.html.

[76]   "Jujiao Beiji zhengduo ganggang kaishi" [The scramble for the Arctic has just begun], CCTV-7, July 24, 2007, accessed January 26, 2015, http://210.27.176.60:8088/Web/Player/SingleVide oPlay.aspx?VideoID=73135 (link discontinued).

[77]   "Zhang Zhaozhong: Meiguo gao haiyang cehui yu zai weilai guafen Beiji" [Zhang Zhaozhong: US Arctic Ocean mapping aimed at carving up the Arctic], Phoenix TV, June 27, 2014, http://v.ifeng.com/mil/annals/2014006/01986320-1f3b-47ce-be29-4c87fb85c5bc.shtml.

[78]   Du Wenlong, a senior researcher with the PLA Academy of Military Science, interviewed in "Dongji Beiji qiaoqiao bian 're,'" [The Arctic is quietly heating up], CCTV-7, February 17, 2013, http://tv.cntv.cn/video/C10524/f2a28d1e2fdc45299d222adeoeaoo4de.

[79]   Zhao Lei, "Officials Mull Nuclear Power for Ships on Polar Expeditions," *China Daily*, February 21, 2013, http://usa.chinadaily.com.cn/china/2013-02/21/content_16241982.htm.

[80]   "Luo Yuan: Hai di cha guoqi xuanshi zhuquan you xianli Diaoyudao ke jiejian" [Luo Yuan: China can learn from the precedent of inserting a flag on the seabed], *Renmin ribao*, August 1, 2013, http://opinion.haiwainet.cn/n/2013/0801/c232601-19213834.html.

maritime strategy. The SOA and the PLAN rotate some of their leading personnel, so polar expertise will overlap between the two agencies.[81] SOA vessels can serve PLAN military-strategic interests while attracting less political controversy than a PLAN vessel operating in the same waters would – a fact not lost on many foreign commentators who speculate about the activities of the *Xue Long* icebreaker in the Arctic.[82] In a time of war, China's polar scientific vessels and bases would fall under PLAN command.

The PLAN is currently represented on China's Polar Advisory Committee by the General Staff Operations Office. This is the PLAN's most senior office, responsible for all naval military orders. In 1984, the Central Military Commission was involved in polar decision-making because the PLAN was providing the vessels for the first Antarctic expedition. The fact that the Central Military Commission is not currently involved in the final decision-making process on polar issues is an indicator that, as yet, there is no significant contribution of Chinese military assets to China's polar scientific activities. At present, China's military is currently short on experience and capabilities to engage in any depth into polar activities. But if the PLA becomes more involved in supporting the logistics for Antarctic scientific expeditions and icebreaking for Chinese Arctic shipping, then it could greatly strengthen its own polar capacities as it helps expand China's polar scientific capacity.

The Arctic's Role in China's Nuclear Deterrence

Although many foreign observers have scoffed at China's talk of being a "near-Arctic" state and think of China as a relative latecomer to Arctic affairs,[83] from a nuclear security point of view the Arctic has long been China's vulnerable northern flank. As Chinese geopolitical strategist Lu Junyuan points out, the trajectory of China's arsenal of land-based nuclear missiles targeted at the United States and Russia transit the Arctic, as do the 450 US ICBMs targeted at China and those targeted by Russia at China.[84] Key components of the US missile defense system targeted at China are also located in the Arctic. There

---

[81] For example, Luo Yuru was both director of the SOA and deputy director in the PLAN Training Department.

[82] See, e.g., Roger W. Robinson Jr., "China's 'Long Con' in the Arctic," *MLI Commentary* (Ottawa: Macdonald-Laurier Institute, September 2013), http://www.macdonaldlaurier.ca/fil es/pdf/MLIChina%27sLongConInTheArctic09-13Draft4-1.pdf.

[83] See. e.g., Nathan Vanderklippe, "For China, North Is a New Way to Go West," *Globe and Mail*, January 19, 2014, http://www.theglobeandmail.com/news/national/the-north/for-china-north-is-a-new-way-to-go-west/article16402962/.

[84] Lu, *Beiji diyuan zhengzhi yu Zhongguo yingdui*, 317–18 and 320–21.

are twenty ground-based interceptors (GBI), at Fort Greely, Alaska, and four more at Vandenberg Air Force Base, California; one sea-based X-band radar for fire control in Adak, Alaska; three PAVE PAWS radars at Clear, Alaska, at Cape Cod, Massachusetts, and at Beale Air Force Base, California; two BMEWS radars in Thule, Greenland, and in Fylingdales, England; and one Cobra Dane early-warning radar in Shemya, Alaska, plus Defense Support Program early-warning satellites. By 2017, the United States will have increased the number of GBI at Fort Greely to forty-four, with proposals to locate more GBI sites on the US East Coast.[85]

The upgrading of the US GBI program from 2013 is aimed at neutralizing Russia and China's nuclear arsenals and electromagnetic pulse weapons, as well as responding to North Korea's tiny nuclear program. But China's new era land-based missiles and submarine-based ballistic missiles could restore its deterrence threat. In 2013, the State Council Information Office issued a report on China's upgraded nuclear arsenal aimed at the United States, highlighting the Arctic trajectory of China's latest land-based missiles (figure 3.1). According to Global Times, "If we launch our DF 31A ICBMs over the North Pole, we can easily destroy a whole list of metropolises on the East Coast and the New England region of the United States, including Annapolis, Philadelphia, New York, Boston, Portland, Baltimore, and Norfolk, whose population accounts for about one-eighth of America's total residents."[86] In 2012, an unnamed "Beijing-based military expert" told China's Global Times, "If China could put a nuclear submarine in the Arctic, it would pose a threat to Europe, Russia, and the United States."[87] In 2014, China's nuclear-powered submarines traveled into the high seas for the first time, voyaging as far as the Persian Gulf. In 2015, when two Chinese submarines and a submarine support ship docked in Sri Lanka, Global Times triumphantly reported that PLAN submarines had successfully broken through the first island chain and predicted that accessing the Arctic Ocean would be the next breakthrough in access for Chinese submarine forces.[88]

[85] Wu Riqiang, "Why China Should Be Concerned by U.S. Missile Defence? And How to Address It?" Program on Strategic Stability Evaluation (POSSE), Georgia Tech Center for International Strategy, Technology, and Policy, 2016, http://posse.gatech.edu/sites/posse.gate ch.edu/files/China_Concerned_WuRiqiang_3.pdf.

[86] "Zhongguo shouci jubei dui Meiguo youxiao de shuixia zhanlue he weishi" [China for the first time possesses effective underwater nuclear deterrence against the United States], Huanqiu ribao, October 28, 2013, http://www.chinadaily.com.cn/dfpd/retu/2013–10/29/content_17065593_4.htm.

[87] "Zhuanjia jiefangjun Beiji bushu yi sou he qian jiu neng weishe oumei" [Expert: PLA deployment of nuclear submarine to Arctic could serve as deterrent to Europe and the United States], Huanqiu shibao, April 11, 2012, http://tom.news.huanqiu.com/Observation/2 012–04/2599934.html.

[88] "Zhongguo heqianting xunhang chenggong tupo dao lian xia yibu Beibingyang."

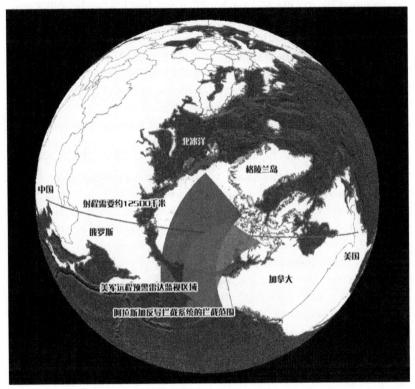

FIGURE 3.1 China's Arctic Missile Route
Source: People's Daily, October 28, 2013. (The online link has been removed from
the *People's Daily* site, but it can still be found on other sites.)

As a nuclear power, China has a no-first-use policy; however, nuclear-armed
submarines could be the decisive factor in ensuring that China has second-
strike capability in a nuclear war. If PLAN submarines can escape detection
when leaving China's near seas, they would have the unique ability to break a
strategic blockade launched by the United States and its Asia-Pacific allies.[89]
Whether nuclear or conventionally powered, undetected submarines would

[89] Andrew S. Erickson and Lyle J. Goldstein, "China's Future Nuclear Submarine Force:
Insights from Chinese Writings," *Naval War College Review* 60, no. 1 (2007), 6.

not be subject to attack by cruise or ballistic missiles, chemical or biological weapons, or electromagnetic pulses.[90]

China now has five nuclear attack submarines, four nuclear ballistic missile submarines, and fifty-seven diesel attack submarines – the largest force in Asia.[91] In 2015, a US Department of Defense Office for National Intelligence report predicted that China would have seventy submarines by 2020.[92] China has been trying to acquire nuclear submarines since the late 1950s. In 1959, the USS *Skate* became the first nuclear submarine to surface at the North Pole. In the same year, Mao Zedong asked the Soviet Union to share the technology to build nuclear weapons with China. After Soviet leader Nikita Khrushchev declined this request, saying that China was protected by Soviet submarines, Mao Zedong declared that China would develop its own nuclear submarine "even if it takes ten thousand years!"[93] China threw its scarce resources at the nuclear submarine project throughout the 1960s, and launched its first rudimentary nuclear submarine in 1974. In 1981, Geng Biao, then general secretary of the Central Military Commission, authorized a budget of RMB10 billion (around US$1.5 billion) to build six nuclear submarines – what became China's Xia-class submarines – with the specific goal of combatting US maritime power. However, Geng's decision was severely criticized by CCP leaders one year later, because the submarines would be defunct even before they were launched. As PLA media sources pointed out in 1982, "they cannot cruise underwater in the Arctic Ocean without being detected by the other side. Thus, these submarines cannot serve as a deterrent force against any of the powerful nations."[94] Geng lost his position soon after these comments were published.

In the early 1980s, Geng's expensive investment in redundant technology was a costly mistake, one which China could not afford to fix. But China's rapid economic growth and technological progress since the late 1990s has changed that situation. China is now steadily expanding its submarine capacities; its nuclear-armed submarines are now able to

90 William J. Holland Jr, "Globalization under the Sea," in *Globalization and Maritime Power*, ed. Sam J. Tangredi (Washington, DC: National Defense University, 2002), 338.

91 Jeremy Page, "The Rapid Expansion of China's Navy in Five Charts," China Real Time Report, *Wall Street Journal*, April 10, 2015, http://on.wsj.com/1DPhZQu.

92 *The PLA Navy: New Capabilities and Missions for the 21st Century* (Washington, DC: US Office for Naval Intelligence, 2015), https://fas.org/nuke/guide/china/plan-2015.pdf.

93 "Jiemi: Wo guo shou suo heqianting dansheng shimo [Uncovered: The story of the birth of China's first nuclear submarine], Xinhua, July 16, 2009, http://news.xinhuanet.com/mil/200 9-07/16/content_11716087_1.htm.

94 "Ba Yi Says Building Nuclear Submarines Unwise," Ba Yi Radio, November 10, 1982, FBIS-CHI-82-219.

operate thousands of miles from home for long periods, and are capable of launching missiles at targets up to 600 miles away.[95] Many experts now agree that China is not far off from developing a credible sea-based deterrent. This changed situation will force the United States to respond with denial, to accommodate China's nuclear capabilities, or else to redefine what the US "extended deterrence" strategy means in the Asia-Pacific in the twenty-first century.[96]

China's Northern Fleet, based in Qingdao, is the PLAN division with Arctic and North Pacific duties and interests. Chinese submarines have been active in the northern Pacific since 2009.[97] China's three Type 094 Jin-class SSBNs are technically capable of operating in northern latitudes, through the Arctic and out to the Atlantic, as well as throughout the Asia-Pacific region. Currently, one of the Jin-class SSBNs is based at Qingdao port.[98] China also has small air-independent, propulsion-powered submarines (Yuan-class S20) that are armed with nuclear missiles that have a 1500-kilometer range. The S20 have low-noise engines and can travel underwater for up to forty days without surfacing, so they are hard to trace. They can perform tasks in offshore waters such as destroying enemy maritime transportation lines, conveying special reconnaissance teams to shore bases or ships at anchor, and attacking enemy ships.[99] Yuan-class vessels are capable of operating in shallow waters and straits as well as the high seas. This makes them suitable for China's near-sea operations, and even for operating in the relatively shallow waters of the Arctic. But recent Chinese news reports suggest that China's upgraded Shang-class (93-T) nuclear-powered attack submarines, first developed in the mid-1990s, are the vessels intended for any foray into Arctic waters.[100]

China's SSBNs already are capable of launching missiles from the Pacific that can reach the US West Coast, and its ICBMs can reach the US East

95 Jeremy Page, "Deep Threat: China's Submarines Add Nuclear-Strike Capability, Altering Strategic Balance," *Wall Street Journal*, October 24, 2014, http://on.wsj.com/14vS3sI.

96 Christian Conroy, "China's Ballistic Missile Submarines: How Dangerous?," *The National Interest*, November 18, 2013.

97 "Zhongguo xinxing qianting chuanguo dao lian chuangxia shui xia zhang hang xin jilu" [China's submarines hit a new record in voyaging past the island chain], *Zhongguo qingnian bao*, April 24, 2009, accessed March 12, 2014, http://news.ifeng.com/mil/2/200904/0424_340_1124208_1.shtml (link discontinued).

98 Hans M. Kristensen, "China SSBN Fleet Getting Ready: But for What?," Federation of American Scientists, April 25, 2014, http://fas.org/blogs/security/2014/04/chinassbnfleet/.

99 "Haijun qiangguo zhuajin yanfa xiaoxing qianting zhengduo qianhai kongzhi quan" [Maritime powers focus on research on shallow water submarines, competing for control of shallow waters], *Beijing Ribao*, May 28, 2009, http://news.ifeng.com/mil/2/200905/0528_340_1179016.shtml.

100 "Zhongguo heqianting xunhang chenggong tupo dao lian xia yibu Beibingyang."

Coast. At some point, in order to acquire operational experience, Chinese submarines – like US Navy submarines – most likely will transit or be based in the Arctic region from time to time. Arctic waters offer unique advantages for submarines to travel undetected. As geopolitical specialist Lu Junyuan has pointed out, the ambient noise of the pack ice renders acoustic listening devices ineffectual, while the opaqueness of the ice defies visual monitoring methods. Satellites cannot locate submarines beneath the ice, and the Arctic environment makes antisubmarine warfare challenging. An Arctic-based submarine could attack targets anywhere in the Northern Hemisphere, and Arctic submarine-launched missiles could strike the United States within ten minutes, leaving no time for the missile defense at Fort Greely to respond.[101]

The PLAN will need to map the Arctic Ocean seabed and acoustics for Chinese navy submarines to operate safely in Arctic waters in future. Since 2010, the *Xue Long* icebreaker has been engaging in oceanic surveys in the Arctic using unmanned submersible robots. In 2014, the PRIC and the Chinese Ministry of Transport published navigation guidance for the Northwest Passage, based mostly on information available from Arctic littoral states.[102] The September 2015 foray of the five PLAN vessels into the Bering Sea and the October 2015 voyage of three PLAN vessels to Finland, Denmark, and Sweden provided an opportunity to try out the Chinese navy's existing capacities in polar waters. China's Antarctic researchers have been studying Antarctic bathymetry – the topography of the ocean floor – for some time,[103] though their research has been restricted by the *Xue Long*'s relatively limited marine research capabilities. During the austral summer of 2015, the *Xue Long* conducted research mapping Antarctic waters,[104] and in July 2016 the SOA's *Ocean 6* research vessel was sent on a year-long voyage to explore seabeds in the Southern and Pacific oceans.[105] Such experience will be useful for mapping submarine and further shipping routes in the Arctic. China's polar science program's new research vessel, which is being built to PLAN specifics, is equipped for bathymetric surveys. The PLAN may be able

[101] Lu, *Beiji diyuan zhengzhi yu Zhongguo yingdui*, 47–49.

[102] Angela Yu, "China's Arctic Guidance Due in October," *IHS Maritime*, January 19, 2015, http://dev.fairplay.ihs.com/article/16232/china%E2%80%99s-arctic-guidance-due-october.

[103] Sun Yunfan, Gao Jinyao, Zhang Tao, Zhou Zhiyuan, and Yang Chunguo, "Huan Nanji quyu gu shuishen yanhua tezheng" [A preliminary study on the evolution of circum-Antarctic paleobathymetry], *Advances in Polar Science* 25, no. 1 (2013): 25–34.

[104] "Wo guo shouci zai Nanji Luosi Hai faxian xin de maodi" [China discovers new anchorage in Antarctica's Ross Sea], Xinhua News Agency, January 9, 2015, http://www.oeofo.com/news/201501/09/list96087.html.

[105] "Chinese Research Vessel Sails for Antarctica," Xinhua, July 8, 2016, http://www.china.org.cn/china/2016-07/08/content_38844466.htm.

to gather polar submarine experience by following the United States and Russia in using its navy's submarines and boats to work on scientific projects.[106]

PLAN submarines heading north from Qingdao face two potential chokepoints before they could enter the Arctic Ocean. The first set of hazards involves the straits of the Japanese archipelago. Chinese submarines accessing the North Pacific can travel via Japan's Soya, Tsuruga, Tsukishima, and Osumi straits, all of which are classified as international straits. In international straits, submarines are not required to travel on the surface of the water and can remain submerged during transit. During the Cold War, Japan claimed only three miles of sea territory along these straits, instead of the usual twelve miles, in order to permit the US Navy to convey nuclear weapons on its aircraft carriers and submarines without breaching Japan's antinuclear policy. In recent years, PLAN vessels increasingly have been utilizing these straits for northern transits.[107] The *Xue Long* also routinely uses these straits for its Arctic expeditions.[108] Beyond Japan, the second hazard for PLAN submarines is the relatively narrow Bering Strait, which has a closed military area on the Russian side and the Tin City radar station on the Seward Peninsula on the American side. From a deterrence point of view, however, China's submarines would not need to transit the whole of the Arctic for Chinese missiles to reach the United States. Once in the Arctic Basin, they could copy the Cold War–era example of US and Soviet submarines and remain submerged in some location outside the twelve-mile zone of other coastal states.

If Chinese submarines did transit the Arctic Ocean to get to the Atlantic, they would face two further potential chokepoints: Russia's Severnaya Zemlya and the New Siberian Islands on the Northern Sea Route, and Canada's Queen Elizabeth Islands on the Northwest Passage. The possible opening of these Arctic sea routes to shipping introduces new military considerations for the PLAN. Article 20 of the UN Convention of the Law of the Sea provides that "in the territorial sea, submarines and other underwater vehicles are to navigate on the surface and to show their flag," if the submarine is to be regarded as exercising the right of innocent passage. On the high seas and in the case where territorial waters are also an international strait, then submarines can transit submerged. However, under UNCLOS,

[106]   "Submarine Arctic Science Programme," National Snow and Ice Data Center, 2016, http://nsidc.org/scicex/.
[107]   Kirk Spitzler, "China Finds a Gap in Japan's Maritime Checkpoints," *Time*, July 18, 2013, http://ti.me/17nyGOw.
[108]   PRIC, ed., *2014 Xue Long Polar Research Vessel* (Shanghai: PRIC, 2014), 5–6.

the regulations for straits used for international navigation are subordinate to those for ice-covered areas. This means that coastal states – in this case, Canada and Russia – can legally put limits on navigation where ice conditions may increase the risk of collision or oil spills.[109] Thus, from the point of view of China, the United States, and the United States' NATO allies other than Canada, the opening-up of the Northern Sea Route as a regular, ice-free sea route in the summer months will not only have economic advantages but also could turn Russian and Canadian territorial waters into acknowledged shipping straits – which would mean that the international-waters rules would then apply for submarine transit.[110]

China is becoming a global strategic power and will defend its interests globally when necessary. It cannot hope to match the military might of the US military and its allies, aircraft carrier for aircraft carrier or missile for missile, so it is focusing instead on expanding its SSBN capabilities and nontraditional areas of warfare such as space, cyber, and electromagnetic pulse, where significant damage can be done with a lesser outlay. Beyond the Asia-Pacific, the strategic global assets that China will defend militarily are its sea routes; its satellite system; resource exploitation sites where Chinese companies have significant investments; and its interests in international territories such as the polar regions, outer space, and the deep seabed. It is already defending key sea routes along the Somali coast and oil installations in South Sudan; we can expect to see more of this in the future as China's strategic economic interests continue to expand. In 2015, for example, the PLA built three landing strips on coral reefs in the South China Sea. All three are capable of landing bomber planes.[111] This new military initiative – the equivalent of China having three air craft carriers permanently stationed in the South China Sea – will greatly expand the reach of China's long range offensive air capacity.

China's polar security and military interests are defensive in nature. However, in the Arctic where Canada, Russia, and the United States are expanding their military presence, China's growing polar military capacities will not be perceived in a defensive light and will be regarded as a threat. Likewise, in the Antarctic, China's increased use of military personnel in

---

[109]   Kristin Bartenstein, "The 'Arctic Exception' in the Law of the Sea Convention: A Contribution to Safer Navigation in the Northwest Passage?," *Ocean Development and International Law* 42, no. 1–2 (2011): 22–52.

[110]   Claudia Cinelli, "The Law of the Sea and the Arctic Ocean," *Arctic Review on Law and Politics* 2, no. 1 (2011), 13.

[111]   Asia Maritime Transparency Initiative, "Airpower in the South China Sea," Center for Strategic and International Studies, 2016, http://amti.csis.org/airstrips-scs/.

logistics will have to be handled carefully in order to be accepted by other states.

CHINA'S STRATEGIC INTEREST IN POLAR RESOURCES

Polar Mineral, Oil, and Natural Gas Resources

China has a strong interest in accessing polar natural resources in both the Arctic and Antarctic, but current policy is to downplay or deny this interest in discussions with foreigners. From 2008 to 2012, the PRIC website displayed detailed maps of the location of Antarctic mineral resources (figure 3.2).[112] When questioned about it in 2012, senior China Arctic and Antarctic Administration officials denied any knowledge of it, but PRIC staff told me that the maps had been put up as "educational materials" for China's polar scientists. When I published a web link to these same educational materials in my 2013 book *The Emerging Politics of Antarctica*,[113] the maps were quickly removed from the PRIC site. Foreigners were not supposed to receive this particular signal from China's preeminent polar research institute, as it is not in keeping with the ban on mineral exploitation in Antarctica. Similarly, during a question-and-answer session at the 2012 International Polar Year meeting in Montreal, PRIC director Yang Huigen repeatedly denied that China had any interest in Arctic mineral resources, claiming that China's sole focus in the Arctic was science.[114]

Yet in contrast to the official reluctance to admit China's strong interest in polar resources to foreign audiences, one of the striking features about Chinese-language information on Antarctica and the Arctic is the high prominence given to the potential resources there. China's Wikipedia equivalent, Baidu,[115] highlights the findings of the 1974 US Geological Survey report on Antarctic mineral resources,[116] and the same information is found on multiple other open- and closed-source publications in China. In a 2005 report

---

[112]　"Nanji youqi ziyuan" [Antarctic oil and gas resources], PRIC, accessed March 12, 2012, http://908.chinare.org.cn:8088/njyq/ (link discontinued); see also China Arctic and Antarctic Administration, "Beijing ziliao: Nanji de kuangcang" [Background information: Antarctic mineral resources], Sina.com.cn, July 14, 2008, http://tech.sina.com.cn/d/2008-07-14/132623 24769.shtml.

[113]　Anne-Marie Brady, ed., *The Emerging Politics of Antarctica* (Abingdon, UK: Routledge, 2013).

[114]　As observed by the author. The question was repeated in both Chinese and English.

[115]　*Baike Baidu*, s.v. "Nanji ziyuan" [Antarctic resources in Antarctica], accessed January 13, 2015, http://baike.baidu.com/view/369379.htm#2.

[116]　N. A. Wright and P. L. Williams, eds., *Mineral Resources of Antarctica*, Geological Survey Circular 705 (Reston, VA: US Geological Survey, 1974).

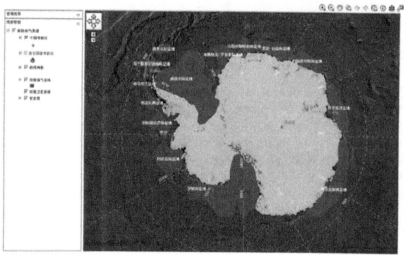

FIGURE 3.2 Chinese Government Map of Oil and Natural Gas Basins in Antarctic Waters. The resource areas are indicated by the lighter gray areas around the Antarctic continent and seabed.

Source: "Nanji youqi ziyuan" [Antarctic oil and gas resources], PRIC, accessed March 12, 2012, http://908.chinare.org.cn:8088/njyq/ (link discontinued).

evaluating Antarctic resources and their potential utilization, PRIC researchers Zhu Jiangang, Yan Qide, and Ling Xiaoliang estimated that there are 500 billion tons of oil on the Antarctic continent and 300 to 500 billion tons of natural gas on the Antarctic continent, plus a potential 135 billion tons of oil in the Southern Ocean.[117] In 2006, Yan Qide described Antarctica's coal reserves as a "black treasure house."[118] In 2009, Chinese Academy of Geological Sciences professor Hu Jianmin told Chinese journalists:

> Antarctica has very rich mineral resources and more than 220 kinds of minerals have been discovered there. The Prince Charles Mountains iron ore reserves are likely to be enough for the world to use for 200 years; Antarctic geologists call "Antarctica Iron Mountain." The Trans-Antarctic Mountains coalfield

[117] Zhu, Yan, and Ling, "Nanji ziyuan ji qi kaifa liyong qianjing fenxi," 18 and 20.
[118] Yan Qide, "Heise jinku shijie tieshan" [Black treasure house, world coal mountain], *Kexue*, 2006, 12.

may be the world's largest coalfield. It is estimated that hidden under the Antarctic ice sheet is over 500 billion tons of coal and the Ross Sea and Weddell Sea basin all have very good prospects for oil and gas resources.[119]

Also in 2009, PRIC staff produced a book-length study investigating the full range of Antarctic mineral resources and their legal status, stating that "when all the world's resources have been depleted, Antarctica will be a global treasure house of resources."[120] Similarly, the 2013 and 2014 annual reports on China's polar policy both emphasized that access to the considerable natural resources at the two poles was essential for the continued growth of the Chinese economy.[121]

Chinese researchers began investigations into Arctic and Antarctic mineral resources as early as the 1970s. Initially, they were only translating foreign research on these topics, but in the past five to ten years, more and more China-based studies have been assessing polar oil, natural gas, and mineral deposits, with maps showing areas that have been surveyed for such deposits (see figure 3.3). Maps of Arctic and Antarctic resources are widely available in Chinese-language publications on the polar regions and on the Chinese-language internet. China is by no means the first country to produce such maps. The United States produced an Antarctic minerals map in 1974 and updated that information with a more detailed map in 1998.[122] In 2016, the US Geological Survey released a report analyzing coal deposits in Antarctica.[123] Likewise, in 1997, Japan's National Museum of Nature and Science published a set of Antarctic resource maps as part of a volume commemorating the fortieth anniversary of Japan's Antarctic science program.[124] However, the ubiquity of Antarctic resource maps in the Chinese internet and printed materials on

[119] "Wei Nanji Geluofu shan huizhi shouzhang ditu [A preliminary geological map of the Grove Mountains], *Dili tongxun*, January 23, 2009, http://news.dili360.com/dlsk/dlzh/2009/0123761 4.shtml.

[120] Yan Qide and Zhu Jiangang, ed., *Nanjizhou ziyuan lingtu zhuquan yu ziyuan quan shu wenti yanjiu* [Research on Antarctic sovereignty and resources rights] (Shanghai: Kexue jishu xhubanshe, 2009), 183.

[121] Ding, *Jidi guojia zhengce yanjiu baogao 2012–2013*, 79; and Ding Huang, ed., *Jidi guojia zhengce yanjiu baogao 2013–2014* [Annual report on national polar policy research, 2013–14] (Beijing: Kexue chubanshe, 2014), 138.

[122] Philip W. Guild et al., *Mineral Resources Map of the Circum-Pacific Region Antarctic Sheet* (Washington, DC: US Geological Survey, 1998), http://pubs.usgs.gov/cp/47/plate-1.pdf; and N. A. Wright and P. L. Williams, eds., *Mineral Resources of Antarctica*, Geological Survey Circular 705 (Washington, DC: US Geological Survey, 1974).

[123] Michael D. Merrill, *GIS Representation of Coal-Bearing Areas in Antarctica*, Open File Report 2016–1031 (Washington, DC: US Geological Survey, 2016), http://pubs.usgs.gov/of/2 016/1031/ofr20161031.pdf.

[124] National Museum of Nature and Science of Japan, *Fushigi tairiku nankyoku ten: Nihon nankyoku kansoku 40shuunen kinen* [The mysterious continent of Antarctica: Japan Antarctic Observation 40th Anniversary] (Tokyo: National Museum of Nature and Science, 1997);

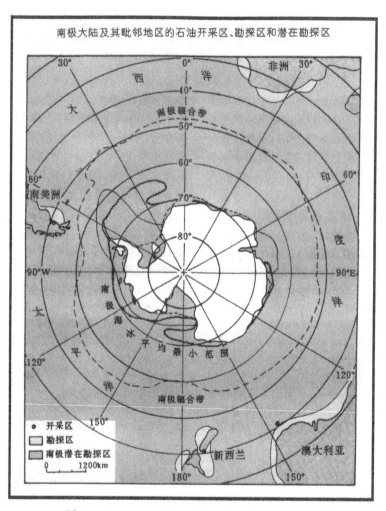

FIGURE 3.3 Chinese-Language Map of Southern Ocean Mineral Resources
Source: Ding, *Jidi guojia zhengce yanjiu baogao 2012–2013*, 57.

the polar regions sends a clear signal of the priority that China places on future access to these resources. Chinese discussion on Antarctic mineral resources glides over the issue of the current ban on mineral exploration and exploitation in Antarctica as if it was just a technicality. Nonetheless, Chinese polar researchers and senior officials do acknowledge that close to 95 percent of

Chinese trans. by Liu Shuyan and Zhou Dali, *Bu ke siyi de Nanji dalu* (Beijing: Haiyang chubanshe, 2002).

Arctic oil and natural gas resources are held on the sovereign territory of the United States, Russia, Canada, Greenland, and Norway.[125] China will need to negotiate access to these resources and pay a fair price for them.

China's expanding polar presence and interest in accessing polar natural resources is directly linked to the CCP's global economic, political, and military goals, and the ways in which these goals interact with China's economic growth. Since the late 1970s, China has looked to the polar regions as part of its solution for resolving its own mid- to long-term energy security concerns.[126] In a classified report published in 2010, PRIC polar strategy director Zhang Xia highlighted the importance of Arctic oil and natural gas for China's needs.[127] Many other scholars believe that engaging in Arctic oil exploration will significantly enhance China's energy security.[128] Other Chinese researchers have identified Antarctica as a long-term potential source of oil and hydrocarbons, one that cannot be ignored.[129]

According to a 2014 report by the International Energy Agency, despite significant investment in renewable energy, global demand for oil and natural gas could grow as much as 37 percent from 2013 to 2040, with emerging markets in Asia, Africa, the Middle East, and Latin America pushing demand.[130] Since 2013, China has been the world's largest importer of crude oil.[131] Seventy percent of China's current energy use is from coal and 20 percent is from petroleum; 80 percent of China's electricity is generated from coal.[132] China's

[125] Lu Jingmei, Shao Zijun, Fang Dianyong, and Wang Xinran, "Beiji juan youqi ziyuan qianli fenxi" [Analysis of oil-gas resources potential in the Arctic Circle], *Ziyuan yu chanye* 12, no. 4 (2010): 73–83.

[126] "Beiji diqu de zhuyao nengyuan he kuangchan ziyuan" [The main energy and mineral resources of the Arctic region], *Neibu ziliao: Renmin Ribao*, no. 188 (1979), 1; see also Lu Wenzheng, "Kuanchan ziyuan yuanjing pingjia" [Long-range evaluation of [Antarctic] mineral resources], *Nan dayang kaocha baogao 1984–1985* [Antarctic expedition report 1984–1985] (National Committee for Antarctic Research, SOA, 1985), 247–49.

[127] Zhang Xia, "Beiji youqi ziyuan qianli de quanqiu zhanlue yiyi" [The global strategic importance of the potential of Arctic oil and gas reserves], *Jidi zhanlue*, no. 2 (2010): 11–17.

[128] Zhang Shengjun and Li Xing, "Zhongguo nengyuan anquan yu Zhongguo Beiji zhanlue diwei" [The place of energy security in China's Arctic strategy], *Guoji guancha*, no. 4 (2010), 64, http://vbn.aau.dk/files/47402669/Chinese_energy_security_Li_Xing.pdf.

[129] Zhu, Yan, and Li, *Nanji ziyuan ji qi kaifa liyong qianjing fenxi*, 17 and 21.

[130] *World Energy Outlook 2014*, International Energy Agency, November 12, 2014, http://www.worldenergyoutlook.org/publications/weo-2014/.

[131] Joe McDonald, "China Passes US as World's Biggest Oil Importer," *Canadian Manufacturing*, October 10, 2013, http://www.canadianmanufacturing.com/manufacturing/china-passes-u-s-as-worlds-biggest-oil-importer-119669/.

[132] Ma Hengyun, "China's Energy Economy: Reforms, Market Development, Factor Substitution and the Determinants of Energy Intensity" (PhD Thesis, University of Canterbury, New Zealand, March 2009), http://ir.canterbury.ac.nz/bitstream/10092/2739/1/Thesis_Ma_Final.pdf.

coal reserves can meet the domestic coal demand for the next eighty years,[133] but in the mid to long term, the Chinese economy is likely to shift the balance of its energy use from coal to petroleum, nuclear energy, and renewables.

International relations specialists Sun Yantai and Wang Haibing have noted that in 2010, China imported 60 percent of its oil and natural gas supply, but by 2020, close to 75 percent of its supplies will come from international sources.[134] Currently, most of China's oil supply comes from the Persian Gulf, Africa, and Russia. Eighty-five percent of the oil shipments come via the Malacca Straits, though China is constructing various oil pipelines through Burma, Russia, and other neighboring states to lessen its dependence on heavily congested SLOCs. Chinese-language materials discussing China's energy needs worry that as the United States currently uses a quarter of all global oil products and China needs more and more, this growing demand may well lead to conflict between the two states.[135] Scholars say that diversifying the sources of China's oil imports and setting up a strategic oil reserve are extremely important for China's economic development.[136]

Despite the ban on mineral exploration in Antarctica after the passage of the 1991 Environmental Protocol to the Antarctic Treaty, between 1991 and 1995 Chinese geologists were still exploring the Antarctic continental shelf's oil and natural gas reserves.[137] In 1995, a study was published on the oil and gas potential of the Ross Sea area.[138] Chinese cartographers at Wuhan University's Chinese Antarctic Center for Surveying and Mapping have been involved in a long-term project to compile information from foreign research on Antarctic oil and mineral resources, as well as that by Chinese scientists, to prepare detailed

[133] Minxuan Cui, ed., *Zhongguo nengyuan fazhan baogao* [Annual report on China's energy development 2008] (Beijing: China Social Science Academic Press, 2008), 34, as cited in Gao Yang, "Energy Security in China: Going Beyond the Traditional Approach," (paper presented at the 5th Oceanic Conference on International Studies, The University of Sydney, 18–20 July 18–20, 2012), 18.

[134] Sun Xuefeng and Wang Haibing, "Zhongguo huoqu quanqiu shiyou ziyuan de zhanlue xuanze [China's strategic choices for obtaining global oil resources], *Dangdai yatai*, no. 1 (2010), 59.

[135] Zhou Tianyong, "Weilai Zhongmei guojia liyi chongtu de kenengxing fenxi" [Analysis of future clashes of national interests between China and the United States], *Lilun dongtai* 1936 (September 30, 2012), 15.

[136] Xiao Jianguo, *Guoji haiyang bianjie shiyan de gongtong kaifa* [Joint development of oil across international maritime boundaries] (Beijing: Haijun chubanshe, 2006), 160.

[137] See, e.g., the project "Nanji dalujia zhong xinsheng dai chenji pendi ji youqi ziyuan yuanjing tance yu fenxi" [Exploration and analysis of oil and gas reserves in the Cenozoic sedimentary basin of the Antarctic continental shelf], PRIC, November 12, 2015, http://www.polar.gov.cn/projectDetail/?id=283.

[138] Wu Nengyou, "Nanji Luosi Hai dizhi yu youqi ziyuan de qianli" [Ross Sea Antarctica: Geology and the prospect of oil resources], *Haiyang dizhi* (1994).

maps of Antarctic resources – the very same maps available on the PRIC website from 2008 to 2012.[139] China's 12th Five-Year Science and Technology Development Plan set the goal of "strengthening marine and polar mineral resources comprehensive investigation techniques."[140] One of China's International Polar Year (2007–9) projects conducted Antarctic seismic research in the vicinity of its Zhongshan Station and Grove Hill, aimed at "providing the basis for Antarctic mineral resource exploration and prospect evaluation."[141] A 2012 Chinese study analyzed the natural gas potential of the Antarctic peninsula and the nearby Weddell Sea.[142] From 2012 to 2016, leading Chinese geologists took part in a government-sponsored project to assess Antarctic resources,[143] a component of an even larger project evaluating polar resources and governance, the Polar Environment Comprehensive Investigation and Assessment Program. The geologists involved were part of the Polar Geology Lab at the Chinese Academy of Sciences, which proclaims on its website that it has a brief to investigate Arctic and Antarctic oil and gas reserves.[144] This long-term, in-depth reconnaissance of Antarctic minerals potential builds on smaller studies done by Chinese scientists in the 1990s and 2000s and a systematic study of the work of foreign geologists. According to an internal document reporting the project's findings, during the project Chinese scientists engaged in "preliminary exploration of mineral resources in Antarctic waters" and "surveyed coal reserves."[145] However, as the majority of the project research is published only in classified government reports – despite the

---

[139] Chinese polar scholar, interview with author, November, 2013.

[140] "Shi'er wu kexue yu jishu fazhan guihua" [12th Five-Year Plan science and technology development plan], Ministry of Science and Technology of the People's Republic of China, accessed March 20, 2014, http://www.most.gov.cn/kjgh.

[141] "Zhongguo keyan renyuan gei Nanji dalu zuo 'CT'" [Chinese researchers in Antarctica do "CT"], Xinhua, December 12, 2013, accessed November 4, 2013, http://scitech.people.com.cn/n/2013/1227/c1057-23961694.html.

[142] Wang Shimin, Kang Changsheng, and Gong Yuehua, "Nanji bandao dizhi tezheng ji xibei bianyuan de youqi ziyuan qiannneng" [The geological structural characteristics of the Antarctic peninsula and the oil and gas potential in its northwestern margin], *Haiyangxue* (2012).

[143] "Guojia caizheng zhuanxiang zhuanti 'Nanji dalu kuangchan ziyuan kaocha yu pinggu CHINARE2012-02-05'" [PRC Ministry of Finance special project exploration and evaluation of Antarctic resources CHINARE2012-02–05], Graduate School of the Chinese Academy of Geological Sciences, accessed April 1, 2014, http://edu.cags.ac.cn/teachercontent.php?iid=476&PHPSESSID=cdd175454888f63d5a291253bbb6b3d3.

[144] "Jidi dizhi yanjiu shi yanjiu shi jianjie" [Introduction to the Polar Geology Research Laboratory], Chinese Institute of Geomechanics, June 21, 2012, http://www1.geomech.ac.cn/yanjiushi/8shi.htm.

[145] "Nanji zhoubian haiyu yu dalu zonghe pinggu" [A comprehensive evaluation of Antarctic waters], *Jidi zhuanying jianbao* 10 (January 2016): 3.

requirement of the Antarctic Treaty that all scientific information be made publicly available, the outside world will not know exactly what the scientists found. China's current level of Antarctic mineral research is at what experts call Stage 2 of basic commercial exploration, which is the stage in mineral exploration when a country or company is acquiring relevant knowledge of oil and natural gas fields prior to beginning exploitation.[146]

A 2010 report on Arctic oil and gas potential recommended that China find a way to become involved in Arctic resource exploration and that it should study the operational experience of global oil companies such as British Petroleum.[147] In 2012, the China National Offshore Oil Company (CNOOC), China's leading oil SOE, bought the Canadian oil company Nexen, which has rights to access substantial oil sands and shale gas in western Canada. In June 2013, Iceland granted CNOOC China's first ever Arctic oil exploration license. This license will enable CNOOC to gain experience in polar hydrocarbon exploration. China wants a foot in the door of Arctic oil discoveries, despite the high costs and environmental risks. Another major Chinese oil company, Sinopec, has also been in talks with the Icelandic government about oil exploration off Iceland's northeast coast.[148] In 2013, China National Petroleum Company (CNPC) partnered with Russia to develop three oil sites in Arctic seas. All are financed by the China Development Bank Corporation, which is well known for its investment-for-oil banking strategy in other parts of the globe.[149] In 2014, CNPC also bought a 20 percent stake in Russia's liquefied natural gas project in the Arctic Yamal Peninsula. In March 2014, China Nonferrous Metal Industry's Foreign Engineering and Construction invested in Greenland's Kvanefjeld rare earth project, partnering with Greenland Minerals and Energy. In 2015, the Chinese mining company General Nice took over the Isua iron ore field in Greenland. In August 2015, Russian energy firm Novatek sold a 9.9 percent share of the Yamal Peninsular natural gas project to China's Silk Road Infrastructure Fund. In 2014, Russian oil firm Gazprom signed a thirty-year,

---

[146] See Egil Bergsager, "Basic Conditions for the Exploration and Exploitation of Mineral Resources in Antarctica: Options and Precedents," in *Antarctic Resources Policy: Scientific, Legal, and Political Issues*, ed. Francisco Orrego Vicuña (Cambridge: Cambridge University Press, 1983,) 170.

[147] Lu, Shao, Fang, and Wang, "Beiji juan youqi ziyuan qianli fenxi."

[148] "Sinopec Looks North for Oil," *China Daily*, June 20, 2013, http://www.china.org.cn/business/2013–06/18/content_29148596.htm.

[149] Rakteem Katakey and Will Kennedy, "Russia Lets China into Arctic Rush as Energy Giants Embrace," *Bloomberg*, March 25, 2013, accessed March 27, 2013, http://www.bloomberg.com/news/print/2013–03-25/russia-cuts-china-into-arctic-oil-rush-as-energy-giants-embrace.html.

US$400 billion deal with China – even though experts say that the deal is unprofitable for the company[150] – but due to low oil prices further planned deals have not been completed and construction on a pipeline has not yet begun.

Because of greater production of shale oil, the United States is increasingly self-sufficient in oil and natural gas, as a result China is a core market for Russian Arctic and sub-Arctic oil and natural gas. Russia needs China's trade and investment to open up this area. If Greenland can generate sufficient income from its natural resources, it will be able to become fully independent from Denmark. Internal Chinese analysis says that Greenland would find it difficult to find any other investor to replace China in terms of mining development and activities.[151] In many ways, the Arctic is a buyer's market for China, but so far Chinese investors are moving relatively slowly to take up opportunities. This is a reflection of currently low global oil prices and the availability of supplies elsewhere, and the slowing Chinese economy. China's strategic interests in Arctic and Antarctic minerals are long term, not short term, and as noted, they are in the preparatory stage of exploration and exploitation.

In 2015, China identified the deep seabed as one of its new strategic frontiers. International Seabed Authority maps show extensive mineral deposits in the seas surrounding Antarctica. The UN Commission on the Limits of the Continental Shelf accepted submissions by claimant states on Antarctic continental shelves. Australia and Norway requested that the Antarctic portion of their continental shelf claim not be considered, leaving yet another unresolved matter in Antarctic governance to a later date. The China Ocean Mineral Resources Research and Development Association has signed three contracts with the ISA to explore polymetallic nodules, polymetallic sulfides, and ferromanganese crusts. (See figure 3.4 for an official Chinese government map that indicates the location of manganese node sites in the Southern Ocean.) One of the three contracts is to investigate undersea metal deposits in an area between Africa and Antarctica,[152] and a SOA vessel set off to explore this area in 2016. China's SOA is in charge of seabed mining as well as polar affairs. Antarctic Treaty System instruments are ambiguous on matters relating to the deep seabed. The 1991 Protocol on

[150] Jack Farchy, "Gazprom's China Contract Offers No Protection against Low Prices," *Financial Times*, August 10, 2015, http://on.ft.com/1I65hbF.

[151] "Gelinglan" [Greenland], *Jidi zhanlue yanjiu dongtai* no. 2 (2013): 14.

[152] "Zhongguo jiang zai Nanji Feizhou jian haidi tan jinshu kuang" [China will explore minerals in the seabed between Africa and Antarctica], *Hexun.com*, July 22, 2011, http://news.hexun .com/2011–07-22/131686468.html.

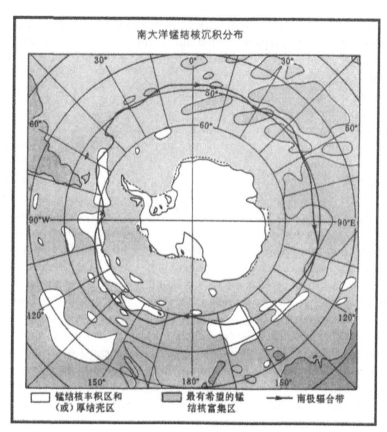

FIGURE 3.4 Chinese-Language Map Showing Manganese Node Sites in the
Southern Ocean

Source: Ding, *Jidi guojia zhengce yanjiu baogao 2012–2013*, 59.

Environmental Protection would not permit a signatory state to engage in seabed
mining, but for nonsignatory states the legal situation is unclear.[153]

Mineral, oil, and natural gas exploration and exploitation are currently
forbidden in Antarctica, but all other resources there are available for potential
exploitation. For instance, China does not have enough water for its people, so
it is interested in exploring the commercial use of Antarctic freshwater ice.[154]
The harvesting of Antarctic ice is not prohibited under the environmental

---

[153] I am grateful for Professor Karen Scott, expert on polar law, for providing advice on this and
other polar law-related points throughout the book.

[154] Chen Yugang and Wang Wanlu, "Shi xi Zhongguo de Nanji liyi yu quanyi" [Analysing
China's Antarctic interests and rights] (*Jilin Daxue Xuebao*), vol 56, no. 4 (2016): 99.

protocol. China is also investigating the possibilities of harvesting wave, solar, and thermal power in the Antarctic as further untapped resources that any nation has the right to exploit on the Antarctic Continent.[155]

Polar Fishing

Polar fishing rights are a further polar resource in which China has a great interest. China has the world's largest fishing fleet, and the Chinese population consumes more marine produce than any other nation. Food security is a top priority in China's national security strategy. The majority of China's distant water fishing, which totals around 4.3 million tons per year, is off the coast of West Africa.[156] China is also a significant presence in fishing in the South and North Pacific. About 120 Chinese fishing vessels are currently operating in the North Pacific, which accounts for about one-eighth of the total number of China's offshore fishing vessels and an output of 26.4 percent of China's overall overseas fishing total.[157] China's state-subsidized fishing fleet has pushed local fishing industries out of the market in the South Pacific and West Africa. China is already active in Antarctic fishing and is keen on becoming involved in Arctic Ocean fishing.[158]

In the 2000s, Chinese-registered boats were involved in illegal fishing activities in the Southern Ocean.[159] As a result, New Zealand and Australia, whose marine territories border on the Southern Ocean, were keen for China to join the Convention on the Conservation of Antarctic Marine Living Resources, the agreement that manages fishing in Antarctic waters, and come under its jurisdiction.[160] In 2006, China acceded to the convention, and it became a full consultative member in October 2007. Surprisingly, China's membership in the Commission for the Conservation of Antarctic Marine Living Resources does not include Hong Kong. This is most likely because the former British colony is the main base of multinational fishing

[155] Yan and Zhu, *Nanji ziyuan lingtu zhuquan yu ziyuan quanshu wenti yanjiu*, 13.
[156] Sea Around Us Project, "China's Foreign Fishing Is Largely Unreported," PEW Charitable Trusts, April 2013, http://news.ubc.ca/wp-content/uploads/2013/05/Research-Summary.pdf.
[157] "Zhongguo Beiji kaocha" [China's Arctic expedition], SOA, July 9, 2012, http://www.soa.gov .cn/xw/ztbd/2012/zgdwcbjkxkc/bjzl_dwcbjkk/201211/t20121129_10348.htm.
[158] "Zhongguo yuanyang yuye qiye canyu Beiji yuye de kexing xing fenxi" [Feasibility analysis of Chinese offshore fleet's participation in the Arctic Ocean fisheries], *Yuye xinxi yu zhanlue*, November 12, 2015.
[159] Megha Bahree, "Blue Waters, Gray Areas," *Forbes*, November 12, 2007; and email correspondence, Antarctic Policy Unit (APU), New Zealand Ministry of Foreign Affairs and Trade (NZ MFAT), September 14, 2007, APU/CHN, Part 3.
[160] Email, APU, NZ MFAT, July 18, 2006, APU/CHN, Part 1.

company Pacific Andes, which through its own activities and those of its subsidiaries is heavily implicated in the illegal fishing of the highly endangered Patagonian toothfish.[161] When it joined CCAMLR, China declared that its membership would not include Hong Kong.[162] This arrangement is relatively unusual, but it is perfectly legal according to the Hong Kong Special Autonomous Region's unique status in the Chinese polity, which permits Hong Kong to establish and maintain a separate international legal personality from the PRC.[163]

The only CCAMLR fishery where PRC-registered boats are currently active is the krill fishery in the Southern Ocean. Access to krill, a valuable food source, will help the Chinese government meet its food security goals.[164] It will also help China expand its biopharmaceutical industries, and develop state-of-the-art marine equipment. China got into krill fishing relatively late and initially partnered with Norway, an experienced polar fisher, to research krill and learn the skill set necessary for operating a commercially viable krill fishery in the Southern Ocean.[165] China now has the third-largest catch of Antarctic krill after Norway and South Korea, and it sends five boats, more than any other state, to the Southern Ocean to fish for krill.[166] China's 2014 catch in the Southern Ocean was 55,000 tons of krill, worth around US$10 million. This is just over 1 percent of China's total distant water fishing of around 4.3 million tons per year.[167] In 2011, the Chinese Ministry of Agriculture announced that the government would continue to expand China's krill fishing, as it is regarded as an underutilized fishery.[168] Then, in 2015, China announced that it planned to double or even quadruple its

[161] Coalition of Legal Toothfish Operators (COLTO), "The Alphabet Boats: A Case Study of Toothfish Poaching in the Southern Ocean," COLTO, Hobart, Tasmania, Australia, 2007, http://www.colto.org/news-archive/the-alphabet-boats/.
[162] Antarctic and Southern Ocean Coalition, "Port Visits of Vessels on CCAMLR's IUU's [Illegal, Unreported, Unregulated] Vessels Lists: Lessons on Port State Performance" (Washington, DC: CCAMLR, October 2009), 6, http://www.asoc.org/storage/documents/Meetings/CCAMLR/XXVIII/Lessons_on_Port_State_Enforcement_2009.pdf.
[163] See Roda Mushkat, *One Country, Two International Legal Personalities: The Case of Hong Kong* (Hong Kong: Hong Kong University Press, 1997).
[164] "Zhongguo yuanyang yuchuan jiang shou fu Nanji bu lin xia" [China's long distant water fishing fleet to fish for Antarctic krill], *Chinagate.cn*, December 4, 2009 http://cn.chinagate.cn/resource/2009–12/04/content_19008988.htm.
[165] Kjartan Mæstad, "Norwegian-Chinese Krill Research in the Southern Ocean," Institue of Marine Research, Bergen, Norway, January 10, 2011, http://www.imr.no/nyhetsarkiv/2011/januar/norsk-kinesisk_krillsamarbeid_i_sorishav.
[166] Ding, *Jidi guojia zhengce yanjiu baogao 2013–2014*, 172.
[167] Sea Around Us Project, "China's Foreign Fishing Is Largely Unreported."
[168] "Woguo Nanji haiyang shengwu ziyuan kaifa qude shi zhi xing jinzhan" [China's Antarctic marine living resources development has made major progress], PRC Ministry of Agriculture

existing krill catch, to between one to two million tons per year.[169] Evaluating the state of the Antarctic krill fishery and potential for expansion was one of the topics of China's 2012–16 Polar Environment Comprehensive Investigation and Assessment Program.[170] Currently, CCAMLR limits the overall annual take of krill to 680,000 tons. This amount could be expanded only if scientific data can prove that more krill can be taken in a sustainable manner.[171] China will have to lobby other states and invest in in-depth scientific research to get what it wants. If China succeeds in expanding to this level of level of fishing, it would pass Norway and South Korea to have the biggest krill catch of any other state active in Antarctic fishing.

China's krill fisheries in the Southern Ocean require a close partnership between government and industry as the fisheries are under strict management from CCAMLR. The Chinese government subsidizes the fishing boats,[172] while controlling the fishing industry in accordance with CCAMLR guidelines. Antarctic krill (*Euphausia superba*) are used as feed for China's aquaculture industries.[173] Krill oil, a source of omega-3 polyunsaturated fatty acids (such as eicosapentaenoic and docosahexaenoic acids) is an approved health supplement in China, and it is also made into food products for human consumption. China's krill-processing is dominated by Luhua Biomarine, one of China's many SOEs going global to secure supplies.

If commercially viable fish stocks develop as a result of an increasingly ice-free Arctic Ocean, Chinese fishing companies will have the right to fish in any region beyond the exclusive economic zones of Arctic coastal states.[174] In 2012, 40 percent of Arctic high seas were ice-free. It was the lowest ever recorded,

---

press release, January 31, 2012, http://www.yyj.moa.gov.cn/yyyyyzj/zhyyyy/201201/t20120131_2 722944.htm.

[169] Xie Yu, "China Steps Up Efforts in Antarctica to Benefit from Krill Bonanza," *China Daily*, March 5, 2015, http://usa.chinadaily.com.cn/epaper/2015–03/04/content_19716649.htm.

[170] "Nanji zhoubian haiyu yu dalu zonghe pinggu."

[171] "Krill Fisheries and Sustainability: Allowable Catch Limits," CCAMLR, April 23, 2015, https://www.ccamlr.org/en/fisheries/krill-fisheries-and-sustainability.

[172] "Nanji lingxia yuye chuanbo yu zhuangbei xiandaihua fazhan zhanlue yantao hui" [Antarctic krill fishing vessels and equipment modernization and development strategy seminar], Hubei sheng guofang kexue jishu gongye bangongshi [Hubei Province Office for National Defense Science and Technology], November 24, 2014, accessed January 29, 2015, http://www.hbgb .gov.cn/sjb/xwdt/ywdt/4812.htm.

[173] Tang Jianye and Shi Guihua, "Nanji lingxia yuye guanli ji qi dui Zhongguo de yingxiang" [Management of Antarctic krill and its implications for China's distant water fisheries], *Ziyuan kexue* 32, no. 1 (2010): 11–18.

[174] Rob Huebert, "Canada and China in the Arctic: A Work in Progress," *Meridien Newsletter* (Fall/Winter 2011–Spring/Summer 2012), 6, http://www.polarcom.gc.ca/eng/content/meri dian-newsletter-fallwinter-2011-springsummer-2012-0.

and subsequent years have also been extremely low. The loss of ice cover means the physical barrier to commercial fishing has now been removed. In 2015, the five Arctic littoral states agreed on a voluntary ban on the expansion of Arctic fishing, but this ban is not binding on other nations. China has not made any official statement on the agreement. This official silence should be read as a rejection of the ban. China is not willing to give up any potential rights it might be entitled to in maritime affairs, but avoids open confrontation. China's fishing interests are likely to expand into the Arctic Ocean in future, if only for geostrategic reasons. Chinese fisheries specialists Tang Jianye (who frequently represents China at polar fishing meetings) and Zhao Qiangqiang point out that China's expansion into Arctic fishing will give China a further excuse to increase its right to have a say in Arctic affairs.[175]

Polar Biotech Research

Chinese polar researchers list biotechnology as one of the many resources ripe for exploitation in the Antarctic.[176] There is no regime to manage bioprospecting in Antarctica, other than environmental management regulations. Essentially, if scientists discover new biological substances or organisms in Antarctica, then the intellectual property rests with them and their funding agencies. China's position on bioprospecting is that the principle of freedom of the seas and common heritage of humankind should be followed.[177] China aims to do more Antarctic bioprospecting in order to acquire more benefits from its investment in Antarctica.[178] China has already collected more than a thousand Antarctic biological specimens with commercial potential and has applied for patents on some of the findings of that bioprospecting, but it is still at a relatively early stage of biotechnology compared to other Antarctic states.[179]

---

[175]   Tang Jianye and Zhao Qiangqiang, "You guan Beiji yuye ziyuan yanghu yu guanli de lifa wenti fenxi" [Analysis on the question of Arctic fisheries protection administration and laws], *Zhongguo Haiyang daxue xuebao (Shehui kexue bao)*, no. 5 (2010), 14.

[176]   Yan and Zhu, *Nanji ziyuan lingtu zhuquan yu ziyuan quanshu wenti yanjiu*, 14.

[177]   Liu Hairong and Liu Xiu, "Guojifa tixi xia Nanji shengwu kantan de falu guizhi yanjiu" [A study on the legal regulation of Antarctic bioprospecting under the system of international law], *Zhongguo haiyang daxue xuebao (Shehui kexue ban)* 4 (2012): 9–14.

[178]   "Guanyu weihu Nanji shengwu yichuan ziyuan guojia liyi de ruogan sikao" [Analysis on how to protect China's rights to Antarctic biogenetics], *Jidi zhanlue yanjiu dongtai*, no. 4 (2012): 5–11.

[179]   Ibid., 10; and "Nanji zhoubian haiyu yu dalu zonghe pinggu."

Polar Tourism

In 2012, an international furor erupted over Chinese entrepreneur Huang Nubo's plan to set up a luxury resort in a remote part of Iceland. Even more negative publicity appeared in 2014, when Huang attempted to purchase land for a similar purpose in Norway's Svalbard archipelago. Huang, chairman of one of China's leading real estate investment groups, Beijing Zhongkun, finally succeeded in purchasing one million square meters of land near Tromsø, Norway,[180] and has been planning further tourism investments in Iceland, Norway, Denmark, Finland, and Sweden. Huang Nubo's investment in Arctic tourism has been a lightning rod for negative discussion of China's rapidly growing interests in the Arctic. As Huang frequently has tried to point out to a disbelieving international media, China is one of the fastest-growing tourism markets for outbound tourism in the world, and through his investments more Chinese tourists will come to Scandinavia and the High North.[181]

So far, however, there is a relatively limited level of Chinese tourism into the Arctic, although Chinese tourism into Antarctica has grown exponentially. Initially, the Chinese government restricted Chinese tourism operators from applying to set up their own Antarctic ventures out of concern about "political sensitivities."[182] However, strong pressure from Chinese tourism industry operators eventually led to a change in this policy.[183] In 2010, senior Chinese Antarctic diplomat Wu Yilin recommended that China encourage Chinese tourism operators to become active in Antarctica in order to take advantage of a legitimate Antarctic "resource" – the pristine environment – and gain market share before restrictions on tourism numbers are introduced.[184] From 2007, a number of travel agencies in Beijing, Shanghai, and Guangzhou began to specialize in polar travel. The current price for Chinese tourists to visit Antarctica is around RMB 80,000 (US$12,000),[185] though discounts can

---

[180] Knut-Eirik Lindblad, "Norwegian Landowner Sells Huge Amount of Land to Chinese Billionaire Huang Nubo," *Nordlys*, May 16, 2014, http://www.nordlys.no/nyheter/arti cle7362483.ece.

[181] Leslie Shaffer and Susan Li, "Chinese Tycoon Bets Chinese Tourists Will Venture Here," Entrepreneur Asia: Power Players, CNBC, April 21, 2014, http://www.cnbc.com/id/101597750.

[182] "Qu Nanji luyou? Xianzai bu xing" [Tourism in Antarctica? Not right now], *Sichuan luyou zhengwu wang*, January 19, 2007, http://news.sohu.com/20070119/n247705552.shtml.

[183] Wang Zipan, "Zhongguo Nanji luyou kaifa tantao" [An approach for developing Chinese Antarctic tourism], *Luyou xuekan* 18, no. 6 (2003).

[184] Wu Yilin, "Guanyu fazhan Nanji luyouye de sikao" [Thoughts on expanding Antarctic tourism], *Zhongguo haiyang daxue xuebao, shehuixueban* (2010): 5–8.

[185] "Nanji you 'Zhongguo wei' jian nong" [Antarctic tourism takes on a Chinese flavor], *Changjiang ribao*, November 11, 2013, accessed November 11, 2013, http://www.hnce.org/ht ml/news/lvyou/3021.html.

bring the price down as low as RMB 8800 (US$1420).[186] In the 2015–16 Antarctic tourist season, there were 38,548 tourists, of which 3558 were from China – 500 more than the previous year. In 2017 China became the second largest source of Antarctic tourists after the United States. Ten years before, only ninety-nine Chinese tourists visited Antarctica. Currently, a New Jersey–based firm with a Taiwanese owner is the main agent for sending Chinese tourists to the polar regions. This company has arranged the tours of about half the Chinese tourists who have traveled there.[187] However, the Chinese government wants to have China-based travel agents and operators working in Antarctica (and the Arctic) in order to make a China "a major tourism nation in Antarctica."[188] Becoming a significant market for Antarctic and Arctic tourists would further add weight to China's polar authority, influence, and presence.

CHINA'S STRATEGIC INTERESTS IN POLAR SCIENCE AND TECHNOLOGY

China is by no means alone among polar states in regarding its polar science as a political activity, but few national program leaders have been as frank about admitting so in public. In 2005, PRIC director Yang Huigen made it clear to Chinese journalists that China's polar science was almost totally strategic, saying, "Without Antarctic bases and expeditions, we would lose the opportunity to develop resources there in the latter half of the twenty-first and early twenty-second century."[189] In the same year, in widely circulated articles in the Chinese media, Yang also said that according to the (nonexistent) "World Treaty on Managing Antarctic Minerals" (*Shijie Nanji kuanwu ziyuan guanli tiaoyue*), Antarctic states would be able to access Antarctic minerals depending on their level of investment in Antarctic science.[190] In 2006, SOA deputy

---

[186] "Ju huasuan bao chuan kai tuan Nanji zuidi 8811 yuan you Nanji" [Charter tours to Antarctica for 8811 Chinese yuan], Chinabyte.com, November 18, 2013, accessed November 21, 2013, http://net.chinabyte.com/413/12778913.shtml.

[187] "Are small ship and expedition cruise marketers ready for Chinese tourists?," Navilogue, January 16, 2014, http://bit.ly/1dZh7Ff.

[188] "Yinggai peizhi zhenzheng de Zhongguo Nanji luyou shichang" [We should foster the development of a truly Chinese Antarctic tourism market], *Zhongguo luyou bao*, July 3, 2014, http://www.henanci.com/Pages/2014/07/03/20140703023333.shtml.

[189] "Fangwen Zhongguo Nanji kaocha shouxi kexuejia: wei shenme qu Nanji" [Interview with China's chief polar scientist: Why go to Antarctica], *Sina.com*, December 5, 2005, http://tech.sina.com.cn/d/2005-12-05/1202782841.shtml.

[190] "Zhongguo weihe xuanze zai Zhili jianshe Nanji bangongshi" [Why China built an Antarctic office in Chile], *Tiexuewang*, November 15, 2007, http://bbs.tiexue.net/post2_2380390_1.html; and "Fangwen Zhongguo Nanji kaocha shouxi kexuejia: wei shenme qu Nanji."

director Chen Lianzeng stated that "Antarctic science is not just a matter of answering scientific questions; it is closely linked with the national interest. One of the key goals of China's polar expeditions is to strive for and safeguard China's national interests and enhance China's substantial presence in the Antarctic."[191] The 2012 report on China's maritime development commented, "Polar expeditions are the foundations for humanity to open up and utilize the polar regions."[192] In 2014 Xu Shijie, the Director of CAA's Office of Polar Planning, commented that scientific research in both polar regions is strategically important because, he said, "Whoever knows the most, will have the most influence."[193] And the 2014 annual report on China's polar policy asserted that "the ability to make use of polar scientific knowledge is directly related to a nation's ability to successfully turn polar natural resources into commercial resources."[194]

Polar Science Strategies and Influences

China is looking for ways to increase its influence in polar affairs and having a high-profile, high-status, polar science program is an important means to this end. Under the current norms of the Antarctic Treaty, new Antarctic players must have an active Antarctic science program in order to be accepted as consultative parties, and only consultative parties can have a say on governance issues in Antarctica. China achieved consultative party status in 1985; in the thirty years that followed it gradually built up the pool of Chinese polar scientists and expertise, but its polar science was seldom groundbreaking. During this period, China did not have a clear strategic national Antarctic science plan, so if a Chinese scientist put together a reasonable proposal to work on the ice it usually was accepted. The main political goal was to have scientists working at China's Antarctic bases. For China, as for other Antarctic states, polar scientists are the central actors on the stage of the national project to promote the state's Antarctic rights and demonstrate that it has legitimate interests. The same situation is now playing out in Svalbard in the Arctic, though under a different set of governance rules. A given project may be

[191] "Chen Lianzeng: Zengqiang woguo zai Nanji de shi zhi xing cunzai" [Chen Lianzeng: Increase China's substantive presence in Antarctica], Xinhua, January 2, 2006, http://news .xinhuanet.com/world/2006–01/02/content_4000473.htm.

[192] Guojia haiyangju haiyang fazhan zhanlue yanjiusuo ketizu, *Zhongguo haiyang fazhan baogao*, 363.

[193] "Nanji jiang ruhe guanlian women de shenghuo?" [How will Antarctica affect our lives?], Xinhua, January 12, 2014, accessed December 1, 2014, http://news.xinhuanet.com/fortune/2 014–01/12/c_125990779.htm.

[194] Ding, *Jidi guojia zhengce yanjiu baogao 2013-2014*, 173.

important to the scientists, but the very act of conducting the science in the polar regions is important to the funding governments.

Since 2005, China has sought to take its polar affairs to a new level, and consequently the expectations of the significance and quality of China's polar science projects have risen. From this period on, China began to set strategic themes for science projects. Climate change was the first major theme; from 2012 to 2016, polar resources and governance became another key theme. More and more Chinese polar projects have begun to fit within these core themes, attracted to the dedicated funding. However, stand-out individual projects such as meteorite gathering or aurora observation can still attract funding, as they enable China to achieve another stated goal of being a leader in polar science.

The ability to produce groundbreaking research in polar science is crucial for any state that wishes to have more influence in polar affairs. The most influential states helping shape current policy in Antarctica – the United States, Australia, New Zealand, the United Kingdom, France, and Chile – produce authoritative science and working papers at Antarctic governance meetings, backing up their policy initiatives. However, states that want to block new policy initiatives in Antarctica do not necessarily need to come up with science to challenge an initiative; they can simply vote against it. China did exactly that at the CCAMLR meetings in 2012, 2013, 2014, and 2015 when it opposed proposals for new Marine Protected Areas in Antarctica. Similarly, in the Arctic, having a significant Arctic scientific program was one of the key factors that the Arctic Council considered in 2013 when debating which new states could have observer status. If the Chinese government wants to bring about a shift in some aspect of global governance with a polar connection – krill fishing, climate change, and the policy on mineral exploitation in Antarctica seem the most obvious issues – then Chinese scientists will have to come up with convincing science to back up their policy positions. In Chinese terms, engaging in meaningful science in the polar regions will grant China the "right to speak" (*huayu quan*) on polar governance matters and the ability to defend its polar "rights and interests" (*quanyi*). Chinese researchers note that participation in Antarctic (and Arctic) affairs also improves the government's "right to speak" on global governance measures.[195]

In addition to the benefits of asserting its own positions, polar science can help China build stronger connections with potential allies. Offering polar scientific partnerships is a form of economic incentive to other states whose support or trust China may want to gain, whether for Arctic or Antarctic policy

---

[195] "Zhongguo Beiji guojia liyi fenxi" [Analysis on China's national interests in the Arctic], *Jidi zhanlue yanjiu dongtai*, no. 2, (2012): 16.

goals or for some other aspect of the bilateral relationship. China's cooperation with Denmark, Finland, Iceland, and Norway can be regarded in this way
in terms of Arctic affairs (and, for Norway, in terms of Antarctic affairs as well).
China's polar scientific partnerships and annual polar strategic dialogue with
the United States can be seen as both polar-specific and a part of broader
bilateral relationship- and confidence-building measures. Hobart, Australia, is
now China's main Antarctic logistics base. China's scientific collaborations
and economic partnerships with Australia on Antarctic affairs are a means to
help silence significant criticism from Australian Antarctic policy specialists
about the potential threat that China's expanded Antarctic activities poses to
Australian interests. Through such partnerships, China also can have access to
strategic polar locations, such as the collaboration with Iceland over a second
Arctic research station. Scientific partnerships with other countries give China
access to strategic expertise or equipment that it is unable to produce or
acquire itself, and helps make China's science more competitive. This was
the case in China's early Antarctic science partnerships with Australia and
New Zealand in the late 1970s, and it is a factor in China's present-day
scientific partnerships in astronomy, ice cores, and geophysics with Japan,
the United Kingdom, and Australia. Nowadays, as China's polar science
program is perceived as flush with funds and has state-of-the-art polar facilities,
China does not even have to seek out scientific collaborations; foreign scientists come seeking Chinese scientific partners or their governments send polar
science delegations tasked with finding ways to partner with China.

China's polar science projects also can help it achieve strategic national
goals. China needs polar science information for its own geostrategic needs
related to shipping, air links, resource extraction, missile positioning and
timing, and weather forecasting. As noted, from 2012 to 2016, a large team of
Chinese scientists and social scientists worked on the Polar Environment
Comprehensive Investigation and Assessment Program, with a five-year budget of US$82 million. In the Arctic, the project assessed resources and envir-
onment in the Bering and Chukchi seas and the Canada Basin, particularly
focusing on sea routes. In Antarctica, the project analyzed marine resources
and environmental issues in the Ross Sea, Weddell Sea, and around the
Antarctic peninsula – all zones where experts have identified the likely
presence of hydrocarbons – and engaged in upper atmosphere physics, paleon-
tology, and geology in the three Antarctic land territories where China operates.[196] The project has produced hundreds of scholarly papers and reports

---

[196] Chen Danhong, "Chinese Polar Activities in 2012/13" (PowerPoint presentation at the Asian
Forum for Polar Science, Penang, October 10, 2013).

(most of them classified) and funded several hundred doctoral studies.[197] The project's objective was to prepare China for the next stage of polar policy-making and strategy. Only by assessing Antarctic and Arctic available resources and governance structure can China decide what the stakes are and what position it wants to take in international negotiations to access these resources and shipping routes.

Much of China's polar science is strategically important to China's short-term goals. Polar scientific research is helping create new biotechnology industries, providing authority for China's perspective on global climate change negotiations, helping China to develop its own Global Positioning System (GPS), and helping to improve China's global status and approval ratings by enabling Chinese scientists to engage in groundbreaking research that could lead to a polar-related Nobel Prize in science. In the Arctic, China's research is centered on the impact of Arctic climate change on China's environment, water mass exchange between the Arctic Ocean and North Pacific on the North Pacific circulation, Arctic fisheries, Arctic sea ice melt, geo-biochemical processes, and a past environment survey in the Arctic Ocean.[198] Meanwhile, China's Antarctic research has achieved a number of internationally recognized breakthroughs, which have included research into changes in the composition of the Antarctic ice sheet, tectonic research (which discovered that the shield of southeastern Antarctica was formed half a billion years ago), research on the average life span of krill (which will assist in fisheries management), research on Antarctic auroras, paleoecologic studies on the Antarctic peninsula examining changes in temperature and penguin populations over 3,000 years, the Grove Mountains meteorite recovery, and research on the paleoclimate ice sheet advance and the retreat of the Grove Mountains. In years to come, Chinese scientists expect to make more scientific breakthroughs, particularly at their base on Dome A in deep-ice drilling and astronomical observations, ice cores in the Gamburtsev Mountains, explorations into the lake under the ice of the Grove Mountains, and further Grove Mountain seismic observation that will help determine the resource potential of the region.[199] China's polar science plan is now part of the national scientific and technological infrastructure and long-term plan (2012–30). The Chinese government aims to accelerate China's scientific and

---

[197] A summary of the project's findings and outputs was featured in the tenth issue of the project broadsheet. See *Jidi zhuanying jianbao* 10 (January 2016): 1–8

[198] CAA, "Science and Data: Projects of Chinese Polar Scientific Research," accessed January 23, 2014, http://www.chinare.gov.cn/en/index.html?pid=science.

[199] Liu Xiaohan, "Chinese Scientists in the Antarctic," Beijing Normal University, April 1, 2011, http://english.bnu.edu.cn/academicevents/33646.htm.

technological infrastructure in the next twenty years, as a stimulus to further economic development.[200]

Polar Space Science

Parallel to the SOA's scientific priorities in the Arctic and Antarctic are other strategic science projects that rely on polar sites. These projects connect with China's wider national security and defense plans. China's seven polar research stations play a crucial role in the development of China's space program; for the monitoring of space flights, space physics, and space exploration; and in helping the PLA enhance its command, control, communications, computers intelligence surveillance reconnaissance (C[4]ISR) systems capabilities. China has invested heavily in a space program and continues to expand it, with plans for a moon landing by 2017 and a Mars mission by 2020.

One important component of China's space program is the roll-out of the BeiDou satellite system. BeiDou is China's equivalent of GPS. It is a dual-use technology, which among other functions will assist the Chinese military in its missile timing and positioning as well as in its C[4]ISR capabilities.[201] C[4]ISR is a crucial capacity of the modern military: it enhances situational awareness in a tactical environment, improves interoperability, and provides surveillance and intelligence capacity. The civil aspect of BeiDou – satellite navigation and positioning – is also an extremely lucrative industry. According to a 2012 Chinese government white paper, by the time BeiDou becomes available on a global scale in 2020 it is likely to earn US$64 billion profit per year.[202] The polar regions are crucial for China to expand BeiDou's reach to global coverage.

China, like a number of other polar states, is able to make use of the unresolved sovereignty of Antarctica to establish space tracking and ground receiving stations for polar satellites, with global coverage, that would be unwelcome on the sovereign territory of other states. China's first polar ground

---

[200] State Council Gazette table of contents, Issue No. 8 Serial No. 1439 (March 20, 2013), The State Council of the People Republic of China (English-language site), http://www.gov.cn/english/official/2013–03/28/content_2364718.htm.

[201] "Beidou li ya GPS zheng shi 5000 yi shichang" [Beidou GPS fights for 500 billion market], Sohu.com, March 21, 2015, http://news.sohu.com/20150321/n410099067.shtml; and Ding, *Jidi guojia zhengce yanjiu baogao 2012–2013*, 64.

[202] "Zhongguo weixing daohang yu weizhi fuwu chanye fazhan baipishu (2012 niandu)" [China's satellite navigation and location services industry White Paper (2012)], Ministry of Industry and Information Technology of the People's Republic of China, September 25, 2013, http://www.miit.gov.cn/n11293472/n11293832/n11293907/n11368277/15643419.html.

receiving station was established at its Antarctic Great Wall Station in 1993. The data collected there had dual civil-military use for improving weather predictions and enhancing China's coastal defense.[203] China's Arctic and Antarctic expeditions rely on Chinese satellites to relay up-to-date weather and oceans data, not only to plot maritime voyages and land-based traverses but also to transmit scientific data.[204]

A BeiDou satellite capable of being received in the polar regions was launched in 2007. The voyages of the *Xue Long* icebreaker into Arctic and Antarctic waters and expeditions into the Antarctic hinterland have been used to test BeiDou's capabilities.[205] In January 2014, the BeiDou system was put to the test when the *Xue Long* was itself trapped while attempting to rescue the Russian research vessel *Akademik Shokalskiy*. A polar-orbiting Chinese military satellite, part of the BeiDou system, was used to identify ice conditions to guide *Xue Long*'s passage through the ice floes. The SOA and PLA jointly coordinated *Xue Long*'s successful exit from its ice trap. The same military polar satellite has been used to help look for the missing Malaysia Airlines Flight 370, which vanished over the South China Sea in March 2014.[206] China installed ground satellite receiving and processing stations at both Changcheng and Zhongshan Stations in 2010[207] and at Kunlun Station in early 2013,[208] and completed further upgrades to the Zhongshan Station facilities in early 2015. Installing ground receiving stations at these locations greatly increases the positioning accuracy of Chinese satellites as well as China's Antarctic mapping capacity, useful for engaging in further mineral

[203] James C. Bussert, "China Taps Many Resources for Coastal Defence," *Signal*, November 2002, http://www.afcea.org/content/?q=china-taps-many-resources-coastal-defense.

[204] "Weixing shuju wei Xue Long hao Nanji kekao tigong daohang baozhang" [Satellite navigation data helps Xue Long's Antarctic expedition], *Zhongguo hangtian bao*, February 14, 2014, http://www.spacechina.com/n25/n144/n206/n214/c639323/content.html.

[205] "Snow Dragon helped assess Beidou positioning thousands of miles away," Xinhua, December 31, 2011, http://mil.chinaiiss.com/html/201112/31/a46896.html; and "Xue Long chuanshang de BeiDou weixing shebei ke yu guonei shouji hufa duanxin" [Xue Long's BeiDou satellite technology enable mobile connection with China's mobile network], Zhang Jiansong, personal blog, July 11, 2010, http://zhangjiansong.home.news.cn/blog/a/01010001BC540ACC5ADCFB3F.html.

[206] Chinese polar scientist, interview with author, August 2014.

[207] "Guojia Nanji 'shiwu' nengli jianshe zhongdian xiangmu Nanji Changcheng zhan, Zhongshan zhan, dimian weixing jieshou chuli xitong" [National 15th five year plan capacity key building project to install satellite ground receiving and processing stations successfully completed], National Marine Environmental Forecasting Center, March 18, 2010, http://www.nmefc.gov.cn/nr/cont.aspx?itemid=2&id=1757.

[208] "Sinan Beidou daohang jieshouji biaoxian youyi" [Sinan Beidou navigation receiver's outstanding performance], *Xi'an Beidou xun*, May 17, 2013, accessed November 19, 2013, http://www.xabdxl.com/xwdt/yjxw/2820.html (link discontinued).

exploration there. And whether in peacetime or during conflict situations, China's polar satellite receiving stations – along with those of other states with similar capabilities in the polar regions, such as the United States and Russia – are crucial for tracking missile launches and enemy satellites.[209] According to the US Department of Defense, the PLA has a large range of imaging and remote satellites that can support China's C4ISR needs by supplying coordinated situational awareness of foreign military force deployments, critical infrastructure, and targets of political significance.[210] China's 2012–13 annual report on polar policy highlighted the role of the polar regions in C4ISR and observed that Antarctic ground receiving stations were invaluable for "preparing for the facilitation or interference of precision missile strikes and for targeting and communicating with various satellite systems."[211] In 2012, CCP researcher Zhou Tianyong noted in a classified paper that "China's space program is rapidly expanding. The development of space satellites, space flights, space stations and modern equipment has profound economic and military applications and whoever has the upper hand in terms of technology systems and programs will have an advantage in future development and warfare."[212]

In 2020, BeiDou will achieve full global coverage by utilizing over thirty spacecraft in orbit.[213] BeiDou-1 had full Asia-Pacific coverage in 2003, while BeiDou-2 rolled out in 2012 with improved capabilities. BeiDou-2 has five open channels and five closed military channels, which makes jamming impossible.[214] The PLA has been using BeiDou for military navigation and weapons targeting; the system also provides the timing function for China's financial and power sector transactions, along with navigation and positioning information for fisheries, forestry, and transportation. As yet, most of China's potential users – civilian and military – still use GPS, as it is more accurate than BeiDou and its technology is widely integrated into existing infrastructure. China will continue to use GPS, but in a time of military crisis it will be able to draw on BeiDou. One anonymous Chinese military specialist told the

---

[209]   Chen and Wang, "Shi xi Zhongguo de Nanji liyi yu quanyi," 99.

[210]   Office of the Secretary of Defense, *Annual Report to Congress: Military and Security Developments Involving the People's Republic of China 2013* (Washington, DC: Department of Defense, 2013), 65.

[211]   Ding, *Jidi guojia zhengce yanjiu baogao 2012–2013*, 64.

[212]   Zhou, "Weilai Zhongmei guojia liyi chongtu de kenengxing fenxi," 15. Zhou is a researcher at the Strategic Research Institute of the Central Party School.

[213]   Stephen Clark, "China Sends Beidou Navigation Satellite to Space," *Spaceflight Now*, April 14, 2011, http://www.amerisurv.com/content/view/8568/.

[214]   James C. Bussert and Bruce A. Elleman, *People's Liberation Army Navy Combat Systems Technology, 1949–2010* (Annapolis, MD: Naval Institute Press, 2011), 161.

Chinese media in 2013 that the dual-use capacity of the BeiDou satellite receiving station in Antarctica might bring the risk that in a future US-China conflict, China's Antarctic bases could be targeted in order to disrupt the BeiDou system.[215] Two international relations scholars, Chen Yugang and Wang Wanlu, also have discussed this possibility, and have advised that for this reason, China should strongly advocate for the continued demilitarization of Antarctica.[216] China's expansion of dual civil-military strategic capabilities into the Arctic and Antarctic, combined with its increased military capabilities worldwide and in particular its increasing use of the PLA in the polar regions, will put pressure on the fragile diplomatic game that interested states play of turning a blind eye to abuses of Antarctic and Spitsbergen Treaty norms.

A further aspect of China's strategic polar interests is upper atmosphere physics and satellite remote sensing. China's planned new base in the Ross Sea will have remote sensing facilities.[217] Remote sensing is used for mineral and oil exploration, marine surveys, military reconnaissance, and mapping. In the austral summer of 2015, a team of Chinese and foreign scientists conducted extensive remote sensing, zigzagging back and forth via airplane across what China calls the "East Antarctic Sector" (see chapter 5).[218] China's Antarctic upper atmosphere physics is also useful for the PLAN's submarine-related research on sea ice noise.[219]

Like the United States, China regards Antarctica as a useful laboratory for preparing for an advanced space program. The engineering required to build a modern research station in Antarctica can be applied in many other extreme environments, including space. During the 12th Five-Year Plan (2011–2015), China set up a polar engineering research network to strengthen and develop the research links between polar and space engineering.[220] Antarctica is one of the easiest places in the world to find meteors. The area around the Grove Mountains in East Antarctica, site of China's fourth Antarctic station,

---

[215] "Zhongguo xinjian Nanji Kunlun shan zhan, Ao zhiku cheng jiang yinfa junshi chongtu [China's new Antarctic base Kunlun, Australian think tank implies it could have a role in a military conflict], 114junshiwang, accessed November 1, 2013, http://lunti.114junshi.com/fang wupinglun/js44045.html (link discontinued).

[216] Chen and Wang, "Shi xi Zhongguo de Nanji liyi yu quanyi," 7.

[217] "Zhongguo jidi kaocha: Xiang guangdu yu he shendi jinjun" [Improvement in the breadth and depth of China's Antarctic expeditions], *Zhongguo haiyang bao*, March 12, 2013, http://www.cmrv.org/home/a/chuanduiyaowen/guonahaiyangdiaochadongtai/2013/0312/201.html.

[218] Project participant, interview with author, April 2016.

[219] Chen and Wang, "Shi xi Zhongguo de Nanji liyi yu quanyi," 7.

[220] "Zhengzhan Nanji, Zhongguo zai xingdong" [China is on the move in Antarctica], *Zhongguo kexue bao*, January 17, 2014, accessed August 6, 2014, http://www.shkpzx.com/822 7/9063/21252.html (link discontinued).

Taishan, is rich in meteorites, as is the location of China's planned fifth Antarctic research station in the Ross Sea area. China is extremely active in collecting meteorites in Antarctica, and as of 2015 it had collected 12,035. This is the third-largest collection in the world, after those of the United States and Japan. Chinese scientists have discovered meteorites from Mars and the moon. Research on meteorites is helpful for understanding the solar system; it also enables scientists to better understand what they will find among igneous rocks when spaceships land on the moon and Mars. China's Lunar Expedition Program has already sent several robotic missions to the moon and plans a manned mission between the years 2025 to 2030. Meteorite research is also useful for comparative planetology and geochemistry – that is, comparing the geology of the earth, the moon, and Mars, and assessing what mineral resources lie there.[221] China has not yet signed the Lunar Treaty, which treats mineral resources on the moon and other planets as part of the common heritage of humankind and therefore unable to be colonized.[222]

China has a strong polar geomagnetics, ionosphere, and auroras research program that benefits from Arctic and Antarctic research. Geomagnetics research is used by militaries to help determine local geomagnetic field characteristics, in order to detect anomalies in the natural background that might be caused by a significant metallic object such as a submerged submarine. China,[223] Russia, and the United States are all prioritizing high-frequency active auroral research programs, investigating the defense-related potential uses of the ionosphere. The ionosphere is important for GPS navigation and radio signals. Electromagnetic pulses can be used to upset, jam, or even destroy, enemy electronics. Polar auroras often interfere with radio and radar signals, and solar flares can interfere with military and civilian communication. Thus, China's ability to develop an independent satellite communications system, improve the safety of its polar navigation in difficult areas such as the Arctic seas, and expand its cross-Arctic air routes all depend on whether it can manage this strategically important concern. Chinese polar scientists are also researching how to harvest aurora-generated energy. Zhongshan Station, Kunlun Station, Yellow River Station at Ny-Ålesund, and the new joint Iceland-China aurora research station are China's key

---

[221] William Cassidy, *Meteorites, Ice, and Antarctica: A Personal Account* (Cambridge: Cambridge University Press, 2007), 126–32.

[222] "Agreement Covering the Activities of States on the Moon and Other Celestial Bodies," United Nations Office for Outer Space Affairs, A/RES/34/68, December 5, 1979, http://www .unoosa.org/oosa/SpaceLaw/moon.html.

[223] Qu et al., *Beiji wenti yanjiu*, 296, discusses the military significance of space weather research in the polar regions.

research sites for these programs. China's Antarctic Zhongshan Station and Arctic Huang He Station are perfectly paired sites for atmospheric physics and space-related research, as they are geographical cognates.[224] Zhongshan and the Svalbard research area are both at 74.5° latitude – the only place in the world where solar flares go into the upper atmosphere – and consequently they are excellent locations for researching auroras.

China's astronomy in Antarctica is potentially groundbreaking. At 4093 meters, China's observatory and base on Dome A is the highest on the Antarctic plateau and benefits from calm, dry, cold, and clear skies. Chinese astronomers hope to research how stars form, the nature of dark matter and dark energy, the origins of the universe, and the question of whether life exists on other planets. The only challenge in achieving this goal is that since 1999, China-based scientists have not been permitted to purchase the US-made state-of-the-art polar telescopes and satellites they require.[225] The US government bans such exports to China under the International Traffic in Arms Regulations.[226] In 2011, the US National Aeronautics and Space Administration (NASA) also cut off funding to any US scientific programs working with Chinese scientists affiliated to Chinese government institutions, universities, or companies.[227] Many US scientists strongly objected to this abrupt policy switch, which came after thirty years of encouraging US-China scientific collaboration. Compounding these restrictions, in 2012 the US Antarctic Program, in direct competition with China's Dome A project, funded a rival space science automatic telescope (nicknamed the "Heat" project) at Ridge A, another strategically significant site only a short snowmobile ride away from China's Dome A outpost.[228] To get around the US import restrictions, a Chinese astronomer at Texas A&M University, working with the Nanjing Institute of Astronomical Optics and Technology, designed China's own advanced polar telescope: the AST3, a fully automatic Antarctic survey

[224] "Jiemi Zhongguo shouzuo Beiji ke kao zhan: Tan Beiji bi Nanji 'shengshi'" [China's first Arctic Station: Exploring the Arctic is "easier" than Antarctica], *Beijing ribao*, July 21, 2004, http://www.china.com.cn/chinese/TR-c/616173.htm.

[225] Toni Feder, "China Is Latest Country to Pursue Astronomy in Antarctica," *Physics Today* 64, no. 1 (January 2011): 23.

[226] Directorate of Defense Trade Controls, "The International Traffic in Arms Regulations," US Department of State, December 16, 2015, https://www.pmddtc.state.gov/regulations_laws/itar.html.

[227] "PRC FAQ for ROSES," Service and Advice for Research and Analysis, National Aeronautics and Space Administration, February 11, 2014, http://science.nasa.gov/researchers/sara/faqs/prc-faq-roses/.

[228] "Exploring the Life Cycle of Galactic Matter from the Bottom of the World," HEAT: The High Elevation Antarctic Terahertz Telescope, Steward Observatory Radio Astronomy Laboratory, 2013, http://soral.as.arizona.edu/heat/.

telescope. China's first AST3 was installed in the 2012–13 austral summer. In 2015, the AST3-2 telescope was installed at Dome A. The telescopes can be used to study supernova explosions, the afterglow of gamma ray bursts, extra-solar planets, the origins of galaxies and stars, and indeed the very origin of the universe.

But China's astronomical program at Dome A also has direct military applications. Infrared telescopes can be used to search for enemy satellites, drones, and missile launches, and identify if they have been shot when targeted. China's use of this technology during a conflict would greatly enhance its defensive capabilities in an air-sea battle in their near seas.[229] This capacity is not unique to Chinese telescopes in Antarctica: all the Antarctic states with advanced telescopes and satellite receiving stations there have similar dual-use capabilities. Meanwhile, seismic research in Antarctica, conducted by many states (including China), can be used to detect nuclear tests.

Astronomical images taken at Dome A will be sharper than images taken anywhere else on earth and comparable with images taken from space. Chinese astronomers believe that these series of telescopes make their base at Dome A the world's best observatory. The telescopes are remotely con-nected to the Nanjing Observatory, so with a click of a button Chinese astronomers can engage in deep-space research.[230] In 2013, China strength-ened its telecommunication links with Antarctica, sending two China Telecom personnel to enhance the satellite communications network of China's Antarctic bases, enabling live transmission of images.[231] Previously, Chinese scientists physically had to go to Kunlun to collect data, and relied on US satellite company Intelsat to facilitate the relay of the research. This arrangement made Chinese data vulnerable to being spied on by the US-led Five Eyes signals intelligence network, which utilizes New Zealand's proxi-mity to Antarctica to spy on Antarctic telecommunications.[232]

---

[229] Polar astronomer, interview with author, August 2014.

[230] Ma Weihong, "Nanji bingqiong A jiang zhuangzhi shou ge zidong yuancheng yaokong wangyuanjing" [The Connection of Dome A's first remote telescopes], *Zhongguo xinwen-wang*, March 25, 2010, accessed November 19, 2013, http://chro.cpst.net.cn/xxkd/2010_03/26 9506719.html (link discontinued).

[231] "Dianxin zhuanjia sui 'Xue Long hao' bu Nanji" [Telecom experts follow *Xue Long* to Antarctica], *Wenhuibao*, November 12, 2013, accessed November 18, 2013, http://wenhui.ne ws365.com.cn/tp/201311/t20131112_1702675.html (link discontinued).

[232] "Snowden Revelations: NZ's Spy Reach Stretches across Globe," *New Zealand Herald*, March 11, 2015, http://www.nzherald.co.nz/nz/news/article.cfm?c_id=1&objectid=11415172; US National Security Agency, "NSA Intelligence Relationship with New Zealand," NSA Information Paper NSA/CSSM 1–52, April 1, 2013, https://fveydocs.org/document/nsa-rela tionship-nzl/.

4

The Party-State-Military-Market Nexus in China's
Polar Policymaking

Multiple government agencies and actors have a stake in China's polar policy-making and participate in China's national delegations to polar governance meetings. China's first Antarctic expedition involved sixty government departments and units. These days, China's bureaucracy is considerably stream-lined, yet at least seventeen agencies participate in polar activities and planning. All of these institutional actors are helping shape, to varying degrees, China's evolving polar strategy. To a certain extent, Chinese commercial forces with polar interests are also helping shape China's polar policy. The seventeen agencies involved in polar affairs reflect the broad parameters of China's polar interests: security, resources, and strategic science. Moreover, China's complex polar interests and the associations that have built up because of them reflect the deep nexus between the Chinese Communist Party, the state, the military, and the market.

THE PARTY-STATE CONNECTIONS IN CHINA'S POLAR AFFAIRS

Under the constitution of the People's Republic of China, the CCP has a leadership role over the whole of Chinese society. China's political system has a dual structure of party and state decision-making bodies whose leadership frequently overlaps. Thus, China's strategic polar policies are decided by the CCP's Politburo Standing Committee (PBSC), headed by General Secretary Xi Jinping. Xi is also state president and head of the People's Liberation Army Central Military Commission. The State Council, headed by Premier Li Keqiang (who is ranked second in the PBSC and is also a senior CCP leader), approves new polar budget items. The seven-member PBSC oversees and approves polar strategic matters, while the thirty-five-member State Council focuses on administrative matters such as funding.

Like all Chinese bureaucracies, China's polar agencies have a CCP branch office incorporated as part of their organizational structure, as do all of China's major corporations that participate in China's polar affairs. In the Chinese bureaucracy, all senior leadership roles are held by CCP members, and polar affairs are no different.[1] The party secretary of each government and quasigovernmental agency in China has as much authority as the administrative leader, and in most cases more. However, illustrating the inseparable party-state relationship in China, polar administrative leaders such as Polar Research Institute of China director Yang Huigen are also part of the CCP leadership team within their organization.[2] The CCP party secretaries at China's polar agencies are in charge of leading strategic policies, as well as personnel and finance; giving them immense powers, as well as opportunities for corruption. The CCP branch office within China's polar agencies is in charge of media management on polar issues and of managing Sino-foreign scholarly contact on polar issues,[3] and thereby acts as a "gatekeeper" on what can be said and which foreigners Chinese polar scientists and social scientists can be associated with. In addition, each Chinese Arctic or Antarctic expedition has a party secretary who is the overall leader of the expedition.[4] The CCP's role in overseas projects ensures the political goals of these projects are understood and upheld.[5] China's state-owned enterprises and other major companies also have CCP branch offices, and the party secretary of these branch offices works closely with the Chinese embassies in their host countries to ensure that CCP policy is followed in the Arctic and Antarctic, as elsewhere.[6]

---

[1]   "Zhongxin lingdao" [PRIC leadership], Polar Research Institute of China (PRIC), 2011, http://www.pric.org.cn/detail/sub.aspx?c=9.

[2]   "Bushu jiaoyu shijian huodong zuo hao ge xiang zhunbei gongzuo" [Briefing on the CCP Mass Line], PRIC, July 5, 2013, accessed June 4, 2015, http://www.pric.org.cn/handler/UploadHandler.ashx?action=DownloadAttach&uGuid=bddc07bb-4fc3-4e7d-b171-ee506f9f8c33.

[3]   "Dang ban zhineng" [PRIC CCP Office functions], PRIC, May 28, 2013, http://www.pric.org.cn/detail/content.aspx?id=559d7429-dd33-4bf9-88c3-2881203ed567.

[4]   "Zhongguo di 31 ci Nanji kaocha dui chengli" [31st Chinese Antarctic expedition team established], PRIC, October 29, 2014, http://www.pric.org.cn/detail/News.aspx?id=b02b179b-36b5-449c-98c6-652457ee109d.

[5]   "Tansuo haiwai dangjian gongzuo xin lu" [Explore new roads for party-building overseas], *Lilunwang*, June 11, 2014, accessed August 14, 2014, http://www.cntheory.com/JCDJGQDJ/2011/614/11614953300CI1FDE278F078J7193B.html (link discontinued).

[6]   "Zhong jiao jituan jiaqiang haiwai dangjian gongzuo" [CCCC Group to strengthen CCP building work overseas], State-owned Assets Supervision and Administration Commission of the State Council, September 19, 2011, http://www.sasac.gov.cn/n1180/n6881559/n10281420/n110282125/n10282230/13828176.html.

CCP members are not only employees; they are Chinese citizens and party members. Those working in the polar regions must follow three layers of control: first, CCP discipline (*dang de jilü*); second, Chinese law; and third, international law. Antarctic Treaty states are supposed to self-police their own behavior in Antarctica by passing national legislation that implements the Antarctic Treaty and applying this legislation to the activities of their nationals active there. But in China, CCP *diktat* overrides national law, and so implicitly it also overrides the Antarctic Treaty and other international instruments. For polar governance, this issue has already appeared as a point of conflict on matters such as transparency. Transparency is a norm in Antarctic policy and is desirable in Arctic governance, but it is not the norm in the Chinese political system.

One of the key methods that the CCP utilizes to ensure policy coordination and implementation within Chinese society is to group policy areas within either a *xitong*—a kind of suprabureaucracy that links agencies in a horizontal as well as a vertical structure—or a *kou*, an organizational unit for narrower policy matters. A *xitong* or *kou* is normally led by a small leadership group headed by a member of the CCP PBSC. The CCP classifies the polar regions—even the Antarctic continent—as marine areas. Therefore, China's polar affairs are managed within the CCP's maritime affairs suprabureaucracy (*haiyang xitong*), which links all Chinese government departments and agencies with maritime interests. Some aspects of China's polar affairs are also managed within the separate foreign affairs (*waishi xitong*), national security (*guojia anquan xitong*), and propaganda and education (*xuanjiao*) *xitong*.

Since the death of Mao Zedong in 1976, it has been the trend in Chinese politics to divide up leadership roles among the senior PBSC leaders so as not to have power overly concentrated in one individual. However, Xi Jinping has broken that trend; in addition to his roles as CCP general secretary, PRC state president, and head of the Central Military Commission, he also heads the CCP Foreign Affairs Leading Group (*Zhongyang waishi lingdao xiaozu*), the CCP Finance and Economics Leading Group (*Zhongyang caijing lingdao xiaozu*), the National Security Council (*Guojia anquan weiyuanhui*), and the Party Leading Group for Comprehensively Deepening Reform (*Zhongyang quanmian shenhua gaige lingdao xiaozu*). As a result, Xi is the most powerful Chinese leader in the past forty years. Moreover, his position at the top of these crucial policy groupings means that all the three core aspects of polar affairs – security, resources, and science – are now under one leader, allowing for a much higher level of policy coordination and policy prioritization than ever before.

Xi Jinping has shown a great interest in polar and maritime affairs, even more so than his predecessors had. From 1979 to 1982, he was personal secretary to Defense Minister Geng Biao, during the years when Geng was making strategic decisions about Arctic-capable nuclear submarines.[7] It is evident that Xi is acutely aware of the strategic importance of both the Arctic sea route and the Arctic missile route to China's security. Moreover, because of the PLA's direct involvement in setting up China's first Antarctic base when Geng was minister of defense, Xi will long have been more conscious than most CCP senior leaders of Antarctica's strategic importance to China as well. One sign of the growing importance of maritime affairs in China in the past ten years, particularly under Xi's leadership,[8] was the creation of the CCP Maritime Affairs Leading Group (*Zhongyang haiyang gongzuo lingdao xiaozu*) in 2012. This group, led by Xi, was established to better coordinate maritime policy among the various government agencies engaged in international maritime activities. It consists of senior officials from China's State Oceanic Administration, Ministry of Foreign Affairs, Ministry of Public Security, Ministry of Agriculture, and the PLA. The day-to-day work of the CCP Maritime Affairs Leading Group is managed by the CCP Maritime Rights Office (*Zhongyang haiyang quanyi lingdao xiaozu bangongshi*).[9]

Since coming to power in 2012, Xi Jinping has made multiple strong statements in support of China's expanding polar program and more widely in connection with the issue of China as a maritime power and China's New Silk Road strategy. At the 18th Party Congress in 2012, where Xi succeeded Hu Jintao as CCP general secretary, he issued the instruction that "the polar regions are an important part of the oceans; all departments should seriously comprehend and thoroughly implement government policies [on the polar regions]."[10] As mentioned earlier, Xi gave an extremely significant speech on China's polar interests during his visit to Hobart, Australia, in November 2014. The speech was not meant for foreign audiences, so only excerpts of it appeared in English. But it was understood in Chinese polar policy circles

---

7   Cheng Li, "Xi Jinping: One of China's Top Future Leaders to Watch," Brookings Institution, 2012, http://www.brookings.edu/about/centers/china/top-future-leaders/xi_jinping.

8   As discussed by Ding Huang, ed., *Jidi guojia zhengce yanjiu baogao 2013–2014* [Annual report on national polar policy research, 2013–14] (Beijing: Kexue chubanshe, 2014), 50–51.

9   Zhongguo yi chengli zhongyang haiquanban xi she hai gao cengci xietiao jigou" [China sets up high-level coordination mechanism the CCP Maritime Rights Office], *Haiyang Zhongguo*, March 2, 2013, http://ocean.china.com.cn/2013–03/02/content_28105606.htm.

10 "Zhongguo jidi kaocha gongzuo zixun weiyuanhui di 15 ci huiyi zai 'Xue Long' chuan juxing" [15th Meeting of polar advisory committee held on *Xue Long*], State Oceanic Administration of the People's Republic of China, October 18, 2013, accessed March 20, 2014, http://www.soa.gov.cn/xw/hyyw_90/201310/t20131018_27552.html (link discontinued).

as marking a new impetus to China's polar affairs, as Xi had described China as a nascent polar great power in public for the first time.[11] Previously, this terminology had been mentioned only by SOA leaders. Following this speech, the polar regions were also officially included in Xi's bold New Silk Road foreign policy direction. The Arctic Northern Sea Route was one of three transportation routes highlighted in Xi's vision for this new Sinocentric order of regional cooperation announced in 2013; the proposal would link twenty-six nations, with China at the center. As maritime affairs become more central in China's foreign policy and economic planning, so too are polar affairs gaining in prominence and public attention.

CHINA'S STATE POLAR BUREAUCRACY

China's evolving polar strategy is effectively an undeclared foreign policy. Yet the Chinese Ministry of Foreign Affairs is not the primary agency setting the polar agenda. Linda Jakobson and Dean Knox's classic study on Chinese foreign policymaking makes the point that China's Ministry of Foreign Affairs is "only one actor" in China's present-day foreign policymaking, and these days it is "not necessarily the most important one."[12] This certainly is the case in China's polar affairs, where the Foreign Ministry frequently plays a relatively minor role compared to other agencies[13] even though it is officially the lead ministry for representing China on polar issues at international meetings.[14] Its role is to draft China's polar-related laws and official statements and coordinate China's participation in international polar governance meetings such as the Antarctic Treaty Consultative Meeting, but it is not a strong voice in devising China's polar agenda. The ministry leads when China must respond to new polar global governance measures such as new agreements within the Antarctic Treaty system, and it joins with other concerned departments to make a joint report of recommendations to China's State Council.

---

[11] On the significance of the speech, see the comments of SOA party secretary Liu Cigui, "Liu Cigui: Kaita jinqu fenyong pinbo cong jidi daguo mai xiang jidi qiangguo" [Liu Cigui: Forge ahead courageously, from polar big power to polar great power], *Haiyang bao*, November 19, 2014, http://www.soa.gov.cn/xw/hyyw_90/201411/t20141119_34122.html; and "Jin zhua jiyu tuidong shiye zai shang xin taijie" [Seize the opportunity to take polar affairs to a higher level], *Haiyang bao*, December 25, 2014, http://www.soa.gov.cn/xw/hyyw_90/201412/t20141225_34741 .html.

[12] Linda Jakobson and Dean Knox, *New Foreign Policy Actors in China*, SIPRI Policy Paper 26 (Stockholm: SIPRI, September 2010), vi.

[13] Chinese polar policymaker, interview with author, October, 2012.

[14] Qu Tanzhou et al., eds., *Beiji wenti yanjiu* [Research on Arctic issues] (Beijing: Ocean Press, 2011), 365.

The State Council then approves the recommendations on the basis of such reports.[15] Within the Foreign Ministry, the Department of Boundary and Ocean Affairs has polar-related responsibilities, but Department of Treaty and Law officials are usually selected to lead China's polar-related delegations. However, even though Department of Treaty and Law personnel attend many international treaty meetings, few of its staff members are posted to the meetings long enough to develop detailed Arctic- or Antarctic-related expertise. China sends only midlevel diplomats as representatives to Antarctic meetings, and unlike Japan and Singapore, it has not yet appointed an Arctic ambassador (though it is likely to do so in the 13th Five-Year Plan [2016–2020]). For Arctic matters, the Foreign Ministry is the lead agency for China's Arctic Affairs Coordination Group (*Beiji shiwu xietiao xiaozu*), which was established by the State Council in 2011, and it has the power to set and synchronize the Arctic policies of various government departments.[16]

Nevertheless, when it comes to setting China's overall polar agenda, it is the State Oceanic Administration, not the Ministry of Foreign Affairs, that takes the lead. The SOA's role is to "organize and lead" (*zuzhi yu lingdao*) China's effort to become a "polar great power."[17] The fact that the SOA established the phraseology "polar great power," which has been used by Xi Jinping since 2014, is a clear indicator of the agency's preeminent role in China's polar strategic thinking.[18] Many SOA polar affairs personnel have been working in the field for decades, and they have an intimate knowledge of China's polar activities. On specific issues such as fishing in the Southern Ocean or the Arctic sea route, other departments will take the lead, but since most of China's current polar activities focus on science – and science is used as a means to achieve China's other polar goals – the SOA inevitably takes the lead in polar policy-making overall.[19]

Fractured authority is a defining feature of contemporary Chinese foreign policymaking.[20] A range of what Jakobson and Knox call "new foreign policy actors" also have been helping to shape China's polar policy, as they have been

[15] Zou Keyuan, "China's Antarctic policy and the Antarctic Treaty System," *Ocean Development and International Law* 24, no. 3 (1993), 247.

[16] Yang Jian, "Beiji keyan yu huanjing baohu dui renlei ju zhongyao yiyi" [Arctic scientific research and environmental protection have great interest for the whole of humanity], *Guancha* (Taipei) 15, November 2014, http://www.observer-taipei.com/article.php?id=511.

[17] "Zhongguo jidi kaocha gongzuo zixun weiyuanhui di 15 ci huiyi zai 'Xue Long' chuan juxing."

[18] "Er lun shenru xuexi guanche Xi Jinping zhuxi zhongyao jianghua jingshen" [Study and implement the important speech of Chairman Xi Jinping], *Zhongguo haiyang bao*, November 20, 2014, http://www.oceanol.com/redian/shiping/2014-11-25/38013.html.

[19] Chinese polar official, interview with author, October 2013.

[20] Jakobson and Knox, *New Foreign Policy Actors in China*, vii.

shaping other aspects of Chinese foreign policy. The external actors helping to shape China's polar policymaking include polar researchers, SOEs with polar interests, and Chinese corporate interests. In future, if the work of Chinese environmental nongovernmental organizations comes to fruition, Chinese public opinion may be a further factor in polar decision-making, as it is in many other aspects of Chinese government policy. Conflicting influences – including nationalism, resource security, a deep sense of inferiority with regard to the outside world, business interests, climate policy, China's maritime strategy, China's internationalization strategy, the need to maintain a high level of economic development, and the desire for international acknowledgment for China's scientific achievements – are all putting pressure on China's polar policymaking.

The current Chinese leadership clearly values polar affairs, but as yet there is a gap between their interests and the bureaucratic arrangements of the various agencies with polar activities. Unlike other leading states with strong polar interests, China lacks one key agency to coordinate all the activities of the other players. China has a large range of government organizations and institutional actors involved in polar policymaking, the international governance of Antarctica, and strategic thinking on the Arctic. These organizations, as well as other prominent actors such as SOEs and major Chinese corporations, have overlapping and occasionally competing interests.

Since 1964, the SOA has been the main government body focusing on polar affairs. From 2008, it has been under the direct control of the powerful Ministry of Land and Natural Resources (*Guotu ziyuanbu*). Among the duties of the Ministry of Land and Resources are the protection and rational use of land resources, mineral resources, marine resources and other natural resources; the management of mineral resources development; and the management of geological exploration and mineral resources.[21] The relocation of SOA to within the Ministry of Land and Natural Resources reflects the long-standing resource emphasis of China's contemporary polar and broader maritime interests.

The SOA coordinates all aspects of China's polar affairs from scientific to strategic matters.[22] It supervises two polar-related subsidiary bodies: the Chinese Arctic and Antarctic Administration and the Polar Research Institute of China. In addition, staff within all of SOA's eleven divisions

---

[21] "Guotu ziyuanbu: jigou" [Ministry of Land and Resources: Organizational structure], Ministry of Land and Resources of the People's Republic of China, accessed May 23, 2016, http://www.mlr.gov.cn/bbgk/.

[22] Qu et al., *Beiji wenti yanjiu*, 364.

work on polar matters.[23] SOA's Institute for Marine Development Strategy is important in polar policymaking, as are its First, Second, and Third Institutes of Oceanography. The role of these agencies is to offer scientific advice on polar governance issues, such as recent proposals to set up extensive Marine Protected Areas in the Southern Ocean and China's participation in deep seabed mining. The SOA is also a key agent in formulating and enacting China's overall maritime strategy, and has very close links to the People's Liberation Army-Navy. The SOA's already high status in the Chinese bureaucracy was raised still further in 2013, when it was restructured and given greater powers, including being put in charge of the day-to-day running of the China National Maritime Committee, which coordinates the policies of all government departments with maritime interests. Since 2013, SOA has also been in charge of the Chinese Coast Guard. The Coast Guard acts as a "grey-water" force, operating in place of the PLAN in strategically sensitive coastal and open ocean areas: for instance, it operates in the East China Sea to manage China's maritime borders with Japan.

China's interagency polar policy coordination is managed by the Chinese Advisory Committee for Polar Expeditions (*Zhongguo jidi kaocha zixun weiyuanhui*), known in English as the Chinese Advisory Committee for Polar Research. The committee is led by a vice director of the SOA, and it has cross-agency functions to advise all Chinese government departments with polar interests, advise the Chinese leadership on polar matters, organize scholarly conferences on polar themes, and evaluate China's polar research program and its outcomes. It helps coordinate, but does not decide, China's official polar policy. In the medium term, in order to better protect China's polar interests and ensure that all agencies "sing with one voice" (*changxiang zhuxuanlü*), China will be likely to set up a policymaking body that will consider the interests of all the various government agencies and will have the authority to declare and administer a long-term polar strategy. In the meantime, the current membership of the Chinese Advisory Committee for Polar Research includes the following ministries and government bodies:

- National Development and Reform Commission (*Guotu ziyuan bu*): Focuses on polar resources; approves polar-related planning;
- PLAN, General Staff Operations Department (*Zongcan zuozhanbu haijun ju*): Represents polar military interests; involved in the new polar research vessel project;

---

[23]   Chinese polar official, interview with author, October 2013.

- Ministry of Foreign Affairs (*Waijiao bu*): Advises the committee on international law; represents China at international polar organizations;
- Ministry of Finance (*Caizheng bu*): Sets the polar budget;
- Ministry of Transport (*Jiaotong bu*): Focuses on polar transportation routes;
- Ministry of Education (*Jiaoyu bu*): Represents polar education in the curriculum;
- Ministry of Agriculture (*Nongye bu*): Focuses on polar fishing interests;
- Ministry of Industry and Information Technology (*Gongye he xinxi-huabu*): Concerned with polar icebreaker, BeiDou satellites, polar telecommunication;
- Ministry of Science and Technology (*Kexue jishu bu*): Supports polar research infrastructure, and polar science planning;
- National Health and Family Planning Commission (*Guojia weisheng yu jihua shengyu weiyuanhui*): Focuses on biotech interests, especially krill oil;
- Chinese Academy of Engineering (*Zhongguo gongchengyuan*): Advises on polar technology, especially the polar icebreaker project;
- Chinese Meteorological Administration (*Zhongguo qixiangju*): Advises on climate change and weather forecasting;
- China Earthquake Administration (*Zhongguo dizhen ju*): Engaged in polar seismics and geomagnetic research, important for the "study of mineral resources" and "monitoring the activities of other countries in Antarctica";[24]
- Natural Science Foundation of China (*Guojia ziran kexue jijin weiyuanhui*): Key funder for polar scientific research;
- National Administration of Surveying, Mapping and Geoinformation (*Guojia cehui dili xinxi ju*): Supervises polar mapping;
- Chinese Academy of Science (*Zhongguo kexueyuan*), Resources, Environment, and Technology Division: Represents polar strategic science;
- Chinese Academy of Social Sciences (*Shekeyuan*): Represents polar social sciences;
- SOA Polar Expedition Office / China Arctic and Antarctic Administration (*Jidiban*): Administrative body of the committee.

---

[24] "Nanji dizhen dici guance" [Antarctic seismological and geomagnetic observation], China Earthquake Administration, n.d., accessed January 29, 2015, http://www.csi.ac.cn/manage/eq Down/09JianCeZhi/IGP/06diliuzhang/06.pdf.

The Chinese Advisory Committee for Polar Research secretariat is the SOA's Polar Expedition Office (*Guojia haiyangju jidi kaocha bangongshi*). This organization goes by the English name China Arctic and Antarctic Administration, commonly abbreviated as CAA. The CAA is in charge of setting China's polar activities development strategy, plans, and policies. It applies for polar expedition budgets; manages China's polar bases, domestic facilities, equipment, and vessels; and is in charge of personnel decisions for polar expeditions. It also helps coordinate China's international polar cooperation activities; coordinates domestic agencies' polar activities; researches major issues in polar affairs; and advises the SOA on polar issues, which the SOA then reports to the State Council.[25] The CAA features six division-level offices: the CAA CCP Secretariat, which doubles as the CAA General Office; Policy and Planning; Finance; Technology; International Liaison; and Personnel. The CAA also manages China's polar training base at Yabuli ski area in Heilongjiang, where polar personnel are able to acclimatize to working in polar conditions.[26]

Although the CAA's list of duties may seem impressive, Chinese polar officials chafe at the organization's lack of institutional power and complain that China has no agency equivalent to the US State Department's Office of Ocean and Polar Affairs or the British Antarctic Survey (part of the British government's Natural Environment Research Council) to decide and lead polar policy.[27] However, this complaint reflects a misunderstanding of the complex polar policymaking process of leading polar states such as the United States[28] or even Russia,[29] whose structures are in fact quite fragmented. The CAA is the equivalent of a secretariat, and has only secondary status within the SOA bureaucracy. It has a forty-person staff, fifteen of whom are in leadership positions. Staff numbers have been relatively static for the past ten years. CAA staffers are very clear on the importance of the polar regions to China's future, but without budgetary resources, decision-making authority,

[25] Wu Jun, "Wo guo jidi kaocha zuzhi guanli jizhi youhua yanjiu" [Research on improving China's polar expedition organizational management] (MA thesis, Wuhan University, 2005), 12. Wu Jun is CAA deputy director, and this master's degree was completed while he was in that role.

[26] China National Arctic Research Expedition, accessed September 23, 2013, http://www.chinare .gov.cn/gljg/xljd.htm (link discontinued).

[27] Wu, "Wo guo jidi kaocha zuzhi guanli jizhi youhua yanjiu," 32.

[28] Heather A. Conley, Terry Toland, Mihaela David, and Natalja Jegorova, *The New Foreign Policy Frontier: U.S. Interests and Actors in the Arctic*, CSIS Europe Program Report (Washington, DC: Center for Strategic and International Studies, 2013), 23–27.

[29] See Marlene Laruelle, *Russia's Arctic Strategies and the Future of the Far North* (Armonk, NY: M. E. Sharpe, 2014).

or policy oversight, they say that they can only make suggestions on polar policy.

China produces several polar-related publications and data collections, although most of these are not available to the general public. CAA's International Liaison Division and the PRIC Polar Information Center jointly compile the quarterly *Foreign Polar Expedition News Report* (*Guowai jidi kaocha xinxi huibian*), a classified bulletin of political and scientific trends in global polar affairs. The factual and comprehensive reporting in the bulletin helps to keep Chinese polar policymakers and scientists up-to-date with the latest polar issues. The bulletin's subject areas provide a revealing list of China's strategic interests with regard to other polar states: polar governance news and reports on meetings; discussions on environmental protection, including monitoring plans; information on logistics, expeditions, private expeditions, tourism, and nongovernmental organizations; commentary on polar resource exploration, including the likelihood of various states in engaging in polar resource prospecting in Antarctica; news on commercial fishing in the Southern Ocean; and reports on Arctic Council meetings.

Since 2012, the Polar Special Project Office, based in the CAA, has published a classified, quarterly two-page *Polar Bulletin* (*Jidi jianbao*) that summarizes current scientific, logistical, and strategic information on China's polar affairs. The role of the Polar Special Project Office is to coordinate and supervise the previously mentioned five-year project (2012–16) to assess polar resources, environment, and governance. The outcome of this project is likely to be a formal declaration on China's national strategy and priorities in the polar regions. Researchers involved in the project had to have security clearances to participate.[30] Most of the published reports from scholars participating in this project are secret and not publicly available.[31]

The classified *Polar National Policy Research Report* [sic] (*Jidi guojia zhengce yanjiu baogao*), released to authorized readers in annual volumes from 2012, summarizes some of the findings of this project. The key agencies involved in putting together policy documents based on that research are the CCP Central Committee Policy Research Office, the SOA Maritime Development Strategy Institute, the National Defense University's Strategic Studies Institute, the SOA East Sea Division, Renmin University, China

---

[30] "Guojia jidi ruan kexue xiangmu guanli guiding" [National polar soft science management regulations], SOA, accessed February 12, 2013, http://www.soa.gov.cn/zmhd/zqyj/201211/P020 121128611162510952.doc.

[31] "'Nan Bei ji huanjing zonghe kaocha yu ping'gu' zhuanying lingdao xiaozu chengli" [Special leadership group for polar environment comprehensive investigation and evaluation set up], *Jidi yanjiu jianbao* 1, 1.

University of Political Science and Law, and the CAA. The involvement of the CCP Central Committee's Policy Research Office in the project is a sure indication that a comprehensive strategy for dealing with the polar regions is under way.

China has shared its polar science in forums apart from these restricted-access publications. In 1999, CAA launched the Chinese Polar Science Database System project, a website with information in English and Chinese to promote the outcomes of China's polar science to the rest of the world – an important task, if China is to have a more prominent role in polar affairs. Countries that lead in Antarctic science also take the lead in Antarctic governance, and it was China's investment in Arctic science that gained China an observer seat on the Arctic Council in 2013. The Chinese Polar Science Database System website boasts that it is one of the country's most inclusive and open databases,[32] and indeed there is a remarkable amount of information available on the site. However, China is still not as open as it could be on its Antarctic activities. Although it is a member of the Scientific Committee on Antarctic Research and is required to provide annual reports on its Antarctic activities to this body, from 1983 to 2009 China provided only six reports.[33] CAA began to provide an annual report to SCAR in 2010 – the same year I first published a paper on China and Antarctica that pointed out that the Chinese government was not providing regular reports to SCAR.[34] But even these reports and other official information are still lacking in detail, at least compared with those of other states such as the British Antarctic Survey, the Korean Polar Research Institute, the Australian Antarctic Division, Antarctica New Zealand, and the US National Science Foundation. This is unfortunate, leading many observers to assume that China might have something to hide. China is also required to provide a preseason and end-of-season report to the Antarctic Secretariat, but the reports it has provided have also lacked information. Since 2012, the Council of Managers of National Antarctic Programs has had a project to bring more transparency to Antarctic affairs by asking COMNAP's member states to provide a full, up-to-date report of their Antarctic activities and capabilities. China's COMNAP report is full of ellipses, underestimating China's actual capacity

[32] China National Arctic Research Expedition, "About Us," Chinese National Arctic and Antarctic Database Center, Shanghai, 2007, accessed September 23, 2013, http://www .chinare.org.cn/pages/aboutUs_en.jsp (link discontinued).

[33] Rosemary Nash (SCAR, Scott Polar Research Institute), email correspondence with author, February 20, 2009.

[34] Anne-Marie Brady, "China's Rise in Antarctica?," *Asian Survey* 50, no. 4 (2010): 759–85.

and budgets in Antarctica.[35] China is not the only COMNAP member to provide incomplete information (some have provided no information whatsoever), but at a time when some commentators have expressed negative views of China's increased Antarctic activities,[36] this lack of transparency is damaging to China's reputation. China's lack of transparency on Arctic affairs is also resulting in suspicion and speculation by the international media and policy analysts investigating China's Arctic activities and intentions.

The Polar Research Institute of China (*Jidi yanjiu zhongxin*) in Shanghai is China's premier polar research facility. Shanghai is the logistics base for China's polar expeditions and the home of many of China's leading polar scientists and social scientists. Whereas the CAA's personnel numbers have remained stable for a number of years, the PRIC is expanding rapidly. When the PRIC was established in October 1989, it had twenty staff, only three of whom were scientists. In 1999, it had 143 staff, 66 of whom were scientists.[37] By 2012, the PRIC's personnel numbers had increased to 154 staff, and it advertised for forty-seven more.[38] In 2016, PRIC had approximately 230 full-time staff and thirty master's and doctoral students working on polar-related projects. Within the next five to ten years, PRIC plans to expand to one thousand personnel.[39] The doubling of staff of the past five years and the planned quadrupling of staff in the near future reflects the new level of China's polar engagement, as China moves from being a major polar state to becoming a polar great power.

The PRIC's main tasks are to lead and organize China's research on polar mineral and natural resources and climate change; organize China's polar expeditions; set up and maintain China's polar bases, vessels, airplanes, vehicles, and museums, manage the logistics for the crew and scientific personnel on China's polar expeditions; collect and store China's polar research data, compile reports on China's polar research, and publish

[35] "About the Chinese National Antarctic Program," COMNAP, accessed July 23, 2013, https://www.comnap.aq/Members/CAA/SitePages/Home.aspx.
[36] The following *New York Times* article is representative: Jane Perlez, "China, Pursuing Strategic Interests, Builds Presence in Antarctica," *New York Times*, May 3, 2015, http://nyti.ms/1Jj8GGK.
[37] *Zhongguo jidi yanjiu zhongxin keyan 20 nian 1989–2009* [PRIC: 20 years of research, 1989–2009] (Shanghai: PRIC, 2009), 1.
[38] "2012 Nian Zhongguo jidi yanjiu zhongxin gongkai zhaopin jihua" [PRIC 2012 recruitment plan], Oiegg.com, November 10, 2011, http://www.oiegg.com/viewthread.php?tid=1083149.
[39] Yang Huigen, "Development of China's Polar Linkages," *Canadian Naval Review* 8, no. 3 (Fall 2012), 32, accessed November 17, 2014, http://www.pric.gov.cn/detail/Gg.aspx?id=f2680129-71be-409b-ab07-2e5b186a55d1 (link discontinued).

China's polar scholarly journal.[40] When compared with the list of the CAA's responsibilities given earlier in the chapter, it is evident that many of the CAA's and the PRIC's duties and interests overlap and even clash, which causes some friction and inefficiencies.[41] Their current heads also follow very different leadership styles. The two organizations have a somewhat competitive relationship, and the tension between them is obvious to foreign partners. In a 2013 personal interview, one national Antarctic program leader whose country has long had close cooperation with China complained, "I never know which one to deal with and who makes the final decisions."[42] Both organizations are equal in status in the Chinese bureaucracy and there is no chain of command between them. Moreover, as the CAA is not formally in charge of managing all polar affairs, there is also some overlap between the activities of other SOA agencies working on polar matters, leading to considerable inefficiency and duplication of efforts.[43]

The differences in style and approach between the CAA and the PRIC may also reflect current political differences and tensions between Beijing and Shanghai CCP leaders and the political culture they foster. The Beijing-based CAA and its leaders have a tendency to be more bureaucratic, in word and in deed, whereas the Shanghai-based PRIC, particularly under its current leader Yang Huigen, is strongly science-focused, outward-looking, innovative, and outspoken. CAA focuses more on administrative support for polar affairs, while PRIC is more focused on polar logistics and science.

Both PRIC and CAA staff have argued for a clearer delineation of responsibilities and chain of command for China's polar affairs,[44] and researchers have been studying the polar administrative structures of various leading polar states.[45] The point of these projects is to assess whether the next stage of China's polar engagement will require a new form of organizational arrangement. Structurally, China's polar administration is a mishmash, combining government-led polar administration (similar to the United States, Australia, and New Zealand) and scientific-led polar administration (similar to the United Kingdom). In 2008, Chinese policymakers recommend that China should copy three aspects of other countries' Antarctic administration: (1) set

---

[40] Wu, "Wo guo jidi kaocha zuzhi guanli jizhi youhua yanjiu," 12.

[41] Ibid., 31.

[42] National Antarctic program leader, interview with author, October 2013.

[43] Wu, "Wo guo jidi kaocha zuzhi guanli jizhi youhua yanjiu," 31.

[44] Ling Xiaoliang, Long Wei, Zhang Xia, Zhu Jiangang, Li Shenggui, and Sun Yi'ang, "Guowai Nanji kaocha guanli jigou yu kaocha guanli moshi de duibi fenxi" [Comparison and analysis of foreign Antarctic expedition organizational management], *Haiyang kaifa yu guanli*, no. 3 (2008): 43–46.

[45] Ibid., 50.

up a special research fund for polar research in China's Natural Science Fund, (2) choose either a government-led or a science-led administration for Antarctica (and Arctic) affairs, and (3) clarify the respective roles of various agencies engaged in polar activities to improve agency performance.[46] A change in the bureaucratic structure of China's polar administration would indicate the key strand of China's polar policy: a political/economic approach or a scientific focus. The current bureaucratic arrangements mix both. China plans to streamline its polar bureaucracy during the 13th Five-Year Plan (2016–2020).[47]

The PRIC has large purpose-built office facilities, staff accommodation, a modest polar museum, and laboratories in Pudong, just across the river from central Shanghai. It also has a separate warehouse for polar equipment and a dedicated wharf for polar expeditions a short drive away from the PRIC offices, in Caolu District on the Huangpu River. These facilities will be expanded in the next five years into a polar campus that will house more offices, dormitories, conference facilities, laboratories, and a larger polar museum. The PRIC also has a Representative Office in Santiago, Chile, that coordinates logistics with the Chilean Air Force to supply China's Antarctic expeditions to its Great Wall Station (Changcheng Base) on King George Island. (Most fresh supplies and, nowadays, virtually all of China's Antarctic personnel reach the Great Wall Station (Changcheng) courtesy of the Chilean Air Force, as they have done since the first Chinese Antarctic expedition in 1984.)[48] In 2015, China set up a similar representative office in Hobart, Australia, to make use of the Australian air and sea links to Antarctica to service its three bases in East Antarctica, Zhongshan, Kunlun, and Taishan, and the new base in the Ross Sea region.[49]

In 2009, the PRIC established the Polar Strategy Division, as "the strategic importance of the polar regions is ever-increasing."[50] The division is tasked with "better coordinating polar science with national

---

[46]   Ibid.

[47]   Liu, "Liu Cigui: Kaita jinqu fenyong pinbo cong jidi daguo mai xiang jidi qiangguo."

[48]   "Nanji 'cha qi' jingzheng jilie zhongguo Nanji ke kao 'nuli kuai pao'" [Antarctic states compete to "show the flag," China works hard to catch up], Xinhua, November 12, 2007, htt p://news.xinhuanet.com/world/2007–11/12/content_7056206_1.htm.

[49]   Michelle Paine, "Memorandum of Understanding with China Set to boost State's Antarctic Sector," *Daily Telegraph* (Sydney), September 13, 2013, http://www.dailytelegraph.com.au/n ews/national/memorandum-of-understanding-with-china-set-to-boost-states-antarctic-sector/s tory-fnjj6o1o-1226718429676.

[50]   Zhongguo jidi yanjiu zhongxin ed., *Zhongguo jidi yanjiu zhongxin keyan 20 nian, 1989–2009* [20 years of scientific research at the Polar Research Institute of China, 1989–2009] (Shanghai: PRIC, 2009), 9.

interests."[51] It aims to improve China's polar policy- and law-making and to give advice on major special projects; its small staff also researches polar politics and economics.[52] The division coordinates the Polar Strategic Research Group (*Jidi zhanlüe yanjiuzu*), a pool of several hundred Chinese social scientists and thirty-four research institutes and universities, engaged in strategic research on research topics set by the PRIC. The Polar Strategy Division publishes the *Polar Strategy Research Bulletin* (*Jidi zhanlüe yanjiu tongxun*), a classified print and electronic publication on polar policy issues that analyses current polar strategic issues. The PRIC also publishes the classified journals *Polar Scientific Trends* (*Jidi keji dongtai*) and *Polar Information* (*Jidi xinxi*).

Compared with its international equivalents, the quality of polar policy analysis published under the PRIC's leadership is variable. Despite the large numbers who have been brought into polar social science research since 2012 when the special project to research polar resources, environment, and governance was launched,[53] China has only a few dedicated polar social scientists or humanities specialists, and none who participate in global polar academic debates. Almost all of those who are participating in polar strategic research are specialists in other fields who have been asked to apply their knowledge to polar topics. Much of the research that is being produced is done by graduate and postdoctoral students on behalf of their supervisors, using secondary source material. Some of it simply translates articles that have already been published in English, without attribution or links to the original source – in academia, this normally would be regarded as plagiarism. Common mistakes and misunderstandings about polar governance are repeated over and over again, such as the myth that the Antarctic Treaty ends in either 2041 or 2048, because new researchers are basing their work on the faulty analysis of earlier scholars. Researchers are often limited to using online, open-source materials for much of their research, which is made even more difficult by Internet restrictions imposed by the Chinese government that block Google Scholar and other databases housed outside China. There are no significant library collections of polar social science materials in China; even the National Library of China has only a handful of sources, and the PRIC Reading Room has very limited and mostly outdated social science and even scientific books and other materials on polar studies. Even domestically produced polar research can be hard for others to access. Some open-source policy discussion by China's polar social scientists

---

[51] Ibid., 7.
[52] Ibid.
[53] "Jidi guojia liyi zhanlüe pinggu" [Evaluation of polar states strategic interests], *Jidi zhuanying jianbao* 10 (January 2016), 4.

is collected in the PRIC's online Polar SoftScience Research Platform, intended for other social scientists and those interested in polar research.[54] Some, but by no means all, of the publicly available research in Chinese academic journals on polar issues is by the authors involved in the CAA- and PRIC-led polar strategy projects. However, many of the key authors in the polar strategy projects have released only classified or limited-circulation polar publications. China also lacks a comprehensive course on polar studies to get emerging scientists and policymakers up to speed with the field.

Yet despite the limited research funds, as polar issues gain more attention from the CCP senior leadership and the Chinese media, the number of social scientists in China commenting on polar issues has undoubtedly grown very fast in the last four years. This is a strong indicator of the increasing significance of polar politics in Chinese policy. Chinese scholars tend to congregate into topics where there is high policy interest, so if more individuals and top-tier research institutions are moving into polar studies that is a sure indication of the importance of the topic to central government. In recent years, multiple universities and government research institutions have set up maritime law and policy institutes or centers and employed researchers specializing in polar matters. Participating institutions include Beijing University, Beijing Normal University, Tongji University, Qinghua University, Xiamen University, Shanghai Institute of International Studies, Wuhan University, PLA Military Sciences Academy, and the Ministry of State Security's China Institutes of Contemporary International Relations. China's pool of polar scientists is also expanding. There are polar science education bases in eight cities in China;[55] the prestigious University of Science and Technology in Hefei; the SOA's First, Second, and Third Institutes of Oceanography in Qingdao, Hangzhou, and Xiamen, respectively; the National Center of Ocean Standards and Metrology in Tianjin; Ocean University of China in Qingdao; the Chinese Academy of Sciences; the Chinese Academy of Social Sciences; Wuhan University; and Dalian Maritime University. The Marine Development Strategic Research Institute of the SOA and the PRIC also supervise master's and doctoral students working on polar topics. China currently has an estimated 500 scientific researchers engaged in polar research spread out over a wide range of tertiary institutions and research centers all over the country, but plans to double the number of polar scientists in the next few years.

---

[54] "Zhongguo jidi ruan kexue yanjiu wang" [Polar SoftScience Research Platform], PRIC, accessed May 25, 2016, http://softscience.chinare.org.cn/index/.

[55] Chinese Arctic and Antarctic Administration, *2010 National Annual Report on Polar Program of China* (Beijing, CAA, December 2010), 80–81.

THE ROLE OF THE PEOPLE'S LIBERATION ARMY IN CHINA'S POLAR AFFAIRS

The PLA is a third major actor involved in planning China's future polar strategy, one whose role is disguised by China's polar science program. China's polar officials always emphasize China's scientific interests in the Arctic and Antarctic and avoid discussing China's security- and resource-related interests with foreign audiences. Article I (2) of the Antarctic Treaty states that "military personnel and equipment may be used for scientific research or any other peaceful purpose," and Article VII (5) (c) requires countries to report details of any military personnel or equipment to be introduced into Antarctica. In 1984, during China's first Antarctic expedition, armed PLA naval personnel helped set up China's first Antarctic station, a fact that was not properly acknowledged in China's report to SCAR at the time.[56] In recent years, PLA personnel have repeatedly participated in China's Antarctic program without their presence being noted in China's annual report to the Antarctic Treaty. For example, in the 2013–14 season, China's Antarctic expedition included a PLA logistics expert who was there to set up the BeiDou-2 global positioning system.[57] Yet in China's 2013–14 annual Antarctic Treaty report, the section of the report where a nation active in Antarctica should report any military activity on the continent was removed altogether from the form.[58] In the 2007–8 season, six PLA experts were sent to work on China's Zhongshan Station to help to build a new pier and a high-frequency radar station. Chinese and international reports commented that the new radar station would be capable of blocking the United States' polar satellites – an important military consideration.[59] The PLA's involvement in this activity was widely – and proudly – reported in the Chinese media. However, China also failed to report the presence of these military personnel in its 2007–8 annual Antarctic

---

[56] First Chinese National Antarctic Research Expedition, 1984/1985, Report to SCAR; interview with first expedition member, 2012.

[57] "Di 30 ci nanji kaocha dui cong Aodaliya deng chuan duiyuan mingdan" [30th Antarctic expedition team Australia boarding group list], PRIC, 2013. Wang Guangdong works at the PLA Logistics Department in the Institute of Military Transport, and boarded the *Xue Long* at Fremantle in Australia.

[58] "Antarctic Treaty Electronic Exchange Information: China 2013–2014," Secretariat of the Antarctic Treaty, 2014, http://eies.ats.aq/Ats.IE/ieGenRpt.aspx?idParty=9&period=2&idYear=2014.

[59] "Zhongguo jun fang zai Nanji juemi wuqi chuji, rang huashengdun kongqian chuchou" [China's secret Antarctic weapon attacked, Washington looks foolish], April 7, 2011, accessed May 2, 2015, http://www.fxingw.com/zgjq/2011-04-07/5689.html (link discontinued).

Treaty, leaving that section of the form blank.[60] Polar equipment and support is another venue for Chinese military involvement. China's Arctic and Antarctic expeditions' helicopter support is contracted to Ha Air, a subsidiary of one of China's top ten military companies.[61] China's small fleet of polar amphibian and all-terrain vehicles used in Antarctica were specially designed by PLA engineers. The manufacturers boast that the vehicles are also useful for "airdrop operations, border patrol, forest protection, antiriot security, disaster relief, maritime rescue, and other special operations" – which makes them useful for both peaceful and military applications.[62]

It is a significant breach of the Antarctic Treaty for a signatory state not to report on the presence and activities of military personnel in Antarctica and the presence of equipment associated with military use. However, China's polar officials know that there will be no consequences for this behavior, as even more egregious breaches by other nations are frequently ignored.

CHINA INC. AND THE POLAR REGIONS

In the polar regions, more so than any other region of the world where Chinese interests operate, the PRC government is employing a "China Inc." strategy to achieve its goals. In the Arctic, China is following a comprehensive, multi-pronged attempt to access Arctic resources, which is linked to China's global foreign investment strategy. Similarly, China is now encouraging a broad range of Chinese scientific, commercial, and individual engagement in Antarctica to underline its legitimate interests and rights there. The Chinese government has offered targeted assistance to Chinese commercial interests that wish to expand their businesses into the polar regions, such as providing shipping charts for the Arctic sea route, sponsoring the scientific research that helped a Chinese SOE expand its krill fishing in the Southern Ocean, and

---

60 "Jiefangjun baopo zhuanjia zai Nanji xiujian gao pin leida zhan" [People's Liberation Army explosives expert built high-frequency radar station in Antarctica], Xinhua, April 18, 2008, ht tp://news.qq.com/a/20080418/000875_1.htm; and "Antarctic Treaty Electronic Exchange Information: China 2008," Secretariat of the Antarctic Treaty, 2008, http://eies.ats.aq/Ats.IE/ieGenRpt.aspx?idParty=&period=1&idYear=2008.

61 "Ha hang liang jia zhi jiusi fu Nanji" [Ha Air complete four missions in Antarctica], Sina.com, November 24, 2005, http://mil.news.sina.com.cn/2005-11-14/1502330881.html; and "Ha hang yu changhe chongzu jincheng yinmi" [Secret restructuring process of Ha Air and Changhe], Sina.com, December 31, 2004, http://news.sina.com.cn/c/2004-12-31/07074678410s.shtml.

62 "Jiefangjun Q ban shuilu liangqi quan dixing che jiang zhengzhan Nanji" [The PLA's Amphibian, all-terrain Q-class vehicle will go to Antarctica], China.com, October 12, 2007, http://military.china.com/zh_cn/news/568/20071012/14389013.html.

publicizing information about the rights of Chinese citizens to engage in economic activities in Svalbard. Polar policymakers say that Chinese oil companies "will do their own research" on the economics of whether or not to invest in Arctic oil, but China's polar program is helping with that decision-making process by facilitating scientific research to assess the extent of polar oil and natural gas resources and publicizing business opportunities. The *Xue Long* icebreaker's crossing of the Arctic in 2012 was meant as a flag to Chinese shipping that the Arctic route is now open.[63]

The China Inc. approach is employed for more than purely political reasons. The Chinese government, like many other rising states involved in the polar regions, is seeking economic benefits for its scientific investment. Extreme climate engineering is cutting-edge technology that will have a global market. For example, in 2015, the 32nd Chinese Antarctic expedition took delivery of the first Chinese-made all-terrain vehicle, made by a Chinese-Singaporean company, Guizhou Jonyang Kinetics. The commercial sector can be useful as an additional source of funding for Chinese polar science. There is considerable private involvement in polar affairs already, and Chinese polar officials would like to involve more commercial interests in their work.[64] In 2012, the Sinopec oil-and-gas SOE entered into a five-year agreement with the PRIC to provide subsidized oil to polar expeditions.[65] COSCO, China's international shipping SOE, has provided funding to researchers on the Arctic shipping route. The iron-and-steel SOE Baosteel donated the steel used to renovate China's Zhongshan Antarctic research station in 2002 and to build the inland Antarctic station Kunlun in 2008.[66] In 2013, Futian Auto provided vehicles for polar expedition teams.[67] During China's 2012–13 Antarctic expedition, companies ranging from a tourism organization to Daqing Oil Field Water Engineering participated as members of the expedition.[68] And in 2014, the China Arctic and

[63] Chinese polar official, interview with author, October 2012.

[64] Ibid.; see also Guojia haiyangju haiyang fazhan zhanlue yanjiusuo ketizu, ed., *Zhongguo haiyang fazhan baogao* [Report on China's maritime development] (Beijing: Haiyang chu-banshe, 2012), 374.

[65] "Zhongguo jidi yanjiu zhongxin yu zhongshihua runhua you zhanlüe hezuo" [PRIC's strategic collaboration with Sinopec], *Runhua you zixunwang*, September 25, 2012, http://www.eworldship.com/html/2012/Manufacturer_0925/59195.html.

[66] "Baogang yuan jian wo Nanji shou ge nei lu ke kao zhan" [Baosteel helped build China's first inland Antarctic station], *Renmin ribao*, October 18, 2008, http://scitech.people.com.cn/GB/8193240.html.

[67] "Futian qiche zhuli Zhongguo di 30 ci Nanji ke kao chuzheng yishi qidong" [Futian Car Company's support for 30th Antarctic expedition kicks off], Sina.com, October 31, 2013, http://auto.sina.com.cn/news/2013-10-31/09491242024.shtml.

[68] "Zhongguo di 29 ci Nanji kexue kaocha" [China's 29th Antarctic expedition], PRIC, November 12, 2015, http://www.polar.gov.cn/expeditionDetail/?id=759.

Antarctic Administration was sponsored by at least twenty-seven companies, which provided products such as heavy trucks, wrist watches, beer, sport utility vehicles, dairy food, cleaning products, nutritional pills, and cold-weather clothing.

For Chinese companies and SOEs, close relations with the SOA and its subsidiaries can be very lucrative, since they are now so rich in funds for new equipment. Laurel Industrial, whose sister company Laurel Films produced the movie *Antarctica 2049* (see chapter 2), has been extremely successful in bidding for contracts from the SOA and the PRIC to provide marine geophysical equipment such as bathometers. Laurel Industrial in turn has provided generous marine geology scholarships and subsidized marine exploration conferences in China.[69] Chinese SOEs are also piggybacking on the Chinese government's plans to strengthen relations with polar states to seize commercial opportunities in the Arctic and Antarctic. In 2015, Chinese defense industry SOE China Import and Export Electronics Corporation was granted the contract to rebuild Brazil's Antarctic base, which had burned down in 2012 – outbidding both a Finnish and a Brazilian-Chilean consortium. The deal was announced just as Chinese premier Li Keqiang visited Brazil, where he signed thirty-five agreements and contracts totaling US$53 million.[70]

Recently, the Chinese nuclear industry has been bidding for China to use nuclear power to fuel its Antarctic bases, as well as for deep sea drilling and for a new polar icebreaker.[71] Like most polar science programs, China spends the bulk of its logistics budget on fuel, and using nuclear power in its Antarctic bases and for its polar vessels would ease its fuel supply problem. The type of fuel system used by China's polar vessels became a hot topic of debate in China in 2014, after the Chinese icebreaker *Xue Long* briefly became trapped in Antarctic sea ice while rescuing the *Akademik Shokalskiy*. Social media and traditional media sources in China were highly critical of China's polar icebreaking capacities, comparing them unfavorably with Russia's six nuclear

---

[69] "Laolei gongsi gei Zhongguo haiyang daxue 180 wang yuan" [Laurel Industries gives China Oceanic University RMB 180,000], Ocean University of China, October 24, 2014, http://211.64 .142.38/xiaoqing/70/69/c5797a28777/page.psp.

[70] "La empresa china CEIEC construirá la nueva base científica de Brasil en la Antártida" [Chinese company CIEEC will build the new Brazilian scientific base in Antarctica], *Sputnik Mundo*, May 21, 2015, http://sptnkne.ws/ncd.

[71] Zhongguo chuanbo zhonggong jituan gongsi di qiyijiu yanjiu suo [China Shipbuilding Corporation 719 Institute], "Xiaoxing fanyingdui zai chuanbo haiyang gongcheng lingyu de yingyong" [The use of small reactors offshore] (PowerPoint presentation, October 2013), http://www.imp.cas.cn/xshy/fydhy/hybg/201310/P020131025602941443921.ppt.

ice breakers.[72] That same year the China National Nuclear Corporation (CNNC) and other military industry groups pitched a development plan for the SOA to invest in a nuclear-powered polar icebreaker.[73] CNNC is a state-owned enterprise that oversees all aspects of China's civil and military nuclear program. If CNNC built a polar nuclear icebreaker for the SOA, it could be the prototype for PLAN nuclear-powered icebreakers in future. The PLAN currently has four diesel-powered icebreakers for port operations. A SOA nuclear icebreaker could be used for polar science expeditions and to support Chinese shipping in the Arctic. Chinese media reporting on the plans for SOA's new polar science vessel pointed out that nuclear icebreakers also could help rescue nuclear-powered submarines trapped by Arctic ice.[74]

Russia uses nuclear icebreakers in the Arctic, and there are no current prohibitions on the use of nuclear icebreakers there. Article V of the Antarctic Treaty prohibits nuclear explosions and the disposal of nuclear waste in Antarctica, but has nothing to say on the use of a nuclear icebreaker in Antarctic waters or use of nuclear power on Antarctic bases. Nonetheless, if China or any other state used a nuclear icebreaker in Antarctic waters, it would be sure to provoke massive controversy among those concerned with preserving the Antarctic environment. New Zealand is a nuclear-free zone and bans all nuclear activities,[75] so nuclear icebreakers are forbidden from accessing New Zealand's ports – and New Zealand has the closest port to China's planned new base in the Ross Sea. Developing a nuclear icebreaker for operations in the Arctic would be a sign that China's ambitions there were reaching a whole new level. So for now, due to "political, social, and environmental" considerations, China will not build a polar nuclear icebreaker. The new polar research vessel will instead utilize environmentally friendly electric power.[76]

72   Du Wenlong, statement to *Global Times*, cited in "Zhuanjia cheng zhongguo jiang shiyong he dongli chuan jinxing jidi yanjiu" [Experts say China will get a nuclear polar icebreaker], *Huanqiu ribao*, February 21, 2013, http://www.cjdby.net/redianzhuizong/2013–02-21/military-28 29.html; and "Zhongguo xinxing (hedongli) jidi kaifa tichu chubu pobingchuan" [China's new (nuclear-powered) polar icebreaker preliminary development plan], *Nanhai yanjiu luntan*, March 17, 2014, http://www.nhjd.net/thread-13458–1-1.html.

73   "Zhongguo xinxing (hedongli) jidi kaifa tichu chubu pobingchuan" [China's new (nuclear-powered) polar icebreaker preliminary development plan], *Nanhai yanjiu luntan*, March 17, 2014, http://www.nhjd.net/thread-13458–1-1.html.

74   "Zhongguo xin pobingchuan jiang zai jinnian kai jian" [Construction on China's new icebreaker will begin this year], January 7, 2014, *Keji ribao*, http://news.kedo.gov.cn/hqsy/zxb d/377223.shtml.

75   See the terms of the 1987 New Zealand Nuclear Free Zone, Disarmament, and Arms Control Act.

76   "Jiangnan zaochuan zong gongchengshi hu ke yi: He dongli huo wei jidi ke kao chuan yi zhong xuanze" [Jiangnan Shipyard Chief Engineer Hu Keyi: Nuclear power could be one

A similarly tactful decision has been made about the proposal to utilize nuclear power at China's Antarctic bases. In the 1960s and early 1970s, the United States had a nuclear power plant at McMurdo Station in the Ross Sea area, but in 1972 it was forced to remove the plant as it leaked fuel and required a major effort to decontaminate the site. Whatever the financial benefits for China (or any state) in setting up a nuclear plant in Antarctica, international public opinion is likely to be opposed to the idea. Thus, despite industry pressure, the PRIC's current preference to solve the fuel problem in Antarctica is to increasingly use renewable energy such as wind and solar energy to power China's Antarctic bases.[77]

There has been a lot of international interest and media coverage of China's economic interests in the Arctic and Antarctic; however, relative to the government's strategic agenda, China's major companies have been slow to take up the opportunities available to them in the polar regions and are still relatively weak in polar capacity.[78] But with such high-level official support, it can only be a matter of time before Chinese companies expand their operations in the Arctic and Antarctica on a big scale, just as they have into other strategic areas of the world identified by the Chinese government.

option for the polar research vessel], *Zhongguo chuanbo bao*, March 5, 2014, http://www.cssc .net.cn/component_news/news_detail.php?id=16613.

[77] "Zhongguo dianli qiye lianhe xiehui: Weilai zai Nanji ruhe shiyong nengyuan" [China Electric Power Association: the future use of energy in the Antarctic], *Beijixing xinwen zhongxin*, May 9, 2013, http://news.bjx.com.cn/html/20130509/433477.shtml.

[78] Ding, *Jidi guojia zhengce yanjiu baogao 2013–2014*, 175.

5

Evaluating China as a Polar Power

China claims to be close to reaching the status of a polar great power. To be considered a polar great power, a state must have a significant presence in the polar regions; high levels of polar scientific capacity and scientific research funding; significant polar economic, military, political, and diplomatic capacity; and a high level of participation in international governance relating to the polar regions. Some of the indicators for power in polar affairs are distinctive to the terms in which states may legally operate in the Arctic or Antarctic. In Antarctica, a signatory state to the Antarctic Treaty may only legally engage in science; fishing, tourism, and other non-minerals-related economic activities; exploration; bioprospecting; and governance. Signatory states have the right to operate in any area of the Antarctic continent and ocean and to set up semipermanent camps and permanent research stations there. But in the Arctic – where there are eight sovereign states, international waters, and multiple non-Arctic states that have an interest in the region – the measures of power and rights of access are more complex. States may engage in the Arctic region as members or observers of the multiple governance bodies that manage Arctic affairs; they have the right to set up a scientific program in the Arctic Ocean, they may be able to negotiate further access for their scientists to the region through bilateral arrangements, and their vessels are entitled to innocent passage in international Arctic waters. The citizens of a non-Arctic state may also be active in the region as investors, tourists, or residents. All of these levels of engagement have to be factored into a consideration of whether a state has "power" in Arctic affairs.

China's polar scientific capacity is a key marker for evaluating China's capacity as a polar great power. The question of which states have polar power is a topic of great interest to China as it seeks to achieve its national goals and maintain its interests in the polar regions. The China Arctic and Antarctic Administration has sponsored a number of research projects evaluating the relative strengths and interests of various polar states that, when combined with other sources, are useful in assessing China's own comparative strength.

EVALUATING CHINA'S SCIENTIFIC PRESENCE IN THE POLAR REGIONS

Since the questions of Antarctic and Arctic Ocean sovereignty, sovereign rights, and resource rights are currently unresolved, many states are jostling to have their interests represented there. A state could construct a case to argue for sovereignty rights in an area where sovereignty is not determined by discovery, by naming geographical sites and mapping, and by continual presence and occupation. In lieu of actually acquiring sovereignty, interested states can protect their rights to have a say in new norm-setting and to secure a share in any spoils from these contested regions by having identified, legitimate interests in the disputed region. Scientific activities are one of the main means by which all states, regardless of their geography, may legitimately engage in Antarctic or Arctic affairs and establish a presence there – which helps explain why so many countries have set up bases in Antarctica and on Norway's Svalbard Island. China reserves the right to make a claim in Antarctica[1] and wants access to Antarctic resources, it wants to take advantage of whatever rights it can garner in the Arctic, and it wants to enhance its right to speak on polar affairs more broadly – all of which it can do by expanding its scientific presence in the polar regions.

In less than ten years, China has gone from being a minor player in the polar regions to becoming a major actor. Although China's annual polar operations budget places it as only a medium polar power, it now has more money than any other polar state to spend on new infrastructure such as bases, planes, and icebreakers. In the past ten years, China has doubled its number of bases in Antarctica (see figure 5.1) and circumnavigated the continent twice, and it has dispatched eight expeditions to the Arctic and set up new bases there. Chinese-language materials clearly express the logic for this rapid expansion. For instance, a 2012 *Polar Strategic Research Trends* report stated:

> In preparation for the future contention over Antarctic resources and sovereignty, China must increase its substantive presence in Antarctica so as to establish the necessary physical foundations for China's Antarctic rights, Antarctic governance rights, and the future opening up of resources.[2]

[1] Yan Qide and Zhu Jiangang, *Nanjizhou lingtu zhuquan yu ziyuan quanshu wenti yanjiu* [Research on the issue of Antarctic sovereignty and resources] (Shanghai kexue jishu chubanshe, 2009), 31.

[2] "Zhongguo zai Nanji guojia liyi qianxi" [Analysis of China's national interests in Antarctica], *Jidi zhanlue yanjiu dongtai* 1 (2012): 16.

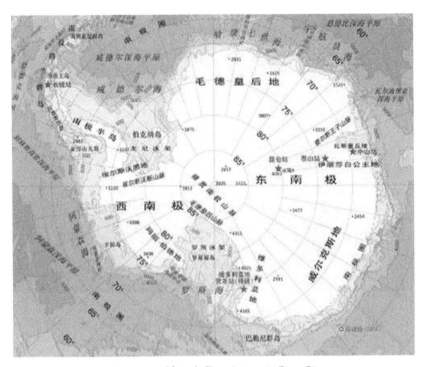

FIGURE 5.1 China's Five Antarctic Base Sites
Source: "Woguo Nanji ke kao jiang xingcheng wangluo xing liti kaocha geju" [Our Antarctic expedition will study the formation of network-based three-dimensional pattern], *Haiyang bao*, February 12, 2014, accessed May 22, 2015, http://www.soa .gov.cn/xw/hyyw_90/201402/t20140212_30492.html.

According to CAA deputy director Wu Jun, science, scientific expeditions, and scientific bases are the main means by which China has expanded its presence in the polar regions; these activities demonstrate China's legitimate interests in polar affairs. As Wu said, "they will be the means to open up resource exploitation in the polar regions in future."[3] Expanding China's polar presence was a core element of the guiding strategy (*zhidao sixiang*) of China's

---

[3] Wu Jun, "Wo guo jidi kaocha zuzhi guanli jizhi youhua yanjiu" [Research on improving China's polar expedition organizational management] (master's thesis, Wuhan University, 2005), 34. See also similar comments that Wu made in an October 2009 interview, "Guojia Haiyang ju jidi ban jieshao geguo Nanji kaocha huodong jinzhan" [SOA CAA reports on various states' Antarctic expeditions], *Xinhuashe*, October 15, 2009, http://env.people.com.cn /GB/10197601.html; and similar points made in a 2012 report, Guojia haiyangju haiyang fazhan zhanlue yanjiusuo ketizu, ed., *Zhongguo haiyang fazhan baogao* [Report on China's maritime development] (Beijing: Haiyang chubanshe, 2012), 363.

FIGURE 5.2 Great Wall Station
Source: "About the Chinese National Antarctic Program," COMNAP,
accessed July 23, 2013, https://comnap.aq/Members/CAA/SitePages/Home.aspx.

12th Five-Year Plan (2011–2015), where it related to the polar regions,[4] and it is important in the current Five-Year Plan (2016–2020). Thus, for interested observers of China's polar affairs, an assessment of China's current polar science capacity is important for evaluating how close it is to achieving the goal of becoming a polar great power and for establishing where its strategic priorities lie.

Antarctic Research Stations

China's first Antarctic base, the Great Wall Station (*Changcheng zhan*), was established on King George Island in western Antarctica in 1984 (figure 5.2). This station is at 62°S latitude, outside the Antarctic Circle. At the time of setting up the base, China did not have the technical capabilities to build on the Antarctic continent itself. The base can house up to fifty people in the summer and twenty in the winter.[5] However, in recent years its scientific

---

[4] Guojia haiyangju haiyang fazhan zhanlue yanjiusuo ketizu, *Zhongguo haiyang fazhan bao-gao*, 371.
[5] Wu, "Wo guo jidi kaocha zuzhi guanli jizhi youhua yanjiu," 47.

activities have been scaled down considerably.[6] In the 2012–13 season, only twenty-four scientists went to work at the base in the summer season and three were left behind to winter over.[7] In the 2013–14 season, twenty-two scientists were there in the summer, while three wintered over.[8] China is now making Great Wall Station beds available to other partner states. Since 2013, China has offered two slots for Thai scientists to enable Thailand to develop experience in Antarctica before it joins the Antarctic Treaty.

Great Wall Station is near to the Antarctic bases of eight other countries, and compared to China's other Antarctic bases it is relatively easy to get to. It is also in the part of Antarctica where the majority of Antarctic tourists visit and is now increasingly being visited by Chinese tourists as part of their Antarctic voyages. So although the base continues to have a modest scientific program, more than any other of China's Antarctic research stations, Great Wall Station is effectively taking on the role of a diplomatic outpost. In 2014, reflecting this changed status, as part of "cultural construction" (*wenhua jianshe*) at the base, a large collection of Chinese cultural artifacts were donated to showcase Chinese culture to visiting foreign dignitaries and tourists.[9] Notably, a large bell from Hanshan Temple in Suzhou was installed as a symbol of "the Chinese tradition of harmony."[10] Great Wall Station is also used to host China's Antarctic arts program, which brings out Chinese artists and writers to experience Antarctica. Many other Antarctic states also have such programs, which create and nurture a national Antarctic culture and add legitimacy to a state's activities there.

China's second base, Zhongshan Station (*Zhongshan zhan*), was set up in 1989 in eastern Antarctica (figure 5.3), close to the Russian base Progress II. Zhongshan is named after the Chinese revolutionary and first president of the Republic of China, Sun Zhongshan (more commonly known by the Cantonese pronunciation of his name, Sun Yat-sen). In the summer, this

6   Chinese Advisory Committee for Polar Research, *Report of 21st Chinese National Antarctic Research Expedition, 2004–05* (Beijing: Chinese Advisory Committee for Polar Research, 2005).

7   *Annual Report to SCAR: China, 2012–13*, Scientific Committee on Antarctic Research (archived website), 2013, http://www.webarchive.org.uk/wayback/archive/20140320231414/http://www.scar.org/about/nationalreports/china/China_2012-13.pdf.

8   *Annual Report to SCAR: China, 2013–14*, Scientific Committee on Antarctic Research, 2014, http://www.scar.org/scar_media/documents/aboutscar/nationalreports/China_2013-14.pdf.

9   "Nanji Changcheng ke kao zhan jinxing wenhua jianshe suzhou cixiu deng ruxuan" [Suzhou embroidery selected for cultural construction at Antarctic Great Wall Station], *Suzhou ribao*, January 26, 2014, http://www.chinanews.com/cul/2014/01-26/5782459.shtml.

10 "Suzhou han shansi 'he zhong' li shang Nanji jinian liang de teshu kekao qingyuan" [Suzhou Temple "peace bell" to commemorate special Antarctic connection], js.people.cn, March 6, 2014, http://www.jspeople.com/html/2014/03/06/293405.html.

FIGURE 5.3 Zhongshan Station
Source: "About the Chinese National Antarctic Program," COMNAP.

base can house up to sixty personnel; in winter, it can support twenty-five.[11] However, in the 2012–13 season, it hosted only seven scientists in the summer and seven in the winter,[12] and in the 2013–14 season, it hosted only three scientists in the summer and seven in the winter.[13] During the 11th Five-Year Plan (2006–2010), Zhongshan Station was upgraded and fitted with new research facilities and living quarters, doubling in size from its original 2700 square meters to 5800 square meters. Increasing the base footprint is one way in which China has demonstrated its presence and status in Antarctic affairs. In 2014, an ice airfield was built at Zhongshan.

China's third Antarctic base, Kunlun Station (*Kunlun zhan*) on Dome Argus (commonly known as Dome A), was officially opened in February 2009 (figure 5.4). According to Chinese analysis, Antarctica has four scientifically and politically strategic sites: the Terrestrial South Pole, the South Magnetic Pole, the coldest location at Dome Circe (commonly known as Dome C), and the highest ice feature at Dome A. Significantly, as Chinese researchers point out, each site is now "occupied" or "held" (*zhanju*)[14] by four of the world's nuclear powers – the United States, Russia, France, and China – which have established permanent research stations on the sites. All four states have significant space and missile programs that require polar satellites and polar receiving stations. During the 1956–57 International Geophysical Year,

---

[11] Wu, "Wo guo jidi kaocha zuzhi guanli jizhi youhua yanjiu," 47.
[12] *Annual Report to SCAR: China, 2012–13.*
[13] *Annual Report to SCAR: China, 2013–14.*
[14] "Wei Wenliang: Jidi rensheng" [Wei Wenliang: Polar life], *Wen huibao*, January 29, 2014, h ttp://whb.news365.com.cn/jjl/201401/t20140129_918528.html. Until 2014, Wei was the PRIC's party secretary and captain of the *Xue Long*.

FIGURE 5.4 Kunlun Station
Source: "About the Chinese National Antarctic Program," COMNAP.

the United States insisted on the right to occupy the Terrestrial South Pole and set up the Scott-Amundsen South Pole Station there. In the same year, the Soviet Union occupied the South Magnetic Pole and set up Vostok Station. In 1992, France set up a summer camp at Dome C, and in 2005 it established the all-season Concordia Station. In January 2008, Chinese scientists succeeded in reaching Dome A after six attempts. Initially, they set up only a weather station and a satellite antenna there.[15] Dome A, like all the elevated sites in Antarctica, is a strategically important site for an airfield. It is useful from the point of view of alternative flight paths to avoid chokepoints; furthermore, unlike coastal airfields located on ice floes such as Williams Field at the United States' McMurdo Station, it will not be affected by melting ice.

Kunlun Station has a floor space of 500 square meters, and it can accommodate fifteen to twenty personnel. But it has hardly had any use since it was opened and at present, should be understood as an empty fort (*kongcheng ji*)

---

[15]   "Liu Xiaohan: Zhongguo qiangzhan Nanji zuigao dian ling meiguo shi liao wei ji" [Liu Xiaohan: China seizing the highest point in Antarctica took the United States by surprise], *Sohu*, January 8, 2009, http://news.sohu.com/20090108/n261650601.shtml; and "Hu Jianmin: Wei Nanji Geluofu shan huizhi shou zhang dizhi tu" [Hu Jianmin: First map of the Grove Mountains is completed], *Dili tongxun*, January 23, 2009, http://news.dili360.com/dlsk/dlzh/2009/01237614.shtml.

meant to advertise China's polar strength and occupy the site so no other nation can take control of it. In the Chinese classic essay the *Thirty-Six Stratagems* (*Sanshiliu ji*), an empty fort is a strategy used to deceive an enemy into retreat. During the 2012–13 season, nine scientists and seventeen support personnel worked at Kunlun Station.[16] However, in the 2013–14 season, no traverse was organized to Dome A and Kunlun Station remained empty. At present, the base is able to house scientists for only two weeks a year, as it takes one month via traverse between Zhongshan and Kunlun stations. A 600-meter landing strip was built at Kunlun in 2010 and hundreds of barrels of aviation fuel are stored there.[17] In early 2016, the first return flight from Zhongshan to Kunlun was made by China's new polar plane.[18] Chinese scientists will now be able to get to Kunlun from Zhongshan in four hours. These improved logistics will enable China to expand Kunlun from a summer base to an all-seasons station before 2020.[19] As a research station, Kunlun can be used for deep ice core drilling, glaciology, astronomy, atmospheric science, weather observation, and geological study of the Gamburtsev mountain range that lies beneath the ice cap.

China's fourth Antarctic base, Taishan (*Taishan zhan*), is inland from Zhongshan Station (see figure 5.5) at a crossroad point en route to Kunlun Station and the Grove Mountains, where China has a field camp. The base was set up in the summer of 2014. Taishan is China's third base on the Australian claim, which is the largest Antarctic sovereignty claim, comprising 42 percent of the continent. The base helps consolidate China's presence in eastern Antarctica, particularly its ability to operate in the Antarctic hinterland – something that the region's claimant state, Australia, currently is unable to do.

Taishan Station was constructed over a forty-five-day period by a twenty-eight-member team in the 2013–14 season. It is a summer-only station, located on the East Antarctic ice sheet about 520 kilometers from Zhongshan, 715 kilometers

[16] *Annual Report to SCAR: China, 2011–12*, Scientific Committee on Antarctic Research (archived website), 2012, http://www.webarchive.org.uk/wayback/archive/20140320231436/http://www.scar.org/about/nationalreports/china/China_2011-12.pdf.

[17] "Woguo zai Nanji nei lu bing gai xinjian fei ying jichang" [Our new Antarctic hinterland "Eagle Airport"], Xinhua, February 2, 2010, http://news.xinhuanet.com/tech/2010-02/02/content_12914702.htm.

[18] "Shou jia jidi feiji chuanyue Nanji zuigao qu" [First polar aircraft crosses Antarctica's highest area], *Beijing Ribao*, January 11, 2016, http://bjrb.bjd.com.cn/html/2016-01/11/content_344150.htm.

[19] Yang Huigen, "The Poles and China: Dimensional Development of Linkage through IPY 2007–2008" (presentation at International Polar Year [IPY] 2012 Conference, April 22–27, 2012, Montreal, Canada).

FIGURE 5.5 Taishan Station
Source: "Steel Structure Building of Taishan Station Finished," CNTV,
January 14, 2014, http://www.china.org.cn/video/2014-01/14/content_31187136.htm.

from Kunlun, and 85 kilometers from China's campsites in the Grove
Mountains. The station has a total area of 1,000 square meters, and can house
a maximum of twenty personnel. Station scientific projects will focus on geology,
glaciology, mapping, atmospherics (weather), geomagnetics, and satellite remote
sensing. Its location facilitates access to Kunlun, the Grove Mountains, and the
Amery Ice Shelf area. A 2013 internal report commenting on the significance of
the new base highlighted the strategic significance of the region surrounding the
base for the future "development and utilization of Antarctic resources."[20]
The distinctive, lantern-shaped design of the Taishan base indicates that China
wants its base and activities in Antarctica to be noticed. CAA director Qu
Tanzhou has said that Taishan "will be open to research by any country."[21]
A key asset of the new base is an ice runway, which became operational at the
end of the 2015–16 season.

   In 2007, a team of Chinese geographers mapped the Grove Mountains,
identifying the distribution of mineral resources in the area.[22] China's field
camp in the Grove Mountains has been in continuous use since 2007, so the
mountains are a further site of continual occupation to which China could

[20] "Di 11 ci nei lu kaocha dui (2012~2013 nian)" [11th inland expedition (2012–13)], PRIC,
       November 12, 2015, http://www.polar.gov.cn/expeditionDetail/?id=755.
[21] Jane Qiu, "China to Break Ground on Antarctic Base," *Science*, December 24, 2013, http://
       news.sciencemag.org/asia/2013/12/china-break-ground-antarctic-base.
[22] "Hu Jianmin: Wei Nanji Geluofu shan huizhi shou zhang dizhi tu."

claim property and access rights to. In the 2013–14 season, six scientists were based there during the austral summer.[23]

China's fifth Antarctic research station, which has the working name of "Victoria Land Permanent Base" (*Weiduoliyadi changnian zhan*), is in the strategically important Ross Sea region where the United States, New Zealand, South Korea, Germany, and France also have research stations. This new research station will significantly consolidate China's Antarctic interests and help bring China to its goal of becoming a polar great power.

China announced that it was going to set up a fifth base in Antarctica in January 2013, after a team of scientists and technicians spent a mere eight days inspecting the Ross Sea area for a suitable site.[24] By contrast, the South Korean Antarctic mission took more than five years to establish the location of the base it constructed in the same region.[25] The site China chose, Inexpressible Island, in Terra Nova Bay, was one on the list of seven possible new base sites in New Zealand's Antarctic claim area that the New Zealand government had handed to China back in 1984, in the hope of getting the Chinese authorities to recognize New Zealand's territorial rights in the Ross Dependency. In 2013, CAA head Qu Tanzhou told journalists that the new base site had been selected because the Ross Sea area will be "one of the hottest locations in Antarctica" in the future.[26] Senior polar glaciologist Sun Bo stated that the new base was located close to areas of "resource potential,"[27] and the Polar Research Institute of China's internal newspaper stated that "resource exploration and climactic studies" would be the main tasks of the base.[28]

Unlike Taishan, which is a summer-only station, China's fifth base will be a permanent one (see figure 5.6). As a result, China was required to submit a Comprehensive Environment Evaluation (CEE) report to the Antarctic Treaty's Committee for Environmental Protection, and receive and respond to the feedback of other Antarctic states with a final CEE to be issued sixty days

[23]   *Annual Report to SCAR: China, 2013–14.*

[24]   "Yongshi di ba tian ba ye: cehui duiyuan xinjian Nanji ke kao zhan xuan zhi ji" [Warriors 8 days and 8 nights: Mapping team reminisce on siting the new Antarctic station], Central People's Government of the People's Republic of China, March 1, 2013, http://www.gov.cn/gzdt/2013-03/01/content_2343061.htm.

[25]   "Jang Bogo Station," Korea Polar Research Institute, n.d., http://eng.kopri.re.kr/home_e/contents/e_3310000/view.cms.

[26]   "Zhongguo jihua 'shi'erwu' xinjian yizhi liang ge Nanji kaocha zhan" [China plans one to two new bases in second five year plan], Xinhua, January 8, 2013, accessed January 8, 2013, http://news.hbtv.com.cn/2013/0108/185695.shtml (link discontinued).

[27]   "Nanji nei lu kaocha kaizhan xuanze xin zhan zhi gongzuo" [Inland Antarctic expedition undertakes to select a new station site], *Zhongguo haiyangbao*, December 31, 2012, http://www.soa.gov.cn/xw/dfdwdt/jsdw_157/201212/t20121231_23478.html.

[28]   *Jidi zhongxin bao*, February 5, 2013, 3.

FIGURE 5.6 Artist's Impression of China's Fifth Antarctic Base
Source: "Zhongyang meishu xueyuan qianyue Nanji di kaocha zhan gainian sheji"
[Central Academy of Fine Arts signs on to Antarctic station conceptual design],
Vision Union, November 12, 2013, http://www.visionunion.com/article.jsp?
code=201311120021.

before it began work on the new base. China's draft CEE for the new base was
published in January 2014. The draft CEE did not mention China's interest in
exploring minerals or other resources in the Ross Sea area; instead, it highlighted climate change research, space science, and remote sensing as key
projects.[29] In breach of Antarctic regulations, in January 2015 the *Xue Long*
icebreaker traveled to the site of the new base and staff began preparations for
it, including depositing ten tons of material, setting up prefabricated accommodation, and building a temporary wharf.[30] There was no public response
from other Antarctic nations regarding China's breach of protocol.

The site identified for the new base is a windy spot, infamous for katabatic
winds. Many New Zealand Antarctic specialists familiar with the area had told

[29] Polar Research Institute of China and Tongji University, "Proposed Construction and Operation
of a New Chinese Research Station, Victoria Land, Antarctica: Draft Comprehensive
Environmental Evaluation," CAA, January 10, 2014, accessed January 31, 2014, http://www
.chinare.gov.cn/en/download/DRAFT_CEE2014.pdf.

[30] "Wo guo kaishi zai Nanji Weiduoliya di jichu choubei di wu ge kaocha zhan" [China begins
preparatory surveying for the 5th Antarctic Base in Victoria Land], *Renminwang*, January 6,
2015, http://scitech.people.com.cn/n/2015/0106/c1007-26334885.html; and Chinese polar official, interview with author, February 2015.

Chinese polar officials that it would be a difficult location in which to build and operate a scientific program. One senior Chinese polar official with whom I raised this point in 2015 dismissed such concerns, saying "the wind doesn't blow there every day." In January 2016, the *Xue Long* returned to the planned base area and an eight-man team of scientists set up an automatic weather station at the base site and engaged in further site surveying.[31] Soon after this expedition ended, Chinese polar officials quietly announced to Antarctica New Zealand and other agencies that China was rethinking the location of the new base. In February 2017 Chinese scientists conducted further surveys and mapping at Inexpressible Island. Multiple reports have now confirmed it as the preferred site for the new base.

The delay in finalizing the base site was due to three factors: a new leadership team at the State Oceanic Administration which wanted to review China's polar plans and priorities; the need to deal with objections raised by US and New Zealand in the first CEE that the base was not necessary from a scientific point of view; and an assessment of scientific priorities for the new base. Funding has been approved for the new base and it will be built within the next five years.

The design for China's Ross Sea base has already been released. It will be a building of around 5,500 square meters, which will make it China's largest Antarctic research station. It is 1000 square meters bigger than South Korea's new Jang Bogo research station in Terra Nova Bay, but it is considerably smaller than the United States' nearby McMurdo Station, which has eighty-five different buildings and can house up to 1500 personnel. China's newest base will accommodate up to eighty people in the summer and thirty people during the winter. The landmark red-and-white buildings have been designed by a team of experts from the Chinese Academy of Fine Arts, Tongji University's Institute of Environmental Science and Engineering, Baosteel Group, and China Shipbuilding.[32]

The Ross Sea base will greatly expand China's international research links with more-established Antarctic research programs in the vicinity – such as those of New Zealand, Italy, South Korea, and the United States – which will help China make a stronger contribution to Antarctic science. China plans to set up an airfield there to link up with its other bases in Antarctica. China could even take

---

[31] "Zhongguo di wu ge Nanji kaocha zhan xuan zhi queding: Renlei hanghai jixian" [China's fifth Antarctic site identification at the edge of the ocean], *Guangming ribao*, February 18, 2016, http://tech.huanqiu.com/news/2016-02/8564120.html.

[32] "Zhongyang meishu xueyuan qianyue Nanji di kaocha zhan gainian sheji" [Central Academy of Fine Arts signs on to Antarctic station conceptual design], *Vision Union*, November 12, 2013, http://www.visionunion.com/article.jsp?code=201311120021.

advantage of the US–New Zealand–Italian–South Korean air and sea logistics pool for transporting scientists and equipment to Antarctica. By sharing its infrastructure, China could greatly enhance others' logistical capabilities as well as its own. In the 2012–13 season, for example, the US McMurdo ice airfield could not operate at capacity because the ice was melting too quickly. China's state-of-the-art logistics capacity will also be a welcome addition to search-and-rescue efforts in the Ross Sea area, which are coordinated by New Zealand.

China now has two all-season research stations (with another to be built in 2015–17), two summer stations, and one permanent camp in Antarctica. China's three most recent bases are all in areas of Antarctica that it has identified as strategically important and rich in resources. The Chinese National Development and Reform Commission document authorizing the budget for the expanding presence in Antarctica emphasized that doing so will enhance China's "political, economic, diplomatic, and military" interests on the southernmost continent.[33]

Arctic Research Stations

China has two permanent research stations in the Arctic, as well as temporary ice stations and a satellite ground receiving station. All have been developed in the past ten years. In 2004, China set up its first Arctic research site, Yellow River Station (*Beiji Huanghe zhan*), at Ny-Ålesund, Norway, where many other non-Arctic states also have established Arctic research stations (see figure 5.7). In Chinese tradition, the Yellow River is understood as the source of the Chinese nation, so the choice of the Arctic base name has particular significance.[34] China's Yellow River Station building is rented from Norway's Royal Company and was originally a dormitory for company workers. The Yellow River Station has laboratories, offices, a reading lounge, and dormitory facilities for thirty-seven personnel in the summer and four in the winter. The base also houses the world's largest space physics observatory.[35] China has the highest occupancy rate for its Ny Ålesund base, more than any other country with facilities there.

[33] "Fagai touzi (2005) 1361 hao" [National Development and Reform Commission (2005), no. 1361], reproduced verbatim in "Jidi kaocha 'shiwu' nengli jianshe ji 'shiyiwu' fazhan guihua gongzuo" [Polar expedition "10th Five-Year Plan" capacity-building and "11th Five-Year" development planning], *Zhongguo haiyang bao*, August 11, 2008, http://www.oceanol.com/keji/jddy/9463.html.

[34] "Tamen cong Beiji huilai" [They returned from the Arctic], CCTV, August 25, 2004, http://www.cctv.com/program/jrgz/20040825/101156.shtml.

[35] Zhong Hui, "Zhongguo, li Beiji geng jin" [China gets closer to the Arctic], *Qianjiang wanbao*, May 16, 2013, http://qjwb.zjol.com.cn/html/2013-05/16/content_2138993.htm.

FIGURE 5.7 Yellow River Station and Ny Ålesund, Norway
Source: "Zhongguo Beiji kaochazhan" [China's Arctic station], CAA, October 23, 2015, http://www.chinare.gov.cn/caa/gb_article.php?modid=04000.

FIGURE 5.8 China-Iceland Joint Aurora Observatory
Source: Anne-Marie Brady, June 2016

In 2012, China negotiated with Iceland to set up a second Arctic research station, on 158 hectares of farmland not far from the northern Icelandic port town of Akureyri (see figure 5.8). The China-Iceland Joint Aurora Observatory (CIAO) will initially research space weather, the northern lights, and variations in the magnetic field, but in time its work will branch out into other fields.[36] In Iceland, land often is held between multiple owners, and ownership of land by foreigners is an extremely sensitive issue, as was shown by the controversy over Huang Nubo's attempt to invest in Iceland in 2012. To get around these problems, the research station's land has been bought by a collection of Icelandic public and private interests, including Akureyri University's Arctic Portal, which formed a company known as the Arctic Observatory and used the company to buy the site for around US$670,000 (ISK 77 million). The PRIC is funding the construction and use costs of the site buildings.[37] The new scientific base will compliment aurora-related work being done at Zhongshan Station in the Antarctic and at Svalbard in the Arctic, as they are in the same longitude. Scientists plan to use the new research station to observe Arctic auroras for two sun cycles, or twenty-four years. The Chinese organizations involved in the observatory include the PRIC; the National Space Science Center and the Institute of Geology and Geophysics at the Chinese Academy of Sciences; the China Research Institute of Radio Wave Propagation; the National Center for Space Weather; the Institute of Space Physics and Applied Technology at Peking University; the School of Electronic Information at Wuhan University; the School of Earth and Space Science at the University of Science and Technology of China; and the School of Space Science and Physics at Shandong University.

China's third Arctic research facility is on ice floes in the Arctic Ocean. Since 2003, China has followed the example of other polar great powers such as Russia and the United States in establishing Arctic iceberg stations (*bingzhan*). These stations enable China to avoid Arctic sovereignty issues while establishing a scientific base useful for strategic science. In 2010, China set up its first long-term Arctic iceberg station at 87°39′ N, 123°37′ E,[38] where it established an automatic weather system and held temporary field camps during the northern

36   "Fréttatilkynning frá Rannsóknamiðstöð Íslands, Heimskautastofnuninni í Kína og Aurora Observatory" [Press release from the Icelandic Center for Research, Polar Institute in China and Aurora Observatory], *640.is*, October 10, 2012, http://www.640.is/is/frettir/frettatilkynning-fra-rannsoknamidstod-islands-heimskautastofnuninni-i-kina-og-aurora-observatory.

37   Chinese polar official, interview with author, October 2012.

38   "Zhongguo di wu ci Beiji kaocha dui zai Beibingyang zhongxin qu chenggong bu fang zidong qixiang zhan" [Successful deployment of automatic weather stations in central Arctic Ocean on 5th Arctic expedition], China Meteorological Administration, November 22, 2012, accessed February 25, 2014, http://cadata.cams.cma.gov.cn/news2/show.aspx?id=772&cid=6 (link discontinued).

summer.[39] As other polar states do, China has set up a new Arctic ice station on each Arctic voyage of the *Xue Long*, as ice conditions often make earlier stations inaccessible or the ice underneath them melts.

China's physical presence in the Arctic is further extended through its satellite receiving stations there. In 2010, the China Meteorological Administration established a ground receiving station for China's meteorological satellites at the Esrange Space Center in Kiruna, Sweden, part of a network of similar ground receiving stations in Beijing, Urumqi, and Jiamusi.[40] The Swedish Space Corporation administers the Esrange Space Center. Esrange is located in a remote area 200 kilometers north of the Arctic Circle and it is useful for rocket launches and tracking polar orbiting satellites. In 2015, China announced that it was setting up a remote-sensing ground receiving station at Kiruna, which became operational in 2017. This Arctic ground receiving station will enable China to access remote sensing data for research on environmental conditions, mineral resource distribution, and climate change in the Arctic and Europe.[41] Also in 2015, at a joint Canada-China Arctic conference held in Beijing, Chinese polar officials told journalists that China was interested in setting up a research station in Canada. Tuktoyaktuk, a coastal settlement in the far northwestern corner of Canada's Northwest Territories, was suggested as a possible location because the area surrounding it is rich in hydrocarbons. The deputy director of China's State Key Laboratory of Frozen Soil Engineering said that when it comes to the Arctic, "We are interested in not only science, but also the technical markets like oil and natural gas. In that sense, we need to have information, access to all this data, in order to make informed decisions."[42]

Increasingly, China is using ice robots, drones, and underwater robotic submarines to carry out scientific research and to extend and maintain

---

[39]   "Beiji fu bing, cheng Zhongguo kekao dui bing zhan" [Chinese expedition's ice station on the Arctic floes], Xinhua, August 3, 2010, http://news.xinhuanet.com/mrdx/2010-08/03/con tent_13956346.htm.

[40]   "National Satellite Meteorological Center," China Meteorological Administration, accessed June 5, 2016, http://www.cma.gov.cn/en2014/aboutcma/organizational/Institutionsu nderCMA/201409/t20140912_260809.html.

[41]   "Zhongguo shou ge jingwai yaogan weixing shuju jieshou zhan jinnian kaigong yuji liang nian jiancheng" [China's first overseas remote-sensing receiving station will start this year, expected to take two years to build], *Guoji zaixian*, March 16, 2015, http://news.163.com/15/0316/16/AK RE774P00014JB5.html.

[42]   Nathan Vanderklippe, "Chinese Scientists Look to Canadian Arctic for Research Outpost," *Globe and Mail*, March 18, 2015, http://www.theglobeandmail.com/report-on-business/indus try-news/energy-and-resources/chinese-scientists-dream-of-arctic-research-outpost-in-the-north/article23527009/.

a physical presence in the Arctic and Antarctic.[43] China's roaming polar robot buoy, first successfully tested in Antarctica in 2014, will send back meteorological data to China via satellite. The information it collects will enhance the safety of China's Antarctic maritime expeditions.[44] China has placed similar robot buoys in the Arctic Ocean.

Polar Scientific Transportation and Communication

If China aspires to become a polar great power, then strong polar transportation and communication links will be essential in achieving that goal. However, until very recently, budget restrictions limited China's ability to invest in top-of-the-line polar transportation facilities, thereby limiting its polar program.

China's annual Arctic and Antarctic voyages are called in English "CHINARE," followed by the number of the expedition. Thus, in 2017, China completed CHINARE 33, the 33rd expedition of the China polar program. In 2005, CAA deputy director Wu Jun explained that the purpose of China's polar expeditions "is to establish a physical presence at the poles and use scientific activities in order to effectively develop and open up resources in the future."[45] In 1999, China launched its first Arctic expedition in the Bering and Chukchi seas, followed by a second trek in 2003 and biannual visits from that date; from 2012, it began to make annual voyages there. China has now completed eight scientific voyages to the Arctic Ocean, going further and longer on each voyage. On CHINARE 30, during the 2013–14 Antarctic summer, China's icebreaker circumnavigated the Antarctic continent for the first time, and it completed this feat a second time during the 2015–16 austral summer. Ninety-five percent of Antarctic waters are uncharted, so China's maritime explorations are a strong indication of China's increased confidence and capabilities in the polar regions. It also is a signal that China is looking to push beyond what other countries have achieved in Antarctica.

According to the CAA's Wu Jun, "polar expeditions are an important public event that connect to China's political, economic, and military interests."[46] Although the home port of China's polar program is Shanghai, each time Chinese scientists set off on an expedition to either the Arctic or Antarctic,

---

[43]   CAA, 2010 *National Annual Report on Polar Program of China* (Beijing: CAA, 2010), 67.

[44]   "Woguo jidi manyou qiuxing jiqiren yijing zai Nanji wancheng shouci ceshi" [Our roaming polar spherical robot has completed the first test in Antarctica], *Zhongguo zhengfu wang*, November 1, 2014, http://www.kaixian.tv/gd/2014/0111/826808.html.

[45]   Wu, "Wo guo jidi kaocha zuzhi guanli jizhi youhua yanjiu," 34.

[46]   Ibid., 49.

a different host port is chosen as the site for major publicity events involving the general public, particularly youth. China's polar expeditions are also used for major public diplomacy events in international ports where their ice vessel docks. Such events help build China's prestige and raise awareness of its newly acquired strengths among Arctic and Antarctic states. In the polar gateway cities such as Reykjavík, Hobart, and Christchurch, the business community and political interests strongly welcome the perceived economic benefits from China's expansion of its Arctic and Antarctic expeditions.

The CAA describes China's current icebreaker, *Xue Long*, as the "world's largest nonnuclear icebreaker."[47] However, the *Xue Long* was originally designed as an ice-strengthened cargo ship, and despite modifications it has many limitations that mean that it neither completely fits the needs of the Chinese polar program nor fits definitions of a true "icebreaker." True icebreakers have specially designed hulls and can break ice up to 3 meters thick at a rate of 3 knots,[48] but the *Xue Long* can manage only moderately thick ice (1.1 meters of ice at 1.5 knots).[49] It is incapable of engaging in meaningful maritime geophysics research, and polar officials complain that this shortcoming is inhibiting China's seabed research at the poles.[50] The ship is equipped with two helicopters, KA-32 and Z-9, which are used for transporting equipment and people, respectively. The *Xue Long* is mainly used for shipping supplies, research equipment, and personnel to Antarctica. As a consequence, conducting marine research forms only a very small part of its duties. On its 2011–12 four-month voyage to Antarctica, only eight to ten days of the trip were devoted to research.[51]

Purchased from Ukraine in 1993, the *Xue Long* has undergone several refits, the latest in 2013. It is estimated the ship can now be utilized for a further fifteen to twenty years. In the latest refit, the cargo-loading capacity was increased from 3,000 tons to 9,600 tons. This signals a change of operation for the *Xue Long*; it will soon go from acting as an all-purpose vessel to carrying out full-time cargo duties, transporting the goods needed to build China's Ross Sea base from 2018 to 2020, and other construction projects such as setting up an airfield at the new base and at China's other Antarctica bases and

---

[47] CHINARE 5, "Snow Dragon," CHINARE 5: Chinese Research Expedition 5, 2012, http://www.chinare5.com/snow-dragon.

[48] Marianne Lavelle, "Antarctic Ship Drama: What Is an Icebreaker, Really?" *National Geographic Daily News*, January 4, 2014, http://news.nationalgeographic.com/news/2014/01/140103-antarctica-ship-icebreakers-science-ice-trapped/.

[49] CHINARE 5, "Snow Dragon."

[50] "Zhongguo jidi kaocha ji xu 'xin Xue Long'" [China urgently needs a "new *Xue Long*"], *Haiyang bao*, December 17, 2014, http://www.soa.gov.cn/xw/dfdwdt/jsdw_157/201412/t20141217_34483.html.

[51] Chinese policymaker, interview with author, October 2012.

transporting Chinese scientists and equipment to and from Antarctic gateway cities such as Ushuaia, Hobart, and Christchurch. While the *Xue Long* focuses on cargo and ferrying duties, a new, purpose-built ice vessel will greatly expand China's polar marine research capabilities.

China is currently building a new electric-propulsion icebreaker that will be ready for use in 2018. A prototype for the ship was designed by Finnish company Åker Arctic. When China's new polar scientific icebreaker is completed, the vessel will have the world's greatest icebreaking ability and research capabilities of its shipping class. It will have shipboard helicopters, cable-actuated bathoscapes (used for bathometry or deep-sea exploration, and also useful for mapping the seabed for Arctic submarine transits), and an underwater detection system (used for seabed mineral resource exploration, and also useful for mineral research in the deep seas of Antarctica).[52] The new icebreaker will be able to cut through ice up to two meters thick and be self-sustaining for sixty days, without the need for refueling.[53]

CAA director Qu Tanzhou has described the new ice vessel as a "mobile research station."[54] As a non-Arctic state with limited rights to access the region, creating a "mobile research station" in the Arctic is a smart way for China to expand its presence and scale of operations without needing to obtain permission from the littoral Arctic states. Until now, the *Xue Long's* limitations have restricted China's ability to launch in-depth scientific investigations in the Arctic and have limited China's chances to conduct in-depth seabed research in Antarctica. When China's second icebreaker becomes operational, its two polar scientific ice vessels will be engaged in polar ocean voyages more than 200 days per year.[55]

Until recently, with very few exceptions, Chinese scientists were required to travel to the Arctic and Antarctic on China's own ice vessel, necessitating a lengthy and difficult sea voyage before reaching their scientific research site. This was one factor in limiting the number of Chinese scientists willing to engage in polar science. In the past few years, increases in China's scientific research funding have made it possible for Chinese scientists to reduce their travel time by

---

[52] "Zhongguo xin pobingchuan huzhi yuchu" [China's new polar icebreaker in contrast], *Keji ribao*, October 17, 2014, accessed January 28, 2015, http://news.szcchy56.com/show-1214.html.

[53] "Shou sou 'Zhongguo zao' jidi ke kao pobingchuan 'pobing qi hang'" [The first "Made in China" polar expedition icebreaker "breaks the ice"], CSSC, November 9, 2012, http://maric.cssc.net.cn/component_news/news_detail.php?id=103.

[54] Wang Qian, "New Icebreaker Planned by 2016: Officials," *China Daily*, January 4, 2014, http://www.chinadaily.com.cn/china/2014-01/06/content_17216579.htm.

[55] "Jidi quyu zhanlue diwei xunsu tisheng Zhongguo jianxin pobingchuan" [China to build a new icebreaker, polar strategic status will improve], *Xilu dongfang junshi*, June 22, 2011, http://junshi.xilu.com/2011/0622/news_343_168393.html.

flying to polar gateway cities and joining up with the *Xue Long*'s voyage to the final destination. Now, the Antarctic research trip traveling time for scientists has reduced even further, as China has become one of only a handful of Antarctic nations making use of airplanes for science on the continent. In early 2015, China purchased a Basler BT-67 cargo plane to work in the polar regions, and it was flown down to Antarctica in November 2015. As the SOA boasts, using military strategic language, China now has "fully self-sufficient land, sea, and air capabilities at the poles."[56] This is a major achievement. Although the United States has a massive number of polar scientific personnel and is strong in polar aircraft and land transportation, its lack of modern polar icebreaking facilities is a crucial structural weakness. Similarly, the Russian Antarctic science program has its own icebreaker, but lacks a dedicated polar plane to operate on the Antarctic continent. China's Basler plane will be used in the Antarctic and Arctic for personnel transportation of up to thirty people, for airborne remote sensing (useful for oil and natural gas exploration), and for atmospheric observations (useful for climate change research). In the Arctic, the plane can be used for flights to China's iceberg station; until now, the only access to the icebergs has been by helicopter on the *Xue Long*'s annual trips. In the Antarctic, the Chinese polar program has built a network of air links between the three Chinese bases over the past five years (see figure 5.9).[57] From the 2016–17, season Chinese scientists will be able to reach Kunlun and Taishan stations by plane, while food and scientific gear will travel by snow tractor traverse.

China is also interested in taking further advantage of existing air links managed by other national Antarctic programs. Currently, there are four main air links into Antarctica: (1) from Chile and Argentina to King George Island, where Chile has an airfield; (2) from New Zealand to the US ice runways at McMurdo Station in the Ross Sea region; (3) from Australia to East Antarctica, where Australia's Casey Station has an ice airfield; and (4) from South Africa to Queen Maud Land, where Norway and Russia have ice runways. China hopes to form an Antarctic air logistics pool with Russia, although so far Russia has only given temporary cooperation.[58] Within the next decade, it is likely that

56 "Wo guo jidi kaocha jiang xin gou feiji xinjian pobingchuan" [China's polar expedition will purchase new airplane and icebreaker], Xinhua, February 3, 2014, http://tech.sina.com.cn/d/2014-02-03/11279140668.shtml.

57 "Zhongguo jiang gou shou jia jidi kaocha guding yi feiji zaojia 9 qian wan" [China's first polar aircraft will be purchased for a cost of RMB 90 million], *Zhongguo ribao*, December 20, 2013, http://news.jnnc.com/mil/2013/1220/284888.shtml.

58 "Bei kao xueshan, mian chao dahai Nanji dalu shang de zhe kuai baodi you sha aomi" [Backed by snow-capped mountains, faced by the sea, this treasure island is rich in mysteries], *Hangzhou wang*, February 26, 2016, http://hznews.hangzhou.com.cn/kejiao/content/2016-02/26/content_6086321.htm.

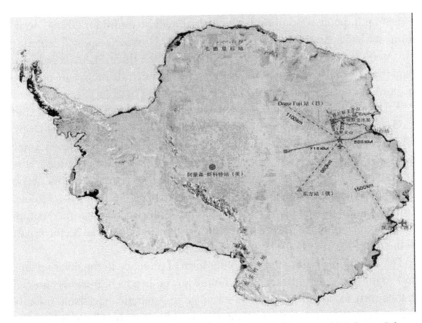

FIGURE 5.9 Map of China's Proposed Antarctic Air Route and Links to Other Airfields: Solid lines indicate China's air route; dotted lines indicate distances to other airfields.

Source: "Zhongguo jidi kaocha: xiang guangdu he shendu jinjun" [China's polar expedition to expand and go more in depth], CAA, November, 3 2013, http://www .chinare.gov.cn/caa/gb_news.php?id=1294&modid=01001.

almost all Chinese scientists will travel to the polar regions via intercontinental flights and then on to their research stations on Antarctic continental flights; the new icebreaker will be used for research, while the *Xue Long* will carry cargo for China's Antarctic expeditions and construction projects.

In 2012, Chinese polar officials told me that in the future the PLA increasingly would participate in China's Antarctic expeditions, citing the example of Argentina, Australia, Brazil, Chile, New Zealand, and the United States, all of which utilize their armed forces in Antarctica for air and sea transportation, cargo handling, and even as station personnel. This decision would be legitimate if China was to publicly state that it is involving its military in Antarctic affairs, but as noted, other than in its first expedition, China has neglected to notify the other Antarctic Treaty states of the PLA's ongoing involvement in Antarctic logistics and strategic science. Increasing the level of involvement of the Chinese military in the Antarctic program will greatly enhance China's Antarctic operating capacity and enable PLA personnel to gain experience operating in polar conditions, both of which will be useful for China's long-term strategic Arctic interests. The five PLAN vessels spotted entering US Arctic territorial waters in the Aleutians and the three PLAN vessels that paid friendly visits to three Arctic states on the Atlantic side in 2015 are only the beginning of PLA expansion into the polar regions.

A nation's Antarctic air and sea capacity is crucial for getting to the ice, but land vehicles are essential for going beyond the vicinity of a base for field trips. China's current inland fleet consists of a relatively modest eleven snow tractors, fifty sleds, and eleven portable cabins.[59] By contrast, the US Antarctic Program has a land fleet of hundreds of vehicles. China's 32nd Antarctic expedition launched the first China-made all-terrain polar vehicle. China has announced plans to develop more China-made polar field equipment, and it will make polar engineering a significant industrial sector as part of the 13th Five-Year Polar Plan (2016–2020).[60]

Telecommunications are yet another form of presence in the polar regions and an indicator of political and economic power. In 2014, China became the first country to provide cell phone coverage in Antarctica, available initially within a 15-kilometer radius of Zhongshan and able to connect internationally, with plans to expand coverage in the next few years.[61]

Polar Mapping and Discovery

Despite being a latecomer in Antarctica, arriving more than 100 years after the earliest Antarctic exploring nations – Russia, the United Kingdom, Norway, and the United States – China has nonetheless managed to make some new discoveries in Antarctica, in territories that earlier explorers previously considered to be too difficult to access. Chinese scientists were the first to properly explore Dome A, the Gamburtsev Mountains, and the Grove Mountains. Below ground, they are making breakthroughs in what lies beneath the surface at Dome A and the Grove Mountain lakes through ice cores. They are also exploring deep space from Antarctica, as well as the Antarctic seabed.

59 "Zhengzhan Nanji Zhongguo zai hangdong" [China on the move in Antarctica], *Zhongguo kexue bao*, January 17, 2014, http://blog.sciencenet.cn/blog-1208826-759893.html.

60 "'Shisanwu' jidi jiang tui san ge zhuanbian zengqiang san da nengli" [The 13th Five-Year Polar Plan will push through three major changes to enhance capacity], *Zhongguo haiyang bao*, October 30, 2015, http://www.oceanol.com/shouye/jdkc/2015-10-30/52443.html.

61 "Zhongguo dianxin shouci zai Nanji kaitong yidong tongxin fuwu" [China Telecom launches first telecom service in Antarctica], *Sohu*, January 13, 2013, http://info.tclc.hc360.com/2014/01/13082845276o.shtml.

The establishment of Taishan Station in East Antarctica has consolidated China's effective hold over a pie-slice–shaped section of Antarctic territory that looks remarkably like the triangle-shaped territorial claims of the claimant states in Antarctica. Through its advanced logistics capabilities, China is able to project its power in this area of Antarctica to an extent to which Australia (which claims this zone as part of the Australian Antarctic Territory) is unable to do. Unlike the seven claimant states of Antarctica (Argentina, Australia, Chile, France, New Zealand, and Norway), all of which have relatively limited hinterland capabilities, China has the ability to continually maintain its presence in this area. Understandably, Australian polar experts repeatedly have expressed unease about this situation, and have urged their government to put more money into Antarctic affairs in order to better defend Australia's Antarctic claim.[62]

China first decided to focus on this sector of Antarctica in 1998, as part of the "East Antarctic Sector Strategic Research Vision" (*Dong Nanji da duanmian yanjiu zhanlüe*).[63] A rare public image of China's "East Antarctic Sector" was revealed in the documents associated with China's participation in the International Polar Year 2008–9. During this IPY, China referred to the area (see figure 5.10) as "PANDA," standing for Prydz Bay, Amery Ice Shelf, and Dome A. The IPY gave a significant boost to China's polar science and presence on the ice. Chinese polar officials point out that the dimensions of this project demonstrated that China's "comprehensive national power and scientific abilities had gone up a level."[64]

China's dominance in this region is further strengthened by a dedicated traverse route from Zhongshan to Dome A via Taishan. Chinese scientists have nicknamed the route "China Boulevard" (*Zhonghua dadao*).[65] The United States is the only other Antarctic state to have established a dedicated long-distance snow road: the 1,601-kilometer-long McMurdo–South Pole Highway, which links the two main US bases. In 2013, China put in a proposal to have

[62] Ellie Fogarty, "Antarctica: Assessing and Protecting Australia's National Assets," Lowy Institute for International Policy, August 3, 2011, http://www.lowyinstitute.org/publications/a ntarctica-assessing-and-protecting-australias-national-interests; Anthony Bergin, "Cold Calculations: Our Antarctic Choices," *ASPI Strategist*, May 28, 2013, http://www .aspistrategist.org.au/cold-calculations-our-antarctic-choices/; and Anthony Bergin et al., "Cold Calculations: Australia's Antarctic Challenges," *ASPI Strategic Insights* 66, October 21, 2013, https://www.aspi.org.au/publications/strategic-insights-66-cold-calculations-australias-antarctic-challenges.

[63] "Zhengzhan Nanji Zhongguo zai hangdong."

[64] Yan and Zhu, *Nanjizhou lingtu zhuquan yu ziyuan quanshu wenti yanjiu*, 34.

[65] "Zhengzhan Nanji Zhongguo zai hangdong."

FIGURE 5.10 Map of China's "East Antarctic Sector": The map as shown here indicates the relative locations of Prydz Bay, the Amery Ice Shelf, Zhongshan Station, Grove Mountain, and Dome A in East Antarctica.

Source: International Polar Foundation, "Zhongshan Station: Hub of Chinese Scientific Research in East Antarctica," International Polar Year 2007–2008, December 10, 2008, http://www.ipy.org/index.php?/ipy/detail/ zhongshan_station_hub_of_chinese_scientific_research_in_east_antarctica

the area surrounding Dome A – 19,764 total square kilometres – designated as an Antarctic Special Managed Area.[66] (The proposed area had been identified in 2008, as shown on the circled area on the PANDA map in figure 5.11.)

---

[66] "Proposal for a New Antarctic Specially Managed Area at Chinese Antarctic Kunlun Station, Dome A," Working Paper 8, CEP 9a, XXVI Antarctic Treaty Consultative Meeting, Brussels, April 2013, http://www.ats.aq/documents/ATCM36/wp/ATCM36_wp008_e.doc.

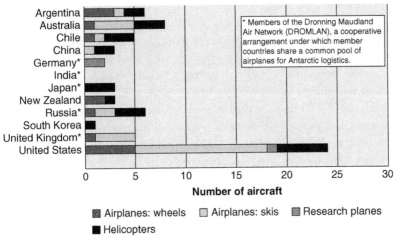

FIGURE 5.11 Antarctic-Purposed Aircraft by Country

Chinese polar scientists and officials commonly (and proudly)[67] refer to this massive territory as "China's Management District" (*Zhongguo guanli qu*) and "China's Great Wall" (*Zhongguo qiang*).[68]

Each country active in Antarctica has the right to name geological sites. A few areas where there has been a lot of exploration have multiple names in various languages. The United States has been prominent in codifying standard names for the main geographical features in Antarctica, as they have been the leader in the modern mapping of Antarctica. Names and the act of naming something correctly (*zhengming*) have deep cultural significance in Chinese tradition. In the past ten years, China has been more active than any other country in exploring new sites and compiling detailed maps of these areas. Chinese names are given to any previously unnamed prominent geographic feature. All China needs to do to have its names accepted is to share its maps with other states and notify the SCAR Composite Gazetteer of the new names and location of the sites. To date, China has had 295 site names recognized in Antarctica. This makes it a middle player with regard to naming rights, ahead of France at 232 but behind Japan at 343, and well behind the United States

---

[67] "17 yongshi chenggong deng ding Nanji bing qiong A" [17 warriors successfully ascend Antarctica's Dome A], SOA, January 8, 2008, http://www.soa.gov.cn/xw/dfdwdt/jsdw_157/201 211/t20121108_16625.html.

[68] Bao Yinghua, "Nanji cehui" [Antarctic surveying], http://drcsm.sbsm.gov.cn/accessory/Se p27,201110500PM.doc; and "Nanji nei lu kunlun zhan ke kao dui 18 ri chufa" [Antarctic hinterland expedition to Kunlun starts on 18th], Heilongjiang Provincial Bureau of Surveying and Mapping, December 9, 2009, www.hljbsm.gov.cn/index.asp?id=1043.

(which has had 13,192 suggested names officially recognized). In contrast to the Antarctic continent, the Southern Ocean is virtually unmapped, leaving plenty of scope for China to make its mark there as it engages in marine surveying.

Chinese geographers say that getting Chinese names for geographical features recognized internationally help to protect China's "Antarctic rights and interests."[69] Chinese geological sites in Antarctica have been named after Chinese cities, famous scenic attractions in China, and scholarly disciplines (for example, "Geologist Island"). Unlike other countries, which mostly name sites after individuals, China has named only one location after an individual: Zhongshan Station (after Sun Zhongshan / Sun Yat-sen).[70] More so than any of China's earlier stations, the choice of names for Kunlun and Taishan stations are particularly significant. Although Kunlun is an actual place in China, it also has mythical associations deeply rooted in Chinese culture. According to tradition, Kunlun Mountain is a Daoist paradise, a place where communication between humans and gods is possible. The Kunlun Range, on the northern boundary of the Tibetan Autonomous Region, marks the outer limits of the old Chinese empire. The new base name was selected by a committee of Chinese polar experts from over 3000 possibilities sent by members of the Chinese public. "Kunlun" was chosen for its "deep cultural associations."[71] The extremely cold, dry, and stable air found at the summit of Dome A is one of the best sites on Earth for conducting a wide range of astronomical observations, from optical to millimeter wavelengths[72] – in a sense, carrying out a dialogue with the "gods." Similarly, Taishan, China's summer-only base, has a culturally significant name with political connotations. The new base is named after Mount Tai, the first of the five sacred mountains in China. "Mount Tai" is also a metaphor in Chinese culture for greatness and hard-to-achieve goals. In 2013, CAA director Qu Tanzhou said that the name was chosen to symbolize the new stage of Antarctic affairs and

[69] "Zhongguo Nanji cehui kexue kaocha 22 nian jiu yu gongxian" [Twenty-two years of achievements for Antarctic cartographers], *Guojia cehuaju guotusi*, November 22, 2007, accessed February 5, 2009, http://www.sbsm.gov.cn/article/ztzl/jdch/jdch/20071100027867.shtml (link discontinued).

[70] *Nanbei dituji* [Atlas of the Arctic and Antarctic] (Beijing: Sinomaps Press, 2009).

[71] "Wo guo shouge Nanji neidi kaocha zhan mingming Kunlun" [Our nation's first continental station is named Kunlun], *Xinlang keji*, October 16, 2008, http://tech.sina.com.cn/d/2008-10-16/09512513402.shtml.

[72] "China: Full Proposals for IPY 2007–2008 Activities," International Polar Year, May 1, 2009, accessed February 14, 2013, http://classic.ipy.org/development/eoi/proposal-details.php?id=313 (link discontinued).

that the building of the base signified the idea of "China standing tall among the nations of the world."[73]

EVALUATING CHINA'S SPENDING ON POLAR SCIENCE

Polar-related budgets are a primary means for evaluating whether a state is a polar great power. As noted, China has three core interests in the polar regions: security, resources, and science and technology. Although it may not be possible to establish the exact amounts that China is spending on polar-related military affairs, or the total sum that Chinese SOEs and other companies have invested in polar resources or donated to build China's polar infrastructure, quite a lot of publicly available data can be found on government spending on polar science–related activities. Since science is the nominal reason for China and other states' expanding polar engagement, China's polar science budget is a useful barometer to the priority the Chinese central government places on polar affairs overall. For China, as with many other states, investing in polar scientific activities is a canny use of government funds. In addition to strengthening a nation's right to have a say in polar governance, polar science can help with the due diligence needed for scoping the resource potential of different areas and meeting strategic needs such as understanding polar shipping routes and weather patterns. As a result, the level of polar scientific engagement and the type of projects funded can indicate the priority that a government places on polar affairs. For the first twenty years of its polar science activities, China's spending was extremely modest, but since 2005 it has made a series of quantum leaps.

National polar science budget figures are notoriously difficult to compile and to accurately compare. Countries have different arrangements for linking polar affairs and different costs involved in accessing the poles, and many states are not fully transparent about their polar scientific spending. China's polar budget is divided into three main spending areas: polar facilities (*jidi sheshi*), polar expeditions and overall operating costs (*jidi kaocha*), and polar research (*jidi yanjiu*).[74] However, these are not unified budgets,[75] as the funds and agencies are scattered among multiple players. Seventeen Chinese government agencies are involved in various aspects of polar science and polar affairs

---

73   "Wo guo jiang zai Nanji jianli de sige kexue kaocha zhan—Taishan zhan" [China will build a fourth Antarctic research station], Xinhua, November 1, 2013, http://www.gov.cn/jrzg/2013-11/01/content_2519523.htm.

74   Qu Tanzhou et al., *Beiji wenti yanjiu* [Arctic affairs research] (Beijing: Haiyang chubanshe, 2011) 365.

75   Wu, "Wo guo jidi kaocha zuzhi guanli jizhi youhua yanjiu," 31.

more broadly; all have separate polar-related budgets, few of which are publicly available. Chinese polar officials appear to be averse to compiling the full spending figures. Even in Chinese-language materials, they reveal only partial figures, omitting to mention what is being left out. China's total current polar scientific spending is thus difficult to calculate with precision. Nonetheless, the available budget figures in China's three categories of polar spending can be used to evaluate its changing level of interest and engagement in the Arctic and Antarctic, and the government's priorities as identified by budget allocations.

Polar Facilities

Even without the precise amounts, it is clear from the new polar science hardware that Chinese polar officials have unveiled since 2005 that China is currently the world's biggest spender on polar scientific infrastructure. The long-standing trend of China's polar policies has been to expand China's physical presence on the ice through investment in bases, boats, and now a plane. By contrast, China has dedicated relatively little money to polar science itself. If, from a political point of view, scientists are the actors on the "stage" of China's polar bases, then the budget allocations indicate that the Chinese government is not overly concerned about what "play" the actors perform or even the quality of their performance; it is enough that they are there. Like many other states active in the polar regions, China continues to prioritize polar presence over polar science.

In the first ten years of China's polar scientific expansion, the main goal was to develop a substantial presence on the Antarctic continent and a reliable supply route. China's first polar research base, Great Wall Station, was built in 1984 at a cost of RMB 20 million (about US$3.8 million).[76] This was a very substantial sum for China in the 1980s. In 1985, the SOA purchased an ice-capable vessel from Finland for US$123,000 to transport China's annual Antarctic expeditions, but unfortunately it quickly proved unsuitable to the task of navigating the extreme ice conditions of the Southern Ocean. China's second polar station, Zhongshan Station in East Antarctica, was built in 1988, at an unknown cost. Zhongshan is twice the size of the Great Wall Station, and from a scientific point of view it is on a more useful site, enabling a steady expansion of scientific programs. In 1993, the government

[76] "Wo zai Nanji jianzhan" [I built a base in Antarctica], *Shidai chao*, October 2001, accessed July 22, 2014, http://www.people.com.cn/GB/paper83/3417/434600.html (link discontinued).

purchased a former cargo boat from Ukraine for US$17.5 million, which was refitted at a cost of US$3 million to become the *Xue Long*.[77] These four major outlays set in place the system of "two stations, one boat" (*liangge zhan yige chuan*), which from the late 1990s and into the early 2000s enabled China to consolidate its scientific knowledge and experience in Antarctica and begin to explore Arctic waters.

From the mid-2000s on, China began a dramatic increase in its polar infrastructure budget, indicating that its senior central leadership was granting a much higher priority to the polar regions. China's budgets are organized into five-year plans. Polar planning has to fit both within that timetable and in the priorities identified in each five-year plan. In 2004, the Ministry of Land and Resources committed more than US$85 million to upgrade China's Antarctic facilities.[78] A 2006 Xinhua report discussing the shift in policy stated that China had now moved into the capacity-building phase of polar engagement.[79] During the 11th Five-Year Plan (2006–2010), China renovated its two existing Antarctic bases, upgraded the PRIC headquarters and wharf in Shanghai, refitted the *Xue Long*, and completed the first stage of a new Antarctic inland station (Kunlun).[80] On a separate budget stream, China built a meteorological ground receiving station in Kiruna, Sweden, in 2010 (cost unknown).

But it was the 12th Five-Year Plan (2011–2015) that really put China on a level of polar infrastructure spending with which no other polar nation could compete. The Chinese government's stated goal in this investment was to bring China's polar expedition facilities "on a par" with those of the other leading players in polar expeditions[81] – in other words, the United States and Russia. At a time when other polar states were cutting back on their polar budgets or struggling to find the funds for core infrastructure needs, China stood out for its phenomenal spending level. During this Five-Year Plan, China invested in a new research station in Iceland (US$3 million),[82] set up

77 "Xue Long hao jidi kaocha chuan [*Xue Long* polar expedition boat], *China.com*, November 29, 2011, http://www.china.com.cn/guoqing/2011-11/29/content_24034393_2.htm.

78 "'Zhongguo jidi kaocha 'shiwu' jianshe ke yan baogao' tongguo zhuanjia pingshen" [China's polar expedition 10th five-year capacity-building plan passes assessment], *Zhongguo haiyang bao*, December 6, 2004, http://wdc-d.coi.gov.cn/dt/041207a.htm.

79 "Chen Lianzeng: Zengjiang woguo zai Nanji de shishi cunzai" [Chen Lianzeng: Increasing China's presence in Antarctica], Xinhua, January 2, 2006, http://news.xinhuanet.com/world/2006-01/02/content_4000473.htm.

80 "Jidi kaocha 'shiwu' nengli jianshe ji 'shiyiwu' fazhan guihua gongzuo."

81 "'Shi'er' woguo jidi kaocha jinru xin de fazhan shiqi" [12th Five-Year Plan: China's polar expeditions enter a new stage], Xinhua, August 2, 2011, http://finance.sina.com.cn/roll/20110802/094510245289.shtml.

82 Vanderklippe, "Chinese Scientists Look to Canadian Arctic for Research Outpost."

Taishan Station in Antarctica (cost unknown), expanded the *Xue Long*'s cargo facilities (cost unknown),[83] updated the *Xue Long*'s engines (US$1.3 million),[84] paid for the design of a new ice research vessel (US$613 million),[85] ordered a Basler BT-67 ice plane (US$15 million), set up a system of marine robots and drones to patrol polar waters (cost unknown), established a polar telecom system (US$577,000),[86] expanded the BeiDou 2 satellite system (US$1.6 billion),[87] and set up a remote-sensing ground receiving station in Kiruna, Sweden (cost unknown).

In the 13th Five-Year Plan (2016–2020), China has announced that it intends to build a new polar campus in Shanghai (cost unknown) with facilities for 1000 polar personnel, build its fifth Antarctic base in the Ross Sea area (cost unknown), and commission Chinese shipyards to construct the new polar ice research vessel (US$193 million).[88] In addition, on a separate budget stream from the SOA's infrastructure projects, other major polar scientific infrastructure projects include the purchase of a new 2.5-meter optical/infrared telescope and a 5-meter Terahertz Explorer (US$150 million) for Chinese astronomers at Kunlun Station.[89]

China is going through an extraordinary expansion in polar capacities over a very short period. No other state has the financial means to expand so rapidly. China now has state-of-the-art polar science facilities at its four (soon to be five) bases in Antarctica and multiple sites in the Arctic; it will soon have a new icebreaker, in addition to the *Xue Long*; and it has two helicopters, an ice plane, and drones and marine robots.

---

[83] "'Xue Long' chuan genghuan zhuji caiyong xianjin dian pen gong gui jishu" [*Xue Long* replaces hoists with rail technology], Yifeng, June 17, 2013, http://news.ifeng.com/mil/2/detai l_2013_06/17/26472854_0.shtml; and China Government Procurement Network, accessed August 4, 2013, http://www.ccgp.gov.cn/eadlynotice/201304/t20130408_2683232 .shtml (link discontinued).

[84] "Zhongguo jidi yanjiu zhongxin 'Xue Long' hao ke kao chuan huifu xing weixiu gaizao chaiyou fadian jizu shebei zhaobiao xiangmu zhongbiao gonggao" [PRIC, *Xue Long* research vessel restorative maintenance and reconstruction of diesel generator equipment tender bid announcement], China Government Procurement Network, August 1, 2012, http://www.ccgp .gov.cn/cggg/zybx/zbgg/201208/t20120801_2258647.shtml.

[85] Wang, "New Icebreaker Planned by 2016: Officials."

[86] Call for bids, China government procurements site, November 24, 2011, accessed July 24, 2014, http://www.ccgp.gov.cn/eadlynotice/201111/t20111124_1892357.shtml (link discontinued).

[87] "Beidou li ya GPS zheng shi 5000 yi shichang" [BeiDou GPS fights for 500 billion market], *Sohu*, March 21, 2015, http://news.sohu.com/20150321/n410099067.shtml.

[88] "Zhongguo jiang xinjian Nanji pobingchuan he 'dayang er hao' chuan" [China will build polar icebreaker and "Ocean II"], *Zhongguo haiyang bao*, August 5, 2015, accessed August 6, 2015, http://www.chinanews.com/gn/2015/08-05/7449557.shtml.

[89] Toni Feder, "China Is Latest Country to Pursue Astronomy in Antarctica," *Physics Today* 64, no. 1 (2011), 22.

Polar Expeditions and Operating Costs

In contrast to the dramatic increase in polar infrastructure spending in the past ten years, China's polar logistics costs have been kept relatively low compared to those of other states. This is actually a strength, rather than a weakness. China's main logistics cost is ship fuel, which accounts for around 90 percent of China's logistics budget. Compared to developed nations such as the United States or the United Kingdom, China has the advantage of a low-wage economy, which keeps personnel budgets low. Until recently, most Chinese scientists travelled to the ice on China's own polar vessel, another major cost saving. Moreover, China's newer polar stations, including Kunlun and Taishan stations, the satellite receiving station at Zhongshan, the Yellow River Station, the Kiruna satellite receiving station, the Iceland aurora observatory, and the iceberg station all use automated data-gathering technology that does not require many scientists to go out into the field, which reduces costs all around. However, with China's expanded number of bases and move to access Antarctica via plane, its logistics costs can be expected to go up considerably in the 13th Five-Year Plan (2016–2020).

From 1983 to 2003, China spent a total of RMB 900 million (around US$110 million) on its Antarctic logistics costs, an average of about US$5.5 million per year. (The actual annual figures were more or less than this amount, depending on variations in spending at the time.) In 2009, a Xinhua report commented that China's Antarctic science was very economical, managing to keep annual polar logistics costs to "several million US dollars" while other countries spent a lot more. Xinhua reported that Argentina spent US$3.5 million, New Zealand spent US$7.5 million, Sweden spent US$7.5 million (a figure that included Arctic funds), Chile spent US$8.0 million, France spent US$26.5 million, the United Kingdom spent US$35 million, and the United States spent $250 million (a figure that also included Arctic funds).[90]

From 1999, China began biannual scientific trips to the Arctic, which increased its logistics costs. In the 10th Five-Year Plan (2001–2005), China spent around US$8 million on logistics alone, but in the 11th Five-Year Plan (2006–2010), the annual polar logistics budget rose to approximately US $15 million.[91] By the 12th Five-Year Plan (2011–2015), the annual operational

---

[90] "Ge guo de Nanji kaocha de touru shi duoshao" [How much does each state spend on Antarctic logistics?], Xinhua, October 9, 2009, http://news.xinhuanet.com/tech/2009-10/14/c ontent_12230013_6.htm.

[91] Chinese polar policymaker, interview with author, May 2012.

budget for China's National Antarctic Program had gone up to US $22 million.[92] Chinese polar officials informed me in 2010 that China's annual Arctic expeditions were 20 percent of the cost of the Antarctic ones, which would put them at around US$4 million per year.[93]

Polar Science Research Funds

In 2012, an *Economist* journalist claimed that China had a larger Arctic research budget than the United States – a laughable statement, as the United States has the largest dedicated polar science budget in the world.[94] China in fact has only relatively small amounts of funding available in dedicated polar science funds. This is a strong indicator that much of China's polar science is still aimed at serving political, rather than strategic, needs. As China's polar administrators complained in 2008, "China's Antarctic-research funds are seriously inadequate, to the point where it is hard to set up significant projects of Antarctic science."[95]

While the polar regions are recognized as being important to China, the opportunities they offer will be available in the mid- to long term, so government-targeted polar science programs are thus only in the exploratory phase. Instead, China provides polar science facilities for scientists and subsidizes logistics costs, then relies on sufficient numbers of the scientific community to be willing to invest in polar knowledge and to garner successful external funding to enable them to engage in meaningful science in the Arctic and Antarctic. As China's polar officials point out, this is a structural weakness in China's polar strategy.[96] If China does move to creating a well-supported national polar science fund, it will be an indicator that polar matters are moving into an even higher gear than before.

As in other aspects of China's polar science budget, the overall budget for polar research is difficult to ascertain with precision as the full figures are not publicly available and there are many Chinese agencies that fund polar science. The polar science funds in the CAA and PRIC budget allocations

[92] "About the Chinese National Antarctic Program," COMNAP, accessed July 23, 2013, https://comnap.aq/Members/CAA/SitePages/Home.aspx.
[93] Chinese polar policymaker, interview with author, July 2010.
[94] Edward Lucas (international editor, *Economist*), interview with senior journalist John Parker, in "Many Voices at the Table," Feast and Famine blog, Economist.com, February 1, 2013, http://www.economist.com/blogs/feastandfamine/2013/02/arctic-politics.
[95] Li Xiaoliang, Long Wei, Zhang Xia, Zhu Jiangang, Li Shenggui, and Sun Yi'ang, "Guowai Nanji kaocha guanli jigou yu kaocha guanli moshi de duibi fenxi" [Comparison and analysis of foreign Antarctic management structures], *Haiyang kaifa yu guanli*, no. 3 (2008): 50.
[96] Li et al., "Guowai Nanji kaocha guanli jigou yu kaocha guanli moshi de duibi fenxi," 50.

are only one small aspect of the polar science fund calculation because most polar researchers must seek their funding from one of the national research funds – which means that they must compete against researchers in many other fields for the available financial support.

The first available figures for Chinese polar science come from 1991, when China had only two Antarctic-related projects worth a total of around US$10,000 (based on 1991 exchange rates).[97] Between 1991 and 2009, various agencies invested around US$44 million in polar science.[98] The main funder for polar projects is China's Natural Sciences Foundation, which funded sixty-three projects between 1991 and 2009; the SOA funded fifty-eight projects and the Ministry of Science and Technology funded forty-five projects in the same period. The China National Basic Research Development Plan, commonly known as the 973 Program, was a further source of polar science funding,[99] as was the marine-focused Special Project 908,[100] while some other projects received funding from universities and local agencies. The current science budget for Dome A astronomy projects is around US$9.8 million, with funding provided by universities and partner observatories.[101] During the 2007–8 IPY, a special year of international polar science projects, China's Ministry of Finance approved a grant of US$5 million for polar science projects.[102] The IPY was the stimulus for China to increase its support for polar science. Since 2006, the Research Fund for the Chinese Polar Science Strategy has given small grants to junior researchers. The CAA also has a separate fund to support Chinese scientists in international research collaborations.[103] The National Social Science Fund, an agency attached to the CCP Central Propaganda Department, has funded three major polar-related social science research projects in the past ten years. The Ministry of Finance has been directly funding a CAA-led project assessing polar resources and governance from 2012 to 2016. This project has a total budget of US$82 million,[104] and both

---

97 PRIC, *Zhongguo jidi yanjiu zhongxin keyan 20 nian 1989–2009* [Twenty years of the PRIC, 1989–2009] (Shanghai: PRIC, 2009), 52–58.

98 Ibid., 52–62.

99 "Guojia zhongdian jichu yanjiu fazhan jihua jianjie" [Introduction to the National Key Basic Research Program], accessed February 13, 2013, http://www.973.gov.cn/AreaAppl.aspx (link discontinued).

100 "Guojia haiyang ju 908 zhuanxiang tongguo zong yanshou mo qing jinhai ziyuan jiadi" [SOA 908 program to ascertain the state of offshore resources], *Renmin ribao*, October 26, 2012, http://politics.people.com.cn/n/2012/1026/c1026-19400553.html.

101 Feder, "China Is Latest Country to Pursue Astronomy in Antarctica," 23.

102 Jing Xiaolei, "Polar Ambitions," *Beijing Review* 36 (September 6, 2007), http://www.bjreview.com.cn/nation/txt/2007-08/31/content_74516.htm.

103 CAA, 2010 *National Annual Report on Polar Program of China*, 58.

104 Chinese polar official, interview with author, October 2013.

social scientists and scientists can access this fund. In 2011, the project allocated US$6 million to researchers, spent US$18 million in 2012, and in 2013 and 2014 US$17 million was spent.[105] In contrast, in 2014 the US National Science Foundation spent US$129 million on polar scientific research,[106] a figure that does not include other scientific research funds available to US polar researchers. In 2015, the recipients and amounts awarded for China's Polar Strategic Fund were made publicly available for the first time, showing that a modest US$174,000 in grants was awarded to be shared between twenty-six projects.[107]

In 2012, the CAA informed the Council of Managers of National Antarctic Programs that China had an annual budget of US$10 million for Antarctic science.[108] In 2013, Chinese polar officials told me that China's annual spend on polar research was around US$16 million, and added that because universities usually matched scientists' funding from these sources, this could bring the figures up to at least $US32 million per year.[109] However, as noted, there are a number of other funding agencies, and the CAA's polar science spending figures do not necessarily incorporate any funding that may have been received from these other agencies. Each Chinese province also has dedicated science projects and funding resources. As a result, many polar science projects have received funds from a combination of sources.

China's dedicated polar research funding does not yet match the capacity of its expanded presence and facilities in the Arctic and Antarctic. Less than 10 percent of China's total polar science spending is devoted to scientific research.[110] China's new facilities will enable China to take its science to a new level, but Chinese polar scientists still must be successful in competing against other scientists for national science and social science research grants. In 2012, polar administrators told me the current system of polar research

[105] Chen Yugang and Wang Wanlu, "Shi xi Zhongguo de Nanji liyi yu quanyi" [Analyzing China's Antarctic interests and rights] (*Jilin Daxue Xuebao*), vol 56, no. 4 (2016): 103.
[106] "Division of Polar Programs FY14 Budget Request," FY 2014 Budget Request to Congress, National Science Foundation, April 10, 2013, https://www.nsf.gov/geo/plr/budget/plr_fy2014.pdf.
[107] "Guanyu zizhu 2015 nian jidi kexue zhanlüe yanjiu jijin xiangmu di gongshi" [Public notice on funding for projects in the 2015 Polar Strategic Fund], CAA, September 30, 2015, http://www.chinare.gov.cn/caa/gb_news.php?id=1630&modid=01005.
[108] "About the Chinese National Antarctic Program."
[109] Chinese polar officials, interviews with author, June 2013.
[110] "Ben bao jizhe zhuanfang Zhongguo jidi yanjiu zhongxin fuzhuren Yang Huigen boshi wo guo yunliang quanqiu kaocha" [A discussion with PRIC deputy director Yang Huigen about China's polar expeditions], *Dalian wanbao*, December 5, 2005, accessed May 31, 2012, http://news.sina.com.cn/s/2005-12-05/00437617786s.shtml.

funding is "not efficient," as polar science is not yet well-coordinated with national policies.[111]

The Significance of China's Polar Spending

Since 2003, when China committed to upgrading its polar infrastructure, China has upped the ante in its level of polar spending and capacity every five years. China is close to achieving its goal of bringing its polar science capacities "on a par" with other leading polar players in Antarctica, and it has the highest level of capacities in the Arctic of non-Arctic states. According to PRIC director Yang Huigen, the next five-year phase of China's polar investment (2016–20) will focus on strategic research looking at Arctic resource utilization and Arctic shipping, as well as assessing the potential of Antarctic mineral resources.[112]

EVALUATING CHINA'S POLAR RESEARCH

Polar scientific breakthroughs are one of the ways in which a nation can build soft power and influence in polar affairs. As a late starter in polar affairs, with limited polar capacity and research team strength, China has had few polar scientific breakthroughs to date. And as recent studies of scientific outputs for the Arctic and Antarctic have demonstrated,[113] China is quite weak in terms of polar science outputs. Beijing is making a major investment in polar research capacity and trying to encourage more Chinese scientists to engage in polar science. Yet despite thirty years of solid effort, China's Antarctic research output is relatively small compared to that of other Antarctic Treaty consultative parties, even smaller than Italy's or South Africa's scientific contribution,

---

[111] Chinese polar official, interview with author, October 2012.

[112] "Zhua zhu jiyu wei jianshe jidi qiangguo er fendou" [Seize the opportunity to work for the creation of a polar great power], SOA, December 17, 2014, http://www.soa.gov.cn/xw/dfdwdt/jsdw_157/201412/t20141217_34481.html.

[113] For the Arctic, see Iselin Stensdal, *Asian Arctic Research 2012–2013: Harder, Better, Faster, Stronger*, FNI Report 3/2013 (Lysaker, Norway: Fridtjof Nansen Institute, 2013). For the Antarctic, see Prabir G. Dastidar and Olle Persson, "Mapping the Global Structure of Antarctic Research Vis-à-Vis Antarctic Treaty System," *Current Science* 89, no. 9 (2005): 1552–54; Prabir G. Dastidar, "National and Institutional Productivity and Collaboration in Antarctic Science: An Analysis of 25 Years of Journal Publications (1980–2004)," *Polar Research* 26, no. 2 (2007): 175–80; and John R. Dudeney and David W. H. Walton, "Leadership in Politics and Science within the Antarctic Treaty," *Polar Research* 31 (2012): 1–9.

and its Arctic research is still in early stages.[114] This is not simply from lack of resources. According to Chinese Antarctic international law specialist Zou Keyuan, China's early Antarctic research was "symbolic," meaning that it mostly served political ends rather than scientific ones.[115] Chinese polar officials repeatedly emphasize that their country's Antarctic program is not just about answering scientific questions; it is as much, if not more, about China's national interests.[116] For the twenty years of its existence, China's Antarctic program suffered from limited logistical capabilities and funding for projects in the field, limitations in computer facilities available to Antarctic researchers, a lack of timely access to relevant scientific literature, and a lack of funding for high-quality scientific equipment.[117] Chinese Antarctic scientist Dong Zhiquan, who led China's first Antarctic expedition in 1983, stated in 2004 that because of such problems, most of his nation's Antarctic research had been derivative.[118] Polar politics scholar Guo Peiqing notes that regardless of the scientific significance of research in Antarctica, engaging in this research and launching expeditions are ways for China (and other nations) to maintain a political presence on the continent.[119]

A 2012 bibliometric analysis by data specialist Wang Xuemei confirms the international research on China's polar science ranking and takes it even further. Wang surveyed leading polar science journals in the ISI Web of Science between 1971 and 2010, and found that China ranked very low in terms of citation rates and output of papers.[120] She found that three-quarters of China's polar science publishing is on the Antarctic, as that is where China has been active for longest. In contrast, since 2009 more than half of Chinese polar social science writing has been on the Arctic, as China comes to grip with the governance arrangements there in a time of considerable change.

[114] Prabir G. Dastidar and Olle Persson, "Mapping the Global Structure of Antarctic Research Vis-à-vis Antarctic Treaty System," *Current Science* 89, no. 9 (2004): 1552–54.

[115] Zou Keyuan, "China's Interests in and Policy toward Antarctica," in *Asia in Antarctica*, ed. Bruce Davis and Richard Herr (Canberra: Australian National University Centre for Resource and Environmental Studies, 1994), 97.

[116] Yu Dawei, "Nanji 'sanji tiao'" [Triple jump in Antarctica], *Caijing*, no. 16 (August 4, 2008), http://magazine.caixin.com/2008-08-04/100087807.html.

[117] J. Cole-Dai, Y. Li, S. Liu, and Z. Zhang, "Antarctica Research in the Polar Research Center of China" (poster presentation at the American Geophysical Union 2003 Fall meeting, San Francisco, December 8–13, 2003).

[118] Yang Jianxiang, "China Takes Bold Steps into Antarctic's Forbidding Interior," *Science* 306 (October 29, 2004): 803.

[119] Guo Peiqing, "Nanji ziyuan yu qi ziyuan zhengzhi" [Antarctic resources and the politics of resources], *Haiyang shijie* 3 (2007), 70.

[120] Wang Xuemei, "Jiu wenxian jiliang de guoji jidi yanjiu jinzhan fenxi" [A bibliometrical analysis of international polar research], *Science Focus* 7, no. 2 (2012): 33–40.

Wang noted that polar-related scientific research is on the increase globally, and most published research comes from international collaborations. However, she found that China is underrepresented in many fields of study, as well as in terms of international polar science collaborations leading to publication. She concluded by recommending that the Chinese government should encourage more oceanographers, meteorologists, geologists, environmental ecologists, biologists, socioeconomists, and political scientists to engage in polar research in order to help China expand its polar engagement.[121]

Yet few Chinese scientists make a career of polar science, and even fewer Chinese social scientists specialize in polar affairs. By 2009, around 4,000 Chinese personnel had visited Antarctica,[122] but most were not scientists. Currently, around 500 Chinese scientists are working on polar topics, but the number is not stable as many young scholars move on to research other topics. China's polar research is scattered in a broad range of fields and there are big generational gaps.[123] A further study, also published in 2012 and commissioned by the CAA, ranked the Antarctic scientific capabilities of various Antarctic states. The authors found that China averaged about twenty-six Antarctic science projects per year, in contrast to Australia's average of 185 projects per year and the US average of 147 projects per year. The authors ranked China 11th in terms of scientific activity, compared to twenty-eight other Antarctic states.[124]

Compared to the current polar great powers, the United States and Russia, China's polar science may serve national goals, but it seldom has been internationally competitive. As shown by the funding model, Chinese polar science adopts a scattergun approach; there is relatively little dedicated funding and, as yet, no central plan. It is mostly aimed at establishing a presence in the polar regions and the right to speak on polar governance. In 2010, scientists at China's research base at Ny-Ålesund, Yellow River Station, conducted around a thousand working days on research, making their base one of the most active in the Ny-Ålesund settlement.[125] But it is quality, not quantity, that

[121] Ibid, 40.
[122] "Zhongguo Nanji kaocha 25 zhounian: Heping liyong nanji yong buguo shi" [25 years of Antarctic expeditions: Peaceful use of Antarctica never dates], Xinhua, October 14, 2009, http://news.xinhuanet.com/tech/2009-10/14/content_12232453.htm.
[123] Chinese polar official, interview with author, October 2012.
[124] Hua Weina and Zhang Xia, eds., *Nanji tiaoyue xieshang guo Nanji huodong nengli diaoyan tongji baogao* [Statistical report on the Antarctic capabilities of the Antarctic Treaty Consultative Parties] (Beijing: Haiyang chubanshe, 2012), 55–86.
[125] Lotta Numminen, "A History and Functioning of the Spitsbergen Treaty," in *The Spitsbergen Treaty: Multilateral Governance in the Arctic*, ed. Diana Wallis and Stewart Arnold, Arctic Papers Vol. 1, 17, http://dianawallis.org.uk/en/document/spitsbergen-treaty-booklet.pdf.

matters in science. China's activities at Ny-Ålesund, like those of other states active there, are as much about establishing an Arctic presence and gaining international recognition for their legitimate Arctic interests as they are about scientific outputs.

This particular depiction also affects how Antarctic scientific activity is presented. Kunlun Station, for example, has advanced telescopes for deep space research that relay their signals back to scientists in China via satellite. The Kunlun astronomy project has involved collaboration among Australian, Chinese, and US scientists. But the Chinese media seldom mention this fact, writing as if the Chinese scientists there were working in isolation. Chinese astronomers hope that the research done on Dome A may lead to a Nobel Prize. To achieve this objective, the project needs a world-leading telescope suitable for engaging in first-class deep space research.[126] But China is unable to purchase US telescopes, which are regarded as the best in the world. The US government has banned the sale of astronomical and other space-related equipment to China, and banned all overall space-related cooperation with China. Until recently, a further crucial factor holding the Chinese astronomers back from reaching their scientific goals has been regular access to Kunlun Station. Chinese astronomers have said that they "have no control" over whether they can access Kunlun Station to conduct their science projects.[127] However, now that China has an air link between Zhongshan and Kunlun stations, access should be less of a problem for China's polar astronomers.

The ice underneath Dome A is over 3,000 meters thick. Researchers predict that the ice cores they can drill there will expand current knowledge about the earth's climate record back to 1.5 million years. This information is important to China's climate-change diplomats as they negotiate over their country's efforts to reduce global warming. The ice core research will also enable Chinese scientists to determine the geology of the rocks beneath the ice, important for understanding the resource potential of the region.[128] China will be in charge of research efforts at Dome A, working in collaboration with teams of international researchers. The first experimental drilling was done in January 2013. China plans to drill for the next five years. If successful, the

[126]   Yang Ji, "Dome A Astronomical Observatory Plan: 2011–2015" (presentation at the SCAR 2010 Astronomy and Astrophysics from Antarctica Scientific Research Program meeting, Xi'an, China, August 18, 2010), http://aag.bao.ac.cn/Academic/xian/ppt/8.18am/yang_ji.pdf.

[127]   Shang Zhaohui, "Updates of AST-3 Survey" (presentation at the SCAR 2013 Astronomy and Astrophysics from Antarctica Scientific Research Program meeting, Siena, Italy, July 25, 2013), http://www.astronomy.scar.org/AAA2013/pdf/Shang.pdf.

[128]   "Hu Jianmin: Wei Nanji Geluofu shan huizhi shou zhang dizhi tu."

research outcomes will give China an unprecedented opportunity to achieve international recognition for its Antarctic scientific research. The ability to produce high-caliber polar scientific research – and have it noticed and cited in the international science community – is one of the key markers of a polar power.

EVALUATING CHINA'S POLAR INTERNATIONAL COLLABORATION

China has an extensive program of scientific collaboration with other polar states. China's international polar collaborations can both help China improve its polar science and reassure other polar states that China has a bona fide interest in exploring scientific questions in the Arctic and Antarctic. A key means to do this is through international collaborations, building on the polar experience and knowledge of various countries. China benefited from scientific collaboration with the Soviet Union in the Arctic in the 1950s and in Antarctica with Australia and New Zealand in the early 1980s. China is continuing to participate in international collaboration and is now also reaching out to help other new players to develop polar scientific capacity, being careful not to become overly dependent on one country for its scientific collaborations. Individual Chinese polar scientific teams have formed partnerships with international polar scholars from a wide range of countries, and China strongly encourages international polar scientific collaboration.

These days, Chinese scientists in the Arctic work with scientists from Canada, Denmark, Greenland, Finland, Iceland, Norway, Russia, and the United States. China has a particularly extensive program of polar scientific and diplomatic collaboration with Iceland. China's new embassy building in Reykjavík has attracted a lot of attention due to its size. Journalists have referred to the building as China's "Arctic embassy"; they claim that the new embassy could house up to 500 personnel, and there is much speculation about China's intentions in building an embassy so large.[129] In 2012, Chinese diplomats told me that the building was planned during Iceland's bubble economy, when costs were a lot higher. The project received a large budget to match costs at the time, but after the collapse of the Iceland economy in 2008 they still received the same amount of funds. They were able to build a much larger building with the money, though staffing levels remain the same – around six or seven diplomatic staff. The Chinese diplomats said that the extra space in the new building will be used for exhibitions. Icelandic diplomats

[129] Didi Kirsten Tatlow, "China and the Northern Rivalry," *International Herald Tribune*, October 5, 2012, http://nyti.ms/1gCRIHg.

told me that the embassy was "built for the future," and said that Iceland-China relations will greatly strengthen if the Arctic shipping route develops. Iceland's ever-closer relations with China have helped Iceland strengthen its dealings with other major powers.

In Antarctica, China has developed a broad program of international collaboration with Australia, Canada, Chile, France, Germany, Norway, Japan, New Zealand, South Korea, Romania, Russia, the United Kingdom, and the United States. China's closest collaborative Antarctic partner is South Korea. In 2013, the two countries signed an agreement for the joint sharing of bases and icebreakers and joint research.[130] By 2018, the two countries will have access to seven bases and three icebreakers between them. Both countries have similar interests in Antarctica, focusing on resources and science, and both are looking at ways to strengthen their presence and authority to speak on Antarctic affairs. China also has strong strategic links with a number of near-Antarctic states: with Australia owing to the need to access China's two East Antarctic bases via the ports of Fremantle and Hobart; with Chile, with whose help China has an air link to its Great Wall Station; and increasingly also with New Zealand, as China expands its Antarctic presence into the Ross Sea area.

EVALUATING CHINA'S PARTICIPATION IN POLAR GOVERNANCE

Since the early 1980s, China has, progressively, joined every polar political, scientific, or economic grouping it could possibly join. China signed the Antarctic Treaty in 1983, was made a consultative party to the treaty in 1985, became a full member of the Scientific Committee on Antarctic Research in 1986, and signed up to the Convention for the Conservation of Antarctic Marine Living Resources in 2007. China has hosted a number of Antarctic Treaty–related meetings over the years, and it hosted the annual Antarctic Treaty Consultative Meeting in 2017. China is also a member of the Hydrographic Commission on Antarctica, which charts Antarctic waters.[131]

In the Antarctic, the governance structures are relatively streamlined, but in the Arctic there are multiple governance organizations. China joined the International Arctic Science Committee (IASC) in 1996 and hosted the annual IASC meeting in Kunming in 2005, the first time it had been held in

---

[130] "Hamjung namgeugseo sonjab-assda, giji gongdonghwal-yong" [China and Korea join hands, joint use of Antarctic bases], *Chosun Ilbo*, November 29, 2013, https://www.kookje .co.kr/news2011/asp/newsbody.asp?code=0200&key=20131130.22010205349.

[131] "IHO Hydrographic Commission on Antarctica," International Hydrographic Organization, May 23, 2016, http://www.iho.int/srv1/index.php?option=com_content&view=article&id=436& Itemid=394.

Asia. China is a founding member of the Pacific Arctic Group (affiliated with the IASC and founded in 2004), a loose grouping of policymakers and scientists linking Asian states with an interest in the Arctic with Arctic states. Russia, the United States, Canada, China, South Korea, and Japan are also members of the Pacific Arctic Group, but China has sixteen representatives with the group, while the United States and Russia have only four each. The group hosts periodic joint conferences on scientific topics and is trying to collaborate on scientific projects and share data.[132]

China is a founding member (from 1997) of the twenty-one-member UN Commission on the Limits of the Continental Shelf, which will make recommendations on the outer limits of Arctic seabed claims. Commission membership is usually limited to a five-year term. China's scientist representative, Lu Wenzhang, is a specialist on seabed minerals; unusually, he has served continuously on the commission since 1997.[133] The International Seabed Authority (ISA) manages mining in international seabed areas. China has representatives on the ISA's Council, Legal and Technical Commission, and Finance Committee.[134] China has been a member of the International Maritime Organization since 1973, and is one of the Class A members of the organization that are able to decide on policy. Despite its strong interests in Arctic shipping, China is not yet an observer (only Arctic coastal states can be members) at the Arctic Regional Hydrographic Commission, which is coordinating bathymetric, biometric, and mapping information of Arctic waters.[135]

China has had an ongoing observer role at the Arctic Council since 2013. The Arctic Council requires all ongoing observers to contribute to Arctic Council working groups. China currently participates in the Arctic Monitoring and Assessment Programme, the Conservation of Arctic Flora and Fauna Working Group, and Arctic Contaminants Action Programme Working Group. These groups conduct in-depth research on migratory birds, black carbon, methane climate pollutants, cryosphere and atmospheric monitoring, and ocean acidification, among other issues. China is also a member of a scientific group attached to the Arctic Council known as the Sustaining

---

[132] See, e.g., "Pacific Arctic Group (PAG)," International Arctic Science Committee, accessed May 23, 2016, http://www.pagscience.org and http://pag.arcticportal.org/.

[133] "Members of the CLCS," United Nations Commission on the Limits of the Continental Shelf, August 8, 2014, http://www.un.org/depts/los/clcs_new/commission_members.htm.

[134] "About the International Seabed Authority," ISA, 2016, https://www.isa.org.jm/authority.

[135] "Arctic Regional Hydrographic Commission (ARHC)," International Hydrographic Organization, April 22, 2016, http://www.iho.int/srv1/index.php?option=com_content&view=article&id=435:arctic-hc-arhc&catid=64:4ircc&Itemid=690.

Arctic Observing Network,[136] which aims to coordinates Arctic scientific data in the same way that SCADAM does for Antarctic scientific data.[137]

Outside of these international scientific and government organizations, China also has a presence on groups that have a more regional or subnational focus. China is represented by Heilongjiang Province at the Northern Forum, a grouping of twenty-four subnational and regional units of Arctic and near-Arctic governments established in 1993. The Northern Forum focuses on economic concerns and the issue of sustainable development in Arctic and near-Arctic areas that are heavily dependent on resource extraction. The forum has observer status in the Arctic Council.[138] China is also a member of the World Winter Cities Association for Mayors, which provides the world's winter cities with a forum to discuss common issues in order to create more livable cities. Seven of the association's twenty city members are Chinese cities.[139] China also is represented in the University of the Arctic, a group of Arctic-focused universities that offer joint programs of study. China Oceanic University, which is administered by the SOA, became a member of the consortium in 2013. China sent a large delegation to the inaugural meeting of the Arctic Circle, initiated by Iceland in 2013, and PRIC head Yang Huigen is on the Arctic Circle advisory board. China is a founding member of the Asian Forum for Polar Science, which works to coordinate the polar policies of China, Japan, South Korea, Malaysia, India, and Thailand.

APPLES AND ORANGES? COMPARING CHINA AGAINST OTHER POLAR STATES

It is commonly said in polar affairs that trying to compare the polar capacity, and influence of various polar players is like "comparing apples and oranges" – it cannot be done. Each country calculates its Antarctic and Arctic budgets differently: some include all logistics costs and some do not, some include scientific research budgets and some do not. Despite requirements for transparency, the full amounts spent are often not publicly available. Nonetheless, many

---

[136]   See "Committees," Sustaining Arctic Observing Network, accessed May 23, 2016, http://www .arcticobserving.org/committees/.

[137]   "Zhongguo kexuejia jiang zai Beiji kexue yanjiu wutai banyan geng jiji juese" [Chinese scientists will play more active role in the Arctic], Xinhua, January 24, 2015, accessed January 24, 2015, http:// roll.sohu.com/20150124/n408043338.shtml (link discontinued).

[138]   See the Northern Forum's Mission and Structure page at the Northern Forum website, http:// www.northernforum.org/en/the-northern-forum/about-the-northern-forum/mission-and-structure.

[139]   "World Winter Cities Association for Mayors – Member Cities," City of Sapporo, April 27, 2016, http://www.city.sapporo.jp/somu/kokusai/wwcam/membercities_e.html.

of the multiple actors and states engaged in polar activities are interested in "comparing apples and oranges" in polar affairs, no matter how difficult the task might be.

China has been particularly obsessed with matching its progress in polar affairs against other players, first pitching to bring itself on a par with the developed states active in Antarctica and within a few years setting the goal of overtaking developed states to become a "polar great power." In 2011, a book-length, PRIC-funded Nanjing University study evaluated the Antarctic activities of various states, examining their scientific programs, scientific outputs, public education on polar affairs, attitude toward environmental protection, level of commercial activities, and participation in the Antarctic system. It found that the United States, United Kingdom, Germany, Australia, Russia, Argentina, and Chile have strong Antarctic presences through their science programs; and the United States, European Union, Australia, Russia, and Japan have a high level of Antarctic scientific publications. It noted that the United States, Germany, United Kingdom, Australia, New Zealand, and Uruguay all emphasize environmental protection in their policies and practices. The report assesses the United States, EU, Australia, Japan, and South Korea as all having a high level of commercial involvement in polar affairs.[140] However, such rankings do not tell the full story of each nation's comparative Antarctic power and influence.

Similarly, China's officially available polar spending figures do not tell the full story of its growing polar power. They do not include scientific research funds, and do not acknowledge the massive sums of money being spent to update China's logistics capacity and presence in the polar regions. As these funds are acknowledged and discussed in internal publications on China's polar presence, this downplaying of China's spending patterns can only be seen as disingenuous. However, as noted above, China is not alone in not making the full figures of its polar investment publicly known. Moreover, it should be noted that some countries active in the Antarctic and the Arctic refuse to publicly present *any* budgets that would reveal the extent of their engagement there.[141]

EVALUATING CHINA'S POLAR STRENGTHS AND WEAKNESSES

In 2014, SOA party secretary, Liu Cigui, responding to Xi Jinping's keynote speech on polar affairs, modestly announced that China would become

[140]   "Zhongguo jidi yanjiu zhongxin jidi ruankexue yanjiuwang 2011" [2011 PRIC Soft science research page], accessed February 13, 2013, http://softsceince.chinare.org.cn/softsceince/index.jsp.

[141]   See "Our Members," COMNAP, accessed June 19, 2015, https://www.comnap.aq/Members/SitePages/Home.aspx.

a polar great power "within thirty years." It was remarkably low-key rhetoric compared to statements that Liu and other SOA officials had made in previous years, but this prudent talk may reflect the fact that the CCP leadership has now finally publicly announced the concept of China as a polar great power. But does China really need to wait thirty years before being classified as a polar great power? The graphs in figures 5.11, 5.12, and 5.13 give only a brief visual

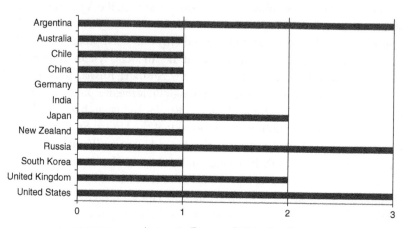

FIGURE 5.12 Antarctic-Purposed Ships by Country

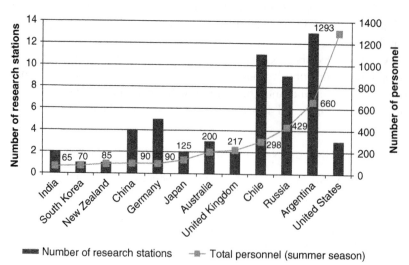

FIGURE 5.13 Antarctic Research Stations and Personnel by Country

indication of China's physical investment in polar resources, compared with that of other polar-engaged nations.

China's Polar Strengths

By the end of the 13th Five-Year Plan (2016–2020), with two ice-fitted ships operational, and use of ice-suitable continental and transcontinental aircraft, China will have achieved its goal of catching up with the operational capabilities of the other polar great powers active in Antarctica – Russia and the United States. According to Chinese media reports, China's enhanced polar scientific transportation capacity will make it "one of the few self-sufficient polar science programs in the world," able, if necessary, to operate even without the cooperation of other polar states. Currently, only the United States and Russia have this level of capacity. As the report notes, this substantial investment in infrastructure will greatly enhance China's ability to pursue its own objectives in the Arctic and Antarctic.[142]

In terms of presence measured by bases, with five bases and one semipermanent research camp spread out across the Antarctic continent (along with the two additional research stations shared with South Korea), by the end of the 13th Five-Year Plan, China will be on a par with the United States and will have overtaken Russia. The enhanced capacity and logistics support also will enable China to take its polar science investment to the next level. Compared to many states, China is still sending only a relatively modest number of scientists to Antarctica; however, the use of robots and other such equipment means that China may never need to send as many personnel to the polar regions as established players have sent.

In Antarctic governance, influential science garners prestige and enhances leadership; it can also help sway governance decisions. If China wants to be an innovator in helping to shape future governance norms in Antarctica or on global issues related to Antarctica (such as climate change), it will need to have the science to back up its position. However, if China's main concern is to maintain the political status quo in Antarctica until such time as the issue of exploiting Antarctic mineral resources comes up for debate again (most likely, in 2048), then it need not make any special efforts to upgrade its Antarctic science. It can simply use its veto to act as a spoiler on any efforts to promote further conservation measures that might restrict its interests – as it did in 2012, 2013, 2014, and 2015 when it opposed bids for new Marine Protected Areas

---

[142]   "Zhongguo Nanji kaocha 25 zhounian: Heping liyong Nanji yong buguo shi."

(MPAs) in Antarctica and helped ensure the Ross Sea MPA passed in 2016 was restricted to thirty-five years.

If China's presence in the Arctic is measured only in terms of scientific logistics capacity and physical presence, by the end of the 13th Five-Year Plan it will have the strongest capacity of any non-Arctic state. In the Arctic, much more so than the Antarctic, polar scientific capacity is only one means to calculate a nation's influence and power in the region. Non-Arctic states' scientific presence in the Arctic is relatively restricted compared to that found in Antarctica: they can only make use of the special status of Svalbard Island, engage in bilateral arrangements with Arctic states, or use international waters for iceberg stations or marine surveys. However, outside players can take on a leading role in Arctic affairs through many other means: through involvement in international governance that touches on Arctic issues, as investors, as buyers of Arctic resources, as users of Arctic waters and airspace (whether for commercial or military use), as sources of foreign labor, as foreign students, and as foreign tourists. In the past ten years, China has become increasingly active in all these spheres of Arctic engagement, and as a consequence it is being courted as a partner by many Arctic states. Thus, Beijing can be a significant player in the Arctic with only a modest investment in Arctic science.

China's Polar Weaknesses

Although China is making a major investment in polar science capacity, at present many of its polar activities are relatively uncoordinated and inefficient. China's polar research is also limited by lack of access to dedicated funds. Research funding is competitive in China, and few funds are dedicated to polar research. A few dedicated polar specialists have devoted themselves to the field, but most scientists who go on China's polar expeditions are only at doctoral or postdoctoral levels and they do not continue in the polar studies field – it is not lucrative or prestigious enough, the results come too slowly, and it is too arduous to obtain such results. These scholars are likely to do one polar-related project and then move on to a new area of research, and this transience affects the quality and the impact of China's polar science. To become more effective, China's polar administration also requires a clearer division of labor and a better mechanism for policy coordination among the various government agencies with polar interests. The lack of a formal strategy document is another point holding back China's polar expansion.

China's polar program may look impressive to many outsiders, but Chinese polar officials continue to talk it down, highlighting its weaknesses. This can be read as a tactical move to increase targeted funding and bring about institutional change, but there is no denying the great strides China has made, as well as the many weaknesses in its polar scientific program. In 2006, PRIC director Yang Huigen revealed in an interview with a Chinese newspaper that behind the fanfare over China's polar success lie some serious structural issues, which as of writing still have not been resolved:

- China's polar science data lacks credibility because of methodological issues.
- Existing published work and new projects are often duplicated. For example, Yang noted that three separate Chinese research teams were researching krill in the Southern Ocean in 2006.
- China's Antarctic science lacks proper data collection, sample storage methods, and strategic planning. For instance, data from earlier expeditions had been saved on out-of-date software that was now inaccessible, meaning that the research had gone to waste.
- China's Great Wall Station has limited use from a scientific point of view.
- In funding, the emphasis is placed on expeditions rather than on scientific projects.
- China's polar activities have an inefficient organizational structure – for instance, ten different work units are involved in approving various aspects of China's polar expeditions.
- Funding for polar activities comes too slow, and comes through various funding agencies that do not prioritize polar research.
- Scientific projects on the polar expeditions often are decided upon at the last moment.
- Polar projects often lack a strategic plan or do not have a sharp focus on the particular polar science topics that will be addressed.
- Despite the requirements of the Antarctic Treaty, not all Chinese scientists who return from Antarctic research are complying with requests to make their data publicly available, and under current bureaucratic arrangements, the PRIC lacks the authority to compel them to do so.
- China lacks mid-career scientists involved in polar research. Polar research was a hot topic in the early days of China's Antarctic activities, but the lack of funding and need for scientists to spend up to five months on ships in order to pursue their research put off most from continuing that earlier interest.

- Chinese media are not interested in reporting on polar science; they report only on expeditions.
- The PRIC needs to attract cutting-edge scientists back to polar research. Most scientists on the expeditions are doctoral candidates; junior researchers come because they are looking for research opportunities, but they seldom specialize in polar research. It takes many years to get an outcome out of polar research, and Chinese scientists want faster results.[143]

Similarly, in 2005 CAA deputy director Wu Jun critiqued the Chinese polar program for a lack of seriousness in following through on scientific plans and a lack of budget accountability.[144] Other weaknesses he highlighted include the lack of central agency to lead and determine polar policy; the lack of a centralized polar affairs budget; the lack of a long-term polar work plan compared to other polar states such as the United States, United Kingdom, or Japan; and the lack of an official strategy.[145] Wu said that China should copy from other polar states and professionalize base management, allowing polar scientists to focus on science.[146] In 2014, CAA director Qu Tanzhou added to Wu's criticisms, commenting that "China is facing a new round of competition for Antarctic resources and interests from a relatively passive position." He continued, "China is still relatively weak in polar science compared to other leading Antarctic states because it lacks a fixed polar expedition and polar research funding budget. Only a relatively small number of scientists work on polar issues, and their numbers fluctuate. China lacks a long-term polar science strategy, while China's polar research management system needs upgrading."[147]

China's polar program has ambitious and visionary bureaucrats and scholars involved in it, and now the support of China's most senior leader, Xi Jinping, but its key weaknesses have not yet been ironed out. Xi's "landmark" November 2014 Hobart speech heralded a new level of impetus for China's polar affairs.[148] The day after Xi's speech, a commentary on the significance of Xi's words made by SOA party secretary Liu Cigui addressed all the concerns that Yang, Wu, and Qu had raised over the years. The CAA-led project to

---

[143]   "Zhuan fang Zhongguo jidi yanjiu zhongxin fuzhuren Yang Huigen boshi" [Special interview with Dr. Yang Huigen, PRIC deputy director], *Dalian wanbao*, January 4, 2006, http://tech.sina.com.cn/d/2006-01-04/1759810860.shtml.

[144]   Wu, "Wo guo jidi kaocha zuzhi guanli jizhi youhua yanjiu," 32.

[145]   Ibid. 31.

[146]   Ibid., 45.

[147]   "Xingzhan Nanji, Zhongguo zai xingdong."

[148]   "Zhua zhu jiyu wei jianshe jidi qiangguo er fendou."

investigate polar resources and governance will provide the groundwork for a more strategic approach to polar affairs in the next ten to twenty years.

IS CHINA A POLAR LEADER?

Is China as a polar leader? Does it want to be? And how can leadership in polar affairs be measured? Dudeney and Walton's research ranked Antarctic states according to their contribution to the typical indicators of demonstrating leadership in Antarctic affairs, such as producing working papers and information papers as part of the Antarctic Treaty consultative process.[149] China ranked low on those measures. Yet China has been steadily acquiring leadership roles in polar governance. From 1991 to 2009, China took on a total of twenty-four leadership roles in various polar governance bodies such as the SCAR, the Asian Forum for Polar Sciences, the IPY, the Pacific Arctic Group, and IASC.[150] China has also been the location for many international polar conferences in the past ten years, which is an important means for an emerging polar nation to build up prestige and influence.[151] As noted, in 2011 the SOA deputy director, Chen Lianzeng, stated that the overall goal of China's current five-year polar plan was to increase China's "status and influence" in polar affairs to better protect its "polar rights."[152] A 2012 report on China's maritime policies stated that China's influence in polar affairs is growing stronger and stronger.[153]

China is interested in being more influential in Arctic and Antarctic affairs and wants to protect its rights, but China is not trying to change anything in polar governance and in the medium term it is strongly in favor of the status quo. China gains considerable benefits from the current arrangements in Antarctic governance. The only areas where it has a clear stance on seeking change are in relation to the exploitation of mineral resources and with regard to Antarctic sovereignty. Chinese policymakers regard it as a "matter of time" before the Antarctic Treaty nations change their policy on Antarctic minerals; they believe that the decision will be made collectively when the technical barriers and financial cost-efficiencies have been overcome, and when other

[149]   Dudeney and Walton, "Leadership in Politics and Science within the Antarctic Treaty," 1–9.
[150]   *Zhongguo jidi yanjiu zhongxin keyan 20 nian 1989–2009*, 134.
[151]   "Zhuan fang Zhongguo jidi yanjiu zhongxin fuzhuren Yang Huigen boshi."
[152]   "Wo guo xinjin jidi kexue kaocha pobingchuan lizheng 2013 nian touru shiyong" [Our new polar expedition icebreaker should be ready by 2013], Xinhua, June 22, 2011, http://news .xinhuanet.com/tech/2011-06/22/c_121566754.htm.
[153]   Guojia haiyangju haiyang fazhan zhanlue yanjiusuo ketizu, *Zhongguo haiyang fazhan baogao*, 364.

global sources of resources have been exhausted. China's position on Antarctic sovereignty is the same as all but seven signatories to the Antarctic Treaty – the claimant states – and like the issue of mineral resource exploitation, this issue also will require a collective decision. Like all the other states active in Antarctica, China is calculating that its best preparation for the future is to increase its physical presence there. Meanwhile, in the Arctic, while China seeks greater influence, it does not claim or seek leadership. Instead, it prefers the phrase "partnership" (*huoban*).[154]

---

[154] "Zhongguo 'huoban guanxi' bianbu quanqiu bushihuoban bu yiding guanxi cha" [States that are not labeled as "partnerships" are not necessarily lacking], Xinhua, June 6, 2013, http://www.chinanews.com/gn/2013/06-06/4900469.shtml.

6

Cooperation or Conflict? China's Position on Points of Contention in the Polar Regions

In September 1983, Guo Kun – China's top polar official – and three other senior officials traveled to Canberra, Australia, to participate in China's first Antarctic Treaty Consultative Meeting. China had signed the Antarctic Treaty in July 1983, nearly thirty years after Chinese scientists had first expressed an interest in being active in Antarctic science. Guo and his team were very excited to be at the ATCM. But Guo's excitement quickly turned to shame and a sense of deep resentment that would stay with him for the rest of his life.

Even though China had signed the Antarctic Treaty several months earlier, it was not yet a full party to the treaty. (China did not become a consultative party until October 1985.) As a result, Guo and the rest of the Chinese delegation were required to sit at the back of the meeting room, without allocated seats, and could only watch the meeting unfold as spectators. The ultimate humiliation – at least in Guo's telling and retelling of the story over many years – was that each time the meeting went into a deliberative stage, a gavel would sound and the Chinese delegation (along with other nonconsultative parties at the meeting) would be asked to "step out for a cup of coffee." In a 2014 television interview, Guo, now in his eighties and weeping as he narrated this indignity, said that he and the other members of the Chinese delegation "walked out in tears." Guo added that after the Canberra meeting, he vowed never to return to another ATCM until China had its own Antarctic base that would secure its "right to speak" (*huayu quan*) on Antarctic affairs.[1]

Guo's painful narrative, which has been repeated in the Chinese media and features prominently in China's polar historiography, puts China's ascent into

---

[1] See the 2014 Phoenix Television documentary "Zhongguo Nanji Changcheng zhan shou ren zhan zhang Guo Kun" [China's first Antarctic Great Wall Station leader: Guo Kun], Phoenix Television video, 35:38, February 16, 2014, http://v.ifeng.com/documentary/figure/2014002/032eac33-d2be-489e-afde-4df734a0921f.shtml.

the world's top polar nations into a broader context that all Chinese can understand and feel in their bones. It is part of a familiar narrative of China as a nation that was long excluded from the top table by Western nations. It matters little in this historiography that the People's Republic of China has been a member of the United Nations Security Council since 1971. The humiliation in Canberra has played into the Chinese Communist Party's narrative of China as a victim of Western imperialism and has given weight to the Chinese government's quest to acquire appropriate status in the revised international order.

As a signatory to the Antarctic Treaty, the Chinese delegation was entitled to attend the meeting, but only consultative parties to the treaty could be in the room when policymaking decisions were being made. Perhaps Guo was unaware of these rules at the time, although he certainly would have been aware of them when he relayed the story to journalists in 2014. Narratives such as Guo's underpin the trope that has appeared repeatedly in the speeches of Chinese leaders and scholars since 2008: that China is somehow missing out on the "right to speak" in international governance and global international public opinion is constantly set against it. The Chinese media has helped frame Guo's story as another instance of China's being denied this right at a polar governance meeting and being given inferior status within a perceived hierarchy of polar nations. The logical response to this historical narrative is Beijing's present-day emphasis on the "right to speak" on polar affairs and assertion of China's polar "rights and interests" (*quanyi*). These expressions are the key political phrases (*tifa*) that have appeared regularly in discussions of China's rapid expansion in polar affairs in the past ten years, and feature prominently in contemporary discussions on China's international role.

The way in which China frames the polar regions is a window into how the government perceives issues of contention in the polar regions. The key frames of Chinese polar affairs are –

- China's past exclusion from polar science and governance;
- The polar regions as a "treasure chest" of mineral resources;
- The polar regions as a global commons;
- The polar regions as a barometer of climate change; and
- The polar regions as a zone for China's emergence as a global power.

Other polar states and interested actors (though less so China) have promoted two other framing concepts:

- The polar regions as a special wilderness area of the world deserving of protection; and
- The negative impact of development in the polar regions.

Arctic governance is in a state of flux, whereas Antarctic governance mechanisms are much more settled and ordered. However, political tension is rising in both regions as many core issues remain unresolved and climate change is bringing new opportunities. China's perspective on polar governance is of interest both to its potential rivals and to those that are interested in working with it. The current main points of contention in the polar regions center around sovereignty, governance, resources, and environmental protection. Although China has not yet issued a formal statement on its Arctic or Antarctic strategy, its position on these contentious issues is available through analysis of open- and closed-source Chinese-language materials.

CHINA'S POSITION ON POLAR SOVEREIGNTY

The Arctic region is a mixture of sovereign territories, internal waters, and high seas. The Antarctic Treaty, by contrast, leaves open the issue of the sovereign status of the Antarctic continent and its surrounding seas. China has been following sovereignty disputes in the Arctic, such as those between the Soviet Union and Norway, since at least the 1970s. China has long-standing concerns about Arctic sovereignty, and during the Cold War it raised public objections about the Soviet Union's behavior in its northern waters.[2] China's current official position on the unresolved aspect of Arctic sovereignty is that the Arctic Ocean is "international waters" (*guoji gonggong haiyu*).[3] However, China's official definition of Antarctic sovereignty is that it is "a continent with no attribution of sovereignty" (*zhuquan meiyou guishu de dalü*).[4] The legal equivalent of this definition is *res nullius*. Bouvier's law dictionary defines *res nullius* as 1. "A thing which has no owner. A thing which has been abandoned by its owner is as much res nullius as if it had never belonged to anyone. 2. The first possessor of such a thing becomes the owner, res nullius fit primi occupantis."[5] Many other nonclaimant states in Antarctica, including the United States, use the term "international space" to describe Antarctica,

---

[2] "People's Daily Raps Soviet Schemes on Maritime Rights Issue," *Peking NCNA*, November 3, 1977, FBIS-CHI-77-049.

[3] "Woguo Beiji kaocha de lishi" [History of China's Arctic expeditions], CAA, April 25, 2008, http://www.chinare.cn/caa/gb_news.php?modid=04002&id=147.

[4] CAA, "Nanji tiaoyue zhong dui Nanji lingtu zhuquan yaoqiu de sanzhong quanli" [Triple rights on sovereignty in Antarctica in the Antarctic Treaty], China.com.cn, n.d., http://www.china.com.cn/chinese/zhuanti/nk/733765.htm.

[5] John Bouvier, *A Law Dictionary, Adapted to the Constitution and Laws of the United States of American and of the Several States of the American Union*, rev. 6th ed. (1856), available online at the "Bouvier's Law Dictionary," Constitution Society, http://www.constitution.org/bouv/bouvier_r.htm.

but this term does not appear in official Chinese sources. Official Chinese sources describe Antarctic sovereignty as having been "frozen" (*bingjie*).[6] Yet this is not the official terminology of the Antarctic Treaty: officially, the Antarctic Treaty preserves the legal "status quo" on Antarctic sovereignty, though it does not define what that status quo was in 1959 when the treaty was signed.[7]

Chinese officials and academics frequently describe the polar regions as "global commons" (*quan shijie de gonggong lingtu*).[8] However, in a paper published soon after the Environmental Protocol was passed in 1991, Chinese Antarctic law specialist Zou Keyuan quoted the private comments of Chinese diplomats, who he says told him that "the Antarctic Treaty System is different in nature from the common heritage of mankind concept" and that "the outside developing countries should face the political and legal reality of the Antarctic Treaty System. The Antarctic resources were like *res communis*, and the 'first come, first served' rule was in application."[9] China appears to be following that understanding in its rapid expansion of Antarctic capacity in the past ten years. According to China's interpretation of Antarctic sovereignty, presence is very importance; as the old saying goes, "possession is nine-tenths of the law." For that reason, China has deliberately extended its physical presence in the polar regions, expanding its scientific, tourism, shipping, investment, and political links.[10]

China's official stance on the Antarctic Treaty and its associated agreements is that they are currently the best means to safeguard China's interests and to ensure safety and security in Antarctic affairs. Yet somewhat contradictorily, China, like Russia and the United States, retains the right to establish a territorial claim in Antarctica.[11] Unlike Russia or the United States, however, China does not publicly state this policy. Russia and the United States made

[6]   "Nanji tiaoyue zhong dui Nanji lingtu zhuquan yaoqiu de sanzhong quanli." See also Guojia haiyangju haiyang fazhan zhanlue yanjiusuo ketizu, ed., *Zhongguo haiyang fazhan baogao* [Report on China's maritime development] (Beijing: Haiyang chubanshe, 2012), 363.

[7]   "ATS – The Antarctic Treaty," Secretariat of the Antarctic Treaty, 2011, http://www.ats.aq/e/ats.htm.

[8]   Wu Jun, "Wo guo jidi kaocha zuzhi guanli jizhi youhua yanjiu" [Research on improving China's polar expedition organizational management] (master's thesis, Wuhan University, 2005), 35.

[9]   Zou Keyuan, "China's Antarctic Policy and the Antarctic Treaty System," *Ocean Development and International Law* 24, no. 3 (1993): 243.

[10] Ding Huang, ed., *Jidi guojia zhengce yanjiu baogao 2013–2014* [Annual report on national polar policy research 2013–14] (Beijing: Kexue chubanshe, 2014), 174.

[11] Yan Qide and Zhu Jiangang, *Nanjizhou lingtu zhuquan yu ziyuan quanshu wenti yanjiu* [Research on the issue of Antarctic sovereignty and resources] (Shanghai kexue jishu chubanshe, 2009), 31.

their position on Antarctic sovereignty known at the time of the signing of the Antarctic Treaty, basing their potential claims on a long-standing history of Antarctic exploration that began more than a century earlier. The China Arctic and Antarctic Administration's official position on Antarctic sovereignty states that the Antarctic Treaty guarantees three rights of sovereignty:

- The right of claimant states to claim they have sovereignty in Antarctica;
- The rights of the basis to those claims; and
- The right to not recognize any sovereign rights in Antarctica.[12]

China's claim of potential sovereign rights in Antarctica is based on Chinese exploration and occupation of sites in Antarctica since the 1980s, and is thus in breach of the rules of the Antarctic Treaty, which prohibit any new sovereign claims in Antarctica while the treaty is in force. Article IV (2) of the treaty states: "No acts or activities taking place while the present Treaty is in force shall constitute a basis for asserting, supporting *or denying* a claim to territorial sovereignty in Antarctica. No new claim, or enlargement of an existing claim, to territorial sovereignty shall be asserted while the present Treaty is in force" (emphasis added). Unlike the seven existing claimant states, and Russia and the United States (which reserve the right to make a claim), China does not have a history of Antarctic exploration before the Antarctic Treaty was signed. Yet China does have effective control over significant areas of Antarctica. Simply by occupying prime spots of Antarctic real estate, such as Dome A, the East Antarctic Sector, and the planned ice-free port and ice runway at its fifth base in the Ross Sea, China is in effective control of these areas and possesses their assets. Even if China later abandons these sites, it retains management rights to the historical ruins – to the exclusion of other states.

China is very sensitive to what it perceives as other states extending their sovereign rights and sovereignty claims in Antarctica. In 2007, Chinese official news sources gave strident, antagonistic coverage of the controversy surrounding the United Kingdom and six other Antarctic claimants that had submitted paperwork (or stated that they had prepared the materials but had not yet submitted them) to support claims for extended continental shelf rights based on their Antarctic claims to the UN Commission on the Limits of the Continental Shelf.[13] China accused the United Kingdom of using the UN

---

[12]   CAA, "Nanji tiaoyue zhong dui Nanji lingtu zhuquan yaoqiu de sanzhong quanli."

[13]   "Yingguo shuaixian daxiang Nanji zhi zheng" "[United Kingdom fires the first shot in Antarctic conflict], Xinhua News, October 22, 2007, http://news.xinhuanet.com/newscenter/2007-10/22/content_6921802.htm.

Convention on the Law of the Sea to gain non-sovereignty-related rights in Antarctica. Underlying the controversy is the fact that the known sites for Antarctic oil and natural gas are in the continental shelf sites that the claimant states want recognized as their own. China's leading polar law scholars Liu Hairong and Dong Yue say that there is a clash between the Antarctic Treaty, which puts aside territorial claims; UNCLOS, which permits them and is the global authority for determining which states own the oceans; and domestic laws, which claimant states use to assert their rights.[14] China is extremely concerned about this issue, which Chinese officials did not pick up on until after UNCLOS was signed.[15] The Antarctic Treaty does not mention seabeds, which leaves room for claimant states to participate in the UNCLOS process.[16] Liu and Dong predict that the issue of Antarctic seabed rights will take many years to resolve.[17]

Since Antarctic sovereignty is currently unresolved, states such as China that do not have a formal claim on Antarctic territory employ well-established patterns of behavior to expand into strategic unoccupied areas of Antarctica and establish a presence there. This expansion gives these states de facto control over the sites they operate in, and will help ensure that their territorial interests are considered in any plans for division. The current situation means that the sky is the limit in terms of China's presence and activities in Antarctica. China, like other major powers without a formal claim in Antarctica, benefits enormously from Antarctica's unresolved sovereignty; if Antarctic sovereignty claims were to be resolved, China's rights would be more limited. Because of China's strong economic growth in the past twenty-five years, Chinese state and private interests have been able to expand rapidly in Antarctica at a time when established players such as the United States, Russia, and Australia are cutting back or barely maintaining their Antarctic programs. The Chinese government does not need to make a formal territorial claim under current institutional arrangements, as China's Antarctic activities, interests, and property rights are protected under the Antarctic Treaty and customary law.

The terms of the Antarctic Treaty guarantee the right of any country with a scientific program to be active in the Antarctic continent. The only

---

[14] Liu Hairong and Dong Yue, "Zhongguo haiyang quanyi falu baozheng shiye zhong de jidi wenti yanjiu" [Polar research from the perspective of legal protection of China's maritime rights and interests], *Zhongguo Haiyang Daxue Xuebao* (Shehui kexue ban), no. 5 (2010): 6.

[15] Ibid., 4; and Zhu Ying, Xue Guifang, and Li Jinrong, "Nanji diqu dalujia huajie yinfa de falu zhidu pengzhuang" [The clash over Antarctic continental shelf delimitation], *Jidi yanjiu* 23, no. 4 (2011): 318–25.

[16] Zhu, Xue, and Li, "Nanji diqu dalujia huajie yinfa de falu zhidu pengzhuang," 325.

[17] Liu and Dong, "Zhongguo haiyang quanyi falu baozheng shiye zhong de jidi wenti yanjiu," 6.

restrictions are on areas designated as special protected areas and sites where other nations have established bases. A national Antarctic program's rights to its existing facilities and equipment are protected by customary law on property; research stations enable states to gain control over their operational area without needing to declare a formal claim. With the exception of the crowded South Shetland Islands and Antarctic Peninsula, large swathes of Antarctic land and coastal waters remain unexplored and unutilized for scientific discovery – and for effective control of any state that can occupy them.

In the Arctic, the situation regarding sovereignty for nonlittoral states is quite different. The Treaty of Spitsbergen permits any signatory of the treaty to engage in economic activity in Svalbard, and also permits scientific research there.[18] Some other Arctic states, such as Russia and Iceland, have also recently permitted non-Arctic states to set up research stations on their territories. In the Arctic Ocean, states are entitled to freedom of the seas in international waters and right of innocent passage in territorial waters. The Northwest Passage is the shortest route between the Atlantic and the Pacific, and the waters surrounding it are controlled by Canada, Denmark, and Greenland. Canada claims the route as its internal waters and thus as subject to Canadian law and control, but the United States and Russia openly oppose Canada's position. Meanwhile, Russia regards the narrowest straits of the Northern Sea Route as internal waters; United States and European Union, which regard these areas as an international strait, dispute this claim. China's position and interests on the Northwest Passage and Northern Sea Route are the same as those of the United States and the EU, but it does not take the lead in disagreeing with Canada or Russia,[19] it does not like to publicize its position on the straits,[20] and so far its official actions in the Arctic Ocean have neither directly challenged the position of the Russian and Canadian governments nor confirmed them.

In the next twenty years, the UN Commission on the Limits of the Continental Shelf will examine the science behind the claims to the outer limits of the continental shelf rights of four of the Arctic littoral states. The fifth Arctic littoral state, the United States, has not ratified UNCLOS, so it cannot participate in these formal claims, though it argues that its seabed rights are recognized under customary law.

---

[18] "The Svalbard Treaty (Paris, February 9, 1920)," University of Oslo Faculty of Law, accessed April 27, 2016, http://www.jus.uio.no/english/services/library/treaties/01/1-11/svalbard-treaty.xml.

[19] Chinese polar law specialist, interview with author, December 2013.

[20] Chinese polar law specialist, discussion with author, April 2016.

Both Canada and Russia have claimed sovereign rights up to the North Pole. The United States' current position is that its rights to the extended continental shelf and to mine the seabed are maintained under international customary law.[21] Only a small portion of the Arctic Ocean – the Gakkel Ridge between Greenland and Siberia, and an area near the Canada Basin – are unable to be claimed by the littoral states. These two small zones will likely be designated as "The Area" and will be administered by the International Seabed Authority. However, as there are overlapping claims to other areas, a political solution will be needed to resolve the outcome. The 2005 Ilulissat Declaration asserted that any territorial disputes would be resolved between the Arctic littoral states, but if they are unresolvable, it is possible that an international agreement would be required, and China could have a role in helping to draft such an agreement.

There has been considerable international interest regarding China's position on Arctic sovereignty. High-profile People's Liberation Army-Navy officer Yin Zhuo once famously stated: "The North Pole and surrounding area do not belong to any state; they are part of the common heritage of humankind" (author's translation).[22] Yin's comments match the official Chinese definition on Arctic Ocean sovereignty. Analysis written for China's polar authorities makes the point that extended continental shelf claims in the Arctic will grant the littoral states only "sovereign rights," not "sovereignty," and that these terms have very different legal meanings. Even if all the various claims are accepted, then large areas of the Arctic Ocean still can be correctly defined as "international waters."[23] China's annual report on polar affairs asserts that "no country can claim to own the North Pole,"[24] and Yin's comments reflect this understanding. However, Yin's statement unfortunately was mistranslated in international media reports as "the Arctic belongs to all the people around the world,"[25] a serious misquote that as of June 2016 has been cited at least 1200 times in authoritative English-language newspaper items, scholarly articles,

---

[21] Steven Groves, "The U.S. Can Mine the Deep Seabed without Joining the U.N. Convention on the Law of the Sea," Backgrounder #2746 on United Nations, Heritage Foundation, December 4, 2012, http://herit.ag/1gzskj6.

[22] "Haijun shaojiang: Kaifa Beibingyang Zhongguo buke 'quewei'" [PLAN General: China should not be excluded from the Arctic], *Zhongguo xinwenwang*, March 5, 2010, http://news.163.com/10/0305/16/611AEFV0000146BB.html.

[23] Guo Peiqing, *Beiji hangdao guoji wenti yanjiu* [Research on the Arctic sea route] (Beijing: Haiyang chubanshe, 2009), 315.

[24] Ding, *Jidi guojia zhengce yanjiu baogao 2013–2014*, 208.

[25] Gordon G. Chang, "China's Arctic Play," *The Diplomat*, March 10, 2010, http://thediplomat.com/2010/03/chinas-arctic-play.

and books,[26] and has been used by many foreign authors to depict China's supposed ambitions to seize control of Arctic territory and resources. The phrase "the North Pole belongs to all humanity" (*quan renlei de Beiji*) often appears in the Chinese media.[27] China, like a number of non-Arctic states, would like to internationalize Arctic issues and is trying to build international public support for this view and influence the frames for debate. Yet Chinese scientific reports on Arctic resources acknowledge that Arctic oil and natural gas reserves are held within the sovereign territory of the United States, Russia, Canada, and Norway.[28]

In 2013, an editorial in the official CCP newspaper *People's Daily* explained what it means when China talks of the Arctic as "belonging to all humanity":

> The land areas of the Arctic belong to the Arctic countries, and its sea areas are governed by those countries. China fully respects those countries' sovereignties and administrative rights in the area. But the Arctic also concerns the whole world in the fields of climate change as well as other global challenges and issues. The shipping lines in the Arctic directly affect international trade and the supply and demand of energy resources.[29]

China's politicking to raise the issue of the Arctic Ocean as the "common heritage of humanity" and Arctic resources as "global resources" can be seen as lobbying the court of international public opinion for the time when a political decision is made to delineate the territory. In the meantime, China's accumulation of Arctic interests and its efforts to gain international acknowledgment for these interests are aimed at securing its seat at the decision-making table for any future political negotiations on the claims.

When China became an observer at the Arctic Council in 2013, it was required to recognize Arctic states' sovereignty, sovereign rights, and jurisdiction in the Arctic. It also was required to recognize both the existing extensive

---

[26]   See, e.g., Shiloh Rainwater, "Race to the North: China's Arctic Strategy and Its Implications," *Naval War College Review* 66, no. 2 (2013): 74; Linda Jakobson and Jingchao Peng, *China's Arctic Aspirations*, SIPRI Policy Paper 34 (Stockholm: SIPRI, November 2012), 15; and James D. J. Brown, *Japan, Russia and Their Territorial Dispute: The Northern Delusion* (Abingdon, UK: Routledge, 2016).

[27]   "Qunxiong liangjian weilie yu Beiji Zhongguo jixu mingque Beiji zhanlue" [Vicious fight in the Arctic, China urgently in need of an Arctic strategy], *Duowei*, July 25, 2011, accessed February 15, 2013, http://military.dwnews.com/news/2011-070025/57938494.html (link discontinued).

[28]   Lu Jingmei, Shao Zijun, Fang Dianyong, and Wang Xinran, "Beiji yuan youqi ziyuan qianli fenxi" [Analysis of oil-gas resources potential in the Arctic Circle], *Ziyuan yu chanye* 12, no. 4 (2010): 73–83.

[29]   "China Contributes to Development of Arctic," *China Daily*, March 25, 2013, http://www.chinadaily.com.cn/opinion/2013-03/25/content_16344255.htm.

legal framework of the Arctic Ocean (including the Law of the Sea) and the fact that this framework provides a solid foundation for responsible management of the Arctic Ocean.[30] These requirements fit China's interests and perspective on Arctic sovereignty: that the Arctic states have jurisdiction over their land territories and the 200-mile zone, while UNCLOS and other international agreements rule the remainder. Unlike the United States, China is comfortable with the agreement's requirements that a percentage of all profits from any future Arctic seabed mining are be shared. As a developing state, China has preferential access to the seabed. China has already taken up two deep seabed mining contracts with the International Seabed Authority, with mining equipment supplied by Laurel Industrial – the same company that is behind the 2015 film on Antarctic mining, *Antarctica 2049.*

In the Arctic, China can see the benefits of cooperation over the competition and friction that would be caused by one or two states monopolizing access to seabed resources or sea routes.[31] To some observers, China's position on the Arctic contradicts its position on its South China Sea territorial claims. However, according to a 2013 Chinese government internal report, there is no contradiction at all between China's policies on the two regions: China has sovereign rights (*zhuquan quanli*) in the South China Sea and expects other states to respect this; similarly, it respects the sovereign rights of the Arctic littoral states in the Arctic Ocean.[32]

CHINA'S POSITION ON ARCTIC AND ANTARCTIC GOVERNANCE

China was made an ongoing observer on the Arctic Council in May 2013. Before then, from 2009, it had been only a temporary observer, and had been required to apply to attend each meeting. Observers do not have voting rights, but they do have the right to propose policies and they can put the money up to finance them. Ongoing observer status grants China the right to attend meetings on a regular basis, allowing its polar bureaucrats to familiarize themselves with the policies of other states and lobby them in support of China's interests. Being accepted as an observer state on the Arctic Council gives China additional credibility as an Arctic stakeholder, an important consideration when governance decisions are being

---

[30] "Observers," Arctic Council, February 12, 2016, http://www.arctic-council.org/index.php/en/about-us/arctic-council/observers.

[31] Chen Muyao and Jiang Haofeng, "Beiji zhengduo zhan zaidu daxiang" [Arctic battle resumes], *Xinmin zhoukan*, September 1, 2014, http://www.cssn.cn/jsx/201401/t20140110_9400 77.shtml.

[32] "Beiji diqu kuanchan ziyuan kaifa liyong xianzhuang fenxi" [Analysis on the current situation for accessing Arctic mineral resources], *Jidi zhanlue yanjiu dongtai*, no. 1 (2013), 4.

made in other international forums such as the UN Commission on the Limits of the Continental Shelf and the International Maritime Organization. Although the Arctic Council is not the venue for the key Arctic governance issues, such as the recognition of sea boundaries or military matters, it is an important organization for Arctic states and interested outsiders to come together to better understand each other's points of view and to have those views taken into account in further decision-making.

In August 2011, an authoritative English-language article clearly stating China's position on Arctic governance appeared in the CCP's official English-language mouthpiece, the *Beijing Review*. This article was later reproduced on the website of the State Council Information Office, also known by its Chinese-only nameplate *Zhongguo duiwai xuanchuan bangongshi* (or the CCP Office for Foreign Propaganda). Although the article was authored by Cheng Baozhi, a scholar at the Shanghai Institute of International Affairs, the views expressed reflected an official position. The article argued for more regulation of the Arctic environment and more clearly established rules of the game for all players, saying that current international law and regional institutions were inadequate for the changing situation in the Arctic region. According to Cheng, "A politically valid and legally binding Arctic governance system has yet to be established. Also absent in the Arctic is a mechanism that can promote all-round regional development and help countries reach agreements on its resources and shipping routes." Cheng singled out the Arctic Five – Russia, Canada, the United States, Denmark, and Norway – which "monopolize Arctic affairs and reject other countries' participation," and said that "it is unimaginable that non-Arctic states will remain users of Arctic shipping routes and consumers of Arctic energy without playing a role in the decision-making process, and an end to the Arctic states' monopoly of Arctic affairs is now imperative." Cheng concluded the article with the following statement:

> In terms of redressing defects in the current Arctic governance system, China will play a critical role given its extensive interests in Arctic research, environmental protection, resource exploration, and navigation. It will intensify Arctic expedition efforts while engaging in the discussions of topical issues such as navigation, environmental protection, tourism, and resource exploration. China plans to make itself heard before arrangements are made, so that its views can be incorporated into any arrangements.[33]

[33] Cheng Baozhi, "Arctic Aspirations," *Beijing Review*, August 30, 2011, http://www.bjreview.com/quotes/txt/2011-08/23/content_385389.htm.

Cheng's article sums up the case that China is making to the Arctic states: that because the Chinese government has been assiduously accumulating a number of interests in Arctic affairs, China will insist on having a say on any new Arctic governance measures that are developed to meet the changing environmental, military, geopolitical, and geoeconomical situation.

Not unlike the Arctic region, Antarctic governance consists of a series of agreements covering areas where states could agree to pass a resolution. Gaps in governance lie in the points where they may not agree, such as minerals exploitation, tourism, biotechnology, and the sovereignty issue. These gaps are the fault lines that constantly bring the Antarctic Treaty into disrepute and eventually may cause it to collapse. Relations between the Antarctic Treaty Consultative Parties are a delicate balance of cooperation on many areas and turning a blind eye in others. Countries that have established Antarctic research stations maintain de facto sovereignty that is unprecedented elsewhere in the world. Antarctica is the only location outside the high seas where any country has the right to locate strategic military technology, such as satellite-receiving stations and telescopes that assist with missile positioning and targeting, without any questions being asked. Antarctica can also serve as a neutral airbase for military airplanes en route to other missions. So for the superpowers of the world, Antarctica is an extremely important strategic "no man's land." However, when the technical and financial barriers to mineral exploitation are resolved, then the fragile balance in relations between the ATCPs will likely go out of kilter. Each country will seek its share, based on its past activities in Antarctica.

Chinese polar policymakers and leading polar social scientists commonly frame the Antarctic Treaty System as a "rich man's club" (*furen julebu*)[34] or a zone for "collective hegemony" (*jiti baquan*),[35] and assert that, in the past, China was a "second-class citizen" (*erdeng gongmin*) within the treaty.[36] Many Chinese analysts believe that the Antarctic Treaty is an inherently unstable, unequal, Cold War–era instrument that does not meet contemporary needs.[37] Chinese policy papers describe Antarctic governance as essentially unipolar, dominated by the United States,[38] even though all of the ATCPs have equal

[34] Guo Peiqing, "Jidi zhengduo weihe xiaoyan zai qi" [Polar conflict: Why the smell of gunsmoke has returned], *Liaowang* 45 (2007), accessed January 31, 2009, http://gbl .chinabroadcast.cn/18904/2007/11/05/2165@1829761.htm (link discontinued).

[35] Guo Peiqing, "Nanji bainian de zhengduo" [A hundred years of fighting over Antarctica], *Huanqiu*, August 1, 2007, http://news.sina.com.cn/w/2007-08-01/104013571315.shtml.

[36] Yu Dawei, "Nanji 'sanji tiao'" [Triple jump in Antarctica], *Caijing*, no. 16 (August 4, 2008).

[37] Chinese polar policymaker, interview with author, September 2014.

[38] "Nanji zhengzhi 'danjihua' qushi" [The tendency of Antarctic policies to be "monopolized"], *Jidi zhanlue yanjiu dongtai*, no. 1 (2012): ii and 19.

rights on the continent. Chinese scholars point out that the Antarctic Treaty system is rife with unresolved tensions between treaty signatories and non-signatories, between claimant and nonclaimant states, between consultative and nonconsultative parties, between developed and developing member states, and among the claimant states themselves.[39] Yet despite the carping about the Antarctic Treaty in Chinese-language debates, China benefits enormously from the current Antarctic governance system. In 2000, a Ministry of Land and Resources report assessing Antarctic mineral resources concluded that the Antarctic Treaty and its various instruments establish the political prerequisites for both "protecting the Antarctic environment and the future utilization of Antarctic resources."[40] China seeks a peaceful and demilitarized Antarctica, the freezing of sovereignty claims, freedom of scientific investigation, the right to the rational use of Antarctic resources, and protections for the Antarctic environment; it acknowledges that the existing treaty protects and maintains all of these aspects.[41]

According to the terms of the treaty, any state can inspect other countries' Antarctic bases, but few devote serious resources to do this. For example, none of the inspections to date have enquired into the use of dual-use civil-military satellite receiving stations by the major powers and some of the medium-sized powers. Moreover, most states ignore the legal requirement to make fully public all their Antarctic activities and capabilities. Many ATCPs are engaging in only low-level Antarctic research that would disqualify them from consultative status within the treaty if the rules were applied properly. This nonaccountable, nontransparent governance environment is as amenable to China's interests in Antarctica as it is to many other states. Predictably, there were no consequences when China broke the rules of the Protocol on Environmental Protection in 2015 and did not respond to the feedback of other Antarctic states with a final Comprehensive Environmental Evaluation sixty days before it started preparatory work on its fifth Antarctic base.[42]

The Antarctic Treaty is very advantageous to the major powers, though less so to weaker powers. It enables China, the United States, and any other country with the requisite economic might unfettered access to the whole of

[39] Ding, *Jidi guojia zhengce yanjiu baogao 2013–2014*, 10–11.

[40] Guojia ziyuan xinxi zhongxin, *Quanchuan ziyuan yu guojia anquan* [Mineral resources and national security] (Beijing: Dizhi chubanshe, 2000), 149.

[41] Chen Li, "Meiguo de Nanji zhengce yu falu" [US Antarctic policy and laws], *Meiguo Yanjiu* (2013), 1, http://ias.cass.cn/show/show_mgyj.asp?id=1429.

[42] "Wo guo kaishi zai Nanji Weiduoliya di jichu choubei di wu ge kaocha zhan" [China begins preparatory surveying for the fifth Antarctic base in Victoria Land], *Renminwang*, January 6, 2015, http://scitech.people.com.cn/n/2015/0106/c1007-26334885.html; and Chinese polar scientist, interview with author, January 2015.

the Antarctic continent and ocean without having to consider the rights of the claimant states. Any country is free to establish as many scientific bases as it can sustain on any area in Antarctica, except locations where other states already have bases or have historical remains of bases. The major players in Antarctica in terms of base numbers – the United States, Russia, Japan, the United Kingdom, Chile, Argentina, and Australia – went through a burst of base-building activity in the Cold War years but are unlikely to expand further due to financial constraints. However, China's recent expansion of facilities in Antarctica shows no sign of slowing. As a result, even though at present there is no possibility of changing the international governance arrangements in Antarctica, China publicly accepts them as it continues to pursue its own interests. The Chinese government's current behavior in various Antarctic Treaty forums is similar to its behavior in many other multilateral organizations and international regimes: it may not like certain aspects of the current order, but it takes what benefits it can. China does not intend to either change or challenge the Antarctic Treaty and consistently acts to oppose any initiatives that it regards as changing the status quo, such as the continental shelf applications of some of the Antarctic claimant states to the UN Commission on the Limits of the Continental Shelf, and initiatives to create Marine Protected Areas in the Southern Ocean.

For the next twenty to thirty years, the Antarctic Treaty will continue to suit the interests of many states with an interest in exploiting Antarctic mineral resources, giving them plenty of time to prepare their capacity to assess what minerals exist there and the challenges involved in extracting them. Long-standing Antarctic diplomat Wu Yilin even said as much in a 2009 paper, pointing out that the upside of the Environmental Protocol's ban on mining exploitation is that it gives China a chance to catch up to other Antarctic states so that in future it can better make use of Antarctic resources. According to Wu, while the overall trend in Antarctic affairs is cooperative, there are some issues of friction and China can take advantage of them to further its own interests.[43] A 2014 report on China's polar activities echoed this analysis.[44] Thus, for the midterm at least, China's expansion of interests in Antarctica requires cooperating with the other Antarctic states. At international meetings on Antarctica affairs, Beijing has continued its official position of upholding the status quo in Antarctic management, and it has expressed alternative point of views at Antarctic Treaty meetings only when defending its own interests.

---

[43] Wu Yilin, "Cong Nanji tiaoyue tixi yanhua kan kuanchuan ziyuan wenti" [Looking at the extension of the Antarctic Treaty system from the point of view of resources], *Haiyang daxue xuebao (Shehui xue bao)* 5, no. 5 (2009), 13.

[44] Ding, *Jidi guojia zhengce yanjiu baogao 2013–2014*, 33.

CHINA'S POSITION ON POLAR RESOURCES

Deciding who can control and access polar resources is a matter of global political and economic importance. As an energy-hungry nation, China is extremely interested in the resources of the Arctic and Antarctic and any possibilities for their exploitation. The notion of "resources" has a broad meaning in the polar regions. It includes oil and minerals, meteorites, the intellectual property of bioprospecting, locations for scientific bases, freshwater, solar power, marine living resources, and polar tourism. But most states fixate on the polar regions' mineral resources, and China is no different. China is currently the world's largest consumer and importer of minerals, and its demand for these resources can only grow. According to training materials for senior leaders at the 2013 CCP Central Party School, over the next twenty years China aims to create an internationally competitive, large-scale overseas mineral development program and its own fleet of offshore oil platforms. China's energy security, future prosperity, and political stability will rely on securing access to global supplies of mineral resources in the next twenty to thirty years. The polar seas are one area where China is planning to expand exploration and mining interest rights.[45]

In the Arctic, China's standard position on the subject of resources, as stated in a classified military journal in 2008 and in other official and semiofficial sources, is that "these resources should not be possessed by a small number of states, they belong to all of humanity, and should be opened up to the whole world."[46] According to china.org, the Chinese government's official website, "Natural resources in the [Arctic] region belong to all the peoples of the world. China has the responsibility, duty and the ability to take part in the peaceful exploration and protection of natural resources there. China's economic and social development already has a demand for natural resources."[47] China wants to purchase Arctic resources and recognizes the ownership rights of Arctic states over these resources.[48]

The situation in Antarctica is somewhat different. For six years in the 1980s, Antarctic states negotiated an agreement that would have permitted Antarctic

---

45 Zhongyang dangxiao shenbuji ganbu jinxiuban (di54qi), "Zhongguo kuangchan ziyuan anquan zhanlue yanjiu" [Research on China's strategic mineral resources strategy], China University of Mining and Technology, May 28, 2014, http://zsd.cumt.edu.cn/09/37/c863 a67895/page.htm.

46 "Beiji junshi zhanlüe jiazhi zhongda" [The Arctic region has major strategic military value], *Bingqi zhishi* (September 2008), 14–15.

47 "Significance of Arctic Research Exploration," China.org.cn, n.d., accessed July 31, 2016, http://www.china.org.cn/english/features/40961.htm.

48 "Beiji diqu kuanchan ziyuan kaifa liyong xianzhuang fenxi," 4–6.

mineral exploitation: The Convention on the Regulation of Antarctic Mineral Resource Activities. China was very active in the convention negotiations, joining with India, Brazil, and Uruguay to form a bloc of developing countries. According to Zou Keyuan, the convention was "the first legal document that recognizes unambiguously the special role of the developing countries in the ATS." During the negotiations, the developing countries demanded special consideration for their interests and equal participation in mineral resource activities, such as compulsory joint venture agreements, and a seat of the Regulatory Committee to be held by a nonclaimant developing country. China was a strong supporter of the convention; the head of the Chinese delegation stated that it would "be justified by history itself. In this regard, I should say that all State Parties to the Antarctic Treaty shall bear a collective and sacred responsibility for implementing this Convention to which we are all committed."[49] The convention was passed in 1988, but because France and Australia did not ratify it, it was unable to be concluded. However, PRIC researchers have not given up on it. They say it should be ratified and brought into force.[50]

Although the Convention on the Regulation of Antarctic Mineral Resource Activities failed to be adopted, its environmental management protocols were repurposed in talks in 1991 and renamed the Protocol on Environmental Protection (also known as the Madrid Protocol). This was ratified by all ATCPs and entered into force in 1998. The Madrid Protocol designates Antarctica as a "natural reserve" and bans any activity related to mineral resources "other than scientific research" until 2048. Any of the original thirty-three signatories can request a review of the protocol at any time, but consensus is required to make any change. After 2048, any modification to the terms of the protocol must be passed by a three-quarter majority of the parties, including "all States which are Antarctic Treaty Consultative Parties at the time of adoption of this Protocol."[51] If a review is requested, then an international conference of relevant states must be held to respond to the request and devise a new instrument of governance. As the numbers of states that have openly stated their interest in Antarctic minerals has been growing since the late 2000s, we can expect that by 2048 a majority of the ATCPs will be willing to accept the inevitability of opening up Antarctica to mineral exploitation. The states that were ATCPs at the signing of the Madrid Protocol are the same

---

[49] As cited by Zou, "China's Antarctic Policy and the Antarctic Treaty System," 245.
[50] Yan and Zhu, *Nanjizhou lingtu yu ziyuan quanshu wenti yanjiu*, 33.
[51] "The Protocol on Environmental Protection to the Antarctic Treaty," Secretariat of the Antarctic Treaty, 2011, 12, http://www.ats.aq/documents/recatt/Att006_e.pdf.

states that in 1988 passed the Convention on the Regulation of Antarctic Mineral Resource Activities and agreed to mining. The 2014 annual report on China's polar policies points out that the Madrid Protocol does not contain any regulations as to what happens to Antarctic mineral resources after 2048.[52]

The limited resource exploitation that is currently permitted and undertaken in Antarctica – fishing, bioprospecting, meteorite-gathering, geological surveying, tourism access, and whaling – is only lightly regulated. Fishing is the most restricted activity, managed by the Antarctic Treaty's Commission for the Conservation of Antarctic Marine Living Resources (CCAMLR), but Antarctica is considered to be an Olympic fishery, meaning that any state has the right to take up fishing there. China's growing transcontinental and oceanic presence in Antarctica will enable it to take advantage of future mineral and marine resources. China's prospecting activities are currently focused on three locations: Prydz Bay, the Weddell Sea, and the Ross Sea region. Antarctic prospecting – given the fig leaf of scientific enquiry – will provide China with an enhanced negotiating position if mineral rights are allocated.

Open- and closed-source Chinese-language polar social science analysis has long been dominated by discussion about Antarctic resources and how China might gain its share. Such analysis has been virtually taboo in the scholarly research of more-established Antarctic powers since the passing of the Madrid Protocol in 1991. In 1998, polar international relations and law specialist Christopher C. Joyner mused that the passing of the protocol meant that the issue of Antarctic minerals resources would not be raised again "for the foreseeable future."[53] Yet unbeknownst to Joyner, Chinese polar analysts and scholars never stopped commenting on the potential of Antarctic resources, even in the years immediately after the passing of the Madrid Protocol.[54] A 2005 paper by PRIC policy analysts Zhu Jiangang, Yan Qide, and Ling Xiaoliang asserted that the rich resources of Antarctica – oil and natural gas, minerals, freshwater, biological resources, and tourism prospects, "as well as

[52]   Ding, *Jidi guojia zhengce yanjiu baogao 2013–2014*, 185–86.
[53]   Christopher C. Joyner, *Governing the Frozen Commons: The Antarctic Regime and Environmental Protection* (Columbia: University of South Carolina Press, 1998), 79.
[54]   See, e.g., Yan Qide, "Nanji ziyuan yu guoji fenzheng" [The international struggle for Antarctic resources], *Kexue* 43, no. 4 (1991): 261–72; Zhu Jiangang, Yan Qide, and Ling Xiaoliang, "Nanji ziyuan fenzheng ji woguo de xiangying duice" [The dispute of Antarctic resources and our countermeasures], *Jidi yanjiu* 18, no. 3 (2006): 17–22; Zou Keyuan, "Guifan weilai Nanji kuangwu ziyuan kaifa liyong de falu yuanze" [The legal principles behind standardizing the future use of Antarctic mineral resources], *Haiyang kaifa yu guanli*, no. 3 (1994); and Zou Keyuan, *Nanji kuangwu ziyuan yu guoji fa* [Antarctic mineral resources and international law] (Beijing: Beijing daxue chubanshe, 1996).

others" – are the main reason for countries to send scientific expeditions there, and that Antarctic mineral, oil, and natural gas exploitation is just a "matter of time." The authors cite the main barriers to Antarctic minerals exploitation in the following order:

- It is difficult to operate in the Antarctic environment; meanwhile, resources in other areas of the world are not yet exhausted.
- Current technology available to exploit Antarctic resources would undoubtedly cause environmental damage. (In an aside, the authors mentioned that such actions would breach the Madrid Protocol, which they erroneously stated ends in 2041.)
- The vexed question of sovereignty over Antarctic resources has not been resolved.

Zhu, Yan, and Ling added that when these three matters are all resolved, resource extraction will begin.[55] They recommended that the Chinese government use the period when mining is banned to engage in strategic research to plan for future Antarctic resource extraction. This is exactly what is now happening. If Chinese scientists are the ones to discover significant mineral resources in Antarctica, then their rights to those resources would be stronger than those of other states. So China's exploration and surveying activities are very important for the future.

Writing in a 2006 paper, Zhu, Yan, and Ling further argued, "The abundant Antarctic resources belong to all of humanity and sooner or later must be utilized."[56] In 2007, polar politics scholar Guo Peiqing pointed out, "No nation or Antarctic researcher has ever negated the possibility that Antarctic resources could be utilized."[57] In 2009, Yan Qide and Zhu Jiangang edited a book-length PRIC research report on Antarctic sovereignty and resource rights, which provides a detailed outline of China's plans to exploit the full range of Antarctic resources. (The study was funded by the National Social Science Fund, a CCP Central Propaganda Department agency.) On the topic of accessing Antarctic oil and natural gas, Yan and Zhu concluded that by the time Antarctic resources become available for exploitation, the experience of mining in the difficult conditions in the Arctic will serve as the prototype for how to overcome any technological barriers. In their

---

[55] Zhu Jiangang, Yan Qide, and Ling Xiaoliang, "Nanji ziyuan ji qi kaifa liyong qianjing fenxi" [Analysis of Antarctic resources, their exploitation, and potential for utilization], *Zhongguo kexue*, no. 8 (2005): 17, 21.

[56] Zhu, Yan, and Ling, "Nanji ziyuan fenzheng ji woguo de xiangying duice," 218.

[57] Guo Peiqing, "Nanji ziyuan yu qi ziyuan zhengzhi" [Antarctic resources and the politics of resources], *Haiyang shijie*, no. 3 (2007): 71.

view, Antarctic oil and natural gas should not be permanently banned from use, and as China has one-quarter of the world's population, it should be entitled to its fair share.[58] Likewise, a 2013 report in the CAA's *Polar Strategy Research Trends* comments that "regardless of how the spoils are divided up, China must have a share of Antarctic mineral resources to ensure the survival and development of its one billion population."[59] Polar resources are likely to be the next big global source of supply after the shale oil and gas boom is exhausted. Shale oil will only marginally affect China's calculus on the importance of polar oil, as China's shale oil is difficult to extract and has high environmental costs.[60]

From the Chinese government's point of view, the 1991 Madrid Protocol simply postponed what Chinese polar policymakers believe is the inevitable opening up of Antarctic resources. Numerous newspaper reports in Chinese have alleged that some countries are already prospecting in Antarctica, under the cover of scientific research,[61] although the reports never list China among those countries doing so. Zhu, Yan, and Ling have also said that since the Convention on the Regulation of Antarctic Mineral Resource Activities was not ratified, the "struggle" for access to Antarctic resources has never abated, and instead become "more complex, secretive, acute, scientized, diplomatized, and legalized."[62] They recommended that in response, China should step up its Antarctic scientific research on mineral resources, focusing on a few key areas known to hold significant reserves in order to help China in its bid to gain rights to these resources.[63] This policy recommendation has been followed up with a CAA-led "strategic mineral resources survey" of the polar regions, which was under way from 2012 to 2016.[64]

Until recently, China did not have the economic and technical ability to exploit polar resources, but double-digit growth since the early 1990s has enabled China to expand its Antarctic capacity expansion to a level at which

---

[58] Yan Qide and Zhu Jiangang, ed., *Nanji ziyuan lingtu zhuquan yu ziyuan quan shu wenti yanjiu* [Research on Antarctic sovereignty and resource rights] (Shanghai Kexue jishu xhubanshe, 2009), 15 and 32–33.

[59] *Jidi zhanlue yanjiu dongtai*, no. 3 (2013): 16.

[60] Chinese polar law scholar, interview with author, September 2014.

[61] See, e.g., "Beiji bingrong dui Zhongguo yiweizhe shenme" [What the melting of the North Pole means for China], cippe.net, July 28, 2008, http://news.cippe.net/news/10054.htm; and "Yingguo shuaixian daxiang Nanji zhi zheng" [United Kingdom fires the first shot in Antarctic conflict], Xinhua, October 22, 2007, http://news.xinhuanet.com/newscenter/2007-10/22/content_6921802.htm.

[62] Zhu, Yan, and Ling, "Nanji ziyuan fenzheng ji woguo de xiangying duice," 217.

[63] Zhu, Yan, and Ling, "Nanji ziyuan ji qi kaifa liyong qianjing fenxi," 22.

[64] Apart from multiple CAA sources, the survey is also referenced in a 2013 CCP Central Party School briefing paper discussing China's strategic resources strategy; see "Zhongguo kuangchan ziyuan anquan zhanlue yanjiu."

no other state can compete. The Ministry of Land and Resources' 2000 report on China's national security and mineral resources says that Antarctic oil and natural gas exploration will likely be opened up when other global oil fields are exhausted, but that for now the Antarctic Treaty and its various instruments provide political prerequisites for environmental protection and the future Antarctic resource use.[65] In the meantime, China's preparations for that future include ramping up its polar scientific programs and investing in polar social science research. Beijing needs to develop the specialist knowledge that will enable its Antarctic representatives to defend its interests. China aims to be in a position to take advantage of any opportunities to exploit Antarctic resources – with trained personnel and infrastructure in place.[66]

CAA deputy director Wu Jun has echoed existing thinking that it is inevitable that Antarctic mineral resources will be exploited one day, when global mineral reserves have been exhausted.[67] PRIC researchers Zhu, Yan, and Ling predict that by the middle of the twenty-first century, the exhaustion of existing oil and natural gas fields could lead to financial crisis and military clashes. They argue that access to polar resources is part of the solution to resolve that future threat.[68] This situation explains why, as Wu Jun states, China's polar science currently focuses so greatly on understanding Antarctic resources.[69] China aims to be prepared for any change of governance situation and to protect its Antarctic mineral resource access rights.

Yan Qide and Zhu Jiangang's lengthy 2009 study on Antarctic sovereignty and mineral resources asserted that access to Antarctic resources "is the foundation of China's future peaceful development."[70] The authors argued that the Antarctic Treaty should permit scientific research to ascertain Antarctic resources and Antarctic resources "should not be permanently frozen." However, they concurred with other Chinese Antarctic analysts that the present ban on Antarctic mineral exploitation will give China more time to prepare for the inevitable change in rules in the middle of the twenty-first century. As Yan and Zhu point out, a state must have a high level of comprehensive power and economic strength to take full advantage of Antarctic rights and opportunities.[71] Xi Jinping's landmark 2014 speech in Hobart, Australia, highlighted the fact that China's comprehensive power

[65]   Guojia ziyuan xinxi zhongxin, *Quanchuan ziyuan yu guojia anquan*, 149.
[66]   Zhu, Yan, and Ling, "Nanji ziyuan fenzheng ji woguo de xiangying duice," 220.
[67]   Wu, "Wo guo jidi kaocha zuzhi guanli jizhi youhua yanjiu," 35.
[68]   Zhu, Yan, and Ling, "Nanji ziyuan fenzheng ji woguo de xiangying duice," 218.
[69]   Wu, "Wo guo jidi kaocha zuzhi guanli jizhi youhua yanjiu," 35.
[70]   Yan and Zhu, *Nanjizhou lingtu yu ziyuan quanshu wenti yanjiu*, 32.
[71]   Ibid., 33.

had finally reached the point where it *could* have full access to its rights in Antarctica.[72]

CHINA'S POSITION ON POLAR ENVIRONMENTAL PROTECTION

One sunny autumn day in 2012, while walking in an obscure and neglected corner of Beijing University, I was astonished to encounter a massive Antarctic boulder placed on a small, dusty mound. The plaque attached to the boulder said that it originated from Zhongshan Station in Antarctica, and was part of a shipment brought back by the *Xue Long* in 2010. Two other boulders were shipped along with it, and they are now in place outside the PRIC in Shanghai and in a park in Harbin. For countries that promote the idea of Antarctica as a natural wilderness that should be protected for the whole of humankind, the act of mining rocks for decoration – indeed, mining rocks at all – would be anathema. When questioned about the boulders, a senior CAA official said (inaccurately) that the Antarctic Treaty does not regulate these activities and, moreover, that China had taken the stones for "the whole of humanity." He argued that environmental regulations in Antarctica should not completely restrict access. Such statements by Chinese polar officials are indicative of a significantly different view on environmental protection in Antarctica than many other states that promote the "wilderness" value of Antarctica. Over the ten years I have been conducting research into China's polar policies, Chinese polar officials have several times asked me to explain (in Chinese) the concepts of "conservation" and "preservation," two terms that appear frequently in Antarctic Treaty documents. The correct translation of these terms in Chinese – *baohu* and *baocun*, respectively – do not have the same level of associations as they do in English, with historical connections to the conservation movement. The changes that the 1991 Protocol on Environmental Protection brought to Antarctic governance are not well understood in China. Chinese policy analysis on it frequently and mistakenly states that the protocol expires in 2041, rather than being up for renegotiation in 2048. Moreover, a 2012 State Oceanic Administration report claimed that according to the protocol's regulations, a state's future access to Antarctic resources will depend on its level of investment in Antarctic science.[73]

---

[72] "Er lun shenru xuexi guanche Xi Jinping zhuxi zhongyao jianghua jingshen" [Study and implement the important speech of Chairman Xi Jinping], *Zhongguo haiyang bao*, November 20, 2014, http://www.oceanol.com/redian/shiping/2014-11-25/38013.html.

[73] Guojia haiyangju haiyang fazhan zhanlue yanjiusuo ketizu, *Zhongguo haiyang fazhan baogao*, 363.

Even though China publicly supports most (but not all) of the new environmental initiatives in Antarctica, its internal position is much more ambivalent. This difference has been apparent in Chinese-language discussions on the Antarctic for a long time, but it has not shown up in any policy action at the level of international governance until recently. However, China's new capacities in Antarctica, increased strategic interests there, and stated desire by senior polar officials since 2011 to exercise China's "right to speak" on any new Antarctic governance measures has brought that different perspective out into the open in a number of situations in Antarctic governance meetings since 2012. In the Arctic, by contrast, China promotes environmental concerns in order to protect its wider interests. International environmental nongovernmental organizations have been an important force at both poles in devising and promoting new protocols to better manage the environment. But Chinese analysis constantly has emphasized that states are the ones that decide Antarctic and Arctic policy, and has claimed that NGOs "challenge" the state-centered governance system at the poles.[74]

China's Position on Antarctic Environmental Protection

In principle, all the land mass of Antarctica and all the sea territories within the 60th parallel are free for any country or its agents to operate in, provided that such operations do not affect the existing scientific bases of other countries. However, as Antarctic diplomat Wu Yilin pointed out in 2009, "43 percent of the 334 recommendations, resolutions, and agreements passed by the ATCM have been related to environmental measures."[75] Since the Madrid Protocol came into force in 1998 and particularly since the protocol's Annex V (which is concerned with area management) came into force in 2002, access to significant areas of Antarctic land and seas has been restricted for environmental, scientific, historic, aesthetic, or wilderness-value reasons. These areas are managed as Antarctic Specially Managed Areas (ASMAs), Antarctic Special Protected Areas (ASPAs), and Marine Protected Areas (MPAs). The protocol further provides for the listing of historical sites and monuments in Antarctica in order to preserve and protect them from damage or destruction. Following the coming-into-force of Annex V, all activities within the treaty area now require prior environmental impact assessments. The protocol brought together existing environmental recommendations that had been

---

74 Ding, *Jidi guojia zhengce yanjiu baogao 2013–2014*, 67.
75 Wu, "Cong Nanji tiaoyue tixi yanhua kan kuangchan ziyuan wenti," 13.

adopted throughout the Antarctic Treaty system; according to Article IV, the protocol was not meant to either modify or supplement the treaty.

Of the restricted Antarctic areas, ASMAs are meant to be managed to "assist in the planning and co-ordination of activities, avoid possible conflicts, improve co-operation between Parties or minimize environmental impacts."[76] An ASPA could be designated in any area of Antarctica to protect outstanding environmental, scientific, historic, aesthetic, or wilderness values, or to enable ongoing or planned scientific research. Permits are required for entry into any ASPA site. MPAs are administered by the Antarctic Treaty's CCAMLR, whose stated task is to "conserve Antarctic marine life."[77] Currently, Antarctica has seventy ASPAs, seven ASMAs, eighty-six registered Antarctic historical sites and monuments, and one designated MPA managed by the commission (with proposals for two more already on the bargaining table), as well as six exclusively marine ASPAs and four ASPAs with marine components.

Although China ratified the Madrid Protocol in 1994 and Annex V of the protocol in 1995,[78] Chinese polar policymakers and analysts tend to regard the more recent tougher environmental protections required for Antarctic activities as a ploy by the established powers to maintain their assets there.[79] Australia, France, New Zealand, the United Kingdom, and the United States – all claimant or potential claimant states in Antarctica, and the same "friendly hands" that partnered to protect their interests through the Antarctic Treaty)[80] – are at the forefront of states advocating for greater environmental protection in Antarctica. Consequently, Chinese officials portray the environmental area management measures introduced since 2002 as a clever form of "soft presence" (*ruan cunzai*) for states that want to seize control over territory in Antarctica and the Southern Ocean.[81] China's polar analysts have said that Antarctic claimant states (or, in the case of the United States, potential

76   "Annex V to the Protocol on Environmental Protection to the Antarctic Treaty," Secretariat of the Antarctic Treaty, 2011, 2, http://ats.aq/documents/cep/handbook/Annex_V_e.pdf.
77   "About CCAMLR," CCAMLR, April 23, 2015, http://www.ccamlr.org/en/organisation/about-ccamlr.
78   "The Antarctic Treaty System: Introduction," US Department of State, accessed June 15, 2016, http://www.state.gov/documents/organization/15272.pdf.
79   Chinese polar officials, interviews with author in Wuhan, Shanghai, and Qingdao, December 2009, and in Christchurch, January 2010.
80   Agenda Paper, Commonwealth Prime Ministers' Conference, 1956, A1838/1495/3/2/1 Part 2, National Archives of Australia, as cited by David Day, *Antarctica: A Biography* (Oxford: Oxford University Press, 2012), 479.
81   Wu Yilin, "Huanjing baohu yu Nanji de 'ruan cunzai'" [Environmental protection and "soft presence" in Antarctica], *Haiyang kaifa yu guanli* 26, no. 4 (2009): 43–45.

claimant states) use MPAs to attempt to secure control of the maritime zone.[82] The term "soft presence" was coined by Wu Yilin, currently China's Antarctic consul to Australia. Wu has said that Antarctic states have been using ASMAs and ASPAs to establish their presence in Antarctica – essential for any future territorial claims.[83] Indeed, PRIC researchers have described the ASPAs as a form of sovereignty claim,[84] and have accused "some states" of engaging in resource exploration under the cover of "scientific expeditions and environmental protection."[85] A 2007 article in the semiofficial periodical *Liaowang* stated that changes in Antarctica's environmental regulations such as the Madrid Protocol "had made the struggle over resources in Antarctica all the more complicated, more covert, and more extreme."[86] A well-informed anonymous opinion piece published in 2014 by china.com – the website supervised by the CCP's Office for Foreign Propaganda – made the point that the United States had been involved in five out of the seven ASMA proposals, and claimed that through these proposals the United States had been able to "control or dominate an area of 48,000 square kilometers" in Antarctica. The anonymous report went on to assert that the ASMA process is a means to prepare territorial claims and described the rush to declare ASMAs and ASPAs in recent years as an "enclosure movement," which China is "not too late" to participate in.[87]

China has indeed set up an ASPA of its own, has joined in on the ASPA and ASMA proposals of other states, and is now proposing its own massive ASMA – Antarctica's largest to date. China's first individual ASPA was set up at Mount Harding in the Grove Mountains in 2008. Along with Australia, India, Romania, and Russia, China participated in setting up an ASMA in the Larsman Hills; and with Australia it set up an ASPA at Amanda Bay in East Antarctica. China also designated a building at Great Wall Station as a historical monument, in accordance with Antarctic Treaty regulations on the protection of historical monuments and sites in Antarctica. China first proposed to set up an ASMA around Dome A in 2013, but the proposal has met

---

[82]   "Nanji Haiyang baohuqu sheli xianzhuang ji qushi" [The current situation and tendencies of the Antarctic MPAs], *Jidi zhanlue yanjiu dongtai*, no. 3 (2013): 1.

[83]   Wu, "Huanjing baohu yu Nanji de 'ruan cunzai.'"

[84]   Zhu, Yan, and Ling, "Nanji ziyuan fenzheng ji wo guo de xiangying duice," 218.

[85]   Zhu, Yan, and Ling, "Nanji ziyuan ji qi kaifa liyong qianjing fenxi," 17.

[86]   Zhang Jiansong, "Zhuanjia chengying zhengzhi Nanji ziyuan fenzheng" [Experts call for facing up to the struggle over Antarctic resources, seven countries put in a request to carve up the territory], *Liaowang*, June 18, 2007, http://news.sohu.com/20070618/n250625161.shtml.

[87]   "Zhong mei an zhan bairehua cong Xue Long hao tuokun kan Nanji quan di zhi zheng" [The hotting up of the secret war between China and the United States: examining Antarctic disputes from the *Xue Long* rescue], China.com, January 13, 2014, http://military.china.com /critical3/27/20140113/18282389_1.html.

considerable resistance from other ATCPs and was rejected by other Antarctic Treaty consultative states at the 2013, 2014, 2015, 2016, and 2017 ACTMs. China's 2014 report on the consultation process for this new ASMA used unusually strong language, raising issues that China considered were of "vital importance ... concerning the operation of CEP and the Antarctic Treaty System as a whole." China's main concern was with the way in which some states were interpreting the Madrid Protocol and Annex V. Its report alleged that the rules used to set up the previous seven ASMAs were different from those that were being applied to China's application.[88] During the 2015 ATCM meeting, one of China's delegates to the Committee on Environmental Protocol thumped on the table and in harsh tones demanded that China's request be met.[89] It is rare to see such displays of emotion at the ATCM, and these reactions reflect the level of resentment and frustration of some Chinese polar officials about what they regard as unfair treatment.

China's Dome A ASMA proposal has five zones and sectors, adding up to 19,764 total square kilometers.[90] The Dome A ASMA would encircle Kunlun Station at a radius of 120 kilometers (for the clean air sector), 10 kilometers (for the buffer zone), and 30 kilometers (for two scientific zones). The operational zone is a rectangular area and is located between them. The ASMA area was first fully mapped out in 2009, and Chinese polar scientists like to refer to it as "China's Management District" (*Zhongguo guanli qu*)[91] or "China's Great Wall" (*Zhongguo qiang*).[92] If the "China Management District" proposal were to be accepted, it would (to use the terms of the 2014 anonymous op-ed cited earlier) effectively put the territory around Dome A under Chinese "control or dominance," making it difficult for other national programs to operate there

---

[88] "Report of the Informal Discussions on the Proposal for a new Antarctic Specially Managed Area at Chinese Antarctic Kunlun Station, Dome A," Working Paper 15, CEP9a, ATCM XXXVII, CEP XVII (Brasilia, April 28–May 7, 2014), Secretariat of the Antarctic Treaty, 2015, http://www.ats.aq/documents/ATCM37/wp/ATCM37_wp015_e.doc.

[89] As relayed to me by NGO attendees at this meeting.

[90] "Proposal for a new Antarctic Specially Managed Area at Chinese Antarctic Kunlun Station, Dome A," Working Paper 8, CEP 9a, ATCM XXXVI, CEP XVI (Brussels, May 22–29, 2013), Secretariat of the Antarctic Treaty, 2015, http://www.ats.aq/documents/ATCM36/wp/ATCM36_wp008_e.doc.

[91] "17 yongshi chenggong deng ding Nanji bing qiong A" (17 warriors successfully ascend Antarctica's Dome A), January 8, 2008, SOA, http://www.soa.gov.cn/xw/dfdwdt/jsdw_157/201211/t20121108_16625.html.

[92] See Bao Yinghua, "Nanji cehui" [Antarctic mapping], accessed March 3, 2015 http://drcsm.sbsm.gov.cn/accessory/Sep27,201110500PM.doc; and "Nanji neilu Kunlun zhan ke kao dui 18ri chufa" [Inland Antarctic expedition to Kunlun Station starting on the 18th], Heilongjiang Provincial Bureau of Surveying and Mapping Geographical Information, December 19, 2009, www.hljbsm.gov.cn/index.asp?id=1043.

other than as a partner with China. It would also close off the possibility of any other state operating an airfield in this strategically significant site. At the 2015 ATCM, other Antarctic states questioned the rationale for the Chinese ASMA, pointing out that Dome A lacked "multinational/multiple operators and multiple activities/multiple use." ASMAs are meant to coordinate the activities of multiple operators in an area, but China is currently the only state working there. To many observers, China appears to be trying to use an ASMA to gain effective control of Dome A, and it is possible that China may try to exclude other countries from operating there. China's Dome A ASMA proposal looks very similar to that used for the South Pole ASMA. Yet Dome A's circumstances are very different from those of the South Pole; the former is used predominantly by Chinese scientists, while the latter is used by tourists, scientists, and numerous state Antarctic programs, and as a result requires additional protections. Overall, to many observers, China's ASMA proposal seemed to be rushed and based on future possible activities rather than a solution for addressing existing problems. China's delegates gave a bristly rebuff to these critiques in the Committee on Environmental Protection at the 2015 ATCM,[93] and a more nuanced plea for its case at the 2016 ATCM,[94] but to no avail.

Yet not all the environmental protection measures China has initiated have been rejected. In 2015, China put in a proposal for a 120-square-kilometer ASPA in the Grove Mountains, noting that the Australian Antarctic program also used this area for research and had a permanent GPS station there, while the Russian Antarctic program had visited the area sometime between 1958 and 1973. The point of highlighting these previous uses was to acknowledge that both states had engaged in discovery and exploration in the Grove Mountains and that Australia had a form of occupation. This ASPA was given fast-track approval by the Committee for Environmental Protection.[95]

China has been vocal in its opposition to new initiatives to set up three separate MPAs: one for the Ross Sea area, one in an area near Prydz Bay close to China's Zhongshan Station, and another in the waters near the Antarctic Peninsula. These new initiatives were first raised at the 2012 meeting of the

---

[93] See China, "Summary of the Comments and the Responds [*sic*] in the Second Round of Discussion," WP048, CEP9a, ATCM XXXVIII, CEP XVIII (Sofia, June 1–10, 2015), Secretariat of the Antarctic Treaty, 2015, http://www.ats.aq/documents/ATCM38/att/ATC M38_atto83_e.doc.

[94] As relayed to the author by nongovernmental organization attendees at this meeting.

[95] "Management Plan for Antarctic Specially Protected Area No 168, Mount Harding, Grove Mountains, East Antarctica," Measure 17 (2015), ATCM XXXVII, CEP XVIII, Secretariat of the Antarctic Treaty, October 31, 2015, http://www.ats.aq/documents/recatt/att578_e.pdf.

Commission for the Conservation of Antarctic Marine Living Resources, and China, Ukraine, and Russia were adamantly opposed. A number of other states neither advocated nor criticized the proposed MPAs. The contentious response to the new MPAs have exposed the lack of consensus on conservation in Antarctic waters and uncertainties about the agenda of the five nations – Australia, France, New Zealand, the United Kingdom, and the United States – that proposed them. The countries that opposed the MPAs in 2012 are not intrinsically opposed to the concept of MPAs as such; MPAs already are operational in the Southern Ocean. But it appeared that some dissenting states regarded these new MPAs as the proposing states' attempt to use environmental measures to restrict the activities of other actors. The dissenters do not share the proposers' view that Antarctica should be protected as an untouched wilderness. This values clash likely will resurface because of the energy security needs of emerging economies, which do not have access to the shale oil deposits that have alleviated the immediate energy concerns of the United States and its allies. As more states eye Antarctic resources, any perception that some states are gaining advantages by stealth will be resisted by others, and this dynamic can block or dilute genuine efforts to protect at-risk habitats. The deep lack of political trust among many Antarctic states, as well as a deep conflict of values and interests, will be hard to reconcile.

Two of the proposed MPAs surround areas where one of China's coastal bases are located and in the area where China intends to set up a new base. Chinese polar policy analysts have told me that they view the MPAs as a disguised form of territory grab, and question why the new MPAs are so big and why CCAMLR is shifting its focus from conservation to protection. A 2013 internal CAA publication claimed that Antarctic littoral states are using MPAs as a means to secure sectoral sea control in the Southern Ocean.[96]

After the 2012 commission meeting, conservationist groups critiqued what they perceived as China's lack of commitment to conservation, and complained that China (along with Russia) used procedural objections to block discussions. They urged that scientific matters should be discussed by scientists, and only scientists should be permitted to attend the next commission meeting.[97] However, a senior Chinese delegate to the commission told me

[96] "Nanji haiyang baohuqu sheli xianzhuang ji qushi," *Jidi zhanlue yanjiu dongtai* no. 3 (2013): 1.
[97] "Outrage as Antarctic Talks End in Failure," Agence France-Presse, November 1, 2012, http://www.rawstory.com/rs/2012/11/01/outrage-as-antarctic-ocean-sanctuary-talks-end-in-failure/; and John Hocevar, "Looking for Hope in the Ruins as CCAMLR Talks Fizzle," Greenpeace NZ blog, November 2, 2012, http://m.greenpeace.org/new-zealand/en/high/blog/looking-for-hope-in-the-ruins-as-ccamlr-talks/blog/42833/.

that from China's point of view, it is "impossible" to separate science from policy and politics in Antarctica. He argued that policy and science are linked, and so decisions based on science must be made by policymakers. China has marine reserves on its own sea borders and understands the need to protect ecosystems, especially spawning grounds. Moreover, he said, Chinese scientists are very pro–environmental protection and for the rational use of fisheries. He pointed out that CCAMLR is a treaty that "both supports environmental protection and allows rational use." China's delegate was concerned that the proposed MPA would restrict fishing zones and add costs to fishing in terms of extra oil needed to travel to open sites, the need to report any transit through the protected areas to the commission, the possible difficulty in accessing open sites, and chance that the weather in open areas could be harsher than that in protected areas. He told me that the MPAs needed to state clearly why there was a need to protect the areas and how much of the area needed to be protected, and that the MPA proposers should provide scientific proof to back up these claims. He said that China supports the idea of MPAs in principle, but thinks that the commission is already doing a good job of maintaining living resources in the Southern Ocean. From China's point of view, the commission already has turned the Southern Ocean into a de facto MPA, so vulnerable marine environments are already protected. The MPA would cover every species in the area, but China questioned the need for this blanket coverage, as not all species are threatened. He told me the MPAs needed to state clearly why there is a need to protect, how much needs to be protected, and to prove it scientifically.[98]

My source told me that China's commission delegates felt that in the November 2012 meeting, there had not been enough time to discuss the science behind the proposals. China needs a long lead time to consider new policy initiatives, but the MPA proposals happened too fast and there were conflicting proposals up until only a few weeks before the meeting. Most of the members of the Chinese delegation are not fluent in English, and they had difficulties following discussions and keeping up with all the circulated policy documents. Chinese is not one of the four official languages of the Antarctic Treaty system (these are English, French, Russian, and Spanish), so Chinese delegates to Antarctic governance meetings often feel that they are at a communication disadvantage. China had asked for more supporting scientific information to back up the MPA proposals and raised this point at the 2012 meeting, but the request caused antagonism and suspicion among some participants who feared that China was being obstructionist. China felt that

---

[98]   Chinese polar specialist, interview with author, November 2012.

many other nations were also unsupportive of the MPAs, so there was a low diplomatic cost in opposing the plan.[99]

Media commentary on the commission meeting highlighted China's interest in fishing as a factor in why its delegates opposed the MPA. But this was only one aspect. China's position on the new MPAs is that the new area designations will change the rules of engagement in the Southern Ocean, and therefore it is a policy issue that should be decided by the CCP government and not by scientists. Additional MPAs are in the pipeline: one for the Weddell Sea, proposed by Germany; one for the Antarctic Peninsula, proposed by a consortium of countries including Argentina, Chile, Japan, Norway, the United Kingdom, and the United States; and one for the Amundsen and Bellingshausen seas, led by Sweden and supported by US and South Korean scientific information.[100]

China's resistance to proposals for MPAs in the Southern Ocean has a historical background. It instinctively mistrusts such proposals made by Western countries, based on the PRC's twenty-two-year exclusion from international governance (1949–71), when the Republic of China held the China seat at the UN. China is suspicious that environmental protection is being used as an excuse for political interests. The antagonism shown to China's proposals during the 2012 commission meeting only made China more resistant, as did New Zealand and Australia's attitude toward Antarctica as their backyard and their perceived possessiveness about it. According to NGO representatives who attended the 2012 meeting, the Chinese delegation did not understand, or did not want to understand, the precautionary approach to conservation. China did not seem to accept New Zealand's explanation that climate change and declining fishing stocks were behind the MPA proposal. China's own fishing stocks are severely depleted after years of overfishing, yet domestic demand for seafood is growing. Expanding deep-sea fishing and krill fisheries was a top priority of China's 12th Five-Year Plan (2011–2015). Chinese fisheries policy adviser Tang Jianye argued in 2012 that China has been very passive in the past in defending its rights to Antarctic fishing and needs to better coordinate the various government agencies with a stake in this issue.[101] To get a fair share of fishing resources in Antarctica and to maintain

---

99   Chinese 2012 CCAMLR delegate, interview with author, November 2012.

100 K. S. Rajgopal, "Antarctica Needs Marine Protected Areas," *The Hindu*, March 13, 2013, http://www.thehindu.com/sci-tech/science/antarctica-needs-marine-protected-areas/article4436120.ece.

101 Tang Jianye, "Nanji Haiyang shengwu ziyuan yanghu weiyuanhui you Zhongguo di 30 jie nianhui" [The Commission for the Conservation of Antarctic Marine Living Resources and China: The 30th annual meeting], *Yuye xinxi yu zhanlue* 27, no. 3 (2012): 200.

untrammeled access to the polar seas for other purposes, China will therefore defend its interests.

China did not block the MPAs again at a special meeting held in Bremerhaven in June 2013. It did not need to, as Russia was adamantly opposed to the MPAs, so Russia took all the blame for the failure to pass the MPAs at that meeting. At the October 2013 commission meeting, China did not oppose the Ross Sea MPA – again, Russia blocked it, so China did not need to say anything – but it did block the East Antarctic MPA proposal of 1.6 million square kilometers in which future fishing activities would have to be approved by consensus.[102] China and Russia again blocked both of the proposed MPAs at the commission's 2014 annual meeting. At this two-week long meeting, one NGO delegate said, China "challenged almost every conservation mandate that was presented."[103] After the 2014 meeting, Andrea Kavanagh, a commission delegate and an environmental conservation director at the Pew Charitable Trusts, angrily described China as "an across the board conservation-spoiler."[104]

It is not completely accurate to portray China in this negative light. China does pay close attention to environment issues in Antarctica. Chinese leaders have made the same pro-environment statements on Antarctica that other international political leaders have made, and Chinese polar officials also have adopted this terminology. China aims to avoid despoiling the Antarctic environment in all its activities as much as is practicable. China addresses environmental aspects in its new capacity-building efforts; for example, all of China's new bases utilize state-of-the-art technology to minimize their environmental footprint. China initially held back on expanding Chinese tourism in Antarctica in the early 2000s, for fear that Chinese tourists might not follow international protocols on protecting Antarctic flora and fauna, and it also highlights climate change as a key research topic for its Antarctic scientists to pursue. Nonetheless, the core agenda of China's interests in Antarctica have always centered on access to available resources, which is an inherently anticonservation, antipreservation stance that contrasts with the position followed by many other states engaging in Antarctica today.

China's stance is highlighted by the keyword that has been used since the mid-1980s to sum up the government's interests in Antarctica: *liyong*. This

[102] Antarctic Ocean Alliance, "Russia, Ukraine, Again Block Southern Ocean Protection," *Scoop Independent News* (New Zealand), November 1, 2013, http://www.scoop.co.nz/stories/WO1311/S00010.htm.

[103] Chinese NGO representative, interview with author, October 2014.

[104] Morag Mackinnon, "China and Russia Thwart Plan for Antarctic Ocean Sanctuary," Reuters, October 31, 2014, http://reut.rs/1wO1VZ6.

term can be translated as "exploit," "make use of," "use," or "utilize," but when it comes to polar matters, it should be understood to mean "exploit." In Chinese-language sources, *liyong* (usually, but not always, prefaced by the adjective "peaceful") has been the key politically correct term to define China's Antarctic activities since October 14, 1984, when Deng Xiaoping used it in an inscription for China's first Antarctic base. Deng's message urged the scientists there to "peacefully exploit Antarctica on behalf of the whole of humanity" (*wei renlei heping liyong Nanji zuochu gongxian*). Deng's phrase has guided China's polar policymakers and scientists ever since, and it is frequently referenced in speeches and documents.[105] Xi Jinping used the word *liyong* twice in his landmark November 2014 speech in Hobart on China as a polar power. Significantly, it was this particular word that was altered by *China Daily*'s coverage of his talk, with "exploitation" changed to "exploration." Although Xi was speaking in Australia, the target audience for the speech was not his Australian listeners, but rather the Chinese public. Xi's speech was meant to justify China's expanded polar presence, massive investment, and expanded scientific program as part of China's efforts to secure future polar resources, which will help underwrite China's continued economic growth. It also was meant to promote China's improved comprehensive national strength. Foreign audiences received only a few sentences from this speech, in terms that would not reveal China's intentions.

At the 2015 CCAMLR, China did not oppose the Ross Sea MPA – Russia took the position as the holdout state – but continued its opposition to the East Antarctica MPA. At the 2016 CCAMLR meeting China proposed the Ross Sea MPA be limited to 20 years, in the end it was passed with a limit of 35 years, meaning the Ross Sea will be free of restriction again about the same time Chinese polar specialists predict a new international agreement will have been negotiated to permit mining in Antarctica. China has not changed its view on MPAs in Antarctica, but may have chosen to "pick its battles" when it comes to the Ross Sea area for now. From 2018 to 2020, it will be building its new base in the Ross Sea area and doing in-depth surveying of the seabed there to look for minerals and hydrocarbons,[106] so it will be keen to avoid offending the sensibilities of New Zealand, the Ross Sea claimant state.

[105] "Shenke linghui 'Nanji tici' gong tui jidi heping liyong" ["Antarctic terms" provide profound understanding of peaceful exploitation], Oceanol.com, October 17, 2014, accessed March 6, 2015, http://epaper.oceanol.com/shtml/zghyb/20141017/74635.shtml (link discontinued); and Ding, *Jidi guojia zhengce yanjiu baogao 2013–2014*, 57. *Tici* also can be translated as "inscription," but here it is being referred to as a guiding terminology set by China's senior leader.

[106] "Zhongguo ke kao chuan 'haiyang liu hao' wancheng ke kao renwu mingnian jiang tingjin Nanji" [Chinese expedition ship "Ocean VI" completes its tasks, next year it will go to

China's Position on Arctic Environmental Protection

On environmental matters and the Arctic, the Chinese government is concerned about climate change and how it will affect China's environment and people. China has identified both problems and opportunities when it comes to climate change in the polar regions,[107] and climate change has been a strong focus in China's polar science in the past twenty years. Warm weather in the Arctic leads to extreme weather patterns in China, from floods to snowstorms, and Chinese agriculture is being affected by the colder winters and hotter summers attributed to Arctic climate change. A sea level rise of only one meter would swamp China's eastern seaboard where close to a third of China's population lives. Weather research conducted at China's Antarctic and Arctic bases can help China better predict major weather events. Accurate weather and ice conditions reporting is also strategically important for countries that operate in Arctic waters for shipping, tourism, scientific expeditions, or resource extraction. The rapidly changing conditions of Arctic ice thus require China to develop better knowledge of the changing environment there.

China's senior polar scientists evidence a high environmental consciousness about the importance of conserving and preserving the polar environment. In a 2004 interview, PRIC director Yang Huigen, who was the first station manager of China's Yellow River Research Station, was appreciative of the environmental protection measures followed at Svalbard and described it as "a model site."[108] Yet since 2005, when China began its "Great Leap" in polar capacity expansion, China's polar policymakers have framed the polar regions as a "treasure chest" of mineral resources and deemphasized environmental values when communicating with Chinese audiences. Yang's December 2014 commentary on Xi Jinping's Hobart speech focused solely on the economic benefits that China could derive from the polar regions.[109] China publicly supports environmental measures in the Arctic,

---

Antarctica], Xinhua, November 11, 2015, http://news.xinhuanet.com/tech/2015-11/11/c_1117101
775.htm.

[107]   Lu Junyuan, *Beiji diyuan zhengzhi yu Zhongguo yingdui* [Geopolitics in the Arctic and
China's response] (Beijing: Shishi chubanshe, 2010), 62.

[108]   "Zhuanfang Beiji zhan zhang Yang Huigen: Yuanshi shengwu shi Beiji de zhuren"
[Interview with Yang Huigen: Indigenous creatures own the Arctic], ScienceHuman.
com, August, 23, 2004, http://www.sciencehuman.com/party/anecdote/anecdote2004/anec
dote200408z13.htm.

[109]   Yang Huigen, "Zhua zhu jiyu wei jianshe jidi qiangguo er fendou" [Seize the opportunity to
work for the creation of a polar great power], *Zhongguo haiyang bao*, December 17, 2014,
http://www.soa.gov.cn/xw/dfdwdt/jsdw_157/201412/t20141217_34481.html.

but worries that these measures may encroach on its interests in Arctic oil and natural gas.[110]

In 2015, the United States, Russia, Norway, Canada, and Denmark signed an agreement banning fishing on the Arctic high seas. The signatories hoped that other major fishing nations, such as China, would sign the agreement. In January 2015, an international meeting on the topic of Arctic fishing was held in Shanghai – an indication that Arctic states recognized the need to get China's support for this initiative. But no support for an international agreement was forthcoming at the meeting. Instead, Chinese scholars proposed that an international commission be set up to evaluate Arctic marine living resources,[111] and advocated the formation of a Regional Fisheries Management Organization to manage fishing in the central Arctic Ocean.[112] China's 2012–13 annual report on polar policies also highlighted the future commercial importance of Arctic fishing stocks.[113] As with the situation regarding the new Antarctic MPAs, China does not want to give up any potential rights. To date, China has not made any official statement on the agreement. Unusually, there was also no news coverage of the agreement in the mainland Chinese media. As the Chinese media has been giving quite detailed coverage of Arctic affairs in the past ten to fifteen years, China's official silence can be taken as a statement of objection to the Arctic fishing ban.

In the polar regions, as elsewhere, China prioritizes development first and environmental protection second. But China is the world's biggest investor in sustainable energy and its development plan is geared toward creating a more sustainable economy. Technological improvements in the coming decades could help China lead the way in environmentally sustainable development – putting Western countries, whose citizens' lifestyles contribute disproportionately to global warming – to shame.

---

[110] "Zhonghaiyou zhongshihua tingjin Beiji chengben huanbao nanti kaoyan qiye yingli" [CNOOC, Sinopec on rising Arctic costs, environmental problems challenge corporate earnings], June 14, 2013, NBD, http://www.nbd.com.cn/articles/2013-06-14/749349.html.

[111] Guo Peiqing, "Xifang eyi jiedu Zhongguo xin zhanlue: Zai Meiguo shuo Beiji bie ti Zhongguo" [The West's malicious interpretation of China's new strategy: When the United States talks about the Arctic, it shouldn't refer to China], Sina.com.cn, September 18, 2015, accessed September 23, 2015, http://mil.news.sina.com.cn/2015-09-18/1401839450.html (link discontinued).

[112] Edward Struzik, "The Future of Fishing in the Central Arctic," *World Policy Blog*, March 11, 2015, http://www.worldpolicy.org/blog/2015/03/11/future-fishing-central-arctic.

[113] Ding Huang, ed., *Jidi guojia zhengce yanjiu baogao 2012–2013* [Annual report on national polar policy research 2012–13] (Beijing: Kexue chubanshe, 2013), 28.

7

From Polar Great Power to Global Power? Global Governance Implications of China's Polar Interests

The polar regions, the deep seabed, and outer space are the "new" New World where China will draw the resources to become a global power. Access to these areas' resources and opportunities is essential for China's continued growth, prosperity, and political stability.[1] China's emerging polar agenda is not only a theater-specific strategy for the polar regions, it forms part of a grand strategy that articulates China's vision for the global order and its role in it, as well as a security strategy that identifies China's national security needs related to the polar regions, and the means to achieve them. Through examining China's polar grand strategy and emerging maritime strategy, we can trace the outlines of the Chinese Communist Party government's strategic moves in the decades to come.

CHINA'S POLAR STRATEGY

China is playing a long game in the polar regions. Keeping other states guessing about its true intentions and interests are part of its strategy.[2] Unlike most other leading Arctic and Antarctic states, China has not published a formal Arctic or Antarctic strategic document, let alone a polar strategic document. In English-language materials, Chinese polar officials repeatedly deny that China has either a broad polar strategy or one specific to the Arctic or Antarctic. Yet in a 2010 Chinese-language interview, Zhang Xia, the Polar Research Institute of China's director of polar strategy,

---

[1] "Fangwen Zhongguo Nanji kaocha shouxi kexuejia: wei shenme qu Nanji" [Interview with China's Chief Polar Scientist: Why Go to Antarctica], Sina.com, December 5, 2005, http://tech .sina.com.cn/d/2005-12-05/1202782841.shtml.

[2] Yan Qide and Zhu Jiangang, *Nanjizhou lingtu zhuquan yu ziyuan quanshu wenti yanjiu* [Research on the issue of Antarctic sovereignty and resources] (Shanghai: Kexue jishu chu-banshe, 2009), 35.

acknowledged that China was "well on the way" to developing a formal polar strategy document.[3] Indicating that a public announcement of either China's Arctic or Antarctic policies is imminent, Xi Jinping's November 2014 speech in Hobart, Australia, also made multiple references to China's polar strategy and its place in China's goal of becoming a maritime great power.[4]

The core themes of China's short- to mid-term polar strategy (*jidi fazhan zhanlüe*) were actually released as early as October 2009 by China Oceanic Administration deputy director Chen Lianzeng and reported in the official Chinese-language media, though not in *China Daily* or other Chinese government foreign-language media outlets. Chen announced that China would follow a three-phase polar strategy. The first phase would focus on building up knowledge and understanding of the Arctic and Antarctic, especially analysis on the impact of the polar regions on climate change, and the extent of polar oil, natural gas, and other natural resources. In the second phase, China would expand its presence in the Arctic and Antarctic, particularly through scientific activities; and in the third phase, China would step up its role in polar governance. During these years, China will strengthen both its polar "soft" and "hard" power. Chen defined polar soft power as a nation's polar scientific activities, while polar hard power was a reference to polar scientific infrastructure. China will seek to achieve major scientific breakthroughs in polar science and encourage more Chinese scientists to research the polar regions. This will help to build China's prestige in polar affairs and enhance its "right to speak" (*huayu quan*) on polar matters. Chen also said that China's polar hard power will expand on "multiple levels" as China acquired new polar research centers, bases, ice vessels, and airplanes.[5]

In the seven years since Chen made this announcement, all phases of the polar strategic plan are well under way. In 2012, China launched a five-year strategic research project to investigate polar resources and governance. China's polar scientific team is steadily growing in size, and its members already have made some significant scientific breakthroughs. China's overall polar scientific capacity and presence now rank among the top three in the world (see details in chapter 8). In 2013, China was finally accepted as an

3   "Zhongguo jiang qidong kaifa jidi zhanlue yifa canyu Beiji kaifa" [China is starting to develop a polar strategy to be able to legally participate in the opening up of the Arctic], Sina.com, September 14, 2010, http://mil.news.sina.com.cn/2010-09-14/1452610787.html.

4   "Er lun shenru xuexi guanche Xi Jinping zhuxi zhongyao jianghua jingshen" [Study and implement the important speech of Xi Jinping], *Zhongguo haiyang bao*, November 20, 2014, http://www.oceanol.com/redian/shiping/2014-11-25/38013.html.

5   "Zhongguo Nanji kaocha 25 zhounian: Heping liyong Nanji yong buguo shi" [China's 25th Antarctic expedition: Focus on peaceful use of Antarctica], Xinhua, October 14, 2009, http://news.xinhuanet.com/tech/2009-10/14/content_12232453_1.htm.

ongoing observer at the Arctic Council. Meanwhile, China's status as a key Antarctic player has risen significantly and is being cited as a justification for other Antarctic players such as Australia and the United States to expand their capacity to keep up.

The next logical step in the Chinese government's long-term polar strategy is to gain global acceptance of China's increasing take-up of its polar rights and interests by releasing a formal, public, document outlining China's Arctic and Antarctic policies. All the other major polar states have issued public strategies for the Arctic, the Antarctic, or both. The environmental and governance situation is shifting in the Arctic, and the Antarctic is going through similar changes. Many Chinese government agencies are involved in polar affairs, and in order to ensure that all "sing with one voice" the government needs a formal document – whether public or not – that sets out its overall polar strategy.

Beijing has never before issued an official foreign policy strategy in an area outside its geographic region. To do so will mark a real breakthrough in Chinese foreign policymaking; indicating that the CCP government is adopting a proactive and confident global grand strategy. Since so many other polar states have articulated their Arctic or Antarctic strategies, China inevitably must do the same in order to build trust – to avoid doing so will engender suspicion about its motives and goals. But China fears that being transparent to foreign audiences about its full polar agenda will lead to even more international resistance toward its polar interests. The CCP government perceives itself as operating in a relatively hostile global environment, at least in terms of its relationships with the Western states that dominate the global system overall and the polar regions in particular. In the meantime, in keeping with China's foreign policy strategy since 1989, Chinese polar officials have advised that in the Antarctic (as in the Arctic) China should learn the rules of the game but maintain a low profile for now.[6] However, Xi Jinping's breakthrough 2014 speech is an indicator that a public announcement of China's Arctic and Antarctic agenda may not be far off.

It is certainly questionable as to whether releasing such a public document will help or hinder China's long-term interests, as the Chinese government clearly suffers from a legitimacy deficit in terms of global public opinion, and not only in the polar regions.[7] It will depend on how such a public announcement is made. If the official strategy paper provides only partial information –

[6] Yan and Zhu, *Nanjizhou lingtu zhuquan yu ziyuan quanshu wenti yanjiu*, 35.
[7] "G20 Countries: Opinion of China," *Global Indicators Database: China 2015*, Pew Research Center, August 2015, http://www.pewglobal.org/database/indicator/24/group/11/.

for example, focusing on China's economic and scientific interests in the Arctic or Antarctic while avoiding mentioning its strategic and resource-related interests – then it will only increase suspicion about China's true intentions. China needs to build trust and cooperation with the current polar great powers, Russia and the United States; strong Arctic states such as Canada and Norway; and strong or influential Antarctic states, such as Australia. Yet China's closest polar bilateral relations so far are with fellow polar outsider South Korea, which has similar polar interests and aspirations,[8] and with Arctic minnow Iceland, which has played the China card to boost its international standing and influence after the disastrous policies in the 2000s that brought its economy to near-collapse. One of the primary barriers to China's enhanced access to the Arctic and Arctic resources is Russia. If China were able to establish a closer relationship with Russia, it could project power into the Arctic much more easily, but the concern for Russia in doing so is that it would weaken its own position and risk being dominated by China.

The CCP government's polar strategy is based on the assumption that China's economic growth will continue, and that this continued growth will underwrite China's expansion into the polar regions and other *res nullius* areas around the world. China's economic growth has slowed considerably since the 2008 global financial crisis. In 2014, Xi Jinping spoke of China entering a "new normal." In economic terms, China is both adjusting to a slower, steadier pace of economic development after decades of double-digit growth, and shifting from an export-led economy to becoming a high-tech, high-value economy.[9] This new economy should be conducive to the high technological needs of engaging in polar, seabed, and interplanetary exploration and exploitation. The Chinese government set growth targets of between 6.5 and 7 percent in 2015; according to official figures, it met these targets, even though the Chinese stock market experienced a massive correction in June 2015 and a further fall in January 2016.[10]

If there was a political crisis in China, leading to a change in government, the odds are that China's ambitious expansion into the polar regions would wither. This is precisely what occurred after the breakup of the Soviet Union in December 1991. Following that date, there was an immediate reduction in

[8] See Anne-Marie Brady and Kim Seungryeol, "Cool Korea: Korea's Growing Antarctic Interests," in *The Emerging Politics of Antarctica*, ed. Anne-Marie Brady (Abingdon, UK: Routledge, 2013), 75–95.

[9] "Xi's New Normal Theory," Xinhua, November 9, 2014, http://news.xinhuanet.com/english/china/2014-11/09/c_133776839.htm.

[10] Mark Magnier, "China Surprises with 7% Growth in Second Quarter," *Wall Street Journal*, July 21, 2015, http://on.wsj.com/1VoOnoS.

funds available for Russia's Antarctic research, and the privileged financial policies that had helped maintain the Soviet Union's economic, political, and military interests in the Arctic also evaporated.[11] What I have described elsewhere as the "collapse thesis" dominates Western analysis of China's future,[12] and the question of how China's political stability might affect the polar strategy cannot be ignored. China does indeed face massive internal and external challenges. But the basic assumption of the CCP's polar planning strategy is that increasing access to military, economic, and scientific polar opportunities will help ensure China's continued economic growth for the next fifty years, and thereby will contribute to keeping the CCP in political power. So far, China's political leaders have weathered China's economic and political challenges, and they continue their detailed planning for China's ongoing growth and prosperity for the next fifty years.

China's Polar Policymaking Timetable

China's polar policymaking timetable can be set out as follows:

Near-term goals: the present through 2021
The year 2021 marks the hundredth anniversary of the founding of the CCP. Xi Jinping has identified 2021 as the date when China's economic development should have advanced to the point that the whole of Chinese society will enjoy a comfortable standard of living as a basic minimum (*xiao kang shehui*). 2021 is also the year when China's 14th Five-Year Plan will be announced. In the years leading up to 2021, China will complete an assessment of polar resources and governance, make a declaration on a formal Arctic and Antarctic strategy, and appoint an Arctic ambassador. China's 12th and 13th Five-Year plans are focused on building up China's polar scientific credibility and infrastructure. China will partner with like-minded states to coordinate common policy and science goals in the polar regions – building a network of states whose interests interconnect with China's in the Arctic and Antarctic as well as elsewhere. The scientific evaluation of Arctic continental shelf limits by the UN Commission on the Limits of the Continental Shelf will continue; meanwhile, mineral extraction in Arctic sovereign territory will expand. Chinese oil and natural gas companies will develop expertise and technological capacity in Arctic oil and hydrocarbon extraction. Chinese shipping corporations will develop Arctic shipping operational requirements and access Arctic routes.

[11]   Irina Gan, "Russia, the Post-Soviet World, and Antarctica," in *Emerging Politics of Antarctica*, ed. Brady, 131; and Marlene Laruelle, *Russia's Arctic Strategies and the Future of the Far North* (Armonk, NY: M.E. Sharpe, 2014), 28.
[12]   Anne-Marie Brady, *Marketing Dictatorship: Propaganda and Thought Work in Contemporary China* (Lanham, MD: Rowman and Littlefield, 2008), 200.

The BeiDou satellite navigation system will expand to cover the entire world. The People's Liberation Army will increase the number of personnel trained in polar operations through greater participation in Arctic and Antarctic polar scientific missions and will invest in polar ice-capable vessels, and Chinese navy boats will increasingly sail in polar waters as part of their global mission. China will engage in a multilevel diplomatic negotiation using state-to-state, people-to-people, and scientific links, so as to lay the ground for activating all its polar rights in the Arctic and Antarctic.

Mid-term goals: 2021 to 2048

During these years, the diplomatic resolution of the Arctic continental shelf issue will play out at the UN Commission on the Limits of the Continental Shelf. Arctic sea routes will become operational four months out of the year. The PLA will develop submarine capabilities to the level of credible nuclear deterrence and be active in supporting freedom of navigation and oversight in the Arctic. The Chinese government will continue its multilevel efforts to secure China's rights and access in the polar regions, partnering and coordinating with other interested states. China's economic development will need to continue to make steady progress in this period, focusing on high-tech, high-value, sustainable industries, and China's own domestic market. January 14, 2048, will mark the fiftieth anniversary of the Protocol on Environmental Protection of the Antarctic Treaty, opening up the possibility of negotiations to establish a new minerals treaty in Antarctica.

Long-term goals: 2049 and beyond

Xi Jinping has signaled that by 2049, the hundredth anniversary of the founding of the People's Republic of China, the goal of China becoming a fully developed nation should be achieved. By that date, China should be a rich country with a strong military (*fu guo qiang bing*), restored to its rightful place in global affairs.[13] Antarctic mineral exploitation treaty diplomacy should be under way in this period. China will continue its multilevel efforts to secure China's rights and access in the polar regions. We can expect a further expansion of PLA capabilities in the Arctic and Antarctic, including nuclear ballistic missile submarines operating regularly in the Arctic Ocean.

China's Polar Tactics

China is currently in the process of formulating its polar and global grand strategy as it adjusts to becoming a global great power. As the policymaking process is under way, we can discern some core methodology being used to

---

[13] "Xi Vows No Stop in Reform, Opening Up," Xinhua, December 11, 2012, http://news .xinhuanet.com/english/china/2012-12/11/c_132034269.htm.

achieve China's polar strategic goals – a core methodology that is applicable to and has implications for other strategic environments.

China's polar strategy requires a peaceful global environment and (especially in the Arctic) a cooperative environment open to increased Chinese involvement in the region. China's self-description since 2011 as a "near-Arctic" state has attracted considerable negative attention internationally. Although Chinese scholars have used this term in an attempt to boost China's authority to speak on Arctic affairs, there was no need for them to make this particular claim. China has legitimate interests in the Arctic region and does not need to use geography to prove this point. Nevertheless, China would be wise to continue to be cautious in the Arctic, to try to avoid offending local sensibilities, and to build partnerships and neutralize hostile forces. In the Antarctic, China is waiting for the time when the question of the utilization of Antarctic mineral resources will be revisited, so until then it is avoiding conflict and forging strategic partnerships with like-minded countries working in Antarctica such as South Korea, or with cash-strapped ones such as Australia or New Zealand. In the next twenty years, we can expect to see China making increasing efforts to extend and strengthen its own coalitions of states such as the Shanghai Cooperation Organization, the Group of 77, the 16+1 China-European Initiative, the Asian Infrastructure and Investment Bank, the more than sixty-five countries that have been invited to participate in China's New Silk Road strategy, and in polar affairs the Asian Forum for Polar Science (AFoPS). China will gather around it a body of states that will vote with it on polar and other strategic matters at international organizations. AFoPS was set up in 2004 in an attempt to evolve a "common vision for polar policy,"[14] so AFoPS states potentially could form a voting bloc within polar governance. For now, the group is just a talk shop, with very little actual cooperation between the various states. China, India, Japan, Malaysia, and South Korea are AFoPS members, while Indonesia, the Philippines, Thailand, and Vietnam are observers. Kazakhstan, Mongolia, and Pakistan, all recent signatories to the Antarctic Treaty, likely will join the group in due course. Four AFoPS members are original signatories of the 1991 Protocol on Environmental Protection, and thus are entitled to request that the ban on minerals extraction be revised after January 2048.

Chinese polar scholars have offered detailed policy advice on specific tactics that the CCP government can follow in pursuing its polar agenda, all of which have been put into effect:

[14] "AFoPS Terms of Reference," AFoPS, accessed June 10, 2015, http://www.afops.org/board/bo ard.php?bo_table=documents&idx=7 (link discontinued).

- Step up publicity and information efforts to respond to any scholarly analysis or journalism that defines China's polar interests as a "threat."[15]
- Join every new polar-related governance group.[16] Track-one-and-a-half and track-two semischolarly and semigovernment activities, such as Arctic Circle, are especially favored.
- Find out what rights to which China is entitled in the polar regions and take advantage of them.[17]
- Use multiple means to indicate China's status and legitimate interests in Arctic and Antarctic affairs, from engaging in polar fishing, tourism, and shipping to conducting more science and participating in all Arctic governance forums. China should also look for new means to gain status in polar affairs, such as setting up its own organizations.
- Seek to raise the international profile of Arctic matters.[18]
- Advocate for and participate in all new measures required to govern Arctic and Antarctic affairs, such as on tourism, fishing, and bioprospecting.
- Coordinate China's policies with those of other observer states in the Arctic.
- Strengthen China's bilateral relations with other polar states, utilizing its economic and political powers to deepen relations. China should take advantage of contradictions between other states to advance its own interests.
- Participate in every possible aspect of opening up the Arctic shipping routes, thus ensuring that China is included in any norm-setting procedures and can extract maximum rights. China should start by using the Arctic shipping route as soon as possible, even if it is uneconomical, in order to enhance its national Arctic legitimacy. Chinese government agencies should invest in Arctic weather forecasting and ice monitoring expertise in order to facilitate Chinese commercial shipping using the Arctic route.[19]

---

[15]   Guo Peiqing and Li Zhenfu, *Beiji hangdao de guoji wenti yanjiu* [Research on the international issues regarding the Arctic shipping routes] (Beijing: Haiyang chubanshe, 2009), 316–17.

[16]   Liu Hairong and Dong Yue, "Zhongguo haiyang quanyi falu baozheng shiye zhong de jidi wenti yanjiu" [Polar research from the perspective of legal protection of China's maritime rights and interests], *Zhongguo haiyang daxue xuebao (Shehui kexue ban)* 5, no. 5 (2010): 6.

[17]   Liu and Dong, "Zhongguo haiyang quanyi falu baozheng shiye zhong de jidi wenti yanjiu," 6; see also Guo and Li, *Beiji hangdao guijie went yanjiu*, 317.

[18]   Guo Peiqing and Sun Kai, "Beiji lishihui de 'Nuke biaozhun' he Zhongguo de Beiji canyu zhi lu" [The Artic Council's "Nuuk standard" and China's path to participation in the Arctic], *Guoji zhanlue*, no. 12 (2013): 135.

[19]   Guo and Li, *Beiji hangdao de guoji wenti yanjiu*, 318–19.

- Use trade access as an incentive to enhance cooperation with key Arctic players.[20]
- Use Chinese scholars to promote China's perspective on Arctic affairs in international forums.
- Be an advocate for the global governance of Arctic affairs, using Arctic science to get a foot in the door of Arctic affairs and using other Arctic activities such as shipping, environmental management, tourism, and energy resources to increase China's level of participation and engagement in Arctic affairs.[21]
- Promote the notion of the Arctic as part of the common heritage of humankind.[22]
- Fund more research on the locations and quantities of Antarctic resources (especially in the seabeds) so that China can prepare for the future.[23]
- Learn lessons from the European Union's experiences in the Arctic, as it, like China, also is regarded as an "outside player" in Arctic governance. Like the EU, China should focus on environmental law concerns and labor laws; engage with indigenous groups, getting them to recognize that China's Arctic engagement is in their interests, and will help improve the economy and their standard of living; utilize multiple global forums to promote China's Arctic interests; increase China's local government interactions with relevant Arctic organizations as a form of diplomatic engagement; utilize participation in scientific groups to be involved in the investigation of the Arctic extended seabed, the opening-up of resources, and commercial shipping norm-setting technical standards; and integrate Arctic cooperation into the EU-China strategic cooperation.[24]
- Advocate the internationalization of Arctic governance, appealing to global concerns and interests, while deemphasizing China's own interests.[25]

---

[20] Cheng Baozhi, "Beiji zhili jizhi de goujian yu wanmei: Falu yu zhengce cemian de sikao" [The construction and perfection of Arctic governance: Reflection on law and policies], *Guoji guancha* 4 (2011): 7.

[21] Cheng Baozhi, "Beiji zhili lilunwang: Zhongguo xuezhe de shijiao" [Probing into Antarctic governance: Chinese scholars' perspective], *Taipingyang xuebao* 20, no. 10 (2012): 62–71.

[22] Cheng Baozhi, "Dangqian Beiji zhili de san da maodun ji Zhongguo yingdui" [Three contemporary Arctic governance contradictions and China's response], *Shijie zongheng* 12 (2012): 73.

[23] Yan and Zhu, *Nanjizhou lingtu zhuquan yu ziyuan quanshu wenti yanjiu,* 35.

[24] "Oumeng Beiji zhanlue de xin dongxiang ji dui woguo de qishi" [New directions in the EU's Arctic strategy, and what China can learn from it], *Jidi zhanlue yanjiu dongtai,* no. 4 (2012): 4.

[25] Cheng Baozhi, "Arctic Aspirations," *Beijing Review,* August 23, 2011, http://www.bjreview.com .cn/expert/txt/2011-08/23/content_386081.htm.

- Learn from other great powers as to how they achieved privileged rights over mineral resources. China should increase comprehensive power and influence over regions with rich oil and natural gas reserves, and adopt a long-term strategy for engaging in the region.[26]
- Do more to educate the Chinese population about the rights and opportunities that China and Chinese citizens can take advantage of in the polar regions.[27]

HOW WILL CHINA'S POLAR INTERESTS AFFECT OTHER KEY ARCTIC AND ANTARCTIC PLAYERS?

China will require international support – or at the very least, lack of opposition to its policies – in order to achieve its core goal of access to all its available polar rights and interests. There is considerable international suspicion and mistrust about China's engagement in the polar regions. An underlying fear seems to be that if China takes what it regards as its share of polar resources, will there be enough left for everybody else? At the same time, the nuclear powers (France, India, Russia, the United Kingdom, the United States, and their close allies) will be keeping a watching brief on how China's military interests in the polar regions might affect their nuclear deterrence strategies. China's polar policies focus on maintaining the government's own short- and long-term interests, such as access to mineral and fishing resources in the polar regions, freedom of the Arctic seas, the expansion of Arctic flight routes, scientists' access to polar regions, and the right to participate in any new polar-related norm-setting. China's interests may conflict with other states that seek similar access, particularly to rights to extract hydrocarbons and other mineral resources. Some of China's interests may also clash with states that seek to preserve the polar environment, especially in Antarctica. Yet as China's polar capacities have expanded since 2005, so too have China's polar bilateral relations. So far, China has been successful in partnering with a range of Arctic and Antarctic states on specific areas of cooperation, such as logistic support and scientific projects, and this will greatly facilitate China's wider goals. The promise of access to Chinese investment, enhanced trade access, and scientific funding is luring states such as Australia,

---

[26] Sun Xuefeng and Wang Haibing, "Zhongguo huoqu quanqiu shiyou ziyuan de zhanlue xuanze" [China's strategic choices for obtaining global oil resources], *Dangdai yatai*, no. 1 (2010): 72.

[27] Wang Hanling, "Zhong Mei shuangfang zuizhong shi zonghe guoli de duijue" [US-China relations will end up in a comprehensive national power showdown], *Zhongguo lunwen wang*, March 26, 2013, http://www.xzbu.com/1/view-4012558.htm.

Brazil, Chile, Iceland, New Zealand, Norway, Russia, and South Korea into closer cooperation with China in the Arctic and Antarctic.

China's increased investment in polar affairs could have some advantages for the traditionally dominant players in the Arctic and Antarctic. In the Arctic, opening up transportation routes and new economic zones will require massive investment and infrastructure development. No one country can achieve this task; it will have to be a collaborative effort between the Arctic states and interested outsiders. An optimistic scenario would be if international leaders can create a consortium to develop safe Arctic shipping, air routes, resource extraction, and communication. A more pessimistic scenario would be one in which various countries go it alone – or, even worse, if lawlessness prevails. The acceptance of China and a number of other non-Arctic states as observers to the Arctic Council in 2013 is an indicator that there is strong potential for cooperation and internationalization to become the norm in future Arctic governance, at least where economic matters are concerned.

China aims to be a polar great power, so how will this plan affect the interests of the United States, the current leading polar great power? China is careful to avoid coming in to conflict with the United States in the polar regions; it is cooperating with it in the Arctic and Antarctic on all areas where cooperation is possible. Since 1999, the United States and China have met for an Annual Dialogue on Law of the Sea and Polar Issues, which focuses on economic and scientific matters. The United States conducts a number of joint science projects with China, although political restraints on technology transfers to China have prevented some polar scientific linkages.

Chinese polar policy analysts find close parallels between US and Chinese Antarctic interests and policies.[28] They believe that there is considerable potential for cooperation between China and the United States in the polar regions, but there is also significant potential for conflict where their interests diverge or clash. Chinese polar scholars have said that getting the US-China relationship right is crucial for China to achieve its polar goals, as it is for its overall global interests.[29] In many ways, the United States and China have essentially similar goals and perspectives in the polar regions, with the exception of polar military affairs. Broadly speaking, this is also China's major point of difference with the United States. China perceives the US alliance structure and forward defense in the Asia-Pacific region as a core barrier to enhancing China's national security.

[28] "Guanyu Zhongguo zai Beiji keyan youxian fazhan lingyu de zhengce jianyi" [Policy suggestions on China's Arctic science priorities], *Jidi zhanlue yanjiu dongtai*, no. 1 (2013): 8.

[29] Ding Huang, ed., *Jidi guojia zhengce yanjiu baogao 2013–2014* [Annual report on national polar policy research, 2013–14] (Beijing: Keji chubanshe, 2014), 59.

In 2013, in meetings with US president Barack Obama, Xi Jinping raised the concept of the United States and China following a "new model of great power relations," meaning that the two major powers could learn from the lessons of the past and partner on security issues instead of competing with each other.[30] Yet Obama did not take up the concept and his successor Donald Trump is unlikely to accommodate China's growing military power and assertion of territorial rights in the East China and South China seas.

China's polar scientific capacity is expanding, while the United States' capacity has been steadily shrinking. The near-term domestic fiscal and political environment prevents the US government from significantly increasing its investment in polar science activities. China's polar military-strategic capabilities are also expanding, while the US defense budget is shrinking.[31] In 2014 the United States spent 3.5 percent of its gross domestic product on defense, but US military spending is likely to drop to 2 percent of GDP by 2025,[32] the same percentage that China spent on defense in 2014.[33] The US Navy is geared toward Pacific operations, not the polar regions. It is strong on submarines, but it has no icebreakers or ice-strengthened vessels capable of sustained Arctic operations. In contrast, the Russian navy is well set up for cold-weather warfare.[34] The US Navy's 2014 Arctic preparedness report mentioned a need to enhance its polar vessel capabilities, but so far no budget has been allocated to that suggestion.[35] China's desire to become a polar great power will expose US weaknesses in the Arctic and Antarctic and may well accentuate tensions between the two sides.

In 2009, a US presidential directive defined the United States' strategic Arctic interests as (1) missile defense and early warning; (2) the deployment of sea and

30 Wang Jisi, "Chinese Perspective: How Is a 'New Model of Great Power Relations' Possible?," *National Commentaries, ASAN Forum*, July 19, 2013, http://www.theasanforum.org/views-on -what-should-come-next-after-the-obama-xi-summit-and-other-introductory-summits-in-2013/.

31 Paul D. Shinkman, "Massive Budget Cuts Would Redefine U.S. Military," *U.S. News and World Report*, February 24, 2014, http://www.usnews.com/news/articles/2014/02/24/pentagons- massive-budget-cuts-would-redefine-the-us-military.

32 "The Long-Term Implications of Current Defense Plans: Detailed Update for Fiscal Year 2008," Congressional Budget Office, March 20, 2008, 3, http://www.cbo.gov/ftpdocs/90xx/do c9043/03-28-CurrentDefensePlans.pdf.

33 "Military Expenditure (% of GDP)," World Bank, accessed September 28, 2015, http://data .worldbank.org/indicator/MS.MIL.XPND.GD.ZS.

34 Lance M. Bacon, "Navy Prepares for Arctic Operations as Ice Thins," *Military Times*, February 11, 2015, http://www.militarytimes.com/story/military/pentagon/2015/02/11/navy- prepares-for-arctic-operations/23230291/.

35 "U.S. Navy Arctic Roadmap for 2014–2030," US Department of the Navy, February 2014, http://www.navy.mil/docs/USN_arctic_roadmap.pdf.

air systems for strategic sealift, strategic deterrence, maintaining a maritime presence, and maritime security operations; and (3) ensuring freedom of navigation and overflight, preventing terrorist attacks, and mitigating any criminal or hostile acts that could increase US vulnerability to terrorism in the Arctic region.[36] According to a 1997 official statement, the United States also has strong foreign policy, national security, scientific, and environmental interests in the Antarctic.[37] The United States has highlighted its interest in maintaining a strong presence in Antarctica in order to maintain strategic dominance there.[38] However, the Antarctic is not high on the policy agenda in Washington, and even the Arctic is relatively low in US domestic and foreign policy priorities. The US government also cannot find enough domestic political support for the United States to sign the UN Convention on the Law of the Sea, which would help protect US interests in the Arctic. It is struggling to pull together a budget to purchase sorely needed polar icebreakers. The United States also has not signed key protocols on tourism management in Antarctica, even though it is the country that sends the largest numbers of tourists there.[39]

Russia, after the United States, is the other great polar power in the world today. China finds working with Russia on Arctic issues challenging, but ultimately China has to find a way to cooperate with Russia, because Russia is China's main gateway to the Arctic. Moreover, Sino-Russian energy cooperation is crucial for helping China achieve its polar economic security goals.[40] Yet Russia's attitude toward China's Arctic engagement is not unified. Some sectors of the Russian government believe that China's engagement in the Arctic will be useful in assisting economic development in the region; others argue that Russian rights to Arctic seas will be weakened by China's increased participation in Arctic shipping. Still others see a military threat in China's expansion into the Arctic.[41] Two-thirds of Arctic mineral resources lie

[36] "NSPD-66 [National Security Presidential Directive 66] on Arctic Region Policy," January 9, 2009, National Security Presidential Directives, George W. Bush Administration 2001–2008, Federation of American Scientists, http://fas.org/irp/offdocs/nspd/nspd-66.htm.

[37] "The United States and Antarctica in the 21st Century," US House of Representatives Committee on Science, March 12, 1997, http://commdocs.house.gov/committees/science/hs y071002.000/hsy071002_0.HTM.

[38] "PDD/NSC-36 – US Antarctica Policy," March 9, 1996, Presidential Decision Directives, Clinton Administration 1993–2000, Federation of American Scientists, http://fas.org/irp/off docs/pdd26.htm.

[39] Rod McGuirk, "The Antarctic Is Left Defenceless to Tourists," *Independent* (London), March 17, 2013, http://www.independent.co.uk/environment/nature/the-antarctic-is-left-defenceless-to-tourism-8537546.html.

[40] Ding, *Jidi guojia zhengce yanjiu baogao 2013–2014*, 207.

[41] "Chinese factor NSR" [in Russian], Morvesti.ru, n.d., http://morvesti.ru/analytics/? ELEMENT_ID=20790.

in Russian territory. Russia requires capital to further develop these resources. China is one of a number of countries invited to participate in joint exploration with Russia. Rosneft (Russia's top oil producer) and Chinese state-owned enterprise Sinopec have been exploring oceanic hydrocarbon deposits since 2010. In the Antarctic, Russia and China have similar views on fishing, minerals exploitation, and the territorial status of Antarctica, as well as a similar approach to staking out influence in Antarctica through a strategic spread of bases. In 2016, Russia and China announced plans for scientific collaboration in Antarctica; however, there are no definite collaborations as yet. The two countries have only a modest level of scientific cooperation in the Arctic.[42] Mutual interest will probably drive Russia and China together on many aspects of polar affairs, but their interests are not completely complimentary. Chinese polar scholars worry that Russia's partnership with China is only temporary, reflecting the current political environment, and warn that the Chinese government should take advantage of this strategic opportunity to get as much as it can out of the relationship.[43]

In the Arctic, the Nordic countries of the Arctic Council (Denmark, Iceland, Finland, Norway, and Sweden) are generally welcoming of China's engagement in the region and support and facilitate China's acceptance as a legitimate Arctic stakeholder. From the point of view of the Nordic states, China can play a useful balancing role to Russian and US power. Nordic states have gained much from China's Arctic interests and increased engagement in the region: obtaining significant trade deals (Sweden, 2012); playing on the situation to enhance bilateral relations with Russia, the United States and the EU, plus garnering a free trade agreement (Iceland, 2013); easing frosty relations (Norway, 2013); setting up a comprehensive strategic partnership (Denmark, 2015); and developing extensive economic links (Finland, 2015). China's investment in Greenland's mineral resources may soon enable the latter to become fully independent of Denmark. Both Iceland and Norway have set up Arctic cooperation projects with China. Norway wants other states to agree that Svalbard is part of Norway. Iceland smarts at the exclusivity of the Arctic five littoral states, so the Icelandic government sees China as a balancing force in Arctic affairs, helping to bring about a "more democratic" approach to Arctic matters.[44] Iceland wants to be the Atlantic-side hub for trans-Arctic shipping; this would favor shipping taking the upper Northern or

---

[42]   Russian polar official, interview with author, June 2016.
[43]   Ding Huang, ed., *Jidi guojia zhengce yanjiu baogao 2012–2013* [Annual report on national polar policy research, 2012–13] (Beijing: Kexue chubanshe, 2013), 140.
[44]   Icelandic diplomat, interview with author, November 2012.

transpolar route, which would avoid Canadian and Russian waters and the sovereignty disputes that go with them.[45] Murmansk is another rival as the site for a potential Arctic hub. However, although the Russian Northern Sea Route will be an important domestic sea route, its waters are too shallow for the size of boats that would be engaging in international shipping. Moreover, existing Russian harbors are congested and its rail system cannot cope with the demand.[46] Norway would also like to host a future Arctic hub location at Kirkenes. For ships following a Northeast route, Kirkenes is indeed a useful stopping point. However, from 2010 to 2016 Sino-Norwegian relations were in the doldrums because of China's displeasure over the Norwegian Nobel Committee offering Chinese dissident Liu Xiaobo the Nobel Peace Prize, so China did not give much support for this option. At present, Iceland looks like the likeliest choice for the main Atlantic-side trans-Arctic shipping hub.[47]

In the Antarctic, China is following a similar strategy of developing close bilateral relations with the less powerful players while avoiding offending the two polar great powers. China has paid particular attention to working with the seven Antarctic claimant states, as any future minerals treaty would require their support.[48] Australia, Chile, and New Zealand all have a history of working closely with China in Antarctica, beginning from the Chinese government's earliest public expression of interest in working there. As China has dramatically expanded its level of activities in Antarctica, so has China's level of partnership with these three countries expanded. China also has strong cooperation with Norway on Antarctic fisheries science, a rare positive spot in this troubled bilateral relationship. Chinese scientists have also partnered with British (as well as American, Australian, German, and Japanese) scientists in their Dome A and Gamburtsev Mountains research.[49] In 2013, China and Argentina signed an agreement to set up a binational nanotechnology center.[50] China supports Argentina's position on the latter's Malvinas/

[45] See *North Meets North: Navigation and the Future of the Arctic* (Reykjavik: Ministry for Foreign Affairs, 2005), http://www.mfa.is/media/Utgafa/North_Meets_North_netutg.pdf.
[46] Chinese polar policymaker, interview with author, October 2012.
[47] Chinese polar policymaker, interview with author, September 2014.
[48] "The Antarctic Treaty System: Introduction," US Department of State, accessed June 15, 2016, http://www.state.gov/documents/organization/15282.pdf.
[49] "The Science Mission, Antarctica's Hidden World," British Antarctic Survey, 2015, accessed July 25, 2015, http://www.antarctica.ac.uk/press/featured/AGAP/science_mission .php (link discontinued).
[50] "Argentina y China crearán un instituto científico de nanotecnología" [Argentina and China will create a scientific institute of nanotechnology], *Telam*, May 6, 2013, http://www .telam.com.ar/notas/201306/20154-argentina-y-china-crearan-instituto-cientifico-de-nano tecnologia.html.

Falklands territorial dispute with the United Kingdom, and has agreed to sell Argentina high-level military technology. The exception to all these cozy arrangements between China and the Antarctic claimant states is France. Sino-French Antarctic cooperation was officially frozen on account of the French government's criticism of China's Tibet policies in 2008.[51] They have not revived since that date, despite Chinese efforts, due to French concerns about the one-sided nature of scientific cooperation plans.

China's emergence as a polar great power is sure to affect geopolitics – for better or for worse – in the Arctic and the Antarctic, as well as globally. Polar affairs are linked to China's quest for international status. Any restrictions on China achieving its polar goals will affect its global interests.[52] In the Arctic, China may help play a balancing role among the various players. China is also the most likely source of the investment funds needed to help open up the Arctic region. But its increased Arctic activities may further exacerbate an existing arms race in the region between Russia and NATO, or split the Arctic players between those that work closely with China and those that do not. Public opinion in the Arctic region is another important factor. If Arctic peoples are uncomfortable with China's engagement in the region, it will have a negative impact on China's interests. And if environmental nongovernmental organizations can build enough international support to oppose the extraction of Antarctic mineral resources or other forms of exploitation in the world's last significant wilderness landmass and maritime zone, then China's long-term goals there will be much harder to achieve.

China's current polar activities are sowing the seeds for long-term interests, some of which will not come into fruition for another thirty to fifty years. Arctic shipping will not be fully operational until the mid-century, and in the same period the question of Antarctic mineral exploitation may be reconsidered. The Arctic and Antarctic, the high seas, and outer space are all arenas where China has indicated a strong interest in being active and having its say in any new norm-setting. According to a report in an internal CCP journal in 2014, China is intensely interested in global governance – not to undermine or overthrow the current order, but to make its perspective known in any new areas of international law and to speak up about aspects of the international

---

[51] Stéphane Foucart, "La question tibétaine gèle une coopération scientifique franco-chinoise en Antarctique" [The Tibet question freezes a Franco-Chinese scientific cooperation in Antarctica], *Le Monde*, April, 25, 2008, http://www.lemonde.fr/asie-pacifique/article/2008/04/25/la-question-tibetaine-gele-une-cooperation-scientifique-franco-chinoise-en-antarctique_10 38506_3216.html.

[52] Guo and Li, *Beiji hangdao de guoji wenti yanjiu*, 320.

order that do not suit China's interests.[53] After years of being excluded from the international system, then adopting a relatively low-key foreign policy, China now wants to have its voice heard on global affairs.

The polar regions, the high seas, and outer space are all areas of the world where participation in global governance is essential. Any unilateralism in these zones will be a clear sign of a state's break with the international order and the established rules of the game. It should be noted that unlike the United States, which has failed to ratify multiple international treaties including on core "public goods" such as human rights, justice, and resource management,[54] China has signed up to, and ratified, virtually all the key instruments of international law and is an increasingly active participant in international regimes moderating global issues. China's polar strategy requires continued economic growth, a peaceful internal and external political environment, and positive global public opinion toward China's rise. To achieve its polar and maritime goals, China will need cooperation from other states, not conflict. So from the point of view of many – but not all – interested nation states active in the Arctic and Antarctic, the wisest response to China's increased interest in the polar regions may well be to find ways to partner with China, to include China in the future governance structure, and to help China succeed in these goals. The greatest opponents to the Chinese government's polar policies are likely to be the global environment movement and China's own nascent environmental groups. Those who wish to moderate China's extractive polar ambitions would be wise to engage with and nurture popular awareness in China of the value of conserving and preserving the Arctic and Antarctic environment.

FROM POLAR GREAT POWER TO MARITIME GREAT POWER

In his 2014 Hobart speech, Xi Jinping made an explicit connection between China's development as a polar power to the even more significant goal of China becoming a maritime great power (*haiyang qiangguo*).[55] The CCP leadership recognizes that in order to become a global great power, China must develop sea power (*haiyang quanli*). In 2014, a lead article in the PLA newspaper *Liberation Army Daily* pointed out that "if China is to become a great power, it must be [powerful] on the high seas, and to achieve this it

53   Ye Hailin, "Wo guo guojia anquan zhanlue linian yu shixian" [China's security strategy principles and implementation], *Da jiangtang* no. 4 (2014): 17.
54   "US Position on International Treaties," Global Policy Forum, July 2003, http://www .globalpolicy.org/empire/26665-us-position-on-international-treaties.html.
55   "Er lun shenru xuexi guanche Xi Jinping zhuxi zhongyao jianghua jingshen."

must have a clear maritime strategy."[56] China is currently developing its own theories of maritime power and developing a maritime strategy. The theories of Alfred T. Mahan continue to be a major influence on China's evolving strategy, as they were in the late Qing and early Republican era.[57] In the 1980s, when PLA-Navy commander Admiral Liu Huaqing laid out a new blueprint for China to gain control over its maritime boundaries and defend the key chokepoints on which China's sea lanes of communication depend, his thinking was greatly influenced by Mahan's writings on sea power.[58] In 2012, a senior Chinese polar policymaker said that while Mahan's theories do not completely fit China's situation, Mahan-ism dominates current Chinese maritime policymaking.[59]

In the 1980s, under Admiral Liu Huaqing's leadership, China adjusted its concept of maritime defense from coastal defense (*jin'an fangyu*), as it had been in the Mao era, to offshore defense (*jinhai fangyu*).[60] The outcome was a steady expansion of the PLAN's role in China's defense and a similar expansion in naval capacity. In 1992, Deng Xiaoping stated that China should "establish a strong navy with a model battle capacity," and added "we do not need too much, but it should be high-level and very modern."[61] As Chinese economic power grew in the 1990s and into the 2000s, so too did China's naval power. In this period, China moved from a maritime strategy of "going out on the oceans" (*zou xiang haiyang, jinglüe haiyang*) to the current one of maritime "offshore battle readiness" (*yuan yang zuozhan*).[62] Hu Jintao first raised the concept of China as a maritime great power at the 18th Party Congress in 2012, just as he was stepping down from power.[63] This goal has taken on even greater prominence under Xi Jinping's leadership.

According to Mahan, a nation's maritime power relies on six conditions: geography, natural resources and climate, territorial size, size of population,

[56] "Jing lue haiyang de san ge zhuoyan dian" [Three-point oceanic strategy], *Jiefang junbao*, October 10, 2014, http://mil.news.sina.com.cn/2014-10-14/0520805377.html.

[57] Zhang Wenmu, *Lun Zhongguo haiquan* [On China's sea power] (Beijing: Haiyang chubanshe, 2009), 78.

[58] Liu Huaqing, *Liu Huaqing huiyilu* [The memoirs of Liu Huaqing] (Beijing: Jiefang jun chubanshe, 2005), 432.

[59] Senior Chinese polar policymaker, interview with author, 2012.

[60] Sun Lixin, "Chinese Maritime Concepts," *Asia Europe Journal* 8, no. 3 (2010): 334.

[61] Deng Xiaoping, *Deng Xiaoping guanyu jianshe you Zhongguo tese shehuizhuyi lunshu zhuanti zhaibian* [Special edition of treatise by Deng Xiaoping on the building of socialism with Chinese characteristics] (Beijing: Zhongyang wenxian chubanshe, 1992), 281.

[62] Liu Zhonghao, "Cong haohan lan shui si lu: lun zhonggong haiyang zhanlue fazhan" [From vast blue waters to the maritime Silk Road: The development of CCP maritime strategy], *Haijun xueshu yuekan* 38, no. 4 (2004): 13-24, http://www.cchere.com/article/557780.

[63] "Hu Calls for Efforts to Build China into Maritime Power," Xinhua, November 8, 2012, http://news.xinhuanet.com/english/special/18cpcnc/2012-11/08/c_131959403.htm.

extent of maritime culture, and political structure. Mahan said that rising states that want to develop maritime power should build big navies to protect their commerce, aim for global markets, and either gain privileged access to resources or establish colonies.[64] The polar regions, the deep seabed, and outer space are all *res nullius* by China's definition, and hence are ripe for such "colonization." Mahan further advocates that rising powers should

- Focus on maritime economics, since production, shipping, and colonies are the key to national prosperity and have long been essential motivators of the policies of maritime states.[65]
- Develop naval supremacy, as this is of critical importance in conflicts between great powers.[66]
- Nurture awareness about maritime issues among the population.[67]

China is currently pursuing all of these strategies. China's maritime goals have moved well beyond defending itself from invasion by sea, and now include ambitions to protect its own sea borders, develop a blue-water navy capable of patrolling the high seas, strengthen its own maritime economy, and take advantage of all available international maritime rights. China's expanding polar program is inextricably linked with these objectives. China's aim to defend its SLOCs will contribute to maritime public goods, but in areas of disputed sovereignty such as the South China Sea, China's goals clash with the interests of other claimant states. Access to shale oil means that the United States likely will become self-sufficient in oil and natural gas by 2035,[68] so the US government may well use its self-sufficiency as an excuse to reduce its global naval presence. By 2035, China will be the world's biggest oil importer.[69] In a best-case scenario, China would step into the role that the United States has played since World War II in protecting global sea routes from piracy and other attacks. From the point of view of the United States

---

[64] Alfred T. Mahan, *The Influence of Sea Power upon History, 1660–1783* (Boston: Little, Brown and Co, 1890), 28.

[65] Ibid., 1, and 28.

[66] Ibid., 1.

[67] Ibid., 29–89.

[68] "North America Leads Shift in Global Energy Balance, IEA Says in Latest *World Energy Outlook*," International Energy Agency, November 12, 2012, http://www.iea.org/newsroomandevents/pressreleases/2012/november/north-america-leads-shift-in-global-energy-balance-says-new-world-energy-outlook.html.

[69] Spencer Dale, "Energy Trends: What's the Outlook for 2035?" *BP Magazine*, February 17, 2015, http://www.bp.com/en/global/corporate/press/bp-magazine/conversations/chief-economist-on-energy-outlook.html.

and many other states, it would be even better if China partnered with the US Navy to do so, thereby demonstrating its position as a stakeholder in the current international order.

CHINA AS A GLOBAL GREAT POWER?

Since he came to power in 2012, Xi Jinping has made several strong statements linking China's expanding polar program to China's rise as a maritime power and the CCP's New Silk Road strategy. The Arctic Northern Sea Route is one of three new transportation routes highlighted in Xi's vision for a new Sino-centric order of regional cooperation that will link sixty-five nations, with China at the center. This new vision, while attractive to many, may well awaken fears of the rise of an illiberal, hierarchical, Sino-centric order: China as the Central Kingdom – the literal translation of its Chinese name, *Zhongguo.*

A new era is dawning in Chinese foreign policy as China's economic growth enables Beijing to move from its past timorousness in declaring itself a global leader and its relative inability to defend its interests to one where it can seek adjustments in the security environment it has faced since the outbreak of the Korean War. Just as the United States did at the beginning of the Cold War, China is now trying to establish its own coalition of states willing to partner with it to form economic and security groupings and alliances: another "hub and spoke" set of alliances, but with China as the hub.

Since the end of the Cold War, Chinese foreign policy has been evolving as China's ability to influence its external environment has improved. After the crackdown on the student protest movement in Tiananmen Square in 1989 and the international condemnation that followed, Deng Xiaoping set out China's core foreign policy strategy as follows: "Be calm and observe the situation; hold our ground; hide our strengths and bide our time; be good at keeping a low profile; don't take the lead, do what you can" (*Lengjing guancha, wenzhu zhenjiao chenzhuo yingfu, taoguang yanghui, shanyu shouzhuo, jue bu dangtou, you suo zuowei*).[70] This dictum became the model for Chinese foreign relations for the next twenty years. But from 1999, after US bombs hit the annex to the Chinese embassy in Belgrade during the war in Kosovo, Chinese foreign policy moved from the post-1989 relatively passive stance to

---

70 "Deng Xiaoping 'taoguang yanghui' waijiao zhanlue de laili" [The origins of Deng Xiaoping's "*taoguang yanghui*" foreign affairs strategy], China.com, March 1, 2012, http://news.china .com/history/all/11025807/20120301/17065999.html.

an "active defensive position."[71] This meant that China would become proactive in both political and economic affairs in order to combat perceived strong attacks from the West on both fronts. In the early 2000s, as China's economic and political power was consolidated, Chinese scholars hotly debated the relevance of Deng Xiaoping's 1989 maxim. After the 2008 global financial crisis, the Chinese foreign policy line was adjusted to focus on the more proactive "do what we can" (*you suo zuowei*) theme of Deng's foreign policy strategy, with the added caution of "don't take the lead" (*jue bu dangtou*). In other words, Chinese foreign policy became increasingly assertive in protecting China's rights.[72] However, China was loath to be seen as taking on a global leadership role, preferring instead to see itself as a "partner" with other nations.[73]

Xi Jinping's administration has taken this assertive foreign policy to a new level, and Xi has seemed less anxious than his predecessors about being perceived as a global leader. Since Xi came to power in 2012, use of Deng's foreign policy maxim has fallen somewhat out of favor and been replaced by a new phraseology. Xi first promoted the changed expression in October 2013, after a conference on China's diplomacy toward its neighbors.[74] At the meeting, Xi stated that China should be more "proactive" (*fen fa youwei*), in this case in diplomatic efforts aimed at China's near neighbors. Chinese state media immediately adopted the expression as a new *tifa* (politically correct term) for China being proactive in various aspects of foreign policy.

As informed Chinese readers well knew, the advice to "be proactive" had a special meaning for Xi because it was part of his personal motto, developed when he was sent to work in the countryside as a young man in the early 1970s. Xi revealed in a 2003 memoir that during those years, his youthful motto was "Be honest, do solid work; be unassuming, get on with things; do not forget the people, be willing to make sacrifices; spare no effort; and be proactive" (*laoshi zuoren, zhashi zuoshi; bu shi zhangyang, zhi qiu shiji; wu wang renmin, gan*

---

[71]　Chen Junhong, ed., *Jiaqiang he gaijin sixiang zhengzhi gongzuo xuexi duben* [A reader of strengthening and reforming political thought work] (Beijing: Zhonggong Zhongyang dangxiao chubanshe, 1999), 169.

[72]　"Xianggang Wenhui bao: Zhongguo junshi 'geng you zuo wei'" [Hong Kong's *Wen Wei Po* newspaper: The Chinese military is "doing more of what it can"], Chinanews.com, January 4, 2009, http://www.chinanews.com.cn/hb/news/2009/01-04/1512366.shtml.

[73]　Wang Yusheng, "Guanyu Zhong Mei guanxi yixie zhanluexing wenti de tantao" [An inquiry into strategic issues and China-US relations], *Shijie fazhan yanjiu*, no. 8 (2012), 13.

[74]　"Xi Jinping: Rang mingyun gongtongti yishi zai zhoubian guojia luodi shenggen" [Xi Jinping: Let the consciousness of a common destiny take root among neighboring countries], Xinhua, October 25, 2013, http://news.xinhuanet.com/politics/2013-10/25/c_117878944.htm.

zuo fengxian; jugong jincui, fenfa you wei).[75] Since becoming CCP general secretary Xi has overseen a renewed opening up of China to the outside world, offering unprecedented levels of trade and investment opportunities to partner states. Under Xi's leadership, China has also gone head to head with Japan on contested territory in the East China Sea; declared a new air defense identification zone over the contested Diaoyu/Senkaku Islands and Sokota Rock (held by South Korea); created seven new islands on coral reefs in the South China Sea and put military bases on them to back up its territorial claims; had a series of spats with the Philippines over territorial issues; rebuffed the ruling of the Permanent Court of Arbitration on the question of its claims on the South China Sea; and been increasingly assertive toward US military air and sea activities in the South China Sea, East China Sea, and North Pacific. All of these actions are aimed at regaining sea and air control in China's near seas, a crucial element of China's emerging maritime strategy. At the same time, under Xi Jinping, China is affirming its commitment to supporting the interests of the developing world, offering loans, preferential trade, and scholarships, and vowing to support their interests in the international system. As Mao Zedong did in the 1950s, Xi is adopting an international relations strategy of "uniting with the majority, while attacking a minority" (*tuanjie da duoshu, daji yi xiaocuo*).[76]

China is now close to meeting all the measures of what defines a global great power: political, economic, and military might with a global reach. But according to many observers, it does not yet act like a great power in terms of its contribution to international leadership during crisis situations such as the Russian intervention in Ukraine or the civil war in Syria. Instead, so far Beijing has been assertive only when it comes to defending its own narrow interests. In March 2015, at the first meeting of China's National Security Commission, Xi stated that while China is stronger than ever before, it faces three great threats: invasion, subversion, and division. Xi also emphasized the risk that China's economic development and stability will be threatened and that the political system will be challenged.[77] China's concept of national security has changed under Xi; it has refocused on sovereignty and incorporates a much more inclusive notion of security, including nontraditional security, political

---

75   Xi Jinping, "Wo de shanshang jingli" [My experience in the countryside], *Renmin luntan*, June 2, 2012, http://news.ifeng.com/history/zhiqing/xiaohua/detail_2012_06/02/14998949_0 .shtml.

76   Ye, "Wo guo guojia anquan zhanlue linian yu shixian," 30.

77   "Jiefangjun fu zongzhang Sun Jianguo shang jiang: Zhongguo you bei qinlue weixian" [PLA Deputy Chief Sun Jianguo: China at risk of invasion], *Liaowang dongfang zhoukan*, March 4, 2015, http://news.sina.com.cn/c/2015-03-04/101031565883.shtml.

security, homeland security, military security, economic security, cultural security, social security, science and technology security, information security, ecological security, resources security, and nuclear security.[78] China must rely on economic growth, political stability, and international partnerships to achieve its long-term goals. Its economic model requires new markets and privileged access to resources, a moderating factor in its foreign policy approach. For a complex range of reasons, ranging from internal and external security to access to the Arctic, China cannot afford to offend Russia, so this is an important aspect to its response to the Ukraine and Syrian crises. The competitive and contentious external environment that China faces in its immediate neighborhood requires the CCP government to take a relatively cautious short- to medium-term approach to its national security, but it will face up to challenges when it feels it must. China is working hard to strengthen its external environment, especially on the periphery. Hence the government's fierce reaction in 2016 to the rejection of its sovereignty claims in the South China Sea by the Permanent Court of Arbitration.

At least until 2021, and continuing through to 2049, we can expect to see Chinese foreign policy verge from being assertive and proactive to being ambiguous and nonconfrontational. Where China cannot affect change, it will make the best out of the current order and quietly pursue its own interests, but if it is possible to create new governance arrangements or it affects its core interests then Beijing will act assertively. China faces a more difficult situation on its immediate borders than the United States did when it became a global superpower at the end of World War II. China has no allies, four nuclear-armed neighbors, and other neighbors that are hedging against it by strengthening their military relations with the United States. Thus, following that advice from Deng Xiaoping on the extent to which China would invest in a modern navy – "We do not need too much, but it should be high-level and very modern" – China is investing in asymmetric warfare and a relatively modest expansion of its naval capacities. It has invested in state-of-the-art electromagnetic pulse weapons, cyber warfare, space warfare, and a small but adequate nuclear deterrent, and has been creating a complex network of China-centered strategic bilateral and multilateral agreements such as the Shanghai Cooperation Organization; free trade agreements with states such as Australia, Iceland, and New Zealand; and less formalized close partnerships with strategically useful states such as Djibouti, Fiji, Sri Lanka, and Zimbabwe. Although the United States spends vastly more on military affairs than any other state, this is more a weakness than it is a strength, as was shown

---

[78] Ye, "Wo guo guojia anquan zhanlue linian yu shixian," 29.

in the last years of the Soviet Union. China is not bogged down in costly wars – since 2002, the United States has spent over US$17 trillion on the wars in Iraq and Afghanistan. China has invested in the capabilities it needs to defend its interests in its core geostrategic zone in East Asia, and is focusing on core sovereignty and security concerns: the status of Taiwan, the South China Sea maritime boundaries, the Diaoyu/Senkaku Islands dispute with Japan in the East China Sea, and the protection of its SLOCs.

China's status as a polar great power is directly linked to its desire to seek a greater global role.[79] So if China succeeds in its goals in the polar regions and consequently achieves its goal to become a maritime great power, then its quest for international status and power will be assured. In 2014, in a widely circulated essay published in a classified journal for senior CCP officials, foreign policy scholar Ye Hailin wrote that "China will become a super power when other states recognize its norm-setting abilities."[80] From the point of view of international relations theory, Ye's conclusion is hardly ground-breaking: super powers are the states that influence international norms. But what is groundbreaking is Ye's matter-of-fact assumption of China's inevitable rise as a global super power. A few years before, when Chinese foreign policy was controlled under the maxim "hide strengths, bide time, and don't take the lead," no Chinese academic would have been so bold or outspoken in an assessment of China's ability to influence the global balance of power, and the concept of China taking a leadership role in global affairs would have been taboo.

Since the end of the Cold War, China has slowly but steadily emerged as a world power. The first few decades of China's rise occurred in an era of unipolarity under the internationally dominant United States. Hence, the questions of how far China's global influence extends and whether China's rise will affect US power is a topic of intense interest to many China politics specialists. China-US relations frequently have been described as the most important bilateral relationship in the world. In 1999, China international relations specialist Gerald Segal's influential *Foreign Affairs* article "Does China Matter?" argued that "China is a second-rank middle power that has mastered the art of diplomatic theater." Segal classified China as merely a "regional power."[81] Fourteen years later, in 2013, leading China politics specialist David Shambaugh defined China as still only a "partial power" in

---

79 Guo and Li, *Beiji hangdao de guoji wenti yanjiu*, 320.
80 Ye, "Wo guo guojia anquan zhanlue linian yu shixian," 1.
81 See Gerald Segal, "Does China Matter?," *Foreign Affairs* 78, no. 5 (1999): 24–36, https://www.foreignaffairs.com/articles/asia/1999-09-01/does-china-matter.

spite of China's economic, political, and military gains. Shambaugh argued that "China is a global actor without (yet) being a true global *power* – the distinction being that true powers *influence* other nations and events. Merely having a global presence does not equal having global power unless a nation influences events in a particular region or realm."[82]

Segal's 1999 assessment of China's global influence is not in dispute, but Shambaugh's 2013 assessment underestimates China's current global influence and power aspirations. China already has massive international political and economic power and influence and is well on the way to developing advanced military capacities that will support further global expansion. By China's own assessment, it already has successfully made the transition from a regional power to a global power.[83] In 2013, in an interview in *People's Daily* discussing why China was setting up a "long-awaited" National Security Council, military strategist Zhang Tuosheng, head of the PLA-backed think-tank China Foundation for International and Strategic Studies, explained that China needed to set up a National Security Council "because global powers have to engage in crisis management and crisis control on a grand scale and need to be able to coordinate key government agencies in a timely manner."[84]

The Chinese government has initiated a number of studies and public projects to examine what China's growing global power means both for China and the international system. Chinese political leaders and theorists have no doubt that China is already a global power, but they differ in how to express that conviction, particularly in terms of China's relationship with the current global hegemon, the United States. In 2005, Zheng Bijian's theory of China's peaceful rise[85] attracted considerable international attention, but eventually was modified as a concept owing to concerns about negative international perceptions. Under the rubric of a "new model of great power relations," Xi Jinping has signaled he wants the United States and China to avoid the historical mistakes followed by other rising and established great powers. But the concept has been met with cynicism by US policy analysts, as

---

[82]   David Shambaugh, *China Goes Global: The Partial Power* (Oxford: Oxford University Press, 2013), 6.

[83]   "Zhang Tuosheng tan sheli guo'an wei: Quanqiu xing daguo yao pin weiji guankong" [Zhang Tuosheng on the establishment of a National Security Council: A global power needs to engage in crisis control], *Renmin ribao*, December 30, 2013, http://politics.people.com.cn/n/2013/1230/c1001-23975187.html.

[84]   Ibid.

[85]   Zheng Bijian, "China's 'Peaceful Rise' to Great-Power Status," *Foreign Affairs* 84, no. 5 (2005): 18–24, https://www.foreignaffairs.com/articles/asia/2005-09-01/chinas-peaceful-rise-great-power-status.

in practice it appears to require the United States to make a number of strategic concessions, while China would make none.

Perhaps the problem in understanding China's current global influence reflects the difference between what the United States defines as global interests and the areas where the United States seeks to influence global government, such as promoting democracy, promoting political and civil definitions of human rights, and using diplomatic and sometimes military pressure in conflict zones around the world. China is not interested in promoting the first two interests, or in promoting its national ideology, though it does promote noninterference in the internal affairs of other countries. According to Peng Guangqian, deputy secretary general of China's new National Security Council, the New Silk Road policies are "beyond ideology." He says that, in contrast to the confrontational policies of the Cold War years, the New Silk Road is focused on economic cooperation, and is aimed at setting new norms in international relations, with the goal of creating a mutually beneficial "community of interests" and "community of destiny" that will help to put an end not only to the bullying of weak states by strong ones but to "all the other political and economic inequalities of the old order."[86]

China has strong global interests and influence on world affairs and seeks more. Its role in the polar regions is a good case study of this. China is the most outspoken advocate of the Arctic as an area of common global interest. In Antarctica, China is one of a number of states that has been raising concerns about how current environmental protection measures in Antarctica restrict existing rights. China's ability to project military power globally, as many analysts have noted, is limited but growing fast. In areas where China does have a global military reach – ballistic missiles, the space program, cyber warfare, and the BeiDou satellite navigation system – polar access is vital. China's growth as a truly global economic, political, and military power is inextricably linked to the Arctic and Antarctic.

China's foreign policy is essentially self-focused, based on economic and political needs. But China is increasingly becoming attractive as a partner to states that want China's trade and investment; that are seeking to balance other major powers, such as Russia and the United States in Europe or Australia and New Zealand in the South Pacific; or that are being overlooked by the West, as is the case for many developing countries in other parts of the world. China is

---

[86] Peng Guangqian, "Yidai yilu" zhanlüe gouxiang yu guoji zhixu zhong gou" [China's New Silk Road strategic concept and the reconstruction of the international order], Xinhua, January 9, 2015, http://world.people.com.cn/n/2015/0109/c157278-26358575.html.

not pushing its own model, but it does offer extensive training programs on this model to officials in developed-world partner countries such as Australia and New Zealand, and in the developing-world states such as Zimbabwe and Fiji. China wants to restore its international status to one where it is a "rich country, with a strong army" (*fu guo qiang bing*), a traditional Chinese saying for describing a great power. If Chinese ambitions are successful, the inevitable outcome is a new Sino-centric world that will make China the core node in a new globalized economic order.

IS CHINA A "RESPONSIBLE STAKEHOLDER"?

In 2005, US deputy secretary of state Robert Zoellick gave a speech to the National Committee on US-China Relations in New York and raised a trope that continues to haunt China's economic and political rise: the extent to which China is a "responsible stakeholder" (*fu zeren de liyi xiangguan zhe*) in the current global order. Zoellick told his audience that for fifty years, US policy toward the Soviet Union had been to "fence it in." In contrast, he said, US policy toward the PRC for the past thirty years had been to "bring it in." Zoellick emphasized that the United States had been extremely generous to China since the mid-1970s, offering technical assistance, intelligence, training, investment, and other cooperation, and that the PRC had benefited enormously from the international system in that period. He then asked China to partner more with the United States to defend and protect that order – instead of undermining it, as he claimed that China did. Zoellick raised other specific concerns about China's international behavior: mercantilism, rampant piracy of intellectual property, counterfeiting, currency manipulation, support for "troubled" states, rapid military modernization, lack of transparency about intentions, and ongoing efforts to "lock up" global strategic resources.[87] From a US perspective, the trends that Zoellick noted in this influential speech have only been accentuated since 2005.

   The Chinese official media did not directly respond to Zoellick's accusation, but within weeks it had come up with a term that better suited China's interests: "responsible great power" (*fu zeren de daguo*). This term is now used continually in official and scholarly publications to refer to China's positive contribution to, and participation in, the global order,[88] including discussions

[87] Robert B. Zoellick, "Whither China: From Membership to Responsibility?," US Department of State (archived), September 21, 2005, http://2001-2009.state.gov/s/d/former/zoellick/rem/53 682.htm.

[88] "Zhongguo heping jueqi jiang zaofu yu shijie" [China's peaceful rise will benefit the world], *Xuexi shibao*, October 10, 2005, http://www.china.com.cn/chinese/zhuanti/xxsb/993425.htm.

on polar affairs.[89] In January 2014 and subsequent months, the official Chinese media gave a high profile to the Chinese icebreaker *Xue Long*'s efforts to rescue the trapped Russian research vessel *Akademik Shokalskiy* as an example of China acting as a "responsible great power." It was promoted to both foreigners and Chinese audiences as an antidote to what Chinese scholars dismiss as "China threat" rhetoric on China's Arctic and Antarctic intentions. The *Xue Long*'s deferral of its own research schedule to rescue the stranded Russian ship showcased China as Xi Jinping would like it to be seen: as a proactive, responsible, constructive, and peaceful contributor to the global order. Three months after that rescue, the *Xue Long*'s assistance in the efforts to recover the downed Malaysia Airlines Flight 370 in the Southern Indian Ocean was a further propaganda coup for the Chinese polar program, as well as a subtle reminder of China's impressive means and will to demonstrate its international role and presence.

Yet China's actions to help the Russian vessel and other acts that China interprets as being those of a "responsible great power" are a far cry from the major changes in behavior that Zoellick and other US leaders are asking from the Chinese government. In August 2014, an exasperated President Obama accused China of being a "free rider" in the international system.[90] The Chinese official media response was swift. The *People's Daily* article on the topic, republished in the US edition of *China Daily* (thus speaking to both domestic and foreign audiences) warned that "US President Barack Obama's recent remarks which accused China of taking a free ride in Iraq ... reflect Washington's arrogance and US's self-declared exceptionalism. The US should not only respect but also get used to China's rising power."[91]

CHINA'S POLAR BEHAVIOR AS A BRIEF FOR FUTURE INTENTIONS

The United States, and the rest of the world, are indeed going to have to "get used to" China's rising power. But since China's foreign policy and foreign policy strategies are not transparent, how can the outside world evaluate the impact that China's rise will have on the global order? China's behavior in polar affairs provides us with many clues to better understand Beijing's attitude toward the international system. Principally, this behavior helps answer the debates over whether Beijing is a "responsible stakeholder," a "status quo

[89]   Ding, *Jidi guojia zhengce yanjiu baogao 2013–2014*, 63.

[90]   Thomas L. Friedman, "Obama on the World," *New York Times*, August 8, 2014, http://nyti.ms /1vnTGVb.

[91]   "US Speaks of Exceptionalism," *China Daily*, August 14, 2014, http://usa.chinadaily.com.cn /epaper/2014-08/14/content_18310752.htm.

power," a "revisionist power,"[92] or a "free rider," and whether it will continue to support current international norms and institutions with its increasing influence. The following common key phrases used in Chinese-language foreign policy discussions give useful indicators of China's intentions at the poles and elsewhere:

Maintain Strategic Ambiguity; Don't Be a Leader, Be Judiciously Assertive (*taoguang yanghui, jue bu dang tou, you suo zuowei*)

China's polar agenda illustrates that Deng Xiaoping's dictum for Chinese foreign policy will still hold true in the medium term. Xi Jinping's new *tifa*, "be proactive," is important, signifying Xi's preeminence in Chinese politics. But intrinsically, it is an extension of Deng's dictum, which remains relevant. China is playing a long game in the polar regions and in other *res nullius* arenas. To achieve its goals, it needs to offer only partial information about its plans until the government is ready to make a move. Although Chinese officials may be unhappy with the status quo in Antarctica or other aspects of international governance elsewhere in the world, Beijing must work within the existing structures and policies for now, a point that Xi made in a speech he gave in Seattle in 2015.[93] The only alternative to this behavior would be breaking international law, a step that China seems careful to avoid at present. But China will act to defend its interests when it feels they are being threatened or whenever there is an opportunity to do so. China's massive increase in comprehensive national power in the past few years means that the government now has the capacity to deal more forcefully with what it defines as core strategic issues, such as territorial disputes with Japan or in the South China Sea.

In a situation where there is no possibility of changing the international governance arrangements, China will publicly accept the situation while still continuing to pursue its own interests. Beijing's current behavior in the Antarctic Treaty system forums is similar to its behavior in many other multilateral organizations. China may not like certain aspects of the current order, but it takes such benefits as it can.

Do, but Don't Say (*zuo er bu shuo*)

CCP domestic and foreign policy has a long tradition of "do, but don't say." China clearly does have an Arctic and Antarctic strategy; it is discussed by senior leaders in information aimed at Chinese citizens and can be observed in China's significant investment in polar capacity and presence since the 11th Five-Year Plan (2006–2010). However, this strategy has not yet been

---

[92]   On status quo states versus revisionist states, see A. F. K. Organski and Jacek Kugler, *The War Ledger* (Chicago: University of Chicago Press, 1980), 19–20 and 23.

[93]   "Full Text of Xi Jinping's Speech on US-China Relations in Seattle," Xinhua, September 24, 2015, http://news.xinhuanet.com/english/2015-09/24/c_134653326.htm.

formalized into an official document, and Chinese polar officials do not talk about it to foreign audiences. Thus, when seeking to understand Chinese domestic and foreign policy intentions, observers should always pay more attention to official actions than to official rhetoric.

Insiders and Outsiders Are Different (neiwai you bie)

Frequently, official statements and internal policy debates in Chinese on polar and other foreign policy issues seem to be disjointed. The CCP has a long-standing policy of giving different messages to different groups, and transparency on policy issues is rare. This behavior is summed up by a phrase often used in CCP foreign affairs: insiders and outsiders are different. Foreign governments and other interested parties trying to understand China's intentions must access Chinese-language sources in addition to official statements designed for foreign ears. Further, they should play close attention when prominent Chinese academics and official public intellectuals such as Yin Zhuo and other military commentators engage in sharp debate on aspects of Chinese foreign policy. Such policy debates reflect the fact that China wants change in some aspect of the international order and it is exploring its options. Situations with this kind of disjunction should be regarded as "watch this space."

Mold Global Public Opinion (suzao guoji yulun)

Information management and persuasion have a crucial role in Chinese foreign policy, and since 2009 China has been spending vast sums on public messaging.[94] As mentioned above, China's foreign policy information management has one message for foreign audiences and frequently a significantly different message aimed at domestic audiences. Those who want to understand Chinese foreign policy and interpret its hidden agenda must be able to distinguish between the level of authority of different media outlets and prominent spokespeople.

"People-to-People" Diplomacy (minjian waijiao)

China has long employed people's diplomacy – the use of nominally independent actors to represent national interests at international events – in foreign policy. To this end, it has been incorporating scientists and social scientists into its polar diplomacy. Social science is formally part of the CCP propaganda system,[95] and science also must respect censorship boundaries. China's polar scientists and social scientists are publishing on China's polar issues within a well-defined script that highlights the polar regions as resource

---

94 Anne-Marie Brady, "Authoritarianism Goes Global (II): China's Foreign Propaganda Machine," *Journal of Democracy* 26, no. 4 (2015): 51–59.

95 Xuexi chubanshe, ed., *Quan guo xuanchuan sixiang gongzuo huiyi wenjian huibian* [Collected articles from the National Conference on Propaganda and Thought Work] (Beijing: Xuexi chubanshe, 1994), 143.

treasure houses and neglects environmental concerns. Their research is essential in helping the CCP government in planning its polar strategy. Scholars are also increasingly being used in track-one-and-a-half diplomacy, as they are a useful means to promote China's position to international audiences.

Total Diplomacy (quanmian waijiao)

The party-state-military-market nexus in China enhances the CCP government's ability to expand Chinese interests in a given region on every level, an approach that Chinese foreign policy theorists call "total diplomacy." Beijing is encouraging multilevel, multiagency engagement in the polar regions, popularizing knowledge about opportunities in the Arctic and Antarctic for Chinese citizens and companies in order to increase China's overall presence and influence and strengthen its "right to speak" on polar affairs. China has been employing similar behavior in Africa, the Southwest Pacific, and South and Central America.

"Face-Seeking" (yao mianzi)

China is a deeply insecure party-state and is seeking to restore and demonstrate its international status. China's national narrative is one of 150 years of victimhood. The CCP government is determined to restore China's international status and prestige, to become a rich nation with a strong military. The polar regions, the high seas, and outer space are convenient locations to demonstrate this new status and "gain face" for China.

Be Proactive (fen fa youwei)

Where the possibility of creating new norms exists, Beijing will be proactive, and it wants a seat at the decision-making table. In recent years, China has shown a preference for action, rather than talk, in its international behavior. Yet in the Arctic, where China is a relatively weak player, Beijing is limited even in terms of the scientific projects it could engage in there. The Arctic's climatic and political environment is changing faster than China can step up its polar capabilities. Consequently, Beijing is signaling its interests now, adopting a firm tone, and asserting its right to have a say in future governance arrangements. This is a new trend that should be closely watched in the polar regions and elsewhere. When it comes to its core interests – in particular, anything that could negatively affect China's rights – China does not shy away from confrontation.

United Front (tongzhan)

The United Front is an old Leninist tactic that the CCP has made good use of throughout its history. Traditionally, a United Front was when a communist party would forge a temporary alliance against a common enemy. In its present use, China is not joining with other states against a common enemy, but rather is uniting for a common short-term goal. In polar affairs,

China has forged strategic partnerships to achieve specific goals, such as when it wanted to become a permanent observer on the Arctic Council. China wants to be a part of norm-setting in new areas of international governance to help protect its own national interests. It is not yet powerful enough to go it alone in norm-setting and must partner with other states. To this end, China has been forming miniature hub-and-spoke blocs of power in the Arctic and the Antarctic.

Look for Points in Common, Put Aside Differences (qiu tong cunyi)

This dictum is associated with the Mao-era foreign minister Zhou Enlai, and continues to be cited by Chinese diplomats as a strategy for managing relations with the West. In the current era, the point in common that China has with other countries is trade and access to the powerful Chinese market. China is using its economic might to assiduously buy friends or quiet rivals, launching new initiatives such as the New Silk Road and the Asian Infrastructure and Investment Bank. In the Arctic and Antarctic, as elsewhere, Beijing seems to have been successful in appeasing some of the concerns about its increased presence by offering generous economic opportunities to other states. Commercial interests have a significant influence on foreign policy in many states, and they are helping to smooth the way for China to achieve its strategic goals. But at what point will states whose political and strategic interests are threatened by China's expansion have to confront the tension between trade with China and national security?

Kill the Chicken to Scare the Monkeys (sha ji jing hou)

China's bullying and isolation of Norway from 2010 to 2017, after the Nobel Peace Prize was awarded to Chinese dissident Liu Xiaobo, was done not only to punish Norway but to set an example for other states of the consequences of publicly displeasing Beijing. In so doing, China shows itself as behaving like a classic great power, throwing its weight around and trying to intimidate smaller states into submission.

Unite with the Majority; Attack Only a Few (tuanjie da duoshu, daji yi xiaocuo)

Under Deng Xiaoping, Jiang Zemin, and Hu Jintao, China tried to make friends with neighboring states and promoted a peaceful global foreign policy. But under Xi Jinping, China is following a policy designed to defend its sovereignty. It is no longer afraid of conflict and is willing to face up to any threats to its sovereignty and national security. This policy approach has already started to play out in the South China Sea with China's dramatic expansion of bases on coral reefs and regular confrontations with Vietnam and the Philippines. In the polar regions, China is uniting with all the Arctic and Antarctic states it can while isolating and disadvantaging any states that disagree with it, such as France or Norway.

Rich Country, Strong Army (fu guo qiang bing)

There is a strong association between economic development and political stability in China's foreign affairs and defense policy. As many have observed, China appears to be fixated on potential resource acquisition in the polar regions and elsewhere. China's drive to acquire privileged access to resources is connected to the CCP government's basic equation for maintaining their privileged position over Chinese society: access to resources will sustain economic development, which in turn will underwrite political stability. China's polar strategy also requires political stability. The achievement of those political, military, and economic goals will enable CCP leaders to succeed in the long-standing goal to make China a rich country with a strong military – in other words a great power.

IMPLICATIONS FOR GLOBAL GOVERNANCE

On the question of whether China is a "responsible stakeholder," a "status quo power," a "revisionist power," or a "free rider," the answer is not as simple as responding to the parameters and value judgments behind those phrases. In global commons such as the polar regions, the high seas, the deep seabeds, and outer space, China is taking advantage of every available right, working within existing governance structures, and finding ways to be part of the solution for resolving disputes. Arctic and Antarctic governance structures necessitate compromise and coordination with other states in order to maximize national interests; because China is unable to act alone to achieve its goals, it seeks cooperation. In areas that China considers to be its own territory, it will defend its sovereign rights. China is adverse to rapid changes in the international system, and it tends to avoid taking the lead in opposing new proposals in order to avoid being blamed if they fail. In polar affairs, as in many other global governance situations, China achieves many gains from the current international order, so to classify it as a "reluctant stakeholder" in such situations is an exaggeration. China certainly would like to shape international governance in certain areas to better suit its own national interests. Its growing economic power, at a time when Western governments are under massive financial pressure, has helped it strengthen its global influence in the polar regions and elsewhere. Where new norms are being forged, observers can expect Beijing to be assertive in demanding a right to have a say.

China is unlikely to directly oppose existing international laws and norms or try to change them. But when it comes to international laws and norms that do not suit China's interests, China will go around them or ignore them. When new international instruments are being forged, China will expect to be part of the consultation process and will go over the new governance measures with a fine-toothed comb. But it will oppose new initiatives only if they directly harm China's interests. China will try diplomacy, coalition building, and (if necessary) intimidation first; true standoffs will be rare.

China is a relatively insecure new great power, both in its internal politics and in terms of the external environment, so it has to be increasingly proactive about defending its interests and ambiguous about what its actual interests are in order to delay open conflict with its potential competitors for as long as possible. China is by no means a reluctant stakeholder in the global order. It is forging its own path of international relations, and its rise as a polar great power is inextricably linked to its transformation into a true global leader.

China does not want to follow in the same global power mold as the United States or other previously dominant states. Chinese contemporary foreign policy phrases aimed at foreigners – "new model of great power relations," "peaceful rise," "noninterference in the internal affairs of other states," "Chinese Dream" – emphasize peace and conflict avoidance if at all possible. As the great Chinese strategist Sunzi pointed out in *The Art of War*, in warfare "the ultimate technique is to get the enemy to submit without actually going to war" (*bu zhan er qu ren zhi bing, shanzhi shan zhe ye*). Thus, in the near future China is likely to show more displays of its growing sea power, such as have been seen recently in the South China Sea and the Arctic, aimed at intimidating rivals and asserting China's rights. Nonetheless, despite its wish for a peaceful rise, China's foreign policy stratagems do not rule out the possibility of conflict. As China's economic, political, and military power grows, it will threaten the interests of other states – and it is preparing for this potential scenario.

8

The Rise of a New Great Power

In 2006, Chinese Central Television launched an epic twelve-part documentary series, *The Rise of Great Powers (Daguo jueqi)*. The documentary was first shown on CCTV-2, a television channel used primarily for national economics education and news. Then, in 2007, it was rebroadcast in prime time on China's preeminent channel CCTV-1, used for the political education of the Chinese nation. The series was devoted to educating the Chinese people about the historical rise and fall of great powers, from the Roman Empire to the United States, and evaluating the lessons that China could learn from their experiences. The program on England's rise concluded with the following admiring statement:

> When a New World has just been discovered, whoever can seize the opportunity, whoever is open to new ideas, and whoever can break away from old ways of thinking; they will become rich and powerful faster. The rules of the game in the New World are that prevailing in sea territories is far more important than prevailing over land territories.[1]

China is now on the path of becoming a global great power, and it is evaluating the past experiences of other great powers. In the 1990s, Chinese policymakers conducted in-depth studies on the lessons to be learned from the fall of the Soviet Union. In the 2000s, they studied the rise and fall of other great powers – such as Portugal, Spain, France, Germany, Great Britain, Japan, and the United States – and the resulting lessons of their experiences. *The Rise of Great Powers* has now been shown repeatedly on Chinese television and widely distributed on subsidized DVDs. The documentary is widely understood as a modern-day political study class for the Chinese population, both

[1] "Di san ji: Zouxiang xiandai (Yingguo shang)" [Episode 3: Into the modern age (The United Kingdom)], *Daguo jueqi* [The rise of great powers], CCTV, November 16, 2006, http://finance.cctv.com/special/C16860/20061116/104051.shtml.

outlining a manifesto for China's future direction and enlisting the Chinese people's support for this endeavor. The documentary themes were first presented to the Chinese Communist Party's Politburo in 2003 as part of its regular schedule of closed-door policy briefings, and then were approved for distribution to the Chinese masses.[2]

For China, Antarctica and the Arctic, the deep seabed, and outer space are the "new" New World; they are rich in resources and opportunities, and ripe for exploitation.[3] The opportunities opening up in these new strategic frontiers favor the great powers, and China is poised to take advantage of every possibility. To better understand this new New World, the Chinese government is incorporating new ideas and breaking with old ways of thinking, as demonstrated by the People's Liberation Army's adoption of Hao Xiaoguang's extraordinary vertical world map.[4] To achieve the CCP's long-term strategic goals, the government is prepared to break with old values and norms where necessary, including setting up military bases on coral reefs in the South China Sea, declaring its own air defense identification zones over contested territory, and nurturing a network of friendly partner countries that are not likely to challenge China's military interests or question the legitimacy of its political system. And the Chinese government, following the example of England in the sixteenth century, has clearly understood that the rules of the game in this new New World are that maritime (and air) control on a global scale are extremely important for any aspiring great power.

From a geopolitical point of view, the polar regions have once again become a site for great power tension and competition. In 2014, Xi Jinping announced that China aspires to be a polar great power. Xi's announcement revealed both a deep need for international recognition of China's position and the Chinese government's high level of responsiveness in spotting a gap in global geopolitics that China has the unique ability to fill. China's thinking on the polar regions demonstrates a level of ambition and forward planning that few, if any, modern industrial states can achieve. The concept of a polar great power is relatively unknown in international relations studies; the United States and Russia, the two current polar great powers, seldom use this term

2   "TV Docu Stimulates More Open Attitude to History, China, the World," *People's Daily*, November 26, 2006, http://en.people.cn/200611/26/eng20061126_325264.html.

3   "Guojia anquan fa cao'an ni zengjia taikong deng xinxing lingyu de anquan weihu renwu" [The draft national security law will increase security in space and other new areas], Xinhua, June 24, 2015, http://www.chinanews.com/gn/2015/06-24/7363693.shtml.

4   The map is located at "Xin shijie ditu" [New world map], http://www.hxgmap.com/images/1106north.jpg. Image used in this book with personal permission of Hao Xiaoguang, May 6, 2015.

to refer to themselves. China's early adoption of this new terminology is yet another indication that China is seizing opportunities, being open to new ideas, demonstrating its willingness to break away from old ways of thinking, and recognizing the opportunities to be found at the poles.

China is not the only country to be turning its attention to the polar regions. Climate change, the shifting global balance of power, and dwindling oil reserves at a time of increasing consumption has led to renewed global interest in the Arctic and Antarctic. The polar regions are of crucial importance to global security. They offer unparalleled sources of food, water, energy, vital transportation links, and strategic military sites. Furthermore, their governance and patterns of human interactions are becoming increasingly contentious: sovereignty, mining, shipping, tourism, bioprospecting, and fishing are but a few of the many points of disagreement, while environmental concerns such as the melting ice sheets have a global impact.

Global economic power has clearly shifted to Asia, with China leading the way. Emerging economies such as Brazil, China, India, South Korea, Malaysia, and Turkey, along with an embattled but defiant Russia, are all interested in taking leading roles in shaping new international instruments that will better reflect their national interests and demonstrate their increased political power. The emerging economies are almost all oil-deficient, so they are looking for new sources of oil and natural gas in the medium term, when their currently available supplies will be exhausted. They also are looking to external resources to resolve food security concerns and to boost economic growth. Changing ice-shelf dynamics brought about by climate change, ever-growing energy demands, and the development of new technologies for extracting oil in the harsh polar environment are all helping to speed up the opening of the polar regions.

The Arctic was strategically significant during World War II and in the Cold War era, but for nearly two decades after the end of the Cold War it became something of a backwater. Climate change brings many challenges to the Arctic, but from the point of view of outside players such as China it brings mostly opportunities: shipping and air routes, sources of energy and minerals, new tourism destinations and other economic activities, bioprospecting rights, strategic science bases, and possible means of strengthening China's defense. The opportunities and the risks that climate change has wrought in the Arctic will require a multinational response; so far, the eight Arctic states have not demonstrated the capacity to respond to this situation on their own. China's level of forward planning, emphasis on "partnership" rather than "leadership," deep pockets, and unquenchable need for natural resources put it at the front of the queue of those non-Arctic states wanting a share in this new arena of power and influence. Despite the desire of the Arctic Five to prevent any further international regimes being introduced in the Arctic, most of the challenges to the region, such as climate change and toxic damage, originate outside of it and thus possible solutions will also come from outside. China is one of many states pressing for the world to acknowledge that Arctic issues are global issues.

Meanwhile, the strategic significance of Antarctica is only going to increase. When the 1959 Antarctic Treaty was signed, the major powers had very limited ability to exploit the potential of Antarctica; it was a major challenge to even get to the continent. Now that the technological barriers to Antarctic exploration are easing, the continent's value has increased exponentially for both the larger and smaller powers. To many states, Antarctica is the "last oil reserve"; to some, Antarctica waters are the "last unspoiled ocean," while others see it as a prime site for prospecting for biological organisms with a commercial application. Antarctica is prized as a neutral territory where any sufficiently equipped nation can locate a civil-military polar satellite receiving station. Antarctica and the Southern Ocean are also air and sea transit routes of last resort should more common air and sea paths be blocked.

Antarctic governance privileges the developed world and allots the spoils to those who came first and those who are the most powerful. In 1959, the main preoccupation of the dominant Antarctic partners was preventing the threat of armed conflict between the two superpowers spreading to Antarctica. But since the end of the Cold War, political ideology no longer divides the world. Arguably, the greatest common global challenges are how to deal with the escalating impact of climate change and the quest for new resources to feed and fuel the world's growing population. The Antarctic Treaty system in its present form is not well suited to deal with these new priorities, and it is questionable for how much longer the period of relative peace and environmental protection secured by the treaty will last. The Antarctic Treaty consultative partners need to face up to the new challenges of Antarctic governance: the pressure on global resources and the rise of new powers that are seeking to reshape the global order to better suit their interests. Emerging Antarctic nations such as China are reaping the benefits of the old order without embracing its vision. The challenge for those states that want to maintain the current order is to increase buy-in to the Antarctic Treaty system and its values, and address perceived inequities and inconsistencies that frequently bring the system into disrepute. Possible avenues forward include introducing more transparency into Antarctic governance meetings and not being afraid to openly address "unmentionables" such as potential challenges to the political status quo in Antarctica or instances when states have broken the existing rules.

EVALUATING THE IMPLICATIONS OF CHINA'S RISE AS A POLAR GREAT POWER

This book has analyzed China's polar behavior as a framework for understanding its global ambitions, its ability to achieve them, and its attitude toward existing norms and governance structures. It also has examined the extent to which existing polar regimes will be able to cope with the changing balance of power and other new pressures. Its aim has been to help policymakers, specialists, and other interested parties better understand the implications of the seismic shift that China's rise will create in the global geopolitical environment. Climate change, globalization, oil interests, and the failure of the United States and a number of other Western countries to continue to invest in the polar regions are all starting to put pressure on existing Arctic and Antarctic regimes. This book has contributed to studies examining this shifting geopolitical environment by evaluating the behavior of a key rising player and exploring structural features within polar governance that may be challenged by the new world order. It has addressed a key challenge facing the major powers and other nations: how to accommodate China's rise, particularly in the politically sensitive and environmentally vulnerable polar regions. In evaluating China as a polar great power, this book has explored a series of questions, which are summarized in the following paragraphs.

Who are the actors in China's polar decision-making? How are the interests of the various Chinese actors with polar interests connected, and to what extent are they coordinated?
Multiple Chinese foreign policy actors have a role in setting China's polar foreign policy agenda. At least seventeen agencies participate in polar activities and planning, and to varying degrees all of them are helping shape China's evolving polar policies. To a certain extent, commercial forces also are shaping these policies. The CCP government's polar policies expose how the tight party-state-military-market nexus operates in China. The CCP's ideological message and legitimacy to rule is bolstered by the promotion of China's existing polar activities and plans for the future. The PLA is a core driver of China's polar policies; polar security, resources, and strategic science interests all reflect PLA priorities. Commercial interests such as Laurel Industries are also thoroughly entwined with China's polar policymaking. The government is adopting a China Inc. approach to the polar regions by

encouraging and assisting Chinese commercial interests to expand into the Arctic and Antarctic. Companies follow their own strategic agendas as they advance government policies. At present, economic interests are not at the forefront of China's polar priorities, and are being used more as a political tool to achieve other goals, but they are sure to grow in importance and have an increasing impact on policymaking as new opportunities arise.

What are China's polar strengths and weaknesses?
In the space of ten years, from 2005 to 2015, China went from being a relatively weak player in polar affairs to achieving parity with most developed countries operating in the polar regions. China is now on the cusp of entering the top tier of polar nations, the polar great powers. China's strengths in this endeavor are its capacity to invest in new infrastructure, its state-of-the-art facilities, and its ability to plan ahead and to adjust to the regions' changing geoeconomic and geopolitical environment. China's current weaknesses are the relatively low quality of its polar research compared with that of other polar states, its low level of contribution to polar governance working papers and working bodies, and its relative weakness in polar-relevant military capacity.

What are China's strategic interests in the polar regions? Will China's rise in Antarctica impinge on the interests of other Antarctic Treaty nations or those that have not yet joined the treaty but have expressed an interest in Antarctica? Will China's growing interest in the Arctic impinge on the interests of the Arctic littoral states? Will China's perspective on the polar issues appeal more widely to other states, helping to shape new global norms?
China's core strategic interests in the polar regions – security, resources, and science – are identical to those of the other two major polar powers. There are no fundamental areas of disagreement between China and the United States on many Arctic or Antarctic issues, but the United States does have some concerns, such as China's prospective polar military interests and the potential impact on US military and political interests of China's growing economic and political polar power. Similarly, Russia can gain great economic and political benefits from China's Arctic interests, and it is not particularly challenged by China's Antarctic activities, but does harbor some concerns on the impact that China's rise in polar affairs may have on Russian national interests.

In the Arctic, China will pay market rates for natural resources and is a potential source of low-cost skilled labor, both of which make it attractive to business interests in Russia, Canada, and Greenland. For nations that will be affected by Arctic shipping, China is likely to be the main international user of the Arctic international routes. China can help fund and construct infrastructure, opening up a previously dormant region. The Chinese government is engaging in proactive diplomacy toward susceptible Arctic states – Iceland, Finland, Greenland, Denmark, Norway, and Sweden – and in doing so it has swiftly gained acceptance for China's role as a legitimate actor in Arctic affairs. At the same time, China has avoided challenging Russia, Canada, and the United States in the Arctic. The Chinese government is trying to find a way to work cooperatively with the Arctic states whose territories contain oil, natural gas, and strategic minerals: Canada, Greenland, Russia, and the United States.

China's view on the expansion of environmental protection controls in Antarctica is shared by Germany, Norway, Russia, South Korea, and Ukraine, whereas Australia, France, New Zealand, the United Kingdom, and the United States support extending controls. China's perspective that the changing Arctic situation is of global concern is accepted by many states, including some on the Arctic Council. China is building a global coalition of likeminded states that will vote with it on crucial issues (and not just polar ones), such as the Group of 77 and the Asian Forum for Polar Science; likewise, it has been enhancing bilateral relations with other non-Arctic states and groups of states (such as the European Union) that share its view on global rights to Arctic resources, high seas, and seabed resources.

Will China demand an upheaval of the Arctic Council to allow itself more of a voice in Arctic governance? Will China demand the establishment of a new Arctic body? Does China support the continuance of the Antarctic Treaty and the Protocol on Environmental Protection? What are China's views on polar governance issues more broadly? What position does China take on key polar policy issues such as sovereignty and the exploitation of resources?
China supports the Arctic Council and other existing governing bodies on Arctic affairs, but insists on having a say in the new governance measures in the Arctic that are evolving to meet the changing environmental, military, geopolitical, and geoeconomical situation. Meanwhile, China, like the United States and Russia – two other major powers without a formal claim in Antarctica – benefits enormously from Antarctica's unresolved sovereignty. China is uniquely able to expand rapidly in Antarctica at a time when other leading states are cutting back or barely maintaining their Antarctic programs. China's activities and interests are protected under the Antarctic Treaty and customary law; where their activities breach Antarctic Treaty rules, such as not reporting military activities or beginning base construction before the full environment assessment process is completed, there are no consequences.

China believes that the Madrid Protocol is useful in the interim, as it will enable China to catch up on its capabilities to take advantage of the potential minerals bounty in Antarctica when a new minerals treaty is negotiated.

As China becomes more powerful, will it attempt to change the existing global order?
China has benefited enormously from the post–World War II international order, including inheriting a permanent seat on the UN Security Council in 1971. It has participated in the formation of core international legal instruments such as the UN Convention on the Law of the Sea. China has made it clear that it wants to be part of any new global decision-making bodies and seeks reform in the international system. For now, in the polar regions as in other global scenarios, China will make the best out of the current order and quietly pursue its own interests, but it will act assertively in any possibility of creating new norms.

Currently, the United States is still the dominant global power, and it is likely to be so for a number of decades. Although it is the greatest challenge to China's rise as a great power, it also has been China's greatest supporter and facilitator of its rise in the past forty years, despite much international criticism across the political spectrum. The United States and China have much in common, and as China becomes more powerful in the international environment both nations are drawn to and repelled by each other. It would take a major policy shift for the United States to dismantle the US-led Asia-Pacific security architecture that China views as an existential threat. Within five years of the end of World War II, the United States was able to regard Japan as an ally in the face of the threat of a greater foe: the spread of communism. But what mutual threat could bring the United States and China together and persuade both sides to perceive each other differently? China's goal is to become rich and strong on the global stage, a new global superpower. China's leaders would like China's rise to be peaceful, but like other great powers before them, they are not likely to shy from using shows of force or actual force when necessary.

RANKING CHINA AS A POLAR GREAT POWER

China now has more money to spend on new polar infrastructure, such as bases, planes, satellite installations, and icebreakers, than any other state. Its rapid polar expansion reflects Beijing's desire to become a polar great power with a voice in the formation of any future governance norms and access to the polar regions' strategic resources, which include not only physical resources but also polar sea and air routes. This access is crucial to China's future economic, political, and military expansion as a global great power, as well as for strengthening and maintaining the CCP government's hold on power. If China succeeds in its goal to become a polar great power on a par with the United States and Russia, then it is also likely to succeed in its goal to become a global superpower, capable of influencing international norms in its favor.

In 2011, State Oceanic Administration vice minister Chen Lianzeng stated that the overall goal of China's polar five-year plan(s) was to increase China's "status and influence" in polar affairs in order to better protect China's "polar rights and interests."[5] So how can China (and other states) acquire "status and influence" in polar governance?

- The quantity, location, and type (e.g., all year, summer-only) of their Arctic and Antarctic scientific bases.
- The quality of their science.
- The size of their polar scientific budget (including operation costs, research funds, and investment in capacity such as bases, planes, icebreakers).
- The number of citizens they have in the Arctic and Antarctic.
- The level and spread of their engagement.
- The number of working papers and new governance initiatives they propose.
- Their level of polar military capacity.

Using Chen Lianzeng's measure of success, if we were to rank China's progress in gaining more "status and influence" in polar affairs, in order of the priorities of China's core polar interests, China ranks as follows:

- **Polar-related military capabilities:** Polar-capable submarines and surface vessels: 1. United States, 2. Russia, 3. China; satellites: 1. United States (549), 2. China (142), 3. Russia (131);[6] nuclear missiles: 1. Russia (1648), 2. United States (1538), 3. China (250).[7]

5 "Wo guo xinjin jidi kexue kaocha pobingchuan lizheng 2013 nian touru shiyong" [Our new polar expedition icebreaker should be ready by 2013], Xinhua, June 22, 2011, http://news .xinhuanet.com/tech/2011–06/22/c_121566754.htm.
6 "UCS Satellite Database," Union of Concerned Scientists, accessed September 1, 2015, http:// www.ucsusa.org/nuclear-weapons/space-weapons/satellite-database#.VqapSvlq97cs. Given here are the total number of satellites for these three states, both officially commercial as well as those designated as "military," because all satellites have dual-use capacities. One example of this dual-use capacity occurred when a Chinese military satellite was used for search-and-rescue duties in the Southern Ocean in 2014 when the *Xue Long* was trapped in sea ice.
7 "World Nuclear Weapon Stockpile: 2015," Ploughshares Fund, accessed March 2, 2016, http:// www.ploughshares.org/world-nuclear-stockpile-report; and "New START Treaty Aggregate

- **Number of Antarctic research stations:** 1. Argentina, 2. Chile, 3. Russia, 4. China–South Korea (per their joint-operations agreement).[8] Measured by China-controlled bases only, China ranks fifth, equal with Germany.

- **Number, location, and type of Arctic bases:** (Arctic states) 1. United States, 2. Russia; (non-Arctic states) 1. China and Japan, 2. South Korea.

- **Quality of polar science (based on citation rates, ranking of journal):** US polar science is preeminent in Arctic and Antarctic studies; China still ranks relatively low on overall quality.[9]

- **Quantity of Arctic science:** 1. United States, 2. Canada, . . . 15. China.[10]

- **Quantity of Antarctic science projects:** 1. Australia, 2. United States, . . . 11. China.[11]

- **Arctic science budget: (operation costs / research funds / capital investment):** 1. United States, 2. Russia; (non-Arctic states) 1. China.

- **Antarctic science budget (operation costs / research funds / capital investment):** 1. China, 2. United States, 3. Russia.

- **Citizens in the Arctic:** (Arctic states) 1. Russia, 2. United States; (non-Arctic states: scientists, tourists, fishers, workers) 1. China.

- **Citizens in Antarctica (scientists, tourists, fishers, and workers):** 1. United States, 2. China, 3. Australia.

- **Level and spread of engagement in Antarctic affairs:** 1. United States, 2. Russia, 3. China.

- **Antarctic working papers:** 1. United Kingdom, 2. New Zealand, . . . 20. China.[12]

- **Polar governance organizations membership and leadership:** China is a member of every polar governance organization it is entitled to join, and it has been taking on leadership roles in these organizations.

Numbers of Offensive Weapons," Bureau of Arms Control, Verification, and Compliance, US State Department, October 1, 2015, http://www.state.gov/t/avc/rls/247674.htm.

8 "Hamjung namgeugseo sonjab-assda, giji gongdonghwal-yong" [China and Korea join hands, joint use of Antarctic bases], *Chosun Ilbo*, November 29, 2013, https://www.kookje.co.kr/new s2011/asp/newsbody.asp?code=0200&key=20131130.22010205349.

9 Ding Huang, ed., *Jidi guojia zhengce yanjiu baogao 2013–2014* [Annual report on national polar policy research 2013–14] (Beijing: Kexue chubanshe, 2014), 159–61.

10 Wang Xuemei, "A Bibliometrical Analysis of International Polar Research," *Science Focus* 7, no. 2 (2012): 35.

11 Hua Weina and Zhang Xia, eds., *Nanji tiaoyue xieshang guo Nanji huodong nengli diaoyan tongji baogao* [Statistical report on the Antarctic capabilities of the Antarctic Treaty Consultative Parties] (Beijing: Haiyang chubanshe, 2012), 55–86.

12 John R. Dudeney and David W. H. Walton, "Leadership in Politics and Science within the Antarctic Treaty," *Polar Research* 31 (2012): 1.

China would like more influence in polar affairs, so what is its position on current and future governance challenges in the polar regions?

In the Arctic:

- **Sovereignty:** Outside the twelve-mile zone, China points out that the Arctic Ocean currently still consists of international waters, and even when the extended continental shelf claims of various Arctic states are resolved, some rights still will be available to nonlittoral states. Resolving Arctic extended continental shelf claims will require a combination of science, diplomacy, and legal action, and China intends to be involved in this process.
- **Sea routes:** China regards Arctic routes as international straits.
- **Strategic minerals and hydrocarbons:** China believes that the Arctic's global mineral and hydrocarbon resources should be opened up to the global market.
- **Fishing:** China wants a regional fishery management organization to manage fishing in the Arctic Central Ocean.
- **Environmental issues:** China sees more opportunity than risk in Arctic climate change.

In Antarctica:

- **Rights:** China wants access to and quotas for fishing, tourism, and bioprospecting. It aims to take up its rights before other states or international bodies attempt to take them away.
- **Environmental issues:** China tends to regard environmental protection as a form of "soft presence" in Antarctica — in other words, a means to control territory.
- **Strategic mineral resources:** China believes that it will only be a matter of time before Antarctic mineral resources are available for interested nations to exploit.
- **Sovereignty:** China regards Antarctica as *res nullius* and open to all the nations of the world.

CHINA AND THE NEW GLOBAL ORDER

Great powers are those that exhibit structural power: the ability to shape and enforce global rules. By default, as a permanent member of the UN Security Council with the right of veto, the People's Republic of China has been a member of this exclusive club since 1971, regardless of the extent of its other capacities. In the polar regions of the world, more perhaps than anywhere else, "structural power" will come from cooperation and participation in existing governance structures, as well as the vision to set up new forms of cooperation such as China's New Silk Road policies. Polar governance involves borders and states, but also requires a level of cooperation between states that is not seen anywhere else in the world.

China's obsession with gaining its share of the spoils of Arctic and Antarctic wealth will pit it against many within the international community, not only those that also crave access to these resources but also those that demand that the world's last great wilderness be protected from exploitation. Yet from a Chinese perspective, China's ambitions are defensive, not aggressive, and it is simply acting to protect its own legitimate interests to feed and fuel its population. In the years to come, China may develop an interest in limiting pollution, resource exploitation, and climate change in the polar regions. In the meantime, it may suffer diminished international prestige and status if it is seen to obstruct policies that a majority of other states deem necessary.

One of the primary aims of China's polar programs is to gain international status and to rise up the ranks of the international system. China seeks international "face" and is making a major investment in global media, entertainment, and other forms of persuasion to obtain it.[13] China has very strong sensitivities to both rank and the concept of "face," which in English is best understood as "to give respect." Imperial China maintained a very hierarchical view of the global order. In the early 1970s, CCP leader Mao Zedong announced the Theory of Three Worlds: the idea that the world was divided into the superpowers, the lesser powers, and the exploited Third World. By the end of the Cold War era and throughout the 1990s, China grappled with how to operate in the US-dominated new world order. But after close to twenty years of double-digit growth in China; the rise of other emerging economies such as Brazil, Russia, and India; and (in the Chinese view) the ebb of US economic and political power, Chinese perceptions of the global order and China's own place in it have adjusted. China wants appropriate international status and recognition for its increased capabilities and intends to acquire a commensurate level of international influence. China's transition from being a regional great power to becoming a great power with global influence requires the CCP government to follow a well-worn path of developing maritime strength; expanding its economic, political, and military presence internationally; building up soft power; and setting up privileged

---

[13] Anne-Marie Brady, "Authoritarianism Goes Global (II): China's Foreign Propaganda Machine," *Journal of Democracy* 26, no. 4 (October 2015): 51–59.

FIGURE 8.1 Still Image from *Antarctica: We're Here!* Documentary
Source: *"Nanji: women laile!"* [*Antarctica: We're here!*], CNTV, *March 1, 2010*, http://jishi.cntv.cn/explore/nanjiwomenlaile/classpage/video/20100301/100860.shtml.

relationships with resource-rich states to provide extra resources to feed the country's growing economy and provide markets for its surplus goods.

WATCH OUT, WORLD: HERE WE COME!

On December 24, 1984, more than two hundred years after human exploration first began in Antarctica, China's first Antarctic expedition landed on the continent. The iconic documentary produced to celebrate this momentous occasion proudly proclaimed "Antarctica: We're Here!" (*Nanji: women lai le!*).

The documentary's promotional image shows a map of Antarctica with a simplified Chinese flag superimposed over it. After decades of planning, China's Five-Star Red Flag has now been unfurled proudly throughout the polar regions.

A new era is dawning in Chinese foreign policy as China's economic growth emboldens its leaders to move from a position of reluctance to declare their country a global leader and a relative inability to defend their national interests, to one where Beijing can seek adjustments in the geopolitical environment that the PRC has faced since 1949. As China's comprehensive national power has grown, so too has its level of engagement in the polar regions. China has gone from being an outsider in polar affairs to its current position as one of the leading players. China's dramatic rise in the polar regions has expanded in parallel with the development of the Chinese economy and China's increasing political and military power. If China succeeds in its core goals at the poles, then its ascendance as a new global great power will be certain. A new global order is emerging and China aims to be at the heart of it.

Index

CPSIA information can be obtained
at www.ICGtesting.com
Printed in the USA
BVOW11s1607120318

510367BV00012B/51/P